PENGUIN B

MALCOLM FRASER PM

Patrick Weller is Professor of Public Policy at Griffith University in Brisbane and Director of the Centre for Australian Public Sector Management. A graduate of Oxford University, he arrived in Australia in 1966, and gained a doctorate from the Australian National University. He is author of *First Among Equals: Prime Ministers in Westminster Systems* (1985), and co-author of *Treasury Control in Australia* (1976), *Politics and Policy in Australia* (1979), *Can Ministers Cope?* (1981) and *Public Policy in Australia* (1988).

MALCOLM FRASER PM

A STUDY IN PRIME MINISTERIAL POWER

PATRICK WELLER

PENGUIN BOOKS

Penguin Books Australia Ltd
487 Maroondah Highway, PO Box 257
Ringwood, Victoria, 3134, Australia
Penguin Books Ltd
Harmondsworth, Middlesex, England
Viking Penguin Inc.
40 Weset 23rd Street, New York, NY 10010, USA
Penguin Books Canada Limited
2801 John Street, Markham, Ontario, Canada, L3R 1B4
Penguin Books (N.Z.) Ltd
182-190 Wairau Road, Auckland 10, New Zealand

First published 1989 by Penguin Books Australia

Copyright © Patrick Weller, 1989

All Rights Reserved. Without limiting the rights under copyright
reserved above, no part of this publication may be reproduced,
stored in or introduced into a retrieval system, or transmitted,
in any form or by any means (electronic, mechanical, photocopying,
recording or otherwise), without the prior written permission
of both the copyright owner and the above publisher of
this book.

Typeset in 10/13 Highland Roman by Midland Typesetters, Maryborough, Vic.
Made and printed in Australia by The Book Printer, Maryborough, Vic.

CIP

Weller, Patrick, 1944-   .
Malcolm Fraser PM: a study in
prime ministerial power.
ISBN 0 14 012974 X
1. Fraser, Malcolm, 1930-   . 2. Prime ministers -
Australia - Biography. 3. Australia - Politics
and government - 1976-   . I. Title.
994.06'3'0924

To my parents, Sam and Irene Weller,
as a small token of appreciation and thanks

CONTENTS

Acknowledgements		ix
Prologue		xi
1	The job and the man	1
2	Harnessing the machine: the system of advice	19
3	'That big bastard': relations with ministers	59
4	'In the bunker': cabinet	106
5	'Duchessing and strongarming': the party leader	148
6	'The highest authoritative source': the salesman	175
7	Axing or taxing: the art of budgeting	214
8	Treating with bandits: the federalist	274
9	'Not without honour': foreign policy	313
10	Decisions, decisions	355
11	Domination and consultation: Malcolm Fraser as prime minister	395
Sources		410
Index		432

ACKNOWLEDGEMENTS

Any project of this type necessarily incurs many debts. I would like to thank Mr Fraser for arranging the access to the cabinet papers and to his personal papers, and Mr and Mrs Fraser for their hospitality at Nareen when I stayed there to interview Mr Fraser. It is important to point out that this access was unconditional; there was no requirement for me to clear with Mr Fraser what I wrote or to show him the text. The access was therefore particularly generous and made the task of writing the book both challenging and enormously entertaining.

I would also like to thank those who gave generously of their time and memories when I interviewed them. Staff of the Department of the Prime Minister and Cabinet assisted me in the four years that this research took. I would like to thank particularly Vicki Buckley and her colleagues in the Cabinet Office and Neil Dwyer and his colleagues in the Parliamentary and Government Division for their courteous and friendly treatment of a visiting scholar and for the persistence with which they sought to meet the often vague requests for files when there were so many other pressing demands on their time.

I would also like to thank Sir Geoffrey Yeend and Mike Codd, successive secretaries of the department, for allowing its resources to be so used.

The Fraser Papers are in the National Archives in Canberra and I would like to thank the staff there for their co-operation. The Lynch Papers were consulted with the permission of the University of Melbourne Archives and I am grateful for Frank Strahan's assistance.

Several people have acted as research assistants during the project. Sue Fraser worked in Canberra, sorting through documents and papers. Colleen Lewis, Jenni Warburton, Michael Brown, Gillian Whitehouse and Melissa Lucas have at different times assisted me at Griffith University. The project was made possible by a grant from the Griffith University Research Committee in 1985 and by grants from the Australian Research Grant Scheme in 1986 and 1987.

Several people have read drafts of the text and given me the advantage of their knowledge and insights. I would like to thank Denis White, Robert Parker, Philip Selth, Glyn Davis, John Wanna, Ciaran O'Faircheallaigh, Christine Smith and Bron Stevens for their help. I trust they have picked up most of the egregious errors.

Kay de Chastel typed much of the manuscript and protected me from too many interruptions. Michelle Redlich, Maxine Lutton, Jan Benjamin, Lenore Olsen and Kay Brown typed and retyped chapters and transcribed many of the interviews. I am very much in their debt for their patience at my ever-increasing requests for help.

Finally, my wife Bron put up with my absence on research trips and my growing obsession with getting the book finished. I thank her for her support.

PROLOGUE

In the election of 14 December 1975, at the age of 45, Malcolm Fraser achieved his ambition. The victory that day returned him to office with the largest majority in Australian history. Fraser's great gamble – the blocking of supply to force the Whitlam government to the polls – had succeeded when the voters swung to support the coalition. If his initial occupation of the prime ministerial post had depended on the secretive actions of the governor-general, he was now elected prime minister as the people's choice.

On 26 February 1983 Malcolm Fraser became Australia's second longest serving prime minister; he had been in office for more than seven years. A week later it was all over: this time a gamble failed. The election he had called eight months early, hoping to forestall the Labor opposition from changing its leader, was lost. Hawke's harmonious succession to the Labor leadership, the necessity to stop campaigning during the aftermath of horrendous bushfires, the continued drought, opposition to the Franklin dam, the state of the economy; these all prevented Fraser from regaining the initiative he had lost even as he was calling the election. He was outmanoeuvred and outcampaigned, though typically he fought hard to the very end. Then he took the blame for the defeat, resigned the party leadership and a month later left parliament.

Between December 1975 and March 1983 were the Fraser years, years when he dominated the political scene, when his word on any issue was seen as final, when the government was often regarded as a one-man band, seen as the Fraser government as much as the Liberal or the coalition government. Largely unchallenged within the cabinet, he fitted the model of a decisive leader and prime minister.

But images change. Defeated heroes are tarnished by their defeat and become easy targets for blame. Since his departure, as time has distanced participants from the immediate events, so too the responsibility for any failings has conveniently been laid on the one person. The Fraser years, argue the free marketeers and the party revisionists, were wasted years. Critics who were in the cabinet or in the party at the time now blame one man. Fraser the hero, the man who led the party to three successive electoral victories and for whom two-thirds of the party voted as recently as April 1982, is now the subject of a Liberal demonology.

Opponents have changed their views too. To most of them Fraser in office was the villain of 1975, the man who bludgeoned his way to power and therefore lacked legitimacy. Nothing he did while in office could remove that stain; he was awarded no credit. Yet time has allowed distinctions to be drawn between the Fraser of 1975 and the Fraser who developed policies for Zimbabwe, for land rights, for multiculturalism, for family allowances and for administrative law, policies that are by Australian standards still radical. As opponents examine the reality rather than just the rhetoric, so this 'eminent person' becomes more respected for some of his actions. Such is the turn of the wheels of political fortune.

Whether reluctant hero or departed demon, both images portray the picture of a prime minister in charge – a dominance that sits oddly in a parliamentary system, for the Australian system of responsible government is collective in its rhetoric, its form and its presentation. Australian government is meant to be based on cabinet and parliament, not presidential or prime ministerial in its style. Two immediate questions emerge: how powerful was Malcolm Fraser and how real was the institution of cabinet government while he was prime minister?

These questions lead to other problems of fundamental importance in the understanding of any leader, either in Australia or elsewhere. First, how do prime ministers have an impact on the procedures and policies of a government – what can they do, and what can't they do? Second, what does an appreciation of the working styles of, and limitations on, prime ministers tell us more generally about the difficulties of governing Australia?

This book examines these problems. It is a study of the way in which Malcolm Fraser acted as prime minister. It is concerned to see how he organised the position, from whom he got advice and what use he made of it, how he ran the cabinet and the party, and how he presented the government through the parliament, the media and at elections. It is concerned as much with the regular routine as with ministerial or political crises because power must be exercised on a daily basis. It therefore concentrates on the means that Fraser adopted, the methods he used to run the government. To ask also what impact procedures have on policy, the details of policy-making in the economic field, in federal-state relations, in international affairs and in some specific cases will be examined. The book provides a portrait of a prime minister in action. It is not a biography, but a study in the exercise of power and influence within the Australian political system.

The book is also concerned, at a more general level, to use the experience of Malcolm Fraser as an example of the difficulties that any leader – indeed any government – must meet in trying to solve the inevitable problems that face it. How much power do governments have and how much can they use (not the same thing by any means)? Do the structures of government and the federal system prevent the fulfilment of the public's expectations? Should the electors demand and expect less, rather than more, from their governments? These questions are not exclusively raised by the Fraser period, but a detailed study of the problems he faced may help us understand more about the way we are governed.

There is no attempt to cover every aspect of the Fraser government or follow through the making of every policy. Such a history would have to be exhaustive; this study is not. Particular events have been selected as illustrations, snapshots of a government. Each episode has been chosen to illustrate the central question: what does it inform us about the workings of Fraser as prime minister and about the processes of government? Style and process are assessed more than the policy outcomes in their own right. Selectivity in the choice of views, anecdotes and policy areas is inevitable in such an enterprise, but that selection has been designed to show all sides of the man, not merely one part of the picture.

Four sets of sources were used in the writing of this book. First there was the public record: the proceedings of parliament, the official statements, the press reports; that is, what the public was told was happening, or what the media were able to discover. These are the traditional sources of political analysis.

Second, I have also used the private papers of Malcolm Fraser that are deposited in the National Archives. They are substantial, with a full collection of official correspondence, and a fairly random collection of papers on different subjects. They illuminate some issues more than others; they provide some dramatic insights. I was granted full access to all those papers by Mr Fraser.

Third, the book is based on the official papers of the period. It has used the records of the cabinet, held in the Cabinet Office, and the files of the Department of the Prime Minister and Cabinet for the whole period of the Fraser government. The cabinet papers include submissions to cabinet, briefing notes, a range of supporting memoranda and the official decisions. They do not include any record of discussion; indeed, as the *Cabinet Handbook* notes, cabinet meetings are essentially meetings without records. The only details of discussions would be found in the notebooks of the cabinet officials. They are primarily *aide-mémoires* to assist the writing of decisions and in no way a transcript; their style varies from person to person. They were not available to the prime minister, or to me. The files of the Department of the Prime Minister and Cabinet

(PMC) were more wide ranging, including working drafts, briefing notes and other details.

Access was granted to any paper that the prime minister saw or in usual circumstances would have seen. This access was arranged for me by Mr Fraser. It is a development of the tradition that allows former prime ministers and ministers who wish to write memoirs to refresh their memory by looking at official papers which they saw while in office. In Australia access has been extended to those scholars who are writing studies such as this, and it has allowed the book to be based on the papers that were actually before the prime minister and the cabinet when decisions were taken. Even though these papers may never tell the whole story, they do assist in providing insights into the actions of the government and remove the need to base reports on what got out, rather than on what exists. I was privileged therefore to be able to use those same documents that will eventually become available to historians under the thirty-year rule. The condition of access was that I should not quote directly from cabinet documents; they are therefore summarised in the text.

Finally, the book is based on interviews, with members of Fraser's cabinet and private office, with senior public servants, with other parliamentarians, with state premiers, with journalists and with members of the business community, around seventy in all. Interviews as a source have both problems and advantages. Some interviewees may have told me what they wished they had said or done at the time, but didn't. Others may have forgotten; after all, the events were between three and ten years before the interviews. Many want to defend their record, explaining their actions in the best light. None, for instance, will acknowledge being scared of Fraser, although all remember that 'several' of their colleagues were!

Where possible, comments have been attributed to individuals; where it was not possible, because I am quoting the views of public servants or because ex-ministers were bolder at the time of the interview than when they saw their comments in typescript, I have indicated the general category of person. These interviews covered both general impressions of Fraser and some specific events.

The impact of interviews is necessarily cumulative. One comment can rarely be regarded as conclusive. As more and more people provide a similar picture, as instances or impressions are checked against each other and against the official record, so they may be regarded as more reliable and accurate. For some parts of the picture interviews are essential; they remain the only way of getting an impression of how Fraser worked with other political actors, of how daily interactions occurred, of how his personality and style had an impact on his colleagues and thus on policy outcomes. In the era of the telephone when notes are rare, the tape recorder is the ally of the researcher. Interviews about recent events are a necessary adjunct to the official records, which will be all that historians have when they are finally released.

Since interviews gradually round out the picture, it is only necessary to quote from a few of them, but they are almost all useful in building up an impression of life in the Fraser government. The final portrait that emerges is likely to be different from the one the public saw; it is the perspective of those who were closest to Fraser, who worked and fought with him on a daily basis; some were friends and allies; others were far less sympathetic.

I had four lengthy interviews with Mr Fraser, between September 1986 and November 1988 (two in Melbourne and two at Nareen). Three of them were spread over two days. It is appropriate to comment, after mentioning both Mr and Mrs Fraser's hospitality at Nareen and the access arranged to the cabinet documents and personal papers, that at no time did Mr Fraser ask to see the manuscript, nor was he offered the opportunity to comment on it. The book is in no way an approved or authorised account.

In painting a portrait of the prime minister in action, the book starts with a close examination of the man and the position he held and then gradually expands the picture: to his network of advisers, to his relations with his ministers, with his cabinet and with his party, and to the way in which he presented the public image of the government. Then the focus turns from the management of institutions to the management of process – making economic policy, treading through the federal minefield, negotiating in the international arena, taking hard decisions in particular areas of policy.

The approach is cumulative, not chronological. It starts with Fraser as an individual and gradually broadens the lens to circles of advisers, ministers, the party and then to the public. The lessons that can be gained by the general accounts of his use of the machinery of government can then be tested against the development of policy. Like complementary transparencies placed one on top of another, the final image should be a complete picture of the prime minister in action.

It is not the Fraser of the public image – a picture of a dominant and determined leader with his mind made up and intolerant of other views, with a history of leaving those who dared to disagree defeated and trampled in his path. Fraser may be best remembered by history for his ruthless drive to power in 1975 and for his dignified but emotional speech of resignation in 1983. The book aims to fill in the picture of the years in between; those Fraser years.

CHAPTER 1

THE JOB AND THE MAN

The job

The position of prime minister in Australia has no formal responsibilities; it is not mentioned in the Australian constitution. The prime minister has few acts of parliament to administer. This minimal recognition illuminates a broader point: government is supposed to be collective, with decisions made by cabinet and legislation passed by parliament. How powerful then is the prime minister? How real is that description of the collective political process?

These questions have been the subject of a long-running debate in parliamentary systems; it asks whether cabinet government still exists or whether it has now been replaced by prime ministerial government. Those who argue that prime ministers are now pre-eminent point to the great powers they can wield. They have the right to select and dismiss ministers. They control the structure and proceedings of cabinet. They allocate extensive patronage. They are protected in parliament by the support of a disciplined party. They choose the date of elections. They are the focus of media attention and are able to manipulate the media. They determine the distribution of functions to departments in the public service and have developed a capacity for co-ordination that gives them access to extensive information. They speak on behalf of their country in international forums. The consequence, it is argued, is that all ministers are the prime minister's 'agents' or assistants. Richard Crossman, the most outspoken advocate of this position, has asserted: 'The post-war epoch has seen the final transformation of cabinet government into prime ministerial government. Under this system "the hyphen that joins, the buckle which fastens" has become one man': the prime minister.

Those who maintain that cabinet government is still a reality emphasise the limitations on prime ministers. They demonstrate that ministers have independence and political strength. They explain that cabinet still makes all the important decisions. They show how powerful departments have the capacity to limit the exercise of the prime minister's prerogatives. Parliament is seen as a real force. Parties do not merely give unquestioning support. The emphasis is on the dispersion of power and the collectivity of the process. Although the debate has been pursued primarily in Britain, similar discussions, usually by journalists, have analysed the impact of prime ministers in Australia and Canada.

However, this has never been done satisfactorily for any country. There are three reasons. First, it is always possible to find examples of particular events to support one or other side of the argument. Since no one proposes either that prime ministers always win or that they never have an impact, that is scarcely surprising. Second, the analysts generally are looking at different parts of the political system. Those who argue that prime ministers have grown more powerful tend to focus on the powers and prerogatives they can wield. Those who accept the premise that cabinet government survives explore the strengths of other actors and therefore the constraints on prime ministers. Different perspectives lead to different answers.

The main reason why the debate has been so inconclusive is that prime ministerial and cabinet government are presented as alternative models of behaviour. Analysts have not defined when the one shifts to the other: when is cabinet government no longer 'real' or how often must a prime minister lose before the government is no longer prime ministerial? Nor could they. The problem is that one model posits individual decision-making and the other collective action. The distinctions in reality are never so clear-cut. It may, for instance, be possible for every decision to be taken by cabinet and yet for the prime minister still to dominate. The two models are points on a spectrum defining the exercise of power, not distinct alternatives.

The power of prime ministers can only be properly understood if the two perspectives are combined, to understand prime ministers in their environment. How influential they are will depend on personal, institutional and intellectual factors. For particular leaders the question is how they use the potential of their office.

Prime ministers' substantial powers can never be exercised without an appreciation of the environment. An observer commented of British prime ministers that 'they accept without hesitation the self-restraint of co-operative government. It is part of the job description'. But the view overestimates the degree to which it is indeed *self*-restraint. A person becomes prime minister *because* he or she is the leader of the party, was elected to that position and can be removed if the party desires. The power is institutional, not personal. Prime ministers are at the centre of a swirling torrent of political forces. They cannot exercise authority in all directions at once; the resources of an individual are limited. Judgements have to be made about which initiative will be pursued, which will be delayed and what the costs of decisions will be. Prime ministers must constantly negotiate and usually compromise. They are not the only actors in the political game; other ministers, business and union leaders, backbenchers, the media, all have to be taken into account. Political support must be gained and then painstakingly retained; it cannot just be demanded and then taken for granted. Governing is for prime ministers a continuous estimation of how others will react to the use of power, and how much effort is needed to achieve a desired end. Prime ministers' power and time are not infinite.

Institutional constraints in part determine what prime ministers can do. The practice and structure of government in

Australia have developed their own history and traditions. Parliamentary government, based on vague and often ambiguous 'Westminster principles', is accepted as a foundation of Australian political life. Those principles prescribe ways of doing things, even if there is still scope for leaders to interpret those traditions to their advantage. Cabinet government is collective; parliamentary procedures are well established. Prime ministers may be able to manipulate the conventions and institutions of government but they seldom create them. Conventions, even if not part of the legal framework, create expectations; whether it is decided to respect or ignore them, that decision has costs.

Institutions have an independent existence too, with their own interests and futures to preserve. Thus the public service brings great advantages to prime ministers: good advice, wide research capacity, an immediate service. But it cannot also be treated instrumentally, as a machine that will instantly respond without an awareness of the proper way of doing things, of tradition and of its own belief in what the best way might be. Institutions such as the public service need to be understood and utilised. Outside government, prime ministers' powers are severely limited. Dealing with state governments, with business, unions and community groups, prime ministers cannot command; they must persuade and negotiate. Even legal powers cannot be exerted with impunity or without political cost; because the federal government has the power to impose its will on state governments does not mean it always will. The antagonisms created may spill over into other policy fields, so ends do not justify the means. Prime ministers therefore enter a political and institutional environment that will shape the way they approach their job and determine some of the choices they need to make.

Prime ministers are captive of their time. They are never blessed with 'the blank sheet of infinite opportunity'. They must face a set of circumstances not of their choosing; they must deal with ever-changing demands; their choices reflect time and chance. They are heirs to a long history, to unwanted problems and to outmoded procedures and institutions. Governing is easy from the outside. Commentators and armchair experts, often with particular ideological views, advocate programs avidly, but without trying to fit them into the general social and political picture. Prime ministers do not have the luxury of ignoring the pressures of the past or the multiple demands of the present; they must be aware of continuity, and struggle with changes beyond their control.

All politicians must to some extent be the captives of the intellectual discussions of the period. Prime ministers cannot be pure pragmatists; every decision is taken because it is designed to have an impact. That impact is calculated on the basis of some theory, however implicit. Ideas are the currency of policy. Prime ministers may try to alter the terms of the intellectual debate; a few may succeed; but they cannot be expected to work outside those traditions and it is unfair to judge them by the orthodoxies or intellectual fashions of another time.

A description of prime ministers' power is elusive. The notional powers and responsibilities are great; so are the political and institutional constraints. Theirs is a position that provides great opportunities, but they cannot be unbounded or unlimited. Two points emerge. First, there can be no job description that has constitutional validity, explaining what is, or is not, proper for prime ministers to do. Comments that prime ministers have exceeded their authority, or become excessively powerful, are based on interpretations of past practices or on views of what the observer wants prime ministers to do. Within the political system such comments are often the complaints of dissatisfied ministers or public servants unable to get their way, but since the position is defined exclusively by convention, there are no 'objective' standards for assessing performance.

Second, no job description can have any political weight; prime ministers will largely determine what they do in terms of what they want. Working within the thoroughly practical constraints created by institutional structures, they will decide what is politically acceptable, what is possible, or what their colleagues will allow them to get away with. No set of rules can determine where these constraints lie because they are constantly shifting, not only when leaders change but also as fortunes rise or fall within the reign of one leader. No one can tell prime ministers how much time they should devote to each of their different responsibilities, how actively they should pursue them at a given moment or which should take priority. The allocation of time must depend on three things: the freedom or the lack of freedom which colleagues are prepared to concede; the political, economic and social pressures of the time; and the personal choices of prime ministers.

These are the dilemmas facing all prime ministers. They cannot merely wield authority; they have to determine preferences. The final exercise of power will depend on the area in which individuals choose to exert their influence. Prime ministers cannot do everything; they have to decide which policies will receive attention, which ministers will be persuaded, which questions will be answered. In part any assessment must relate to the individuals. How do they use their position to influence policy outcomes? How do they organise their time and calculate the best ways for governing? How do they gain and maintain support? What jobs do they do and what do they leave to others? But it must also concern the choices the environment forces on them. How do they react to the political pressures? How do they take their opportunities, shape the debate, or change the political agenda? The job is defined by the individual and the environment. Understanding the individual needs an appreciation of the context and its opportunities.

One simple example can make the point. Liberal prime ministers in Australia have the power to select their ministers. In principle that authority is absolute; in practice it is fettered by several requirements. National party ministers will be nominated by the National party leader, as part of the price of coalition. The prime minister must take into account demands for representation from the Senate, from each of the states and from the internal factions. The ministers must include most of those who hold a powerful position in the party. The prime minister will only really exercise a free choice in selecting the last few members, and in deciding which one or two people to leave out. Thus the potential appears great, but in reality it is constrained.

These analyses touch on important political questions. At the narrowest, what is the influence of the 'great person' in history? How does political style have an impact on public policy? Does an individual have the capacity to change the direction of a nation? An examination of policy outcomes does not explain *how* results were achieved. That needs an analysis of style and political technique. A leader's style is often difficult to isolate and describe. It relates not only to behaviour in crises but also to the daily running of government business. Style refers to the skilful manipulation of others, the capacity of a leader to inspire or persuade, the way in which decisions are made, the techniques that the leader uses. In other words, it examines the *means* of government, rather than the ends.

Yet even 'great people' must exist in an environment that will affect their choices. If a narrow approach to the subject of executive leadership illustrates the use of opportunities, a broader one explains how leaders are constrained by the institutional limitations. Leaders must both interact with their immediate environment – with their colleagues, with officials, with pressure groups – and meet the broad wishes and expectations of society. That environment must shape their style and their effectiveness. If the 'great person' approach asks what leaders can do, the slightly broader view asks what they can get away with and to what extent they have real choices about the way they act. Leadership is about individuals in a context: the right person for the job; the person who takes advantage of the condition he or she finds. There are no universal leadership qualities, applicable with equal effect to all circumstances.

Two American books provide useful examples. Fred Greenstein's study of President Eisenhower, *The Hidden Hand Presidency*, sought to resurrect that president's reputation by illustrating that the bumbling and bland exterior was part of a systematic and deliberate exploitation of the position. He describes the techniques that Eisenhower adopted: the careful choice of language, the system of staffing, the use of intermediaries. Robert Caro's monumental *The Lyndon Johnson Years: The Path to Power* is the first volume of a biography. It analyses the way that Johnson used his opportunities and manipulated his way to political success by emphasising his care for detail, his campaigning techniques, his courting of the powerful, his incessant work. Caro seems to have developed an ambivalence to his subject: a contempt for the man's cynicism and a reluctant admiration for his capacity to deliver. Although this first volume only takes LBJ's story to 1942, it provides brilliant insights into the political methods he adopted and shows a political master in action by illustrating how style influenced outcomes.

The strength of these two books is that Greenstein and Caro explain the methods that their subjects adopted to achieve their ends. They place them in the confines of an institution and ask how they took their opportunities and to what degree their actions were shaped by institutional demands. The prime ministership is also essentially a shell. It provides some roles that must be undertaken, but no rules for determining how they should be played. It offers other roles that can be pursued to a greater or lesser extent.

What matters is not the individual alone or the office, but the interaction between personality, institution and circumstance: how the potential is realised. There is no study of an Australian prime minister's working style (nor, that I am aware of, any sustained study of prime ministers' style in any other country; biographies tend to give little attention to the routine).

This book will therefore explore the way in which Fraser used the position of prime minister and the way in which the political institutions and the broader environment moulded or limited his opportunities. It is not a biography or an assessment of his record, but a study of power in its context, of Fraser as prime minister. Understanding what he was able to do can lead to a better appreciation of the potential of prime ministers in Australia.

The man

Malcolm Fraser was born on 21 May 1930 into a family with a political tradition. His grandfather had been one of Victoria's original senators in 1901. Fraser came from a wealthy family and was brought up for his first thirteen years on the family station in the Riverina. Then his father bought the comfortable property Nareen, in Victoria's prosperous Western District. Fraser went to school at the Establishment bastion of Melbourne Grammar. At the age of 19 he bypassed the local universities and went directly to Oxford, where he obtained a degree in philosophy, politics and economics. He returned to Australia in 1952 and almost immediately became involved in politics. In 1954 he won Liberal selection for the Labor-held seat of Wannon. In an election where there was a general swing to Labor Fraser made a marginal seat even closer; he lost by a mere seventeen votes. In 1955 with the assistance of the preferences of an anti-communist Labor candidate Fraser won with 59 per cent of the vote. He was 25. Since then the seat has been regarded as safe, for Fraser always worked hard to sustain a lively network of branches and represent the local interests.

On the backbench Fraser was an assiduous worker, determined to master a range of subjects. However, not surprisingly for one who entered parliament so young, he had to wait for ten years for his promotion to ministerial rank. Not until Sir Robert Menzies retired and was replaced by Harold Holt did Fraser enter the ministry, responsible for the army at a time when the Vietnam war divided the Australian community.

He first made his mark on Australian politics when Harold Holt disappeared in the surf off Portsea in December 1967. Fraser combined with two other junior members of the party, the whips Dudley Irwin and Malcolm Scott, to mastermind the campaign that took John Gorton from the Senate to the leadership of the party and thus the prime ministership. Fraser reaped the benefit of the successful campaign. He was promoted to the cabinet as minister for education and science in 1968 and then to the senior post of minister for defence after the 1969 election. As a minister he was active and effective; in Defence he insisted on testing all views that were presented to him and developing an appreciation of the need for broad strategic thinking. While his permanent head, Sir Arthur Tange, thought that Fraser at times sought advice that confirmed his views, Tange also appreciated that it required a man with energy and breadth of vision to assert the need for a co-ordinated approach to Defence planning. He was by 1970 widely regarded as a future leader of the party, and by Gorton as a potential successor.

By 1971 many ministers were dissatisfied with Gorton's style of leadership and the relations within cabinet had become strained. Crisis erupted when Fraser told journalists that he found the army briefings on the situation in Vietnam inadequate and that he was given additional briefs from the Joint Intelligence Organisation. The army felt that its efficiency had been challenged and the chief of staff sought Gorton's assurance that the government did not accept those allegations. The breach between Fraser and Gorton only became complete when Gorton declined to deny reports that the army chief of staff had also accused his defence minister of disloyalty to the army and its minister, Andrew Peacock. Accusing Gorton, in turn, of disloyalty to a senior minister, Fraser resigned.

He did not only use the events of the recent past to justify his decision, he also attacked Gorton's style. Using words that were thrown back at him a decade later, he condemned Gorton's refusal to work through the cabinet. Fraser claimed that Gorton 'has a dangerous reluctance to consult cabinet, and an obstinate determination to get his own way. He ridicules the advice of a great public service unless it supports his view'. He condemned Gorton because his 'unreasoned drive to get his own way, his obstinacy, his impetuous and emotional reactions have imposed a strain upon the Liberal party, the government and the public service'. The way in which Gorton worked and the procedures he adopted were targets of Fraser's criticism. So too was his failure to defend a senior minister against press attacks.

When the party failed to pass a vote of confidence in Gorton, he resigned as prime minister and was replaced by William McMahon. Fraser was left to languish on the backbenches. Gorton had surprisingly been elected as deputy leader and was able to maintain a veto on Fraser's appointment to the ministry. When Gorton resigned a few months later, Fraser contested the deputy leadership of the party. He came third and was then reinstated to the cabinet, once again as minister for education and science. In that position he again made a sleepy department active and was partly responsible for increases in funding to universities and non-government schools. However the coalition was finally defeated in December 1972.

In opposition Fraser contested both the leadership and the deputy leadership of the Liberal party; in neither contest did he do well. In the leadership contest he was eliminated on the third ballot, with less support than either Billy Snedden or the former attorney-general and minister for foreign affairs, Nigel Bowen. The party did not easily forgive those who had rocked the boat and created some of that instability that had led it to defeat. He was instead shadow spokesman first for primary industry and then for industrial relations. Both appointments were intended to be difficult and he worked hard to come to grips with issues in those areas.

He used the period both on the backbenches and in opposition to expound his views on the proper role of government and the way in which it should be run. His Deakin lecture in 1971 was the first such vision, but they became more frequent in opposition. In 1975 he expressed the importance of the need to maintain 'long-established conventions of political behaviour' if government was not to become 'arbitrary, haphazard and even dangerous'. He defended cabinet government as essential and wise, condemning the process whereby prime ministers act on the advice of one or two colleagues and arguing that the cabinet system would lead to better decisions than one person acting individually. He emphasised the importance of proper consultation and procedure, thus providing a set of criteria against which his own performances could later be judged. In an ANZAAS address in January 1975 Fraser reasserted his belief that in society it should be individuals, not governments, that make decisions about their own future. Government expenditure needed to be reduced, centralism reversed, the private sector encouraged and industrial disputes settled in a new legal framework. Fraser was deliberately presenting a comprehensive Liberal program. He also identified himself with the Menzies tradition by visiting the retired leader.

Stating his position clearly was also a means of marking out an alternative position from the 'me-tooism' that had marked the electoral opportunism of the Liberals in the 1974 poll. It meant that Fraser was regarded more and more as the only alternative leader of an unimpressive opposition. The reputation of the leader, Billy Snedden, slipped, particularly after the defeat of the coalition in the election they had forced in 1974. Desperate for electoral victory and a sense of direction, change in the leadership became more palatable to the party. In November the first attempt to replace Snedden, masterminded by Fraser's long-time friend and Victorian MHR, Tony Staley, failed – though not by a substantial margin. A second challenge seemed inevitable. Fraser's statements of support for Snedden were carefully conditional. In March 1975 another potential contender, Andrew Peacock, argued that the party should meet to settle the issue and end the speculation. This time Fraser had the numbers. The position of leader was declared vacant by 36 votes to 28 and then Fraser defeated Snedden in a straight contest by 37 votes to 27. He became the party leader. He immediately stated that: 'if a government has the numbers and can maintain the numbers in the lower house, it is entitled to expect that it will govern for the three year term unless quite extraordinary events occur'. The comment, like those of the previous months supporting Snedden as leader, was carefully phrased: an apparently clear statement with a caveat that could be brought into play at any time. Fraser was always cautious and precise in his statements. They repaid detailed attention.

The timing of his success was propitious, as the Whitlam government almost immediately began to collapse. The loans affair, the sacking of senior ministers Jim Cairns and Rex Connor, the swing to the Liberals in the Bass by-election: these were all pointers that indicated that the Liberals would win if only they could force an election.

At the same time Fraser as leader continued to expand his ideas on the role of government and his views of a Liberal vision. In the Sir Robert Menzies lecture in Perth on 25 September, Fraser explored the relationship between the 'government and the people'. There were, he argued:

Serious limitations on the ability of governments to produce the better life . . . It is fundamental to Liberal beliefs that the power of government ought to be used to establish the circumstances in which people can act according to their own wishes and assist those in need, who would not otherwise obtain assistance.

He interpreted Labor ideology as identifying community and state as one, and declared that by contrast the Liberal watchwords would be freedom and concern:

Individuals should not become dependent; they should have choice in matters of concern. Governments should exercise restraint, while providing incentives for achievement.

This was the vision he tried to portray, the promised land that he offered in the weeks leading up to the 1975 election.

In October, in the greatest gamble of his political life, Fraser used the Senate to stop supply in an attempt to force the government to the polls. Whitlam refused to resign or to call an election, declaring the Senate's action unconstitutional. The tension and pressure grew. It was an exercise in political brinkmanship, as everyone waited to see which side would crack. It was not certain how long all the Liberal senators would agree to hold up supply. Then on 11 November, Remembrance Day, the governor-general intervened, sacked Whitlam and installed Fraser as caretaker prime minister. Fraser immediately sought a double dissolution, using as justification the thirty-six bills which the opposition he led had blocked in the Senate. Amid uproar parliament was dissolved. Fraser campaigned without making many promises; pointing to the economic mess was adequate as a general strategy. But some commitments had been made: Medibank was to be maintained, tax indexation would be introduced within the next three years. The Liberals won a massive electoral victory and received a large majority in both houses.

December 1975 was a difficult time to come into government. The economy was in disarray; inflation was still high; unemployment was increasing. Although the Labor government had taken steps to address the problems, their policies had not yet had a chance to make an impact. Overseas the influence of the oil shock was still determining the directions of national policy.

Intellectually the decline in the belief of the efficacy of government had not yet begun. IMF intervention in the affairs of Western nations, notable later in the demands for cuts in public expenditure that were to accompany assistance in Britain in 1976, were still in the future. The belief in deregulation and monetarism did not sweep Western nations until the late 1970s, although Fraser had had lengthy discussions with Milton Friedman, the architect of monetarism, in 1975. The determination to cut expenditure as the centrepiece of economic policy, later espoused by Reagan and Thatcher, was not universally accepted. Although the Labor treasurer Bill Hayden had reluctantly started along that track in the 1975 budget, Fraser was perhaps in advance of the trend in his fervent public espousal of reining in public expenditure. He also tried to reduce the expectations of government, although he still believed in the value of government intervention on suitable occasions. Fraser had to tackle the problems with the available weapons of economic thought.

Further, he had to accept the consequences of his means of coming to office. For the whole of the Fraser years the events of 1975 hung over the government like a cloud. Those events had been divisive; many electors regarded Fraser as illegitimate, as having stolen the reins of government from the properly elected party. They maintained their rage; but directed it primarily against the sorry figure of the governor-general. Even so, Fraser was never forgiven for his part. Whatever he did was, in the eye of many of the electorate, tarnished by the means by which he came to office.

For Fraser and his ministers the desire to heal those wounds, to avoid further splits in the community, was to be a consistent brake on the government's activities, a factor in ensuring that the government's rhetoric was often harsher than actual actions, to the constant regret (articulated primarily in retrospect) of some Liberal partisans. That the image was always one of ultra-conservatism and confrontation was in part due to the legacy of 1975, a legacy that Fraser could never, and can never, escape.

Fraser's approach to politics

Fraser was impressive, tall (6 ft 5 in. or 195 centimetres) and domineering. He had a physical presence: 'They all think he was tough because he was tall and big; you can imagine the effort of smiling', claimed one former minister (who was sufficiently overawed even in 1986 to be concerned lest Fraser found out what he had said in the interview). He was not prepared to show any public emotion as he ground on at his job 'like a piece of stainless steel drawn out to its point of snapping'. Being prime minister was not meant to be easy, although (to complete the original quotation) at times it could be delightful. He enjoyed the position and the challenge. He was immensely hard-working, driving himself and those around him with a determination that seldom flagged. The days were there to be filled, the position was to be used. His advisers were expected to work hard, but they always knew that Fraser himself was prepared to work harder.

The prime minister worked from a suite of offices in the corner of the temporary – and now deserted – Parliament House. Down the corridor from the House of Representatives chamber, the suite included the Cabinet Room and accommodation for his private staff. It was the centre of executive government in Australia.

Fraser set the schedule – according to his criteria. He combined his perceptions of what was important with what others thought significant and then decided what should be fitted into his timetable. The calendar and the clock were mere inconveniences. As one official argued:

You had a Malcolm Fraser cabinet, really . . . making few allowances for even as traditionally accepted things as public holidays. If Carlton were playing in the grand final, that was on the schedule because it was part of Malcolm Fraser's calendar; it wasn't on the schedule because it was part of the sporting calendar because that was generally ignored.

For Fraser politics was his life. He had been an MP for twenty years, and had worked hard during that time. He was shy with people he did not know, but disguised it by being competitive and often aggressive. With his staff and colleagues he found it difficult not to take even into his few private moments the argumentative style he adopted for politics. Dale Budd (who worked for Fraser for three separate spells, two as principal private secretary while he was prime minister, and who was perhaps the ultimate ministerial minder) was a great admirer of Fraser. He believed 'one of his strengths was his desire to talk out issues with people face to face. He did not resort to letters'. Yet he appreciated that

It's almost impossible to have small talk with him. I've often thought that if you were talking idly to him about what was his favourite TV program and you said 'I enjoy watching Minder', he'd say 'why do you think Minder's a good program?' Any sort of topic he would tend to pursue very hard.

He covered his shyness by talking, thinking and acting politics all the time. He had a few friends, like Tony Street and Doug Anthony, with whom he could relax, but he could even be tense at social events. When his staff held an informal party to celebrate his fiftieth birthday, David Barnett commented in his speech of tribute that 'You're not the easiest person to work for'. 'It's all voluntary', retorted the prime minister, 'I'm not here to make you people feel good'. When he had planned a day's trout fishing in Canada, he made several calls to check and double-check that everything was properly arranged. Whatever he did, he pursued hard, with great vigour. It was usually politics.

Fraser thrived on crisis and activity; he believed that government needed to solve problems immediately and urgently. While he was a minister, one of his permanent heads had asked him to use the term 'urgent' more sparingly on his requests to the department. Even when there was no immediate need, Fraser set tight deadlines requiring action or response. It was not his style to allow problems to solve themselves, or to let external forces determine the results. He would not let crises peter out by themselves; he wanted options and choices. He believed the government should at the least have a position with which to react to any circumstance. He both believed that governments were trying to do too much and wanted governments involved where they could be constructive.

Fraser's views of leadership may be derived from his appreciation of an article written in 1973 by David Kemp (later the head of his private office). Kemp argued that leadership should be more than mere image:

The first and most important relationship is between leader and followers, not between leader and the public ... the man who cannot unify and lead his colleagues in parliament and in the organisation cannot make a successful appeal to the electorate.

The leader needed to exert authority so that people would entrust their careers to him but it could only gradually be built up. A strong leader was not afraid to consult where necessary, because consulting was only seen as a sign of weakness by those who were not secure. But, Kemp argued, the ultimate source of authority for a leader was his role as expounder of a philosophy or ideology which commanded common consent and adherence in the party. Over time a leader who relied only on pragmatism would run into trouble; there was a need for assumptions to be spelt out. Kemp saw the need for a leader and a philosophy to be inseparable:

the effective leadership of an opposition party requires authority, and leadership in the restatement of the basic guiding principles of policy is potentially an important source of that authority.

Maintaining unity, the right to lead in philosophical debate and the use of authority were in Kemp's view the functions of a successful leader. Fraser certainly accepted that advice in determining his approach, even if he did not spell it out. In government he was able to add the powers of the prime minister to those of party leader.

Fraser was often prepared to elucidate general principles, yet inevitably his actions were primarily oriented towards specific problems. Philosophical principles could be used instrumentally as a means of justifying decisions. Philosophy might act as a framework; issues were to be settled on their merits. The prime minister's position was to be used to solve immediate crises. Asked how he approached the prime minister's role, Fraser saw the need for immediate action, a requirement to use the power, not to philosophise on the role of the leadership or the functions of the prime minister. He recalled:

I hadn't sat down and said 'Well, I am prime minister, what do I do now?' I was in an environment where there were a number of major priorities to be addressed. They were really all in the first instance economic, so the economic departments had to be made to pull together. I suppose the first thing was the structure of government and the structure of the cabinet committees.

Priorities were dictated by the problems and by the methods needed to solve them; the philosophy provided a broader, but not always determining, context.

Colleagues and other observers thought he had a very clear notion of how to exercise power. One official explained:

He had always planned to be prime minister. He had a very professional approach to decision-making. He had worked out in his own mind the contribution that could come from the bureaucracy, party, ministers, advisers and how they fitted into a total support group for the prime minister. He understood their propensities to look after their own interests.

Power meant duty and responsibility. Colleagues equated him to the lord of the manor or the country squire, with responsibility to protect and nurture his tenants. That required hard work. Peter Baume claimed he had an inner value system that required him to work seventeen hours a day as a sign of toughness, commitment and determination which would eventually be rewarded in heaven. One colourful image claimed Fraser: 'walked through darkling landscapes with fire in the hair'.

Active, dedicated, determined, unrelenting, often tense and aggressive – these are the best descriptions of Fraser's personal style. He was also able to harness the formidable power of the prime minister's advisory machine to provide him with great advantages in the development of his ideas on policy. These advantages helped him develop to its full potential the position of prime minister and exercise his power.

CHAPTER 2

HARNESSING THE MACHINE

THE SYSTEM OF ADVICE

Prime ministers need help. They cannot do everything. They need help as chairperson of cabinet, as head of government and as leaders of political parties. Ministers have their departments and often see issues from a narrow departmental perspective; their interests are specific. Party officials have primarily an electoral responsibility. Yet prime ministers must consider policy and electoral aspects; they must set them into a broader social and economic framework and into a set of priorities. Their perspective is unique; as a consequence so is their need for help.

Information is a necessary foundation for power. If prime ministers are to understand problems, the facts that underlie them, their relationship to other issues and the range of solutions, they need sound, accurate information. Prime ministers are increasingly required to range across all government activity. They have formal authority for very little; they have general responsibility for almost everything. They need to know what is going on, which areas are likely to become politically sensitive or damaging and what can be done. They may need to act or comment on any aspect of government activity, often with little notice.

An examination of the fit between prime ministers' needs and the organisations that provide them with support and information is a suitable starting point for an assessment of prime ministers' power. Those bodies are the foundation on which all other activities are built; their structure and style can explain the way prime ministers work. Yet even at the outset significant choices need to be made. Deciding what structures are required depends in part on the way prime ministers see their role – as mediator, policy initiator, chairperson of cabinet. The leaders' emphasis is likely to be reflected to some extent in the form of those bodies that provide them with support. Several sets of institutional arrangements are possible; all of them combine non-partisan public servants and partisan political appointees in the advisory system.

The notion that prime ministers need partisan or departmental help is fairly new. There is no agreement on what that support should be or how it should be organised. About the need for aid for presidents there is no debate, because they are elected as individuals. Prime ministers are the head of a team, each member of which has specific statutory responsibilities. Prime ministers need to make the system work smoothly. The question is therefore whether advice should be designed to assist the ministers as a collectivity, so that they can better assess the problems, or whether it should be designed for the prime minister as an individual, so that he or she can direct the system. The rhetoric of cabinet government remains collective, yet the needs of prime ministers are individual. The balance between individual and collective support has to be settled for each leader, although the tendency – inevitable in the climate created by the modern media – is for support for prime ministers to be increased and to be designed for them as individuals. Prime ministers must always appear to know what is happening; their supporting and advisory units must reflect this need.

Fraser always appreciated these pressures, but he wanted the system to do more so that he could understand and influence whatever cabinet discussed. He developed a network of advisory bodies that not only served the collectivity of cabinet, but also provided him with the information and advice necessary to maintain his position at the head of government. Those bodies were designed to keep him in touch with what was happening, and to meet his demands. Fraser was constantly the source of policy initiatives, derived from his experience, from his own ideas and from his conversations outside government. He needed machinery that would react quickly and would thrive on the pressures he created.

Part of the advisory network he developed was formal and worked directly to him: the private office and the Department of the Prime Minister and Cabinet (PMC). The former was partisan and temporary, appointed by Fraser and working around him in his office in Parliament House; the latter was staffed by career officials, non-partisan and permanent. Other public service bodies such as the Public Service Board and the Office of National Assessments worked officially to him but in practice were slightly removed from daily directions. More distantly he could, working through his ministers or through his private office, tap the resources of any section of the public service. He also maintained a network of private contacts – political, social and business – that he used continually.

Each part of the system was consciously used for different, if often overlapping, purposes. While the public service might advise on policies or problems, the private office was needed to place them in a broader philosophical or political context. He used his network constantly, effectively and ruthlessly. His authority and his capacity to win arguments about policy were based not just on his position, but also on his access to and mastery of information. He knew as much, and often more, about important policy areas as the responsible ministers. He had considered possible solutions to important issues before they came to cabinet.

By the time a decision on any important issue was made, Fraser would have consulted widely. No one knew precisely with whom the prime minister had discussed the topic or what had been said to him. No one was able to exert any monopoly over access to the prime minister and thus control the flow of information. That result was deliberate. He argued:

In political terms I believe there is safety in having advice from different sources. If you get two points of view, you're more likely to make better decisions, because if there are political difficulties that need to be overcome, or argued through, you're prepared for them before they hit you. To me it's just prudent management.

A multiplicity of advocates left Fraser free to test all the propositions.

He was conscious that he must never be left in a position where he could be 'captured', whether by a group of advisers, a line of advice, a timetable or a schedule of engagements determined elsewhere. To remain his own master, he had to determine the allocation of his own time, his most valuable resource. Fraser's strategy was to leave himself free from the danger of being directed by others; he was determined to keep control.

The machinery of advice

To appreciate how effectively the system of advice strengthened Fraser's position, it is necessary first to understand the way these supporting bodies worked and how they perceived their roles. Explaining their organisation and the service they provided to Fraser illustrates both the atmosphere in which he worked and the process by which he developed his ideas.

The private office

Before 1972 prime ministers worked without the support of an office that had much capacity to provide advice on policy. Whitlam was suspicious of the public service and thought PMC inadequate to provide the support he needed; initially he therefore created a private office that could offer political advice and maintain a broader perspective on the government's progress. As the capacity of PMC developed, particularly when John Menadue was appointed as head of the department in late 1974, the influence of the private office declined. Nevertheless the precedent of a strong private office had been created by Whitlam.

Fraser maintained the enlarged office and honed its

operations to a new sharpness. In 1976 he designed the office with assistance particularly from David Kemp, a political scientist from Melbourne University who had joined his staff in opposition. Kemp came from an established conservative family; his father had founded the conservative think-tank, the Institute of Public Affairs, in Melbourne. David Kemp worked closely with Fraser, who trusted him and felt able to talk to him about all the issues on the agenda. As Kemp explained, the prime minister's role was to integrate the government; the office helped to do that job by maintaining a perspective that was close to his and that therefore understood his requirements. It was developed 'to help the prime minister control the apparatus of government and the political process'. The result was unique because it took account of the pressures of the Australian political system. In 1976 Dale Budd had examined the alternative models adopted by prime ministers in similar political systems. He paid particular attention to Pierre Trudeau's powerful prime minister's office in Canada. He concluded that the differences between the political systems were so great that little could be gained by continuing detailed comparisons. Fraser's office was thus developed to meet his demands and Australian conditions.

The formal structure of the office and its personnel changed several times during the Fraser period, as the embryonic ideas of 1976 crystallised, but there was a basic shape. The office was divided into three sections: an administrative unit responsible for maintaining the flow of paper, for organising the timetable, for following up requests; a policy unit that wrote speeches, commented on policy proposals and acted as a sounding board for some of the prime minister's ideas; and a press office that interacted with the press gallery and tried to assist in presenting the government's policies to the public. The office had nineteen staff in 1976; by 1981 there were about twenty-four. Only ten of the number could be seen as advisers – the five policy advisers, three press officers and two senior departmental officers – although the growth in the advisory staff was the main reason for the increase in the office's size.

Functional divisions in the office were artificial; the senior five or six members of the office were never constrained by formal roles. They offered advice across a range of issues. After all, their purpose, like the reason for the office's existence, was to assist the prime minister personally and through him, but *only* through him, the government. The office existed, as Kemp and Budd put it, to do the things that the prime minister would do himself if he had more time; it was meant to be an extension of the prime minister, able to see problems from the unique perspective of the prime minister.

The office seldom had time to co-ordinate its activities so that it worked as a single unit. Proposals to hold formal planning meetings of the office staff were never effective. Partly it was a matter of finding the available time; meetings couldn't be held while the prime minister was there. If Fraser was in Canberra, meetings would have to start very early in the morning, often after a very late night. However more importantly, the office was reactive, meeting the daily needs of a prime minister who ranged widely, and unpredictably, across all the government's activities. Planning the distribution of work or developing an office strategy did not suit the style of the man the office served.

Several different people headed the office. Kemp left for a chair in politics at Monash University in 1976 and for a time a public servant and diplomat, Michael Cook, took over. But when the office ceased to provide regular support during the 1980 election on the grounds that such activity was not proper for a public servant, it was decided to revert to clearly partisan appointees. Kemp came back for a second spell in 1981 and, over the objections of PMC, he was given the equivalent status to a permanent head, but after family tragedy he returned to Monash. Fraser regarded his departure as a great loss because he thought Kemp had 'no peer as an exponent of Liberal political thought'. A second Monash political scientist, Denis White, was already a principal adviser and then became director of the office, but he never developed the same reputation as Kemp as an influence in policy matters.

In February 1982 when the treasurer asked for his office to be increased in size and in the level of its staff, PMC explained to the prime minister why such a move would be inappropriate. In so doing, it made explicit the principles used to justify the private office's staffing structure. The prime minister's office derived from:

The task of the prime minister to provide political and administrative leadership of the government;
The responsibility of the prime minister which properly encompasses all portfolios;
The value to the government of retention of full time independent advisory staff, centralised for functional and administrative reasons in the prime minister's office.

While the last point may be arguing a specific case, legitimising what Fraser wanted, the general description provides the basic justification for the working of the private office.

Of the three sections, the administrative unit organised the prime minister's timetable. The way in which it was done provides an insight into the pressures on all prime ministers. The schedule had to be organised some time in advance. Invitations, either to specific events or asking him to visit when in the vicinity, were common, and the unit had to decide which should be declined immediately and which should be considered. It was often difficult to pin Fraser down to decisions about attending events that were months away. As he recalls: 'You'd start with a reasonable schedule worked out a long time in advance; and then things would come up that seemed to be desirable'. The schedule became very full. Both Fraser and Budd now argue that too many invitations – to party functions or to business dinners – were accepted, making tremendous demands on the prime minister's time without bringing any distinct political or national benefits. It became, for instance, almost traditional that Fraser would address annual meetings of Chambers of Commerce, yet there was little political advantage in speaking to such groups of the converted.

A prime minister's time is the most valuable commodity in Canberra, yet Fraser's program was always cluttered; there was no regular routine. Some events, such as the briefing for question time, occurred whenever parliament was sitting, and cabinet met at a predetermined time, but the rest of the schedule was flexible. Two examples are given below to illustrate the number of meetings, discussions and activities a prime minister must attend.

PROGRAM FOR WEDNESDAY 30 MAY 1979

08.00 am	Meeting with senators in Party Room
09.00 am	Meeting concludes
09.10 am	Ellicott [minister]
09.20 am	Street and Macphee [ministers]
09.35 am	Telephone interview – Radio station 5DN – Courdeaux
09.50 am	Interview concludes
10.00 am	Puplick/Martin/Teague [backbench senators]
10.30 am	Party meeting – followed by Clarrie Millar [National party backbencher]
1.30 pm	Question time briefing
2.15 pm	Question time
3.20 pm	Depart Parliament House
3.30 pm	Call on the Governor General
5.00 pm	Pre-budget consultations with National Council of Women of Australia, Women's Electoral Lobby, National Women's Advisory Council, Women's Action Alliance and Women's Welfare Issues Consultative Committee
6.30 pm	Dinner at the Lodge with members and senators
8.00 pm	Monetary policy [cabinet committee]
10.00 pm	Peacock [minister]

PROGRAM FOR THURSDAY 18 FEBRUARY 1982

08.00 am	Cabinet. Bulletin photo??
09.15 am	Question time briefing
10.00 am	Question time
11.00 am	Dr Kobayashi, Chairman, Nippon Electric Company
11.30 am	Handover of South West Tasmania declaration by Professor Manning Clark and Dr Bob Brown
11.45 am	Mr Kenneth Wiltshire, Chairman, Australian Heritage Commission
12.15 pm	Father Lini [prime minister of Vanuatu]

12.45 pm   Depart Parliament House
1.00 pm   Arrive AGL Trunk Receiving Station (Federal Highway)
           Met by:
           Mr David Anderson, Chairman AGL; Sir William Pettingell, Director, AGL; Mr John Robinson, Director, AGL; Sir Robert Norman, Director; Mr Mike Davis, Director; Mr Stephen Carney, Stephen Carney & Associates.
           Prime Minister escorted to podium
           Mr Bruce Connery (Manager, AGL Canberra) introduces the Chairman
           Prime Minister speaks (6 minutes)
           Mr Anderson escorts Prime Minister behind podium and invites him to unveil a plaque
           Prime Minister then escorted inside a small enclosure and invited to turn on the gas
           Invited to stay for quick lunch
1.45 pm   Depart
           Return to Parliament House
2.00 pm   Howard/Viner/Departmental Officers [ministers]
3.00 pm   Sir Peter Baxendell and Mr Kevan Gosper, Shell
3.30 pm   Mr Holgate, Premier of Tasmania
4.00 pm   Mr Tonkin, Premier of South Australia, and Mr Howard [minister]
5.00 pm   Mr Bjelke-Petersen, Premier of Queensland, and Dr Llew Edwards
6.00 pm   Lord Shackleton, Chairman of the Cook Society, and Sir John Mason [British High Commissioner]
8.15 pm   Mr Howard and Governor of Reserve Bank
8.45 pm   Mr Howard/Governor/Treasury and PMC officers

Yet even these schedules are misleading because they provide no more than the skeleton of the day's program – the initial proposal. Political events could suddenly interfere. On 18 February Hawke called Fraser a liar in parliament; Fraser interrupted his meeting with the Heritage Commission to respond and came back almost shaking with anger (but there is no mention of the hiatus in the notes recording the meeting). Even when there was no crisis, some people were summoned; others asked for meetings; and advisers or colleagues rushed in and out. A few people – Anthony and Lynch among the ministers, Budd, Kemp and Yeend among advisers – could walk straight in at almost any time. Other ministers could usually get in to see the prime minister within hours, backbenchers within a day. Budd, or the other office administrators responsible for controlling access to Fraser, was responsible for deciding what issues were important, and which people could wait. Those who worried the prime minister with trivia had to be delayed. The picture is less of a controlled and carefully scheduled set of meetings, more of the bustle of the railway station, with issues emerging and disappearing, with people bringing information, giving advice or receiving orders, with views being exchanged. On any day, argues Budd, the prime minister might have had contact with up to a hundred people, face to face, on the phone, in parliament, in kerb-side interviews, at dinners. It was impossible to keep a record of whom the prime minister spoke to. No one tried.

Fraser had always maintained a network of contacts throughout different parts of the community, and he would use them frequently to ask for opinions, extract information and test ideas. One such contact has gone down in political folklore. In the months of crisis in 1975 one caller used the pseudonym 'Mr Williams' when ringing Fraser's office. At the same time the opposition was gaining intimate details about the Whitlam government's loan raising. Legend has muddled the two events, with Canberra gossip nominating several candidates from the Treasury as 'Mr Williams'. 'Mr Williams' was in fact Bob Santamaria, using a name that he had adopted for many years when he rang political leaders; he wanted to keep his closeness to the leader of the opposition confidential. The name gained a certain poignancy as one of the miners' leaders in the 1949 strike had been named Williams. 'Mr Williams' therefore provided no information on the loans affair or Treasury documents. That material was collected primarily by Lynch's office; who was leaking to Lynch, and whether that person was in Treasury, is another matter.

THE SYSTEM OF ADVICE

Fraser sought constantly to maintain links with the business community. He would talk to them on the phone and invite them to dinner at the Lodge. In July 1977, for instance, he held a dinner party at short notice to which four leading businessmen – Arvi Parbo, Ken Myer, Brian Inglis and Rod Carnegie – were invited; he thanked them afterwards for acting as a 'sounding board' and sent them additional information for comment. Fraser both talked and listened at these functions, being as keen to extract ideas and reactions as to express his own.

When the prime minister arrived in the morning he would reel off a list of people he wanted to talk to and give the order in which he wished the calls to be made. He would also give a list of items on which he wanted further details. He might seek comment on an extract of a letter, without saying who wrote it, or he might be reacting to an idea. For instance on 30 June 1977 he asked for details about the salary of the high commissioner to the UK; a report on the progress made by a task force on ASEAN; a brief on EEC protective devices and on steel exports; a brief on a cabinet decision about schools; a draft message to South-East Asian leaders; a brief on whaling; information about ministerial overseas visits; a brief on a 'home loans boost' article in the *Australian Financial Review*; a brief on flat rate tax; a list of correspondence on South Africa; and details of the Administrative Review Committee's recommendations on departmental libraries. The range was diverse. The office provided him, later in the day, with a check-list of his requests, a method that allowed him to follow up his inquiries if he chose and certainly allowed the office to press the department for action. He was constantly throwing off ideas, requests, and demands for information; he had an inquisitive mind. He recalls Yeend once saying to him: 'You have an idea on a tractor and then send us round the world' (that one concerned trade negotiations).

The administrative unit was also responsible for ensuring that the prime minister's reactions flowed back to the department. Fraser wrote little himself, perhaps fortunately as his writing is difficult to interpret, but he annotated widely. 'To cabinet', or 'Anthony', 'Lynch' or some such direction. As Barnett put it:

It was extraordinarily interesting. You'd get these notes back, with a tick or an initial to show that he'd read it. Sometimes you saw the corner torn off and you knew he'd been thinking about it. Sometimes Budd had to get crumpled balls of paper out of the corner of the room and send it back to the department with 'PM has seen' on it.

These annotations represented decisions, or at least recognition. The flow of paper was constant.

The administrative unit was also responsible for dealing with the prime minister's correspondence – some 40000 letters a year. They were categorised and answered. A record of the subjects was maintained so that Fraser could be kept informed about the subjects and slants of the correspondence. Routine responses were drafted in PMC by the ministerial correspondence unit. On items of government policy, such as its approach to South Africa or tax evasion, a standard group of paragraphs was formulated and cleared with the prime minister. It was consistently updated to take account of new developments. Some letters were sent off to the responsible ministers for reply. Budd himself would often draft a dozen letters a day on the politically sensitive items.

Yet the process never became routine; Fraser would not accept without amendment the proposed answers he was given. Drafts were often sent back, with demands that they be shortened or softened, or that the 'threatening tone' be removed. Sometimes Fraser even provided paragraphs he wanted included in the new version. In one note to the department, relating to a swag of letters that had congratulated him on his 1980 electoral win, he demanded specific changes to some sixteen replies; some of the drafts were too unsympathetic, some changes were to make the letters more humane, some did not make the point adequately, some were too long, some did not answer the correspondent's questions. Fraser was conscious of their impact. He always ensured he signed replies to children, which could be seen as politically useful.

Even where there was no immediate political or electoral benefit, Fraser was often far more sensitive to the problems of individuals than his public image suggests. One of his ministers,

Wal Fife, catches the detail with which he could become concerned:

His staff rang me one night and asked me to go up and I walked in the door and he was sitting back going through his mail, the unmistakeable two big feet on the table. He knew it was me coming in and he didn't change his stance. I sat down and read the letter. It was a letter of woe from a lady about a hundred miles from where I lived and she had all sorts of problems: illnesses, children problems, husband out of work, two old cars to take the children to school. Nine out of the ten problems – and there were more than ten problems – were state matters. She finished up saying 'there's probably not much you can do for me, but I feel better for having told you my worries'. There was a draft reply there to say just that. 'Well, we are very sorry but they are state issues'. He said: 'She's upset. I can't just tell her they are state issues; how far is that from where you live? Will you see her?' I said I'd see her, as long as it was not next week. So his letter was changed to say: 'Well, really they are state issues, but I've asked Fife to try to see you in the near future . . .'. He could have signed that letter, but he thought I can't write back and tell her I can't do anything.

The second part of the private office was the policy unit. One of its functions was speech-writing. The notion that Fraser's speech-writers, particularly David Kemp, were the puppet-masters, putting words or philosophy into the mouth of the prime minister, is clearly wrong. Denis White, who was both speech-writer and later director of Fraser's office, argued that

writing speeches was like a river that flows on and on, with various bits dropped off from one speech to another and other bits added on. About every month or six weeks there would be a major one. Typically the normal speech had a major economic content in it and that's what tended to be like the river . . . the big themes were likely to be there.

The initial writer would do a draft, pass it around the office and then present it to Fraser. Then it would come back for redrafting. Sometimes he would say that he wanted more substance, other times some philosophy to justify the stand. Then he'd say it was just words and needed more facts and figures. The speeches were never completed in isolation. The office would get Treasury or some other department's input, depending on the subject matters. The final draft would be cleared with other ministers. The process could be enormously laborious, wearing and even irritating, but the advisers all argued that the speech was better at the end of the process and reflected his views. Petro Georgiou recalls: 'He used to go into numerous rewrites so that it would suit what he wanted to say. It was an awful process, but the product was better and conveyed more of what he wanted to say'.

Speeches were designed both to 'sell' the government and to maintain the offensive by controlling the political agenda. Central themes often lasted for some months, and then Fraser would indicate the need for some changes. He seldom initiated the content in any detail, although when concerned about the onset at the 1982 recession he dictated a first draft while driving out to the Canberra airport. Luckily there was a secretary in the car. He just 'rattled off a whole lot of pretty much perfect sentences that had themes'.

At no stage were the speeches imposed on Fraser, or accepted by him as they stood. It is, after all, difficult to put words in a man's mouth if he doesn't agree with them or insists on understanding everything he is talking about. Speeches were regarded as important statements of government policy. Fraser, always careful with words and skilled in using the small print, was the final arbiter. As Cliff Walsh explains, 'I never felt I was writing something for Malcolm Fraser; you were writing something by Malcolm Fraser'. The insistence on detail, on evidence rather than the flowing phrases or grand visions, was a consequence of the type of speech Fraser liked. Colourful wordsmiths like Alan Jones did not last long because their styles were too different.

The second function of the policy unit was advice on policy issues; its impact is more difficult to identify. Fraser surrounded himself with people of ability. Three political scientists – David Kemp, Denis White and Petro Georgiou (all formerly from Melbourne or Monash universities) – were on his staff. So were two professors of economics, Cliff Walsh and John Rose. Fraser also drew at times on the advice of foreign affairs expert Owen Harries. His advisers could help him react to issues as they emerged. He trusted Kemp implicitly and saw him as the person who could put the policies into a philosophical framework. John Rose and Cliff Walsh, working in tandem with the treasurer's economic adviser, John Hewson, frequently sent him notes on economic issues. PMC would often be told to liaise with them on particular issues. Rose and Hewson were sometimes unofficially invited to attend the Monetary committee of cabinet; they were therefore able to have a direct impact on that crucial cabinet committee.

The actual carriage of proposals in the office depended on both expertise and availability. Rose was responsible for economic matters; Georgiou gave advice on migrant and multicultural issues. Taking responsibility meant developing expertise and thus in turn greater involvement. It was possible for a member of the office to initiate proposals; Rose, for instance, proposed changes to the procedures for the selling of government bonds. He and an official from PMC started the chain of events that led to the Campbell inquiry into the financial system. Then they had to 'sell' ideas to Fraser because action needed Fraser's imprimatur. The private office staff could only act with his support.

More generally, as Kemp explains, the private office was responsible for ensuring that the technical advice took account of political values to which the party subscribed. As Kemp argued:

The private office should be political. A large part of government is good politics, not just winning but policy leadership, defining goals and making sure the priorities of the government are right.

When the facts were disputed, or when technical arguments seemed to push in a direction that was antipathetic to party philosophy, the task of the private office was to point these implications out. Decisions at the top are concerned with electoral, technical and political factors. Party philosophy and electoral expediency interact. The role of the private office was to ensure that, when the prime minister had to make a decision, all the relevant material was available.

To Fraser the office was a resource to be used. Members of the private office eventually did anything the prime minister wanted. Trusted members like David Barnett and Alastair Drysdale, the two press officers, were not exclusively concerned with media relations. Often everyone's advice was sought. For example, in 1978 the prime minister wanted comments on which countries should be visited, and what the impact of those visits might be. Different members of the office suggested a range of countries, from Brazil to the Soviet Union, and Barnett even passed on a suggestion from *Sydney Morning Herald* journalist, Peter Bowers, that Fraser should visit the Antarctic. When the possibility of an early election in 1977 was raised, all members of the office gave their assessment of the advantages and disadvantages. The office reflected Fraser's interests and was at its most useful when staffed by those Fraser trusted, particularly Kemp, Budd and Barnett. In those cases it could really act as an extension of his own position and personality.

The Department of the Prime Minister and Cabinet

For many years the main function of PMC was seen as assisting the smooth running of government. It was responsible for servicing cabinet, planning the parliamentary program, organising ceremonies and honours and providing some general support for the prime minister. It had little explicit policy involvement although the role it filled before 1973 can easily be understated. After 1974 it gradually developed the expertise to provide direct policy advice to the prime minister. The department's strength was increased when Whitlam appointed John Menadue as its secretary and he began to pull together the somewhat chaotic threads of policy-making that characterised the Labor government.

That process continued after 1975. Because Fraser was interested in everything, he needed a department that had the capacity to provide advice or comment on anything. The department became an exciting, frenetic place to work, with the opportunity to brief the prime minister and thus have an impact on policy. Fraser believed it had an important role to play. He argued that specialist departments got so close to issues that they missed important implications, failed to ask important questions and wanted to push a barrow. The prime minister needed a group who could suggest what questions needed answering and could then work through the prime minister, letting him decide how far to push them. He argued that PMC 'was a protection against inadequacy and a protection against a department or minister deliberately trying to push something through cabinet without the full story being told. It was invaluable'.

Government departments have the advantage of being flexible organisations. Because they often have no formal objectives but to serve their minister, they can be reorganised fairly readily to meet changing needs. This is truer of PMC than others because it usually has no programs to run or legislation to implement. Parts of the department are fairly fixed; the Cabinet Office is required to run the cabinet system, accepting and circulating papers, recording and distributing decisions. Other functions, such as ceremonials, the support of the prime minister in parliament and the development of the legislative program, are necessary in some form, but outside these ongoing functions there is no logical form.

The structure of the department constantly changed. At times it looked like a public service in miniature, as it reflected the whole range of government activity. Its organisation shifted regularly to meet the concerns of government and the new interests of Fraser. Some divisions remained essential: Cabinet Office, Parliamentary and Government, Operations, International, Trade and Industries and Economic. Others could be created or abolished. Revenue and Development disappeared; Communications was created. More importantly, the allocation of responsibilities could shift between the policy-advising divisions to meet the changing requirement for advice.

The department provided a range of services to the prime minister. Every cabinet submission was accompanied by a PMC brief. The brief followed a standard format. It began with a specific recommendation, suggesting support for the proposal, no support or support on certain conditions. It then summarised the background and listed the issues that had to be decided. Briefs were usually contained on one page, and almost never took more than three. They allowed the prime minister to concentrate on the important issues that were to be contested. Although the private office complained that the briefs sometimes arrived too late, their standard was usually high. As issues developed so the briefs changed, with the new recommendations following Fraser's indications of the way he wanted to go. Their impact varied. On occasion the final cabinet decision reflected the amendments the department recommended; at other times the minister's proposals were still accepted; often neither were. Neither the prime minister nor the department regarded it as crucial that PMC should always win.

The department constantly had to respond to the demands of the prime minister. It organised answers to the list of inquiries sent over every day by the private office, relying on the advice of the relevant department where it could but, if time was too short or if that department did not respond with the alacrity the prime minister required (and answers were often demanded by the evening of the same day), then PMC had to draft the note on its own. One such list was sent on 21 September 1977:

I would be grateful for a report on the following matters by the close of business today.
Transport: What is involved in dropping air navigation charges for owners of light aircraft in pastoral areas?
Post & Telecom: For people in pastoral areas who have no mail service, what would be involved in reducing telephone, telex and telegram charges?
Treasurer: What duties and taxes are there on four-wheel drive vehicles and farm bikes? What would be involved in taking duties and taxes off for primary producers? If this is done, how can 'Toorak farmers' be prevented from buying the vehicles? Some States have a primary producers registration – I think in Victoria producers are limited to one vehicle.
Is there any duty on aircraft – sales tax or customs duty? Some aircraft are used for mustering cattle, inspecting fences, etc.

Education: Special isolated children benefits: what is the component with means test, and what is the component without? How many people qualify for the means tested part in pastoral areas?
Primary Industry: Some time ago there was a special incentive to try and persuade people to use good bulls in the Northern Territory. How did the scheme work and was it successful?

This list may read like a squatter's agenda, but others were more related to economic matters.

The process was often reiterative; a note went to the prime minister, a query or a request for further information came back, further briefs went across. Fraser queried and challenged, both generally and specifically. The development of policy was evolutionary, over a number of briefs and responses, and across a number of people. For instance, on 15 February 1980:

Briefing - Current Issues
The Prime Minister made the following comments:
Brief No. 21 - Honeymoon Creek Uranium Project
The Prime Minister is unclear as to the link between the statement in the first paragraph that the project proposal has been rejected; and the general provision for flexibility in the administration of foreign investment policy where the desired level of Australian equity cannot be attained. In the light of this he is unclear as to the current status of proposal.
Brief No. 26 - Rail Electrification Studies
The Prime Minister would like to see the Terms of Reference for both studies (Sydney-Melbourne and general electrification). He commented that the Government was seeking advice not on *whether* to proceed, but on how to do so.
Brief No. 22 - Hobart-Christchurch Air Services
The Prime Minister commented that he would like this matter speeded up.
Brief No. 34 - Introduction of Teletext
The Prime Minister would like further advice, please, with respect to the criticism of the Teletext decision and the claims that better systems are available. He would also like advice on how the Teletext system compares with that provided by Claridges Hotel during his recent stay.

No one in PMC expected the first note to be the end of a matter.

The department was required to monitor Fraser's speeches and answers in parliament; in April 1976 he asked the secretary of his department to institute a system whereby, if he said in parliament he would seek further information, it would be provided the same day, even if only as an interim measure while further research was completed.

The process was continuous, running through all seven days of the week, and at any time of night. Senior officials were used to being summoned at all hours. Explanations of terms or practices, comments on policy proposals, forecasts of possible events, reactions to the ideas of others, indeed advice on anything that the prime minister was interested in – these were the daily causes of interaction between PMC and its master.

One respected and senior adviser summarised the process:

The way he would use advisers in the bureaucracy generally was to ask a series of questions or have cabinet ask a series of questions. If he didn't like the answer, it's 'go away and do another report' and the same question almost would be asked again . . . And he'd go on until he got the right answer and it tended to be the answer he wanted.

But at the same time he had little patience with normal bureaucratic processes. The same adviser continued:

One weakness was that I don't think he had much real perception of bureaucratic processes at all. He'd say 'Can I have a report on that by Thursday morning?'. This was Monday afternoon and so we can. But it won't be as good as what you could have got by next Monday. No matter, give it to him by Thursday morning. Then by Tuesday afternoon, he was saying 'well, can you give me a quick run-down on what's going to be in that report?'. For somebody who was trying to measure deadlines or time available against what could be done in the meantime, he was almost an impossible man to work for.

These examples can be balanced by demands for papers which were then not considered for two or three days. That could be frustrating for public servants who had worked over the weekend. Yet on balance most of those who served him in PMC respected him. As a senior official said, 'When you put something to him, you knew it would get a fair run. They are the compensations for the department and its officers' – influence in exchange for pressure and inconvenience.

PMC officials were among the closest of the prime minister's advisers. Fraser had three permanent heads of his department. The first, John Menadue, had been Whitlam's principal private secretary when he was leader of the opposition, a Labor candidate and then an executive for the Murdoch newspaper empire. Fraser kept him on, although many of his ministers retained some suspicions about his earlier political sympathies. Menadue had begun to build up the strength of the department under Whitlam and continued that process for Fraser.

In October 1976 Menadue was appointed as ambassador to Japan and was replaced by Alan Carmody, then head of the Department of Business and Consumer Affairs. Carmody had a 'can-do' philosophy. Anything the prime minister wanted should be provided, and as soon as possible. As Fraser recalls:

Carmody wanted to make sure the department serviced the PM even better than the PM wanted. Nothing pleased him more than when he'd have a piece of paper on my desk which he had done for me before I asked for it.

Carmody was brash, aggressive and demanding, pushing himself and the department to meet demands that could be infinite. Eventually the pressure was too much; he died of a heart attack at his desk.

For the final five years the permanent head was Geoffrey Yeend, a career public servant who had spent thirty years in PMC. He was the antithesis of Carmody: calm, unflappable and always conscious of what was needed and what was possible. He tended to play down the role of PMC. He was also better than Carmody at explaining to the prime minister why he couldn't have what he wanted, or why something couldn't be done. When asked, for instance, why the department shouldn't draw up a series of alternative tax schedules to test the impact of various potential changes, Yeend retorted that it would be a large project that would be time-consuming and a waste. The prime minister did not insist.

None of the permanent heads attempted to monopolise access to the prime minister; they recognised that his interests were too broad and given Fraser's style they were aware that they could never succeed. Behind Yeend and the other permanent heads was a platoon of able public servants. In the economic area were Ian Castles, perhaps the most respected policy analyst in the department, Ed Visbord and Michael Keating. In general policy areas there were Tony Ayers, John Enfield, Michael Codd and Alan Rose. All six of these later became department heads. Several division heads also made rapid progress through the ranks of the public service. They all had direct access to the prime minister. Whereas notes to the prime minister may have been 'signed off' in final form by officers lower down and sent direct to his office, around a dozen officials could be expected to brief the prime minister directly and regularly.

The department was quite prepared to accept that it was involved in giving alternative policy advice. Yeend has commented publicly:

We do not feel inhibited in what some might interpret as the role of second opinion. Our branches have built up an understanding of policy issues and an expertise in co-ordination; our officers are sought out for their advice and assistance. We have scope for probing and proposing.

He argued that PMC

is a tool of government that can be used in a very direct and telling way in ensuring that government policies are got under way, that changes in direction are made, that there is a responsiveness by the public service as a whole to new instructions and change of style.

Yeend believed that PMC should give support to the fulfilment of one main duty of the prime minister: the maintenance of a sense of direction and cohesion in government. That required, of course, that Fraser provided a sense of direction.

Yeend and his colleagues argued that PMC was not exclusively concerned with the position of the prime minister; it was also required to serve the cabinet. Yeend stated that

it is not our business to have ministers surprised in the cabinet room with questions they have not anticipated, or be faced in the cabinet room with propositions they have not considered.

Wherever possible, PMC officials argued, they would consult the responsible department, and let it know what the objections might be.

However, at times they were instructed otherwise. Fraser would give two or three people or groups the same task to do, and require them to act independently. Rather than receiving an agreed wisdom, he wanted to see to what extent their proposals might differ. It was, thought a senior member of the private office, one of the only ways of getting work out of the public service. Fraser was prepared to develop, and profit from, creative tension.

The PMC briefs were for the prime minister alone. As one official commented, with respect to a memo on the Olympic boycott in 1980:

We are aware that [to give a copy of the note for the PM to the minister] would be a departure from the existing policy of not giving out copies of advice given to the PM, but we consider that in this case an exception should be made.

Primarily as a consequence of Fraser's use of the department, PMC was often criticised by ministers and other officials. There was a constant tension between its traditional collective role and its support for the prime minister. Far from merely 'holding the ring' to see that due process was followed, PMC played an active and interventionist role. One minister declared that its members did not have the expertise to challenge the experience and knowledge of departments, but they did it nonetheless. Another feared it had become the quickest route to the top ranks of the service after several PMC officials were appointed permanent heads. Peacock in particular publicly condemned the department when he resigned in 1981; he argued that it 'challenged the authority given ministers by section 64 of the Constitution. It places deep strains on the public service because it sets public servant against public servant'.

PMC was a useful scapegoat. If ministers lost they often didn't want to blame the prime minister, so they blamed the department. Yet PMC largely gave what it was asked for: advice on almost all issues. The problem for ministers was often that PMC was more tuned in to political realities than their less sensitive departments. PMC was assertive in interdepartmental committees and its interventions in discussions were often conclusive. Departments and ministers recognised the value of Fraser's support in cabinet. If, therefore, PMC expressed an opinion that was taken to be the prime minister's likely view – even if Fraser had not explicitly said anything – why not concede and reach some suitable agreement? Officials are conscious of the ability – or inability – of their minister to win in cabinet. Rather than risk defeat there, they will often compromise in the hope that the prime minister will support their case. PMC developed a reputation for power and often arrogance that made it unpopular.

Senior ministers, however, supported the need for a strong department. They argued that Fraser was well served, and needed to be well served. Nixon argued that the use of PMC was reasonable, as long as the ministers were strong enough to stand up to the prime minister, and the advice was professional and thorough. Weak ministers or woolly advice would, and sometimes in Nixon's view did, create difficulties. Another minister argued that PMC was regarded as meddling only because sections of the bureaucracy didn't like others knowing what they were doing. Therefore PMC was necessary as a useful check on narrow departmental views. Those ministers who saw value in a strong, active prime minister also saw the need for a strong department that would allow the prime minister to be well briefed.

Relations between the private office and PMC were generally harmonious. There were moments of tension. John Rose recalls being told that, if he chose to work from the private office, the department would 'cut his throat'; but when he still went, he did not feel isolated. There was tension in 1981 when David Kemp, as director of the office, insisted on the status of permanent head, a standing which Yeend found difficult to accept. PMC may not have wanted a strong private office, but it recognised its existence and the need for co-operation both because they needed access and because they respected the quality of the other's advice. The two bodies differed sometimes on the propriety of the department undertaking directly political roles. In 1979 Mike Codd, then deputy secretary, refused to reprint and circulate a speech made by Fraser at a party function; he claimed it was made by Fraser as political leader and not head of government. In 1981 he questioned whether the government should host ethnic functions; in this instance the private office disagreed and was told to 'get on with it' by Fraser. There was a distinction between the political office and the department. Yet PMC officials acknowledged that the private office had expertise and served the needs of the prime minister; the private office knew its access to information was generally through the department. Both were responsive to the needs of the prime minister, the office even more than the department. The prime minister needed both.

And all the other officials

The prime minister had a range of other bodies on whose advice he could call. He drew up the administrative orders that determined what departments existed and what responsibilities they had; he was responsible for determining the numbers of staff departments could employ. The Public Service Board gave him advice on pay and conditions in the public sector, on industrial relations and on staff numbers. Although much of the detailed work was in fact undertaken by ministers assisting the prime minister in public service matters, the prime minister could intervene where he chose. Fraser was always responsible for final decisions on staff ceilings, because only the prime minister had the authority to impose them on his colleagues.

Further, since prime ministers represent the government, in a sense they can have all departments working for them in that they can call for advice or options from any point in the service. Fraser used this advantage, working through PMC or the private office. The benefit was that, within the capacity of the line department, he received advice from those who nominally had the required expertise. However, the effect of a direct request from the prime minister to departments unaccustomed to them was often a paralysis, with other things being dropped until the immediate demand was met. Fraser would also use more than one department to provide alternative perspectives on the same problem. In 1980, for instance, he asked for a Treasury view on a PMC economic forecast. In budgets he would ask the Department of Employment and Industrial Relations for comments on Treasury forecasts on unemployment. He checked and rechecked every piece of advice.

Fraser was accused of creating further tension by his appointment of permanent heads. The choice of head of department belongs effectively to the prime minister. Under the Public Service (First Division Officers) Act, passed in 1977, a committee of permanent heads, usually chaired by the chairman of the Public Service Board, drew up a short list of candidates. The government could ask that names be added to the list. A candidate chosen from the list was described as 'established' and appointed till retirement. If the government chose figures from outside the list, they were 'non-established' and appointed for a fixed term or for the duration of the government. The purpose of the legislation was to distinguish between 'political' and 'career' appointees.

Yet the process of committee consideration and their recommendation was sometimes little more than a formality. When the Department of Employment and Industrial Relations was split, the committee met to recommend a person who had already been chosen. In 1977 a committee was created, and reported at the one meeting; there was no search for suitable appointees. Senior ministers were often consulted about the possible choice; those who had not met the recommended candidate were given a chance to meet and talk. Had they strongly opposed the choice, they had an effective veto. In a few cases junior ministers might have had a person imposed on them. Not all new permanent heads had previously met the prime minister. It is not possible to determine precisely what qualities the prime minister was looking for; a public servant developed a reputation for ability, strong advice and efficiency, either with the prime minister or with other senior ministers, that made him stand out.

Fraser was also criticised because many senior officers in PMC were appointed as permanent heads: Alan Woods to National Development, Ian Castles to Finance, Tony Ayers to Aboriginal Affairs and then Social Security, Mike Codd to Industrial Relations. It was suggested that he could thereby build up a network of loyalists within the bureaucracy through whom he could work, bypassing his ministers.

That accusation is untrue. Indeed Fraser was often reluctant to see them go. He regarded Castles as invaluable, yet felt he could not stand in the way of the career prospects of an officer who deserved promotion. Codd was also a close and trusted adviser. Yet in neither case did he approach these officials thereafter without their minister's knowledge. Certainly if they were summoned to cabinet or came to his office with their minister, he would seek their advice and, because he knew them well, value it. He also had a shrewd idea of what they thought. However, he was, according to his officials, conscious of the fight he had had in 1971 when Gorton had bypassed him and was not inclined to do it to his ministers. Besides, he knew that if he had tried to contact them without informing the minister, they would tell the minister. The professionalism of public servants required that they serve their minister, and only through him or her, the prime minister. While there is no doubt that the public service network, based on PMC, continued to work, Fraser did not utilise it directly.

Then there was his network of outside contacts, people whom he met at business lunches, at party functions, at official occasions. He often brought back to the department ideas that had been planted in these meetings and which he then wanted to explore or test. Denis White recalls that 'he could often say get X's view and the name would be a surprise'. He knew how to work his network.

Fraser's contacts were therefore wide; he sought advice constantly and refused to listen only to one source. Said a senior official: 'That is the system. The prime minister will talk to ministers, perhaps one or two, the department, the private office, Treasury, Finance'. There was never a danger of anyone creating a monopoly of advice.

Harnessing the advisory machinery

Fraser's use of the advisory machinery was based on his approach to politics. It was total. He tried to ensure that institutions served the government, while he was never the captive of any part of that machinery. He had no illusions that they could be used instrumentally, like a well-oiled machine. He appreciated that departments, actors and advisers all had their own interests, their own views. An official commented:

He understood institutions and, since he did not give his trust and loyalty and confidence to anyone, it led to a style of operations that meant he got advice and comment from a wide group. He would not readily, if ever, entrust himself or his government's reputation to any one of these institutions. He consulted different institutions in different ways, being aware of their abilities, and how to exact a fair response because people knew they had something to gain. He knew what advice represented and could synthesise the responses.

He was prepared to work harder and for longer hours than anyone else. He expected his advisers to be available when it suited him. One senior PMC official provides an idea of the pace:

He would ring, invariably about a quarter of an hour after I had got to sleep, and like other prime ministers who would be working through their papers, drop to one somewhere in the middle and would assume that you have been working through precisely the same file and reached the same paragraph on the same paper. And his question would be 'what are we going to do about eggs?' Well, you would have to say,' what are you looking at?' and you would have to nail that down before you started. But he would read [at] those sorts of hours and he would expect an answer, even if you had to wake him up.

Another recalls being rung at 1.40 a.m. on Christmas Day. At the end of the discussion, after he had proposed that Fraser get more up-to-date details from another officer, he wished Fraser a 'Happy Christmas', and received a somewhat grudging response. However when Fraser duly rang the next officer at 2.00 a.m., he started by wishing him a 'Happy Christmas' before asking for the information he wanted. Not even Christmas was sacred.

It was not only public servants who were expected to be available. A PMC officer recalls a meeting at the Lodge in the early hours of the morning, where Fraser asked his officials to get Sir Roderick Carnegie on the phone. When they protested that it was the middle of the night, he retorted that he was sure Carnegie would be prepared to talk to him. He was (although how reluctantly is not recorded). Even foreign guests were not exempt. A PMC duty officer was told after midnight to ring a senior CHOGM guest to arrange a game of tennis for early that same morning.

His advisers were prepared to put in long hours of work because they knew that he did not ask them to do anything by way of hours and effort that he was not prepared to do himself. They were therefore constantly on the alert, mentally preparing for the demands of the prime minister. His style 'forced people to defend him from the moment they started to read their papers at breakfast; what am I likely to be asked about this or that?'. The pressure both kept them on their toes and made them conscious that they were serving a leader who took nothing for granted. The prime minister determined his own schedule; everyone else was required to fit into his framework.

Fraser always wanted immediate reactions. Budd claims 'When something was on his mind, he wanted to talk to people straight away. He would never leave something for a couple of hours or until tomorrow'. Even routine events were approached with an urgency that then turned them into major issues. An official remembers that 'It used to be a standing joke that if there wasn't a crisis, he'd organise one. If there was nothing running hot, it was almost as though he was bored'. To Budd 'he created urgency where none existed, leading to gruelling exchanges'. In the early hours of the day that the report of the Review of Commonwealth Functions was to be presented to parliament,

Fraser was going through the papers with a group of officials and staff. An association of ideas reminded him of another issue he wanted explored, so he asked for information. But he said, totally unconscious of its impact, 'There's no rush about that; the morning will do'. The pace never slackened; the expectations never relaxed. Pressure was always there; Fraser's impatience was legendary, his demands continuous. When an issue was on his mind he wanted action immediately, wanted to talk at once. It took the weight of a Yeend or an Anthony to suggest that things could be done more slowly – and get away with it.

But the impatience could lead to poor results. Fraser often wanted to make immediate responses when it might have been preferable to say that he wanted to consult. When the TV affair broke (see page 91), he wanted a statement made at once, even though he was told that it would take two days to collect the files. He was not prepared to tell the press he did not yet have an answer; that pressure may have increased the tension.

The tactic was perhaps a matter of balance. Impatience had costs, but possibly some advantages – for Fraser at least. Petro Georgiou considered that setting deadlines was the only way a prime minister could maintain control over the mass of material and decisions:

He'd say 'I'd like something and I'd like it now', which prima facie is not maximally productive, and it was something that, when you are actually on the spot, you didn't appreciate very much. But when you got away from it, you began appreciating it was one of the ways he could cope with a mass of inputs without generating a whole autonomous system of recollecting things. It was one way he could make sure the array of things he was moving on actually didn't escape his attention span.

Fraser's own explanation is that when he first became a minister, in the Department of the Army, he would give instructions to his officials but then nothing would happen. So he began to insist on regular reports. 'The idea of putting in deadlines grew out of this experience. To guarantee that something would happen, you need a follow-up system. If you're going to have a follow-up system you need deadlines'. Then there was the different question of how short the deadlines should be, and whose criteria should be used. Fraser realised the deadlines he set were often uncomfortably tight for public servants, but argues that 'if they had been light enough for comfort, they probably wouldn't have hit political deadlines'. He rarely forgot requests, so the system worked fairly well.

The workload was horrendous and tremendously varied. Looking back it is easy to isolate and then follow through threads of policy, and to explore their ramifications. Prime ministers do not have that luxury; they must deal with several diverse pressures at the same time. For instance, in the first half of 1981 Fraser had to deal with the review of commonwealth functions, the debate on the Sinai force, the 35-hour week campaign, the Peacock resignation, the budget preparations. Each of these was a sensitive and politically important issue and is described elsewhere in this book. Yet they were not isolated or discrete. Fraser had to shift, almost hourly, from one item to another. As he put it:

The papers that come over your desk are dealing with entirely different subjects. You can't avoid that. The person who can only think of one subject at a time sensibly is not prime ministerial material . . . You've got to be able to switch.

Prime ministers need instant recall of what has occurred and what stage the debate has reached if their briefing is not to become repetitive and at times pointless.

Amid this torrent of paper Fraser had an ability to distil briefs quickly. Officials said he had the capacity to 'cut through the bullshit' and go to the heart of a problem, often pinpointing the crucial paragraphs and then appreciating the implications at several levels – the political, electoral, policy levels – at once. Further, once he had been briefed he remembered what he had been told and could bring the relevant information into an argument. As Budd recalls:

The reason you lost so many arguments with him was that, supposing there were two sides to an argument and maybe they were finely balanced, ten points for and ten against; if you went in and you were on the 'for' side you might in the heat of the moment remember five of your points. He'd remember all ten of his.

Fraser kept his points clear, distinct and under control.

The public image often presented a decisive and dogged prime minister with his mind made up. In private the senior ministers saw a different picture because decisions were not taken lightly or quickly. Fraser was not cavalier in decision-making, a criticism that he had levelled in the past at Gorton. Staley claims:

He spent a lot of time agonising over decisions big and small. Maybe you can predict the decision in hindsight, but going through the process was a hard road, a hard and rocky road with him coming to the view it would be proper and appropriate.

Peacock also recalled the lengthy consideration: 'People didn't realise just how long he would agonise; reiteration after the decision was made led them to believe he had always felt that way'. Decisions required consultation, consideration and review. A prime minister, thought Fraser, should not allow cabinet to make a decision without having a clear notion of where it was going and what would eventuate.

Fraser was interested in ideas, but not in a detached sense. 'The force of a good idea' was a constant catchphrase, but he was concerned about their policy and political implications; 'Always solutions, solutions; there must be options', remembered a senior official. 'In a crisis', claims Kemp, 'he was interested in workable solutions, in what to do about it; information was designed for that end'. He was not a philosopher, but a practical person concerned with doing something. Ideas were to be used, not savoured. Certainly he liked to relate particular solutions to more general values; the speech-writers were sometimes told to 'put a bit of philosophy' into a speech, but in day-to-day discussions attention was directed to making progress. If political philosophy sometimes seemed muddled and inconsistent, it was because it was for use, not for show. Time was too short for anything else.

The process of analysing advice before reaching those

decisions was often rugged and tortuous. Fraser always wanted to understand why someone made a recommendation. He wanted more than hunches or strong feelings; he wanted a set of arguments that could be explained to justify reaching the conclusion. Wal Fife recalls:

He was never satisfied with what your view was, he always wanted to know why you held that view, e.g. if he was asking you what you felt was the correct date for the next election, he wasn't so much interested in the date, he wanted to know why. He wanted to test your reasoning.

Indeed often he was less interested in the result than the process as that gave him the opportunity to assess the quality of the adviser. Fraser thought the prime minister should be able to understand all the possible implications of an action. Although that could never be finally achieved he continued to search at least until he was persuaded. He needed to be briefed on the options and possible outcomes and he did not trust any one individual to forecast those outcomes; therefore he chose to satisfy himself by testing advice to the utmost. Once he was convinced the answer was right he then wanted to have it confirmed and sometimes asked for yet more opinions. An adviser was surprised that a man who had won two massive electoral victories so 'constantly sought reassurance', to have his views supported and endorsed before decisions were finally taken. One colleague argued that he wanted to make 'absolutely certain that he knew the tiniest pitfall, fault, trouble, detail of every decision'.

Testing and analysing options are obviously necessary for a leader. It was not the objective that angered his colleagues, but the ruggedness of the way he did it that created problems. He tested ideas by arguing a case and by questioning. Faced with a problem, Fraser would pick a line and pursue it doggedly, persistently. He would in effect adopt a stand and require others to explain why it should not be adopted; and he would stick to his case and only later agree it was indefensible. As a process it could be irritating, almost infuriating. There is one account of an adviser coming out of the prime minister's office seething with rage. Pointing to a white wall, he said 'See that wall, it's black'. However, at the end of the day Fraser might back off a proposition he had been defending dogmatically.

All advisers were treated the same way. Fraser enjoyed putting people under pressure and testing their capacity; his colleagues disliked the approach. He would seldom allow a lengthy, let alone a discursive, presentation; he wanted answers quickly. His questions were often skilful. If he wasn't sure what he wanted, on a subject like electricity pricing, claimed Denis White:

He would rather ask ten or twenty questions such as, what was the average increase in power over the last six months? and a series of questions revolving around the same topic, all on comparisons of state power charges. When the answers to the ten or twenty questions came back, he could pick out which one might be significant. He had a very great skill with a scattergun approach to find out some key information – he had a nugget of information he was after. By asking a whole series of questions and insisting that each be answered, it certainly prevented the wool from being pulled over his eyes.

On other occasions he would ask a specific and precise question; if that wasn't answered, he would retort that that wasn't the question he had asked. He was always probing and pushing.

Fraser was furious if he was let down; not unreasonably, as he was the person who had to act as the government spokesman and he, not the adviser, would be accused of misleading the public or the parliament. He could be angry even if the error might have been his. A staff member recalls:

The day the government announced the purchase of the VIP fleet of 707s, he decided to fly down to Melbourne that afternoon. The cameras were out at Fairbairn waiting to record this moment, the first time the prime minister used the fleet. It turned out the appointments weren't all that official. It was run on the ABC that Fraser had used the VIP fleet that day; he hadn't seen the premier, he hadn't done this, but he'd been in his office – he was actually going to a wine tasting but he drove straight past when he saw journalists waiting outside. In Canberra that night he was furious the press had found out and he wanted to know why. David Barnett said it was on his program and he had told a couple of people. Then followed the most horrific earbashing I think I have ever heard in my life, with David Barnett, myself and Fraser, really sounding off in an extremely emotional and heavy language.

Yet ten minutes later he called us down to his office on another matter entirely and said 'That's finished, that's over; I want you to look at this bit of paper, give me your views'. Almost as if it hadn't happened, totally calm, totally on the ball.

He was impatient with careless or slipshod work. It was dangerous to bluff because the adviser would never know how much information Fraser had. He was always likely to be aware of the last set of figures; if the adviser was to get a point of view accepted he either had to be as well informed as the prime minister or comment that, regardless of what the figures were, the political issue was still unchanged and still had to be addressed.

It was better to acknowledge ignorance and to come back later with accurate information, than to pretend that the answers were known. His questioning would soon lay bare the threads of an ill-founded argument, and possibly at the same time do irreparable harm to the reputation of the adviser. As a PMC official said:

If you had a good working relationship with him, he would be understanding, as understanding as any prime minister is. If someone felt very strongly and tried to offer him a view when they clearly didn't understand the matter, he didn't like it. If he asked you a question and you said 'I don't know the answer, I'll have to check', he would respect you for that. He'd develop confidence and then you came back to give him the answer. The first rule is not to give advice until you've done the checking. As long as Fraser knew that you would have done your homework and been as thorough as you could in the time you were given, if there was a mistake he wouldn't complain.

The atmosphere in an advisory session was often tense. Fraser appeared autocratic in manner, occasionally speaking through gritted teeth, tense and demanding answers, sometimes defending maverick cases, always probing. It is not surprising that some advisers were nervous, others scared; or that many performed well below their best. Some officials were so intimidated they didn't put their case well; they were not at ease, jumbled their argument, left parts out – and that often without the prime minister doing anything. He was polite to public servants; one adviser claims he only heard him swear once in seven years. He merely questioned every proposition they put, believing they would perform better that way. He could be scathing: 'Have you listened to a word I said?' . . . 'You've obviously got no understanding of the issue'.

Fraser readily acknowledged that he has an interrogative style:

My sons say that too. Because when I go home and ask what's happening on the farm, they say this. I'd ask about a few other things they wouldn't mention. It's just the way I'm built, I suppose. But if you want to find out about what's going on, you've got to ask. It's awkward when people don't know the answer.

His preparedness to argue a point made many advisers think that he'd had already made up his mind and was just trying to discredit alternative arguments. The reality was that often he hadn't. If he had a sneaking suspicion that his views were wrong, he wanted to test them. He did it by forcing others to argue. Unless the adviser understood the mechanics of the process, he'd think Fraser didn't want to know what he was trying to tell him. That was one of the limitations of the style; too many didn't appreciate the process. The tension was too great for effective performance.

Many officials bore the scars of a session with the prime minister. Because he believed in challenging their arguments, he paid little or no attention to the impact of prime ministerial ire on their feelings. His style bruised egos; it made people aware of their inadequacies; they felt hard done by and didn't understand what had happened. The justification that time was short and that the prime minister should not be bothered by irrelevancies might be generally accepted as valid; it did not alleviate the problem of individuals. It was not, claimed his close colleague Tony Staley, 'a pretty sight to behold as he would grind people up'. Too often, faced with this barrage, advisers gave way too early. Although he naturally liked to win an argument, Fraser did not like advisers he thought he could push around. He wanted people who would stand up for what they thought; he didn't want advice from those he did not respect. Indeed the more often advisers saw the prime minister – and that meant primarily those in the private office and PMC – the more they appreciated that Fraser was prepared to listen and often to change his mind. A member of the office claimed: 'I never saw a situation where, if there were good arguments, Malcolm was not swayable. But they had to be good arguments, not just strength of feeling'. A respected adviser commented: 'if you gave back as good as you got, he would give you a good hearing and have more respect for you'. A few claimed that if his mind seemed set they would not argue the case then, but would come back at a later date and try again; but the number who recognised this was small. There was a need to distinguish between the interrogation and the final decision. Advisers believed 'As long as he kept arguing a point, he was still interested in what you had to say. The only real sign that he rejected your advice was when he stopped talking about it'. Dale Budd stated:

He had an immense capacity to understand issues and see the consequences several steps down the track. He was tough to argue with, but he expected people to state their point of view strongly and to test his own views. When he was persuaded to change his mind, he would pursue the new course as vigorously as he had previously defended the old.

Understanding that distinction, appreciating the value of pressing on, was the difference between those whom Fraser respected and those he ignored or easily dismissed. The less the contact, the more dogmatic and closed-minded Fraser appeared to be. One consequence may have been that advisers needed a style as combatative and argumentative as his if they were to gain his confidence. Jim Carlton has commented that 'one of his weaknesses was that he wasn't good at accepting advice from mild people. He liked to clash'. He may well have excluded useful options as a result. Yet people like Street and Yeend, to take one minister and one public servant as examples, were both able to get their views across at times; it depended on their reputation and the quality of their advice. Fraser always sought a range of advice from those he respected, but was not interested in other people's. He was not as concerned with maintaining some artificial balance as with answers that could be tested and found satisfactory.

Working for Fraser was working in a hot-house. He often spoke gruffly, or abruptly, to his staff. He was demanding, impatient, and could hector. Yet he developed among the staff a remarkable sense of loyalty. In part it was because, when he was wrong, and particularly if he then castigated someone for it, he would apologise in some way, even if only by a nod of the head. In part it was because he accepted that people would make mistakes; if the adviser acknowledged it, he would not bear grudges. He might bawl someone out, and five minutes later call them back into the office and ask their opinion on another issue as though nothing had happened.

Indeed, some staff were used to ease the tension that Fraser created. He was prepared to admit that others were needed to soothe the feelings that he had trampled over. Reducing the atmosphere of crisis could only be done by others; it was not Fraser's style. Budd recalls:

He realised he tended to heat up situations and he looked to a number of people as a calming influence. I was one of them. I often found myself being called in because there was some problem going on and in fact not being given anything to do.

Fraser appreciated the benefit of having around people like Yeend who would quietly point out the difficulties of proposed actions.

The implications

The advisory system had its problems. The pace was frenetic, with deadlines that were often too short to allow ideas to be worked through. Management by crisis could squeeze out due and careful consideration. It could lead to misunderstandings of what was required and what was done. Asking several people to provide comments on the same issue could lead to duplication and a waste of scarce resources. Demanding an immediate response which required public servants to work throughout the weekend, and then failing to take the issue up for two or three days, could lead to anger and frustration, and thus to charges of inconsiderate arrogance. In other words, the demands of Fraser put pressure on the information systems and bureaucratic structures that they could only meet with difficulty.

Moreover, the bruised egos of advisers were seen as a sign of poor personnel management. Advisers did not work well, or put their case adequately, when they were intimidated. Adversarial processes and creative tension may bring out good answers from tough advisers, but inhibit those of advisers less used to such a bearpit.

On the other hand the style of operation had some advantages. Fraser's style allowed him to test those around him; it was intended to make people perform, to make sure they analysed their policies and presented them. It needed a man like Fraser, working all the time, to get the benefits out of it. While prime minister, Fraser was respected for his political nous. He had usually been successful; if he was to continue he needed to know what was going on. Too shy to jolly ideas out of people, too determined to relax, his style was to contest and argue. Since his interests spread across the government's activities he needed to work fast and to stick to the point.

How necessary such an advisory system may be will depend in part on the perception of the office that a prime minister brings to it. If the prime minister wishes to maintain a close interest in the activities of the government, to understand all the implications of decisions that cabinet may make and to try to integrate them into the government's priorities, then clearly a powerful PMC and private office are required to provide the necessary detail. If, by contrast, a prime minister is more concerned to act as a director or political manager watching the ministers without becoming involved in, or questioning, most of their policy, the demands on the advisory systems may be less, as alternative assessments of policy are not required. Fraser's conception of the office fits the first description, while Hawke's appears nearer the second. As a consequence Fraser chose to be involved in a broad range of detail and developed an advisory system that could serve that need. It was designed to ensure that he received a range of advice and was the captive of no one.

Fraser did not use the system in isolation from others. He did not talk to his advisers and then to his ministers or cabinet; they were all likely to be involved at the same time, as part of the swirling currents of people, ideas and options that are part of the political system. Nevertheless the tough and bruising process of briefing provided the foundation for his influence elsewhere – particularly among his ministers and in cabinet.

CHAPTER 3

'THAT BIG BASTARD'

RELATIONS WITH MINISTERS

P rime ministers are not presidents. They do not have the constitutional right to make all decisions. Their ministers are as much their colleagues as their subordinates. Individually the ministers have formal and legal authority to make decisions within their portfolios. Collectively they work with the prime minister in cabinet, the forum in which most decisions of importance are likely to be made.

Ministers are never all ciphers. They will include most of the senior and talented members of the party. Some may represent states or factions and have a power base in the party; others may have reputations that require they be listened to. They direct many areas of policy. Working as a group they can determine what cabinet does. Any cabinet will include several who want to become prime minister, either by peaceful succession or by removing the incumbent.

Ministers have the potential to wield power. They can limit prime ministers' power – if they choose to try, if they have the capacity, if they have the support. That is the crux of any debate. The arguments that sustain the notion of prime ministerial power tend to argue either that ministers limit prime ministers' power or that they are merely their 'agents'. The truth may be different from both propositions. Ministers may have the potential to influence the prime minister but not the courage. It will depend on their calibre and on the style and strength of the prime minister. Therefore the reality of that power must be tested empirically, not just stated categorically. It will differ from time to time, as some ministers or groups of ministers will be stronger, more cohesive and more influential than others.

It is wrong, however, to regard prime ministers and ministers as necessarily antagonistic. They are meant to be part of the same team. How closely they work depends on the degree to which prime ministers choose to become involved in the details of particular portfolios and the extent to which the ministers accept their right to do so. An understanding of the interaction between leader and led requires a detailed knowledge of the way government works. Attention is usually given to the points of high drama: the appointment of ministers, the dismissal or resignation of individuals, major policy decisions. Yet these are simply very public examples of a relationship built up over a longer period of time and maintained. Ministers interact with the prime minister constantly, both individually and in cabinet. How they react in a crisis will be determined in part by that relationship. The daily contacts provide the foundation on which actions in times of crisis are built. Ministers have to coexist long beyond any one case; few issues are in themselves so important that they are worth risking good relations with the prime minister. Every contest will need an estimate of gains and losses and will depend on the confidence and standing of the minister. The prime minister's influence on policy is determined by the way in which this regular relationship between prime minister and minister is defined, not by the use of dictat.

Prime ministers have a range of formal sanctions or rewards when they deal with their ministerial colleagues. The appointment and dismissal of ministers is the prerogative of Liberal leaders. All prime ministers have the right to promote, reshuffle or demote. Prime ministers decide the range and importance of the ministers' jobs. The Administrative Arrangement Order, which creates and abolishes departments and distributes functions between them, is the sole responsibility of prime ministers. They decide who the ministers are and what they do.

In Australia the prime minister's powers are restricted when there is a coalition government. In this case the prime minister does not select all the ministers, nor are all of them members of the same party and thus able to be readily removed. National party ministers owe their position to their party leader and their loyalty to their party. They provide within the government a group which, whether or not it acts in a united fashion, is set apart from other ministers.

Patronage gives prime ministers influence over those in office and those who hope to get there. Yet that power does not necessarily buy obedience, and nor do prime ministers want it to. Good ministers are valuable because no prime minister can do everything. Incompetent ministers lead to bad government. If prime ministers are to stay in office for long they need to mould the ministers into a team, to work with them, to develop co-operation, loyalty and direction.

This chapter will examine the relationship between Fraser and his ministers as individuals: it will explore how he selected ministers, in what circumstances some were dismissed, and how the responsibilities were distributed. After identifying the sources of power it will show how they influenced the relationship, and their consequences for policy outcomes. The next chapter will examine the activities in cabinet – how Fraser as prime minister interacted with the ministers as a collectivity.

The selection of ministers

Traditionally Liberal prime ministers are powerful because they give the ultimate reward of patronage: a place in the ministry. It does give them control over the future of their colleagues, but not totally. Prime ministers are constrained in their choice of ministers. Some colleagues have positions in the party that cannot be ignored. They may be the leading representatives of the states, the most able senators, or representatives of a point of view or faction. Some have high reputations, others bring the weight of history to their side. In building a cabinet none of these can be ignored.

Fraser was aware of this, even after his sweeping electoral victory. His shadow executive in opposition had been large. When he beat Snedden for the leadership he retained the fifteen Liberals that Snedden had chosen ten months earlier and added five of his own. As there were a further nine Country party shadow ministers, the opposition front bench had thirty members in all. In the selection of his first ministry of twenty-two people, Fraser was faced with the problem of who should be left out, rather than who should be included. Three of the five he added to the shadow executive in March that year were kept in: four of Snedden's choices were excluded, so were four members of the Country party shadow cabinet. Two of those excluded, Liberal Don Chipp and the Country party's Tom Drake-Brockman, had previous ministerial experience and had been members of the inner shadow cabinet. Only two Liberal outsiders were appointed – one of them was the new member for Bass, Kevin Newman, whose sweeping by-election victory in July 1975 had been the harbinger of the December landslide.

What criteria were used for selection? It was difficult for anyone, even Fraser, to be precise. It is a matter of judgement about who will be able to cope with the pressures of the job:

If you are going to choose ministers on a personality basis, or whether you get on with them, with a relatively small parliament you will be in grave trouble, because it will be seen that you are doing that. You have got to make the decisions on the basis of ability. Fred Chaney told me he was surprised when I asked him to do a job. He knew that I knew that he hadn't voted for me. I thought that was irrelevant. We were in the one party. He was an able young man and thoroughly competent. If you have any other approach, it's just not going to work.

Fraser looked at their record and assessed what they could do. For instance, he picked John Howard 'out of the ruck' when Lynch suddenly resigned in 1977, because Howard had performed effectively as minister for special trade representations and could debate well: a necessary quality in the middle of an election campaign. As Fraser puts it:

You think that the guy can do the job without having enumerated the particular things about him that led you to that conclusion. You are just convinced in your own mind and that's your judgement of people.

Every state was represented, but only in the ministry. Tasmania, for instance, returned five Liberals from five seats, and deserved representation, but Tasmania and South Australia never produced ministers who were promoted to cabinet. The available people did not have the political clout, the talent or the support of the prime minister to justify their promotion.

The balance between the parties in the coalition was never much of a problem. Fraser frequently recalled Menzies's comment on his retirement that the maintenance of a stable coalition had been one of his greatest achievements. He took a similar view and insisted that the relationship with the National party leader, Doug Anthony, was one of the vital factors in the success of the coalition government. The agreement never had to be written down; it was based on an accepted give and take:

There was pretty much an agreed formula over the years between the two parties; there were only variations at the margins. If I had a good reason for something, Doug wasn't going to be a stickler. He'd say, 'Well, all right, this time there is an adjustment; I will expect you to remember this'. And I did.

Anthony was also conscious that in 1975 and 1977 the Liberals had a majority in the House of Representatives in their own right and the Country party were in the coalition by invitation.

Prime ministers cannot afford to have too many potential rivals on the backbench, particularly in Australia where they can be easily challenged for their position as party leader. One or two rivals at most can therefore be left out. Those who were excluded in 1975 were as significant as the actual choices. The most notable was the articulate Don Chipp, the shadow spokesman for social security. Fraser and Chipp were the antithesis of one another in political style and in their attitudes to social policy. In retrospect the decision to omit Chipp may have been a mistake, as he left the party and formed the

Democrats, who then stripped the government of its Senate majority. Many ministers felt, with all the advantages of hindsight, that it would have been better to have kept Chipp within the government.

The reasons given for excluding people provide insights into Fraser's approach. He saw it as important that people could be trusted. To play as part of the team included a preparedness to accept defeat in cabinet or the shadow executive. If, for instance, a shadow minister had been unable to carry a proposal through the shadow executive, and then called in the president of a state division to try to reopen the question, he indicated an inability to accept the validity of his colleagues' collective decisions and forfeited their trust. Once Fraser made an initial judgement about a person's ability or trustworthiness, that opinion was difficult to shift.

Fraser did not select ministers entirely on his own. He consulted widely with his senior colleagues about whom to include and whom to exclude. Anthony was drawn into the discussion, and not only on coalition choices; the party leaders in the Senate provided views on the most suitable candidates there. The senior party members from each state had their opinions canvassed about their state colleagues. Those whom Fraser trusted implicitly, like Nixon and Street, may have been used as sounding boards. The final choice was Fraser's, but the process of selection was not random – there would have been no surprises for senior colleagues. Even if Fraser made the formal decision, others knew that they had been involved, and indeed that their views may have been important. As Fraser comments: 'A willingness to consult your senior colleagues indicates a willingness not to proceed with the decision'. It also muted later criticism.

After 1975 changes were fairly constant, as ministers fell from office or left deliberately. Of twelve cabinet ministers in office in January 1976, only seven (four Liberals, three National party) were still there when the government lost office in 1983, though two of these (Andrew Peacock and Ian Sinclair) had had a spell on the backbench and Nixon had announced his retirement. Only five of the twelve outer ministers lasted the distance. Five ministers both entered government after 1975 and left office before the government fell.

Promotion and change in ministries are necessary to maintain enthusiasm and initiative. If the ministers are drawn from different age brackets, then there can be a regular flow of retirements or replacements, as Menzies had throughout his term, to allow the influx of new talent. But the Fraser cabinet was young and all of a similar age. In 1975 Fraser himself was forty-five; only two ministers, Cotton and Carrick, were over fifty-one. It was a cabinet that could expect a long life, if it was assumed that the retention of office was the summit of a politician's ambitions. In principle, as Fraser remarked, everyone believes that ministers should place the government first if the prime minister wants them to depart the scene or take a less important job – but not when it applies to them!

Yet there was a high rate of attrition. Sixteen ministers left office, three of them (Garland, Robinson, Ellicott) having been out and then in again before the final break. As a consequence there were often vacancies, always important for backbenchers on the fringe of the ministry. Deciding on replacements may be hard for a prime minister, particularly when a government has 127 senators and members and thus many more aspirants than positions. Each choice can make an enemy of a person overlooked. The prime minister had again to take some account of state representation, but also to seek out what talent was available. There will always be disputes about ability, but very few of those passed over by Fraser have since made a mark in opposition. Nor did he ignore those who criticised government policy; Jim Carlton, a leader of the backbench ginger group of economic rationalists known as the 'dries' after 1980, was added to the ministry in 1982.

Access to the ministry was crucial to most backbenchers who had entered parliament with any ambition. Peter Baume, Neil Brown and Jim Carlton all recall discussing their futures with Fraser after they had been passed over in a ministerial reshuffle. They wanted to know if they had a future in politics – a ministerial future. Fraser, aware of the pressures from his own ten years on the backbenches and recalling a similar discussion he had had with Harold Holt, never promised anyone a job, but he did encourage them. He suggested that they should hang on, and pointed out that circumstances in politics could change quickly. One was promoted three months after the discussion when a ministerial crisis led to sudden resignations; all three became ministers.

National party ministers were selected by Doug Anthony. The 'big three' – Anthony, Sinclair and Nixon – were tough, experienced and selected themselves; they also made up the National party entitlement in the cabinet. Ralph Hunt was an obvious fourth. Given the strength of the party in Queensland, some representative had to be found from there – Evan Adermann, Tom McVeigh, David Thomson and, for twenty-four hours, Senator Glen Sheil were selected, all holding only junior portfolios. After the departure of Senator Webster in 1979 and the replacement of Senator Scott in 1980 there were no National party ministers in the Senate. National party appointees were discussed with Fraser; he had a veto but never felt inclined to use it.

Promotion within the ministry occurred primarily because a minister was seen to be performing well. In part that relied on performance in cabinet, in part on a broader reputation. Fraser recalls:

Your department would be of some use. Your permanent head has got to know what other permanent heads think about their ministers' administration, how they are going and whether there are problems. You start to get worried if ministers are accident prone and if things are getting into the public domain that indicated back-seat administration; or if members can't comply with cabinet decisions about getting submissions forward at the time cabinet had asked for them.

An impression of competence was important. Some promotions – Howard, Chaney and Baume stand out – were very fast. Howard performed well when the ill-fated wages-price freeze was suddenly handed to him in June 1977 and later as EEC negotiator. Chaney and Baume had handled the sensitive area of Aboriginal Affairs with skill and tact and were then shifted to more senior cabinet positions. Other ministers were appointed at an earlier date but never promoted to cabinet.

The prime minister's power to choose ministers always had

an impact on backbenchers; they wanted to have their efforts noticed and appreciated. The prime minister was the recipient of a flood of letters from backbenchers. Some were flattering – perhaps to excess: 'Truly a great speech of Churchillian proportions' wrote Michael Hodgman, MHR from Tasmania, in one of his more restrained protestations of fealty. Others were less exuberant, but still intent on illustrating their support. A few challenged Fraser on points of policy and John Hyde constantly attacked Fraser's economic policy, particularly his record of public sector cuts. Hyde's letters were cogent and critical. There was a concerted attack on the government's policy on tax evasion. Criticism and debate were not lacking, even from those who hoped to get ministerial preferment. The range of tactics recalls the advice given to Richard Crossman by Nye Bevan:

You know, Dick, there are only two ways of getting into cabinet. One way is to crawl up the staircase of preferment on your belly; the other way is to kick them in the teeth. But, he said, for God's sake, don't mix the two methods.

Some backbenchers could have benefited from heeding that advice. Expectations, however remote, played their part; they were expectations that Fraser would not deny, even if he would never confirm them. Therein lay the source of his power.

Reshuffles and the administrative orders

Prime ministers decide what jobs ministers will do. They also are responsible for decisions about the structure of the government: what departments will be created, what functions each department will fulfil. The two powers are complementary. Those allocations will depend on a balance between ministerial qualities and administrative logic. Sometimes the need to put ministers into slots will appear to predominate; at other times the problems caused by administrative failure will demand action.

There were no shortages of proposals for administrative change in 1975. Sir Henry Bland argued the need for a broad-ranging reconstruction of institutions. He believed there were too many departments and too much control of state government spending. He advocated the abolition of two highly-criticised and 'trendy' Labor departments, the Department of Urban and Regional Development and the Department of the Media. Several different sets of possible departmental arrangements were considered, with Fraser making the final decisions; for instance, he changed the name of the Department of Agriculture back to its original name of Primary Industry. Doug Anthony, as deputy prime minister, chose the powerful departments of Trade and Resources. The second was a trade-off, because Fraser wanted a separate Industry department to break up the old Trade and Industry empire run by former deputy prime minister, John McEwen. In general, the departmental structure announced in December 1975 reflected a continuity with pre-1972 names and thus a break with the Whitlam government. The symbolism was important. Fraser also juggled with the names of permanent heads. He added some, crossed others out in a striking indication of the power the prime minister has over the future of senior officials. Fraser had not only worked with many senior officials in the public service; for a long time he had lived in Canberra, having bought a luxurious house (which he only sold in 1973 when he went into opposition) comfortably situated just behind the Lodge. Many of his judgements were based on intimate early experience.

The allocation of portfolios is indicative both of limited options and policy choices. Senior shadow ministers were generally given their shadow positions; the National party retained its traditional areas of transport and primary industry. There were a few sudden switches: Guilfoyle had been shadow minister for education and became minister for social security. The widest options were in the junior positions, yet even there some people, such as Ralph Hunt as minister for health, got particular jobs as much because they filled the hole in a jigsaw, as because they had skills or expertise.

Some of the choices had clear policy messages. Tony Street, for instance, was given the post of minister for industrial relations. He had been briefly an assistant minister for labour in the McMahon government and had been involved as shadow minister in developing industrial relations policy. Street's views on industrial policy were known; he believed that, although governments could create the structures within which industrial relations could be operated, they could not legislate for compliance. That required consultation and negotiation. Fraser argued:

We really believed in 1976 that divisions in Australia needed healing and, whatever the legacies, however difficult that might be, we ought to pursue that approach and try the ACTU with consultation.

Street's appointment ensured that any proposals coming from the minister would reflect this attitude – one that accepted the value of the 'industrial relations' club. That did not mean that the government's policy was predetermined; the final choice remained with cabinet. However cabinet was unlikely to reject consistently the advice of the responsible minister, particularly one who was close to the prime minister. The decisions of December 1975 reflected both the new policy directions of the government, particularly in the abolition of some of Labor's departments, and the available talent. The skill lay in matching the two.

Thereafter alterations to the administrative arrangements were caused either by the need to change the ministerial mix or to solve administrative problems. Although the latter was nearly always the publicly expressed justification, changes for the former reason were common. As one official remembered, the changes were:

Sometimes to create a few jobs, sometimes to show that things were happening, sometimes because he was dissatisfied with the way things were working and the expectation of improvement. But I don't think there were any deep-seated principles.

Further, fitting the last pieces together was often completed in a hurry, so that announcements could end the speculation and rumours. In 1980 one permanent head, Sir Richard Kingsland, complained that he had heard the name of his new minister over the radio and asked why he had not been properly informed. A PMC official responded:

I am sure you will appreciate that changes in the ministry and in the machinery of government are often finally determined at the last minute with the announcement wanted very quickly; thereafter there is then very little time to give advance notice to those affected.

The allocation of the final positions occurred, therefore, with a remarkable haste for so important a decision.

Industrial relations again provides one example. By 1978 the burden on the minister had grown as unemployment had risen. There were plausible policy reasons for allowing a minister to concentrate on industrial relations rather than employment schemes and other policies. In a meeting with the chairman of the Public Service Board and the secretary of PMC, Fraser spoke of the need for greater emphasis on industrial relations and youth affairs. Fraser and Lynch discussed various alternatives with the officials. The chairman of the Public Service Board, Bill Cole, emphasised the disruption that would be caused by a split, and argued that, if the main concern was a lack of leadership in the department, it would be easier to change the permanent head. Fraser nevertheless insisted. The decision to split the department into Industrial Relations and Employment and Youth Affairs was largely based on the need to lighten Street's load, but it had to be presented in such a way that it was not seen as a demotion for Street. Fraser resisted the suggestion that a broader change might camouflage the altered position of Street and justified the change by reference to the government's desire for a new initiative. The pressures were more political than administrative, yet the administrative problems then emerged in the long confrontation that took place between the Public Service Board and the new department over its structure. For seven months the dispute continued, with the department trying to draw Fraser in on its side, a move described by Yeend as 'smart alec'. One consequence of the ministerial change was long administrative inertia.

In 1982 the two departments were reunited. Peacock had replaced Street as minister for industrial relations briefly before his dramatic resignation and then was replaced by Ian Viner. Although an industrial lawyer, Viner was probably the only minister for industrial relations not in sympathy with the 'industrial relations club'. When Peacock resigned and Viner was mooted as his replacement, George Polites rang Doug Anthony to see if the appointment could be stopped, but Anthony reported that Fraser's mind was made up. Viner was never accepted by the 'club', in part because its members believed he lied to them, in part because he was never able to catch the mood of the prime minister or the community. The administrative problems of co-ordination stimulated the demands inside and outside government for change. A new permanent head was appointed in December 1981 and the two departments were rejoined under Macphee, whose acceptance of the need for consultation before change was similar to Street's. Again the choice of minister had an impact on the policy; in this case administrative and political problems led to a policy change.

In other instances reshuffles had a political dynamic. In 1979, after a few years of constant change in the form of Medibank, health was seen to be an issue on which the government was doing poorly; party polls suggested that votes would be lost. A new minister was needed to salvage the wreck. Michael Mackellar recalls being summoned to the phone in the kitchen of a Greek restaurant and the ensuing exchange: '"I want you to be minister for health." "Why, what have I done wrong?" There was a dead silence. He wasn't renowned for his sense of humour'. Mackellar was not given any instructions on how to approach the job, but he had a reputation for wrapping problems in cotton wool. Health as an issue duly went off the political agenda, not to surface again until after the 1980 election.

Proposals for administrative change were constant, with ministers often arguing a case that would strengthen their own position. In 1977, for instance, Senator Cotton argued that the Department of Business and Consumer Affairs served no useful purpose and its responsibilities should be split, with PMC taking over the IAC, Administrative Services, getting Housing and the Narcotics Bureau, and with most of the remainder going to his Department of Industry and Commerce. That eventually occurred when far-reaching changes were made in May 1982, after the two ministerial vacancies caused by the 'TV affair' were coupled with the external demands to remove Viner from Industrial Relations. On that occasion several drafts of possible administrative orders were sent to the prime minister, the first on 6 May, and they were gradually refined. The Department of Business and Consumer Affairs was finally abolished. The Department of the Vice-President of the Executive Council, a department with three staff and no separate permanent head, was created to keep the former minister for defence, Jim Killen, in cabinet.

A second change in 1982 saw part of the Department of Defence hived off into a Department of Defence Support. Fraser needed to find a position in which to put Viner, who had been unsuccessful as minister for industrial relations and whose credibility was low. This case provides a useful insight into how ideas about machinery of government can gradually emerge. The notion that the Department of Defence was too large for one minister to control had a lengthy history, although its minister, Jim Killen, believed otherwise. He had written to Fraser in 1979 arguing that a second minister was not needed. Nevertheless, in November 1980 PMC proposed a Defence Supply Department which could be responsible for defence factories, and in April 1981 Phillip Lynch also suggested a Department of Defence Supply. The idea of a second department was therefore constantly being floated. In 1982 a committee was examining the structure of the Defence Department; Fraser asked the chairman of the committee, John Utz, to indicate whether its current thinking supported a second department. He was told that it did; thus Fraser had external authority to use as a justification for the decision. The secretary of Defence, however, commented in a letter to the chairman of the Public Service Board that he was not in favour of the proposal; he listed four pages of problems that he thought a split would cause, while its only advantage would be the creation of a new portfolio – but to no avail. The Department of Defence Support was created to provide a backwater and non-cabinet position for the demoted Viner. In 1982 the political demands of a harassed ministry were predominant, yet, as usual, the public explanations were couched in terms of efficiency and administrative need.

Not all administrative changes were derived from ministerial problems. The most dramatic change to the machinery of government decision occurred on 18 November 1976, when Fraser announced his decision to split the Treasury, a decision whose genesis is normally attributed to an article written by Ken Davidson of the *Age* on 10 November and reputedly based on a leak from the Treasury. Davidson had claimed that at an economic committee of cabinet the prime minister had only just been talked out of a devaluation. The split was interpreted as an act of pique. It was far more considered than that legend suggests.

Fraser had considered a split of the Treasury in December 1975, but he thought that the changes made at that time were already extensive enough. During 1976 he had not always been happy with the quality of the economic advice he was receiving and the Treasury had strongly contested the introduction of family allowances. More importantly, he had sent three letters to the treasurer, asking that the Treasury make available to his department the information on which their economic forecasts were based. He received no response and the Treasury continued to fight to retain its monopoly on economic advice. In September Fraser complained to the secretary of PMC about the quality of briefing notes on economic submissions. He was ready to demand change, as the evidence in Chapter 7 illustrates.

On Friday 5 November a group of ministers (not a cabinet committee) discussed the state of the dollar with two Treasury officers, Sir Frederick Wheeler and John Stone. The debate was clearly vigorous. The same day Fraser called over the chairman of the Public Service Board, told him that he was unhappy with the performance of Treasury and wanted more resources and emphasis directed to budget management, forward estimating and the provision of timely information for the government. He had no particular views on what structures might be best. Only the prime minister, the treasurer (it was always agreed that Lynch would keep both departments) and the secretary of PMC were aware of the request. A batch of material was thus collected for the prime minister, with the work starting some five days before Davidson's article on 10 November; it may have confirmed Fraser's determination to act, but it was not the catalyst for change.

The prime minister read the briefing material over the weekend of 13-14 November and was most attracted to the option of splitting Treasury. The chairman of the board pointed out the disadvantages, but Fraser was too disenchanted with Treasury to be persuaded. He said that the treasurer would retain both departments. On 15 November Wheeler, the secretary of Treasury, was informed and in a series of notes to his minister argued against the split, while accepting that it could be made to work. Bill Cole, the commonwealth statistician and a former Treasury officer, was brought in to advise on the details. The prime minister wanted to be given final details by midday on Friday 19 November.

Suddenly, at 9.30 a.m. on Thursday 18 November, Fraser asked for a detailed note and a press statement by 12.15 p.m. that day. He finalised the detailed division of responsibilities between the two departments and then demanded the draft of a public statement by 3.00 p.m. It was taken in to him while a cabinet meeting was in progress and Fraser's amendments to the draft were conveyed out of the Cabinet Room by Carmody. The prime minister had added to the draft statement the names of the two permanent heads, Wheeler and Cole. The final statement was made at 5.45 p.m. Only two Treasury officers had been informed; the remainder were told of the split by Wheeler at a meeting held at the same time as Fraser spoke in parliament. The surprise was complete. In the ensuing two weeks the details of personnel and functions were eventually settled. On 28 November the government devalued the dollar by 17 per cent.

The split of Treasury was made for policy and administrative reasons, not to solve ministerial problems. A separate minister for finance was not appointed until after the 1977 election. The split was designed to break the monopoly on information that Treasury held, to provide alternative resources of economic advice, and to centralise the expenditure control functions. Based on the desire of the prime minister to be briefed more broadly on economic matters, it was a classic instance of the prime minister asserting his authority in administrative arrangements.

Dismissals and resignations

Prime ministers can sack ministers. In a coalition government prime ministers have the absolute right to demand the resignation of Liberal ministers. In theory no reason has to be given, no excuse found. It is enough that the prime minister wants a change.

The reality is different. In Australia prime ministers prefer not to keep powerful opponents on their backbenches. It is easy to remove leaders in the Australian parliamentary system; it requires a vote in the party room, and no more. Opponents can act as catalysts for revolt, or as the centres of organised dissent. The Australian preference is to find jobs outside politics – from governor-general to consul-general – to buy off internal opposition or create ministerial vacancies. In the twenty years before 1983 only one cabinet minister has been fired simply because he wasn't up to the job, although others have been demoted, or offered demotions, to the outer ministry. Fraser was not a ministerial butcher who ruthlessly cast aside the incompetent. Indeed many of this colleagues thought he should have been much tougher, removing many of the less efficient ministers. Fraser commented, by contrast, that: 'If a minister has given good service to the party and to the government of Australia, I think he has earned some sort of right to the possibility of a graceful and good retirement'. And anyway, he did not want to cause a by-election, added one cynical observer. Whatever the reason, there were no sackings of senior ministers just because their performance was inadequate.

Yet the Fraser cabinet saw constant changes. Three junior ministers were dropped in 1980. One cabinet minister, Ivor Greenwood, died. Four – Robert Cotton, Vic Garland, Jim Webster and John McLeay – were given overseas appointments. Three chose to leave politics, as a consequence of illness (Phillip Lynch), frustration (Robert Ellicott) or a desire for a change (Tony Staley). Eric Robinson refused to serve when offered a demotion in 1980, having resigned in 1979 for a week in an unexplained fit of pique. Vic Garland and Ian Sinclair were forced to stand down when facing court action. It was not a picture of stability.

Fraser did not initiate all these movements. The dismissals were his decisions. He could not have been surprised by Robinson's refusal to serve when he offered him a position outside cabinet but he had often found that, as minister for finance, Robinson was not briefed on issues when they were discussed; he was a lazy minister and not held in high regard. Fraser encouraged the overseas appointments as a means of creating some movement in the ministry without having to sack anyone. After the 1980 election he asked some ministers what their long-term plans were. When McLeay said that he would like to stand down in a year or so, he was persuaded to take an overseas appointment immediately; that allowed a new person to be given a job when new blood was clearly needed.

However the most striking crises were forced on Fraser by circumstances beyond his control. Precisely because he was struggling to regain the initiative, these cases – the resignations of Phillip Lynch, Reg Withers, Andrew Peacock, Michael Mackellar and John Moore – provide the clearest insight into the way that Fraser interacted with his ministers in times of crisis.

Lynch

The Lynch case in 1977 exploded into public view during the election campaign. Phillip Lynch was accused of having taken advantage of his position as treasurer to benefit from land and property deals. Questions had been asked in parliament in late October but the answer that Lynch gave, after discussions with Fraser and Tony Eggleton, the federal director of the Liberal party, had been designed to avoid an extension of the charges. In the meantime Lynch's press secretary had tried to defuse the issue by providing background information to journalist Laurie Oakes with Lynch's side of the story. It seemed to work but then in mid-campaign the issue re-emerged with radio reports restating the charges. The difficulties were exacerbated by the fact that Lynch was in hospital, recovering from an operation. There were two bursts of frantic activity: the first on 16–18 November when Lynch was persuaded to resign as treasurer; the second in the week after the election when it became necessary to see if Lynch was cleared of the charges and could be reinstated.

When on 15 November the ABC program 'AM' ran the story that Lynch had benefited from land dealing while treasurer, the prime minister asked for and received a statement of explanation. Fraser was not satisfied; he discussed the issue with senior colleagues because it threatened to blow into an electoral storm and he felt unable to answer likely media questions satisfactorily. When he held a press conference to discuss the opposition's economic policy, he was asked instead a series of questions on Lynch's business affairs. Unable to respond, he got increasingly annoyed and demanded a further report, but it was agreed that the initiative for the report should be seen to come from Lynch's office, not from the prime minister.

When the report was still not available by 17 November, the prime minister impatiently demanded its immediate delivery. During the day he had rung round his ministers to obtain their views. At 6.30 in the evening he summoned Andrew Hay, Lynch's principal private secretary, to a meeting which was also attended by Peter Nixon, Tony Staley, John Howard, Tony Street and Tony Eggleton, and complained about the likely electoral consequences if, as he feared, the rumours couldn't be put to rest. He argued that the only solution was for Lynch to stand aside as treasurer. The others in the room agreed, giving the impression that the party was unanimous. Fraser produced two draft letters of resignation, in one of which Lynch would assert he had done nothing illegal but that he was standing aside in the party's interest. Fraser also rang Lynch to tell him that the issue was killing the party; he argued that unless Lynch stood down, the issue would dominate the headlines and that the government would lose. For Lynch to stand aside would be understood by the Australian people. Lynch argued to Eggleton that he had widespread support in the party. Fraser was later to deny this, naming state organisation leaders as agreeing it was proper for Lynch to stand down.

Then Nixon joined Eggleton as mediator. On the phone to Hay at 3.30 a.m. he was given Lynch's view that as there was no evidence of impropriety, Lynch had to have a reasonable letter of resignation. Nixon commented that Lynch was too concerned with tying the prime minister in; he was relaying the conversation to the prime minister, sitting in the same room. When the phone was handed on to Eggleton, he pointed out the need to avoid charges of cover-up.

The next morning, 18 November, Nixon saw Lynch in hospital, primarily to help draft letters of resignation. Lynch wanted a short letter for public consumption and a longer private letter for the record. He thought that his colleagues had shown less loyalty than might have been expected and complained that he had not been consulted by phone or defended. Nixon pointed out that without details a defence was difficult.

Both sides ensured that their views were known; Lynch complained that stories were being fed out by the prime minister's office but his own staff were doing the same. Hay noted that Brian Buckley, Lynch's press secretary, was 'to get out that support swells for Lynch; telegrams flowing like confetti'. Above all Lynch was angry because Fraser had never sought to meet his advisers, or hold a full cabinet meeting. He worked through other colleagues. Fraser refused to be locked into any supporting statement; he would not make any commitment to reinstate Lynch as treasurer, as he thought in those circumstances the resignation would be seen as a cynical electoral ploy. Finally a form of words was agreed and rapidly released.

The resignation killed the story and Fraser was returned with a massive majority on 10 December. He was then faced with the question of whether to reinstate Lynch as treasurer and support his re-election as deputy leader. It depended on whether Lynch could clear himself from any charges. Even before the election, while his statement was being prepared, senior ministers had informed him that the prime minister might want to receive independent outside advice. Meanwhile others were gathering in Lynch's defence.

On 12 December Lynch rang Fraser to tell him that the statement was ready and he wanted it released as soon as possible, but he thought Fraser should see it first. Fraser argued that he wasn't an accountant and that he wanted a couple of people, preferably QCs, to give him a recommendation on whether it was acceptable. Lynch wanted to discuss it face to face; Fraser said he did not intend to give it his stamp of approval without additional advice. Lynch became very angry, pointing to rumours that Snedden, Peacock, Howard and Street were being mentioned as possible deputy leaders. They both complained about press reports of the meetings that had occurred during the days leading to Lynch's resignation. Lynch objected to the idea of QCs examining the statement, declaring that clearing his name was more important than the deputy leadership. He wanted Fraser, as 'the bloke I work for', to make up his own mind. Fraser was not willing to be seen as both judge and jury. Lynch's final comments were: 'God, we've sweated problems together before; I haven't seen you for four to five weeks. Ultimately you've got to say something . . . either you're satisfied or you're not. And if you are satisfied with it, my reputation's upheld. If not, it's destroyed'. On that tense note the conversation ended. In a letter drafted to the prime minister that day, Lynch complained that Fraser had not treated his deputy properly, that he had not met him or publicly defended him. The letter ended: 'The buck stops at your desk and you cannot stand aside from it . . . There is no legal point at issue. It is for you to take a judgement'.

The point about QCs was reiterated to Hay, and then Street and Nixon were brought into the discussion to consider the report at Nareen. The next morning Fraser, Lynch, Street, Nixon and Hay met at Fraser's mother's flat in Melbourne. Lynch claimed that, although he had not 'called around', he had got a lot of support and that the prime minister would not be well served as deputy by Snedden and Peacock, who were rivals, or by Street and Howard, who were too close. Fraser said he still had reservations about the statements and wanted a QC's advice. Finally, the names of two QCs were agreed.

Later that afternoon Fraser suggested an additional condition: since the final decision concerned ethics as well as legality, he wanted to get the advice of a senior figure like Sir Henry Bolte (former premier of Victoria), Sir Paul Hasluck (former Liberal minister and governor-general) or Sir Howard Beale (a cabinet minister under Menzies) on whether Lynch had 'acted at all times consistent with his high responsibility in the position of treasurer'. Lynch refused; it was the prime minister's responsibility. Nixon was brought into the discussion but acknowledged that it was now too difficult; he thought he could be of little use in such a direct confrontation.

On 14 December the phone-around continued. Fraser got Robinson to ring Lynch to deny he was running a Street-Howard ticket for deputy. Eggleton was also involved. Eventually Hay and the selected QC, Stephen Charles, flew to Canberra. When Hay and Charles went into the prime minister's office, Fraser had also called in Withers, Howard, Chaney and Hyde; the latter two, both backbenchers, had been organising the Lynch defence. They had written to all backbenchers, putting their case. Withers and Howard, both lawyers, argued that Lynch had done nothing wrong, or even unusual. Fraser had also asked Richard Searby, QC, to provide a private opinion. Searby concluded that there was no legal impropriety. 'How injudicious it was appears to me basically a matter of political judgement, involving to some degree what is to be expected of a politician (particularly a minister) by way of standards, and what you as prime minister expect of your ministers'. He concluded that only Fraser could be the real judge.

After Fraser had cross-questioned the QC, Stephen Charles, he announced that he was satisfied; since Charles's advice was more broadly based than just a legal opinion and included comments on ethics, he said there was no need to go further. It still took two days, with the assistance of Withers and Nixon, before a final statement was agreed between the prime minister and Lynch, while Lynch's staff were careful to ensure that the press constantly knew what the situation was.

On 14 December Fraser also declared that he saw no need for a ballot for the deputy leadership and, with his deputy cleared, finally set a date for the party meeting. In the meantime Lynch discussed with his staff which portfolio he should take, with the options eventually being narrowed to Treasury or Industry and Commerce. The prime minister did not mind which. With the assistance of the whip, the prime minister sought a vote on the deputyship without debate and stressed in the party room that the whole matter should be put to rest. Lynch defeated Killen, the only other nominee, by seventy-one votes to twenty and then took up his selected portfolio of

Industry and Commerce. The crisis was over and he remained as deputy until April 1982.

The Lynch incident illustrates the characteristics that Fraser brought to crisis management during the term of his government. First, there was a strong appeal to propriety. Fraser insisted that high standards should be maintained by his ministers; he liked to contrast his government with Whitlam's, arguing that he had a better notion of *how* the high standard ought to be applied. As early as February 1976, after being offered what he saw as preferential treatment when he came through customs, he had reminded ministers that they should not expect special treatment on these occasions. 'I consider it most important that all Australians on their return from overseas journeys receive equal treatment', he wrote. The prime minister was of course to be the judge of what was, and what was not, proper; in making judgements he took into account a range of judicial opinions and media reactions.

Second, Fraser liked to work through intermediaries. He did discuss problems with those concerned, but also used others in whom he had confidence to talk to the ministers in trouble. Nixon and Street were the most common, although Lynch was in other instances to defuse angered ministers. To use intermediaries was sensible in that it prevented a crisis that already existed from being exacerbated by direct confrontations. Discussions of compromises, searches for acceptable forms of words, establishment of working arrangements: these could be negotiated more readily when a refusal to accept was not a direct blow to the minister's leader. The use of intermediaries also illustrated another facet of Fraser's character. He was always ready to confront a person in policy arguments, but was uncomfortable in dealing with those individuals on personal matters. Intermediaries removed the necessity for personal confrontation or too close personal identification with the negotiations. It was both good tactics and a means of avoiding awkward situations, but to those in trouble it appeared as bad personnel management, an inability to 'relate' to others in trouble, an unpreparedness to take hard decisions in the presence of the person most concerned. Lynch's greatest complaint was that he had been unable to meet Fraser alone to discuss the options.

Third, Fraser never acted alone. Before final decisions were made, he collected support, from other ministers, from party officials, from the media. Sackings were eventually seen as cabinet decisions, not the individual act of the prime minister. He consulted, encouraged others to express their views, and sought their agreement before decisions were announced. It may have been that his own mind was already made up; in 1977, once the media coverage of Lynch's financial affairs exploded, he believed that Lynch had to stand aside. However he did not simply demand the resignation; he collected support to indicate that it was a government, not just a personal, decision.

Finally, decisions in time of crisis were often made under pressure, amid a cacophony of phone calls and summonses to meetings. Activity was continuous; assessments were consistently made of the changing situations. The events of 17–18 November, where calls were exchanged in the early hours of the morning, were not atypical. Certainly crisis management demands constant action, but the continuity of the activity, the constant pressure, sometimes appeared to turn up the temperature when a period of calm was perhaps needed.

These characteristics: the demand for propriety, the use of intermediaries, the collective involvement, and decision-making under constant pressure, can also be identified in the other ministerial crises that undermined the Fraser ministry.

The Withers affair

In December 1977, at the declaration of the poll for his new federal seat of Fadden, the Liberal deputy whip, Don Cameron, claimed that there had been improper interference by senior ministers in the redistribution of Queensland seats to influence the names of electorates. His target was Eric Robinson, about to become minister for finance and the power of the Queensland Liberal party. Early in January Fraser met with Senator Withers (the minister under whose auspices the Electoral Office worked) and asked the attorney-general, Peter Durack, and the solicitor-general to report on whether there was enough evidence to justify action. On 9 February Durack and the solicitor-general concluded that there was not.

In April, however, Cameron tabled in the House of Representatives a series of affidavits that documented the initial charges and extended them. In a rush, and in Durack's absence, the Durack report was tabled. Cameron's allegations were discussed twice by cabinet (once supplemented by ten outer ministers and the other time by six) on 10 April; later an informal meeting of Fraser, Withers, Durack, Yeend and Eggleton decided to refer the allegations to the law officers. Further meetings to examine progress were held on 16 and 17 April. On 23 April, after the law officers had recommended further investigation, a small meeting at the Lodge, including Fraser, Anthony, Withers, Sinclair, Street, Nixon, Robinson, Staley, Carrick, Howard and official advisers, decided to establish a Royal Commission. Durack was given a day in which to draw up the terms of reference and find a judge. Fraser was of course heavily involved; his final approval was needed for the terms of reference. He wanted to keep them as narrow as possible, but he insisted that they include not only 'legality', but also 'propriety'.

On 23 April Withers mentioned that he had phoned Keith Pearson, the chief electoral officer, to discuss the name of one Gold Coast electorate. The government had wanted the redistribution completed quickly, to clear the way for a possible election in 1977. When the phone call was brought up in evidence and the propriety and legality of Withers' actions were called into question in the commission, another meeting at the Lodge on 28 May agreed to extend the terms of reference; Fraser, Lynch, Carrick, Howard, Nixon and Durack were the only ministers present. The government was reacting, quietly to the first set of charges, but then almost in a panic, over-reacting particularly in the tabling of the initial report. 'Panic stations', claims Durack in direct reference to this case, 'was a feature of the Fraser government from time to time.'

Thereafter the outcome was very much in the hands of the commissioner. Once the terms of reference for an independent inquiry are set, the government can do little. Nor could it effectively have refused to extend those terms when it became evident that Withers had rung the chief electoral officer and suggested the name of an electorate be changed. Eventually, in August, the commissioner reported, clearing Robinson but accusing Withers of committing an 'impropriety'. The commissioner did not suggest that his action in ringing Pearson was illegal but concluded that, because he was seeking political advantage, it was improper.

Withers held an unusual position in the Liberal hierarchy. He was cheerful, breezy, irreverent and totally pragmatic. Crucially, he had held the wavering Liberal senators together in the last days of the 1975 crisis; his leadership in the Senate had been important in gaining Fraser the prime ministership. Now, in August 1978, he refused to admit that he had done anything wrong in speaking to the chief electoral officer. He argued that the report magnified the incident out of all proportion. Called down to Nareen, he refused to resign, telling Fraser that, if he wanted him out, he would have to sack him. Fraser felt that, having established a royal commission, it was not possible to ignore a finding that was so explicit and damning. A prime minister had to be seen to act, if standards of government were to be maintained. If a resignation was offered, then a prime minister could decide whether to accept it, but there could not be an arrangement that it would not be accepted; that would make the process a charade.

With no agreement reached at Nareen, the participants moved to Sydney, where cabinet was scheduled to meet. Fraser held a series of ad hoc committee meetings, interspersed with other committees that considered the budget presentation. The schedule was hectic:

7 August
9.10-9.23   Ad hoc committee (live sheep export)
10.18-12.53   Ad hoc committee (budget presentation)
1.45-5.45   Ad hoc (senior ministers discussing McGregor report)
5.55-6.55   Ad hoc (budget presentation)
6.55-8.00   Ad hoc (McGregor report)

8 August
10.25-10.40   Cabinet (Discuss pharmaceutical benefits,

                        health statistics, nuclear safeguards – agreement
                        with Philippines)
10.45-11.30   Ad hoc (budget presentations)
2.35-3.20   Ministry (McGregor report)
4.25-5.45   Ministry (McGregor report)
5.45-6.03   Cabinet (health matters considered under the
                        line)

No officials were present at the meetings of the ad hoc committee on the McGregor report on 7 August. It decided (with the decision actually written three days after the event) that it had no alternative but to accept the findings of the report and noted that the prime minister and Lynch were to discuss the consequences with Withers. Refusing to resign, Withers was sacked. The membership of the ad hoc committee was significantly limited. Ten cabinet ministers attended; Anthony was overseas; Peacock (in Brisbane negotiating the Torres Strait agreement), Killen and Guilfoyle were not included. Viner and Hunt were called into the second meeting for a short period.

When all the ministers attended the meetings of the cabinet or the ministry on 8 August, their attention was drawn to the relevant sections of the McGregor report; Peacock vehemently argued that he should be allowed time to read the full document. He did not get it. On the same day the full ministry agreed to release the report and noted the action taken. On 13 August an ad hoc committee considered the prime minister's statement and on the next day cabinet agreed to the draft, leaving the final text to be settled by Fraser, Howard, Nixon, Viner, Durack and Chaney.

The decisions were made amid a growing party revolt as backbenchers became involved. On 7 August the government whip in the Senate reported that ten Liberal and all the NCP senators had argued that no case existed for the dismissal of Withers. John Hyde sent a telegram to the prime minister; Michael Baume rang his office; Fred Chaney sent a carefully argued three-page summary examining the options. The House of Representatives whip reported the efforts by Fred Chaney and John Hyde to generate support.

Fraser's advisers also presented views. Eggleton spelt out the three options: that in the light of the 'referee's' decision, the minister should go; dispute the finding; or accept the finding, but decide the 'impropriety' was a technicality that did not require resignation. One paper argued the pros and cons: 'Propriety – removing minister' compared to 'Politics – toughing it out'. The general tenor of the advice was that to ignore the 'umpire's' decision would be received poorly in the electorate. The private office also prepared a defence for the prime minister against charges (raised by Robinson) that Fraser had known of Withers's phone call since January and therefore was implicated in the whole affair. The brief presented a detailed chronology explaining when Fraser became aware of events and what actions were taken in response. Fraser's justification for the action remains the same: 'If a government rode roughshod over the Royal Commission report, it would be very difficult to again be regarded as a government of principle'. Fraser saw the government being forced to react to a problem identified by an independent report.

Yet Withers, not the most disinterested of observers, is sceptical that in any of these crises Fraser was being pushed into anything. He commented:

Malcolm was not a sacker; he was always blameless and always the victim of circumstances. He would so rearrange things that he had no option but to take the dreadful step. He would convince himself that in the national interest, he had no option . . . pressure from his own organisation, the backbench, the premiers would force him into a position where he just had to do this . . . The fact that he had worked them all up to the position where he had to do it was a bloody irrelevance. A very good worker on people.

It was indeed true that once a crisis had erupted, Fraser was constantly organising support, advice and where possible a consensus. It was against his nature to let control drift. But it is also true that none of the crises began at his behest. He never sacked any cabinet ministers because they weren't up to it.

Here again were all the Fraser characteristics of crisis management. A strong sense of propriety, and the need to protect the reputation of the government. A determination to draw others into support, in this instance by gradually expanding the circle of committed, from a few confidants to a cabinet ad hoc committee to the full ministry. Meetings were held one after another, until the decisions were reached. Propriety, commitment and pressure were the watchwords of the crisis.

Peacock

The resignation of Andrew Peacock in April 1981 shook the Fraser government more than any other issue. Peacock was the heir apparent, the successful foreign minister who represented the liberal wing of the party in popular image. That there was always tension between Fraser and Peacock was well known, despite the fact that in relation to foreign policy they had rarely differed.

In 1980 tension had erupted within the government over the derecognition of the murderous Pol Pot régime in Kampuchea. Peacock wanted to withdraw recognition immediately, while Fraser preferred to delay. At the CHOGRM meeting in New Delhi, Singapore's Lee Kuan Yew had strongly opposed derecognition and on the plane to Singapore had argued the case with Fraser and Peacock. Back in Canberra, on 10 September Fraser released a copy of Lee's press statement that was critical of Peacock. On 23 September cabinet agreed not to change its position but indicated that the decision was only to hold for the short term (the decision was made when Peacock was in New York but substantially accorded with his recommendations). When Peacock was not able to raise the issue again he threatened to resign – on the very day that Fraser was calling the 1980 election. Nixon acted as mediator and smoothed over the chasm for the time being, but Peacock's threat to the government, holding a gun to its head, was not readily forgotten. After the election Peacock challenged for the deputy leadership, losing to Lynch by only thirty-five votes to forty-seven.

As minister for industrial relations Peacock was not always in sympathy with the attitude of the government, preferring negotiation to the hard line taken by the government over the 35-hour week and being particularly disturbed by Fraser's rugged treatment of ICI (described in Chapter 10). Peacock had been opposed to cabinet's action in using RAAF Hercules to fly stranded passengers across the Tasman during an airline strike; he wanted to continue discussions.

The final catalyst was again a matter of alleged improper behaviour, apparently minor in itself, that expanded into a confrontation. On 10 April 1981 Barry Simon, Peacock's principal private secretary and a former MP, criticised the government's policy towards ICI during the struggle against the 35-hour week. Fraser insisted that Simon be sacked. He rang Peacock to express his view and several other ministers did the same to provide a united front. Indeed Simon offered to resign and Peacock first refused to accept the resignation. As David Barnett indicated to Fraser: 'If Andrew has indeed refused to accept Barry Simon's resignation, then the matter could well turn into an issue between you and him'. On 14 April Peacock eventually complied, but in a fury and teetering on the edge of resignation himself. At the same time, a story was run in the *Australian* that Peacock had threatened to resign over the government's attitude to the derecognition of the Pol Pot government in Kampuchea, a story which Peacock then believed had been leaked by Fraser to discredit him (although more recently he has regarded Fraser's office, rather than Fraser, as responsible). Intermediaries, most notably Peter Nixon but also Killen, Guilfoyle and Anthony, tried to persuade him to stay. They failed as the attempted compromises did not satisfy anyone and Peacock resigned on 15 April, the day after Simon. He claimed:

I believe the prime minister has engaged in acts of gross disloyalty to me and my office. The prime minister has allowed false and damaging reports to be published about me in my capacity as a senior minister. He has bypassed the system of government by acting with a manic determination to get his own way. I find the constant disloyalty and erratic acts of behavior intolerable and not to be endured.

He went on to echo Fraser's comments about Gorton almost exactly a decade before: 'He has a dangerous reluctance to consult cabinet and an obstinate determination to get his own way'. He agreed to explain his actions in the House of Representatives when it reconvened two weeks later. This circumstance was different from the earlier crises because Peacock was no longer in office. During the Pol Pot disputes the previous year Peacock was still a minister and Nixon was able to act as a link. Now that Peacock was on the backbench Fraser had to prepare to defend himself publicly and minimise the damage that could be done to the government.

Fraser organised his defence in three ways. First, he brought into line the full weight of the ministry. On 15 April cabinet declared its support, and Anthony and Lynch issued a press statement which declared that Peacock's fight was not just with the prime minister, but with the whole cabinet. Fraser participated in the drafting of the statement; in particular he excised all references to Kampuchea. Nixon recalled for the record the discussions he had with Peacock in September 1980 when acting as negotiator over the derecognition of Pol Pot. Street issued a press statement as former minister for industrial relations, denying that the minister's position had been constantly undermined. The ministry denied that Fraser tried to override cabinet and claimed that every other cabinet minister had expressed the view that Simon had to go. Support for the prime minister was collective.

Second, Fraser made himself available to put his case. On 15 April in his doorstep interview he had declared Simon's resignation to be inevitable. On the day of Peacock's resignation, he gave background information to journalists. After Peacock resigned Fraser gave a press conference that drew attention again to the Anthony–Lynch statement and denied that any undertakings were made. On 16 April a further doorstep interview was held and Fraser also went onto the John Laws program to get his message across.

Third, Fraser prepared responses to anything that Peacock might say in his parliamentary statement. Peacock was permitted to recall from the Cabinet Office, following the normal practice, submissions which he had presented to cabinet. His office not only called for the ones they wanted to use, such as those on the derecognition of Kampuchea, but also some blinds that were intended to mislead. PMC guessed what might be brought up. The Cabinet Office calculated what subjects the Co-ordination committee of cabinet (a body of which Peacock was particularly critical) had considered, how many of Peacock's submissions were not accepted (only 6 out of 272 were said to be significantly altered by cabinet while he was minister for foreign affairs, and 4 out of 17 while minister for industrial relations). It collated all the decisions of the Kampuchean and 35-hour week debates (8 and 30 respectively). It recalled in detail the proceedings that led to Withers's sacking, and many other issues which might be used. For instance, one note recorded that after the Foreign Affairs and Defence committee had agreed to appoint Sir John Kerr as ambassador at UNESCO, there was a debate about whether the prime minister or minister for foreign affairs would announce it. Peacock did not want to. Another note described the process of writing cabinet decisions, arguing that in only three or four cases a year would the decision be shown to the prime minister. Each potential accusation was listed with a possible response.

By the time the debate was held all the necessary data had been collected. As a consequence, during the debate Fraser was able to refute in some detail the specific charges of Peacock; his ministerial colleagues defended his management of cabinet, and the use of the Co-ordination committee. Although Peacock cleverly used the same words as Fraser had done a decade earlier in his assault on Gorton, the debate degenerated into a repetitive litany of the government's general credits and faults.

The issue did not end there, of course. With an heir apparent on the backbench, the question was not whether a challenge would take place, but when. Destabilisation continued for the next year; rumours and head-counting were constant. When Fraser forced a direct challenge, he won easily. Six months later, with Eggleton acting as the peacemaker, Peacock was back in the ministry.

Yet the cost to the government, the instability it caused, the divisions it created, did irreparable harm. The government had entered its third term in crisis and never recovered its air of stability. In retrospect both Fraser and Peacock acknowledge that they should have talked more about their disagreements, that issues were allowed to fester until it needed only a spark to set them alight. Fraser brought the collective weight of cabinet to bear at the stage where positions were too firm. The cost was the loss of government stability.

The TV affair

The final resignations from Fraser's cabinet almost appeared as farce. On 5 October 1981 one minister, Michael Mackellar, had brought a television set through customs. His customs declaration card was actually signed by one of his staff and said 'no' to the question of whether he had a TV, although he was holding one under his arm. After a discussion with a customs officer on whether the TV was a colour set, he was hustled through by a more senior officer. If it was a colour set (it was), he owed duty; if it was black and white, he did not. Mackellar argues that he said it was colour and was still waved through. The minister responsible for customs, John Moore, was warned of the incident on the same day by his permanent head; he was advised to ring Mackellar and to ask what kind of TV set it was. Moore rang Mackellar and chided him for his actions. He then told his permanent head that he had stressed the seriousness of making inaccurate statements and that he wished it to be the end of the matter. The department assumed that that decision meant the set was black and white, and regarded the matter as closed. It was this lack of communication that caused the problem; with Mackellar thinking his statement at the customs on the fact that it was a colour TV was adequate, while others assumed it was black and white because Moore wanted the matter closed. On 13 October Mackellar wrote acknowledging the inconsistency between the customs declaration and his TV set. He stated that he was anxious to fulfil his legal obligations and asked what duty he was liable to pay. None was requested. Six months later allegations emerged from within the customs officers' union that senior officers had tried to cover the incident up. Here was a case where one minister appeared to be in breach of that 1976 circular demanding that ministers receive no preferential treatment in customs, and where another had not insisted adequately on the letter of the law being fulfilled.

When the allegations were published in April, Fraser told the two ministers to get their story straight and explain what had happened. A first draft of a statement was regarded as unacceptable as it seemed to leave Mackellar alone in trouble. Their fortunes were becoming inextricably linked. The issue became confused as it was never clear what each of the ministers had asked or did and should have known. Fraser kept pushing for a statement that would clarify everything. It never came because there was no agreement. One of the main problems was that the non-ministerial participants and the relevant files were scattered; to collect all the information would take three or four days. Fraser was not prepared to wait and explain to the media in the meantime that he did not know the answer; he wanted a resolution achieved immediately. His impatience probably exacerbated the situation. Two days passed. The pressure grew.

After the weekend the media began demanding resignations, arguing that ministers should abide by the same rules as ordinary citizens. Cabinet met on and off throughout the Monday; a group of ministers, including Howard and Durack, met the two ministers in trouble and it became evident that they would stand and fall together. The difficulty lay in accepting that ministers could be forgiven even for small but clear transgressions. To charges that the prime minister was requiring standards of propriety which were too high, Fraser responded:

Some of my colleagues would find it difficult to understand the distinction which a prime minister has to maintain between loyalty to values and loyalty to people . . . If he is not loyal to the values that are important who else is going to be.

Eventually it was decided that the ministers should go. The stories were just not credible. Cabinet held a general discussion about the approaches to be taken in parliament. The unanimous media condemnation was seen as crucial. If the errors were mundane, that was precisely why they were seen as so damaging. Propriety, intermediaries and collective actions were again the hallmarks.

These were not the only resignations. Although the memory is primarily of Liberal disasters, two National party ministers were forced out. When, after a year of speculation, he was finally charged in a New South Wales court, Ian Sinclair stood down (but not until he was charged). Senator Glen Sheil was sacked when, within twenty-four hours of being sworn in, he publicly challenged the government's policy towards South Africa. Fraser's letter was blunt: 'In the circumstances in which you have expressed views contrary to the Government policy, I regret it is not possible to proceed with your appointment to the Ministry'.

But other ministers who faced political problems were defended by Fraser: Fife when the Narcotics Bureau was seen to leak; Howard and Durack when the Costigan inquiry revealed a multitude of tax evasion schemes and a call-girl racket allegedly run from the deputy crown solicitor's office in Western Australia. In none of these cases was there evidence that the ministers had personal knowledge of the maladministration and they were not required to resign.

The most notable exception was Fraser's defence of Peter Nixon in September 1982. Nixon was condemned in a report on the meat export industry by Justice Woodward for failing to pursue his ministerial duties. When he saw the report he rang the prime minister and offered his resignation. He claimed that he believed his record to be sound and that the facts did not warrant resignation, but it would be a contentious political issue. Fraser asked him to hold off and not tell anyone but Anthony, but he appreciated the directness of the offer:

Some ministers will say when they start to get into trouble that if you ever feel I need to resign, just tell me. And you know he won't because in the end he made himself more important than the institution.

Most officials did not see how Nixon could be saved. In a marathon effort Fraser went through the evidence, satisfied himself that the information given to the inquiry did not justify the accusation and then constructed a defence that he pursued in parliament. He emphasised that Nixon's offer of resignation was proper, but that he was not obliged to accept it. Fraser recalls:

I don't think I have ever done more work in a couple of days. It was on top of whatever else we were doing. I wasn't going to take on a judge and be cross-trumped. And I wasn't. So I not only read the report; I read the supporting evidence for all the bits that were relevant to what I wanted to say.

There may have been additional motives: Nixon was the government's most adept troubleshooter – straight, trusted and reliable. The times too were not auspicious: the government was shaken by earlier scandals and now by the Costigan revelations. It could not afford to lose such a senior minister. Yet the defence of Peter Nixon, particularly when compared to the treatment of earlier Liberal ministers, caused further dissatisfaction. It was seen as a double standard, a refusal to apply the same conditions to one Royal Commission as the other. The conclusions seemed as damning of Nixon as they had been of Withers. Even if there can be justifications for the different reactions, they were not convincing to those who had suffered or watched others demoted. Fraser's closeness to the National ministers, already a point of contention since Peacock's resignation, was merely emphasised.

The impact of patronage

The prime minister's power over appointment and dismissal may have several impacts in terms of subordinating the ministers' interests to those of their leader. For those awaiting office there was a constant need to assess their relationship with Fraser, to be noticed but not necessarily to be regarded as an uncritical supporter. There was a need for a balance between constructive criticism and merely becoming irritating. Some criticised and were promoted; other critics stayed on the backbench. It depended on the opportunities. But for those who knew they were unlikely to reach the front bench under Fraser, the choice was to continue to prod, as John Hyde constantly did, or to consider prospects under an alternative leader.

For those in cabinet, fear of dismissal was not likely to create uncertainty, as Fraser did not sack senior ministers – unless they got into serious trouble. That was a constant concern. As

Michael Mackellar said: 'You always had a sense you were living on the edge of a precipice and could topple over at any time'. A mistake could lead to dismissal if it involved the minister personally. Fraser's treatment of ministers gradually exacerbated these problems. His insistence on propriety, his use of intermediaries, his collection of support – all are eminently defensible, but each led to a deterioration in his relations with ministers who did not think he returned the loyalty he demanded.

Was that sense of propriety too high? Kemp is surely correct to say that if a prime minister fails to act, the ministers' standards must become the leader's standards. Yet the standards were often rigorous, and the conclusions more terminal, than those of other governments who have preferred to ride out the political storms. That determination to be seen as maintaining the highest of standards can be interpreted in part as the constant search for legitimacy. 'What exaggerated his sense of propriety', says David Barnett, 'was the nature of his accession to office'. Because he had lambasted the Whitlam government for its ministerial standards, Fraser argued that a high level of propriety was required. (Yet the dismissal of Reg Withers in 1978, for the 'impropriety of a phone call', was seen to be out of proportion to the offence and to be the first sign of instability in the government.) Ministers sometimes thought Fraser moralistic and Calvinistic, even posing, and the political cost high – unnecessarily so. Perhaps the Queensland state government provides a cautionary tale. If the prime minister does not set the standard, no one will. The judgement finally is a political one – what is required must be determined by the prime minister.

Yet even if ministers agreed that Fraser alone could determine the required standards, the way in which they were applied often made the situation worse. Again, there are always occasions when, as Fraser notes, 'it wasn't always appropriate for the prime minister to be directly involved'. But in these crises while Fraser did meet ministers in trouble or talk to them on the phone on their own, with Withers even visiting Nareen to discuss his case, Fraser also worked through intermediaries. Again the choice of actions is a matter of balance between an arm's-length decision and personal intervention. To his ministers his failure to call them in and thrash out the problem more directly was regarded as regrettable, a sign of poor management of people, of an inability to deal easily with people when the case being debated was the minister's future and not a policy issue.

Ministers did not deny that the prime minister had the right to fire, but they were often uncomfortable that he insisted in locking in all the others so that the sackings were either effectively endorsed by cabinet (as in Withers' case or the TV affair) or the prime minister was supported by cabinet (as after Peacock's resignation). He always gained that support, but often only after a lengthy argument and fights with backbenchers. It had costs. As one adviser remarked about his style more generally: 'If a prime minister insists on getting support from ministers, he eventually will lock them in. But if you club people to death that way, it's worse than just riding roughshod over them and making decisions yourself'. This is more so in the case of ministerial crises where Fraser had the authority, accepted by all, to make the decision himself.

Further, the way in which support was collected slowly as the crises unfolded meant that the political repercussions were greater. It was a gift to the opposition, which was able to keep the pot simmering and to build a picture of a government constantly in turmoil. In all the cases the crisis filled the headlines for days, when a more decisive, but less consultative, action might have ended it.

As a consequence of these crises, of the reputed double standard, and of the unease that was exacerbated by their frequency, the tension between leader and led grew, the gap widened. There was no reservoir of goodwill when the tide turned. Even without lowering his high standards – and prime ministers need high standards for no one else can impose them – Fraser's handling of ministerial crises detracted from any solidarity that he tried to develop in his ministry. Withers provided a scathing comparison with Anthony: 'Doug stuck by his mates, while Malcolm let them hang on the wire all day before machine-gunning them!' That at least is how the victims saw it, and perhaps what other ministers feared.

The prime minister and his ministers

The structure of the system gives prime ministers both institutional power and the capacity to wield personal power. Institutional power accrued from Fraser's hold over the reins of promotion. Those outside office wanting a job, those in office wanting promotion, all knew that their future was in the prime minister's hand. One junior minister, John Hodges, frankly admitted it:

Junior ministers who are ambitious are worried about their future. You don't have to be a favourite of the prime minister, but you have to be reasonably well regarded if you want to get on. There was a degree of fear, caused by Fraser's superior attitude.

John Moore was even more biting:

Liberals are scared for their jobs until they get some security. But unfortunately in politics that Biblical saying 'put not your faith in princes' is true. When the TV affair came, I knew what the saying meant.

Those who were promoted knew that they owed their rise to the prime minister. It did not mean that they were cowed or silent, but according to one colleague:

Howard had a very rapid advancement in politics with a decided amount of good luck and not a lot of track record . . . You look at that very rapid advancement and the bottom line was 'you support me on the tough decisions'. A number of times I saw Howard support him on a decision, when in the office he was adamant that he would go in fighting for another position . . . Howard's hard line had faded by the time the vote came round to his part of the table.

Yet as Howard became more firmly established, as his position in the party became more secure, particularly after he was elected deputy leader, he argued more readily and independently. Once Withers had been sacked, ministers knew that anyone was expendable. Fraser may not have created the reason or the conditions but, although many thought that Withers' offence (if indeed they thought he had committed any offence) was trifling, the prime minister removed the powerful baron in the Senate.

Ministers were therefore conscious that they needed both to keep out of trouble and to do a good job: the former to survive, the latter to get promoted. But what constitutes a good job? It does not really matter how anyone but the prime minister defines that answer. It was his conception of the role and his appreciation of the minister that was crucial. Ministers were therefore always sensitive to the prime minister's demands and wishes; if he wanted something, that was reason enough to react. One adviser comments that Fraser was the only leader he knew whose summons had ministers literally running to the office. Ministers were conscious of the need to react quickly. Fraser was constantly making demands or queries of his ministers. 'Did you know there was a long queue in the social security office at X? Why?' Or he asked for a report on the rumour that social security officials were advising people in Western Australian schools how to get the dole. Or Budd would write to a minister that: 'The prime minister thinks you ought to be asked a question on union election irregularities'. Or tell a minister that Fraser wanted a question on industrial disputes in the building industry to be asked.

Fraser was the centre of the wheel, spinning off requests and ideas. He would pass on proposals and seek answers. He didn't often tell ministers what to say; he sought reactions, or asked for information for cabinet. Paper flowed constantly to ministers' offices as they were bombarded with the wishes that flowed from Fraser's active and fertile mind. His edicts usually demanded some action.

Often he would demand a cabinet submission. When the boat people started to arrive, he asked for a consolidated paper on refugee policy. He required the treasurer to bring forward terms of reference for the inquiry into the financial system. On 23 December 1982 he wrote to Howard that cabinet discussion on passports touched on the possibility of introducing universal social security or identity cards and noted that a strong case for some unambiguous form of identification could be made from social security and taxation returns. He acknowledged opposition on grounds of invasion of privacy and asked Howard to take the running in the development of a proposal. Ideas from one discussion could lead to the exploration of others. Fraser's interest was often the impetus for action.

His interest in the administration was extensive; almost as a hobby he would dip in here or there. A senior official of PMC said:

While others would go and paint a painting, play with their kids, listen to music, Malcolm Fraser seized on the hearts of government administration. He'd look at an area and develop knowledge of an area that would arrive in the agenda, perhaps stimulated by an odd comment elsewhere . . . He would suddenly ask a question in cabinet.

The minister of course would be astounded and unprepared. The image of omniscience and total involvement would become more developed. Ministers never knew when or where he would show an interest next, or what his attitudes would be. As a consequence they were constantly kept on their toes, in some cases very nervously.

Consultation was continuous. He was prepared to contact his colleagues at the same odd hours as he contacted his staff. Wal Fife recalls:

On Good Friday I was walking from the back paddock and the telephone was ringing. My wife said, 'I wonder who's calling us today?' I said 'it can only be one person'. I was right. On another occasion when he rang at 2 a.m. I was wide enough awake to say 'I was waiting for your call'.

But the consultation was part of a real effort to extract agreement.

Fraser, said Withers, was a persuader, not a basher. He wanted to convince ministers. To do so he would argue extensively, and often vigorously, testing his ministers as much as he tested his advisers. As long as his ministers understood the style, they could debate an issue at length. Chaney commented that in his early days of dealing with Fraser he always made a note of what he wanted to say before he saw Fraser, so that he did not forget the essential points. Others were more nervous; once Fraser stated a view they were inclined to think the argument was ended, and they backed off and conceded their case. Sometimes they even agreed with rather extreme statements or proposals and found themselves isolated when Fraser changed his line of discussion. Timidity could be dangerous.

Fraser needed ministers to defend their cases: 'A minister was no good unless he was prepared to say what he thought fearlessly. You are not going to make the right decisions otherwise'. Argument was essential to ensure that all aspects of an issue were exposed. Yes-men were of no value. Said Fife: 'He had less chance of staying in office if the people around him said "Yes PM" all the time'. He had little patience with ministers who did. The stronger ministers accepted that he could be persuaded to change his mind. If a senior minister firmly held views on his portfolio, Fraser would seldom ride over them; Carrick's constant opposition to the reintroduction of tertiary fees meant that he always prevailed over proposals from the Department of Finance, and Fraser did not push for change. He did not often have the time or capacity to overcome a serious, senior and fighting minister. He would listen. Even if Withers' style was perhaps unusual:

Malcolm's a difficult bugger, but you could often reason with him by saying: 'Look, Malcolm, you're being bloody stupid.' He'd say 'Why?'

It illustrated the widely held belief that there were ways of getting a point across. He would not cut off ministers who had a really good argument, rather than just strength of feeling. He was prepared to change his view, a point recognised only by those who had the force of argument to win, although Dick Hamer thought at times he 'was listening with attention in order to tell you where you were wrong'. Those he promoted quickly were those who held strong views and argued. No one – except perhaps Doug Anthony – was exempt from the process of argumentative attrition.

Yet within the framework of consultation ministers sometimes wondered whether the reasons behind it were exclusively about an exchange of ideas. It was part of gaining a consensus. Chaney remembers:

He used to consult me a lot; I eventually got around to the rather queasy feeling that he had a pretty fair idea of which way I'd go and consulted me sometimes as part of a calculated drawing together of the majority he wanted.

There is no doubt that Chaney was partly right. After working closely with ministers, Fraser could usually calculate what their reactions would be and how strongly they would hold to them.

Consulting was a means of gathering support. Withers claims:

He was continually in touch by phone 'Oh, Charles, I'm terribly worried about this'. 'Well, Malcolm, you just have to do it'. 'Thanks Charles'. Then 'I had no option. Charles Court said on the telephone that I really must do this'. So that if you enquired far enough you'd find that he'd initiated everything. When he told the story it was as though they had initiated it and pressured him. Very good prime minister, Malcolm. Especially for getting his own way.

Since usually no one knew precisely whom Fraser had consulted, no one was as certain about where others stood as Fraser. He sat at the centre of a circle of discussions.

He adopted a process of gradually extending circles to exert his influence. He persuaded one group, then used its support on a larger group, and then ever outwards. Those two political operators, Nixon and Withers, recognised the skilful process. Nixon argued that he drew around him a group whose judgement he respected; others who he thought brought nothing to the argument he left out; then he skilfully used to lock people in, starting with a handful in his office. Withers says:

He was a great believer in the slow process of locking in . . . He did it in my case and he did it time and time again. He'd get four like-minded people together. Then he'd set up an ad hoc committee of cabinet of another three people and we'd say 'well, the four of us agree on it', so he'd got seven. Then in cabinet he had seven out of twelve. Then he'd have a full ministry meeting and of course you've got the numbers there. And decisions are 'unanimous'.

Others ministers also saw it as a careful and deliberate process, but his staff were not so certain:

Malcolm was strong and didn't need to resort to that tactic on a lot of issues when in fact he did adopt that approach. If he didn't need to do it for political reasons or for solidarity reasons, I think on a number of occasions he did it for actual advice reasons. It's not to say it was always the basic motive, but if it was only for power-mongering, then he did it a lot for someone who was very jealous of his own time and his capacity to do other things. He was more concerned with seeing if something had been overlooked.

The process of expanding circles could thus be used for a range of reasons. Fraser had few close colleagues; he did not always accept ministers' expertise. He liked to puzzle his way through, to understand the implications for the government. Even when he accepted the targets a minister set, he wanted to know precisely how he or she was going to get there. He was not easily satisfied.

That style had costs. Fraser could be very thoughtful about his colleagues: sending personal notes, insisting that their family problems be looked after, requiring in 1976 and thereafter that at least one week of the August school holidays coincided with a non-sitting week. He could also be thoughtless and excessively demanding. He paid no attention to personal feelings when pursuing an argument. David Kemp claimed:

He would tear shreds off ministers. Fraser was so devastating that nobody could stand up to him. He didn't curry favour with his closest supporters. If he tore shreds off someone, it was because they hadn't thought the thing through, or made a mistake, or what they said was contradictory. He went for weakness because it was weak, not to humiliate. He wanted the issue sorted out.

However, the consequence was bruised feelings and often dissatisfaction. The presence of a man's peers and juniors was no bar to a devastating criticism of a less than totally satisfactory performance. A senior official commented: 'Malcolm didn't have great sensitivity about relationships with ministers or indeed anyone else. He wouldn't be trying to snub someone. He just wouldn't think'.

Tony Eggleton would chide him for his impatience, for his inability to suffer fools and his poor treatment of individuals. But he explained it:

He just had something to say; he didn't wrap things up, and he'd be rather curt and down to earth. It was just him getting on with the job, with timetables to meet and assuming everyone would understand.

He was a man who argued the issue most of the time.

Bruised egos were seldom eased by thanks. Fraser worked hard, made massive demands and showed little gratitude. His close colleague, Peter Nixon, argued:

Fraser's problem was he expected from everybody the absolute best performance and would not praise anybody for a good performance — or very rarely — because he took it for granted. He expected absolute loyalty and didn't feel the need for patting people on the head.

Fife thought he should have talked to people after a strident cross-examination in order to ease their feelings, but he didn't often do so. Ministers who had less contact, or less self-confidence, found the process overbearing and regarded him as a bully and a poor manager. They felt that there was seldom any sense of a team: 'there was Malcolm and there was us'.

Yet on occasion he could turn on the charm. He could be persuasive when he chose, much better on a person-to-person basis than in public. Margaret Guilfoyle commented that he would 'soften you up, look very earnest and give you no room to move'. In the course of a crisis he would talk to ministers one by one to ensure they were on side. He could be pleasant to those whom he held in low regard, because he did not expect them to improve. He could even ease the defeat of senior ministers. Chaney recalls:

He didn't always play fair. On one major change each time I won, he asked me to resubmit. He kept the argument going and built up a majority and then he had me. Then he said 'Fred, you can always bring this forward again . . .'. I mean, really bloody duchessed me. He did it quite well.

Fraser certainly liked to win arguments; that was natural for a competitive and determined character. But he was often dissatisfied with winning them by default, dissatisfied because it meant that the arguments had not been adequately discussed. The exceptions were when he had already decided what the best policy was – which was not as often as people made out.

His style had several consequences. The first was the need for mediators, who could calm the ruffled personalities or quietly point out to Fraser some of the emerging problems. The most often used were Lynch and Nixon. Lynch was good at listening to problems and, in his own way, passing on the messages. Nixon was regarded, by Liberals as much as by his own party, as straight: 'tough, honest, direct', 'what you see is what you get', 'Nicko didn't owe the bastards anything', were three Liberal comments. Because he both had no leadership position and a reputation for standing up for himself, many ministers took their problems to him. In the early years Withers played a similar role in the Senate. Ministers could take their policy problems to the prime minister; almost none felt able to face him with personal problems (perhaps because his style was the cause of them). As one put it: 'He didn't engender confidence to go and say "I've got a problem". He didn't develop trust'.

Ministers appreciated his willingness to work, and that meant that they were often prepared to let his views predominate in all but the cases where they felt most strongly. One official believed:

There was no other minister in that whole period who was prepared to make the same investment in the process. They all had other values which they put higher than being a minister. Fraser had a simpler set of values; they revolved around being prime minister. So whenever it became clear that Fraser was going to make a maximum investment in something, you could see the cost benefits tick over in everybody else's mind. 'The bastard wants to go 24 hours a day for three months on this. I'm certainly not going to stand the distance. I might as well see what I can get out of it now.'

They respected his success and his determination; as one adviser put it, 'his sheer record of being right most of the time'. It was a respect tinged with fear. An official recalls:

There was a minister one day who had done something bloody stupid and Fraser really tore him apart. As we went out, this minister said 'he's a bastard . . . but he's a capable bastard!'.

Yet they also criticised his style, thinking that he was often too involved. 'His strength', claimed Senator Baume, 'was that he knew about everything, his weakness was that he knew about everything'. Many ministers claimed he interfered too much; although the critics were those very ministers who often themselves wanted to be involved in the affairs of other portfolios. Interference and control are the two sides of the same coin.

Ministers sometimes doubted his loyalty towards them as individuals, and thought that Fraser showed a double standard, treating National ministers with greater leniency then Liberals. Some grew to appreciate his character; others objected strongly. When Eric Robinson resigned briefly in 1979, he commented 'I can't work with that big bastard any longer'. Loyalty was given for Fraser's success, his drive, his determination. He got support as prime minister, rather than as an individual. That was a consequence of his style, his imperious treatment.

CHAPTER 4

'IN THE BUNKER'

CABINET

Cabinet lies at the heart of government in Australia. Its roles are multiple: to determine government priorities, to settle disputes, to allow the exchange of information, to arbitrate between ministers, to decide on policy, to mesh political and bureaucratic perceptions. Cabinet exists above all to settle what is too hard to be dealt with elsewhere. It is collective because the principles of collective responsibility require collective decision-making. Decisions of cabinet are the currency of the government – ministers are required to participate where requested, and thereafter to support the decision in the party or in public. If they cannot accept the principles of collective responsibility, they may resign.

But even if publicly unanimous, cabinet has always been a forum in which decisions are contested. It is not a judicial body that considers issues on the basis of some notion of objective evidence; it is the place where values, strategies, policies and ambitions compete, where tactics and personalities may be as important as any intrinsic merit of the case. Open discussion of issues is essential and participation is desirable. Cabinet's proceedings can be rugged, because they determine important issues. Prime ministers, however, do not always get subservient cabinets. Nor usually do they want them. An argumentative, challenging and intelligent cabinet is more likely than one individual, however talented, to see the implications of decisions by bringing several minds to bear on a problem.

Prime ministers can control the workings of cabinet. They determine its agenda, chair the meetings and summarise the decisions. They decide what committees will exist, what their powers will be and what they should do. Yet they are also actors in the cabinet, with ideas to pursue and interests to promote. In an environment where many ministers are concerned to fight for the narrow interests and perspectives of their departments, prime ministers alone can be responsible for maintaining a broad view or a sense of direction, and ensuring that the detailed decisions fit within that framework.

But do they necessarily dominate cabinet? The most frequent answer given by political analysts is that prime ministers get their own way by bypassing the cabinet forum, by taking decisions elsewhere and not allowing the cabinet ministers to participate. That is, they control policy outcomes by circumventing cabinet discussions. That view understates the symbolic importance of the cabinet framework and its traditions; it overemphasises the idea of cabinet as a precise group of identifiable people. The form of cabinet is important because cabinet government is often used as a synonym for proper process. But how those processes will be interpreted is the responsibility of prime ministers. Part of the task is to define which meetings and decisions will be included under cabinet's legitimating rubric. Cabinet can be seen as a process, rather than as a single formal body. Managing cabinet then is central to any prime minister's success. Prime ministers, contrary to normal expectations, may work more effectively through the cabinet than by trying to ignore or circumvent it. That is because of the weight of the collective voice.

Fraser came into government publicly committed to the institution of cabinet and the processes of cabinet government. He had condemned Gorton in 1971 because Gorton had bypassed cabinet. Fraser argued that cabinet was an important institution and that the use of proper procedures was essential for good government. The centrality of cabinet was to Fraser more than a mere constitutional necessity; it had been publicly and constantly pronounced as an article of faith. Under his leadership cabinet met regularly and considered the critical issues. However it was also politically convenient: Fraser understood the value of collective action, the advantages of drawing his ministers into decisions and the strength of cabinet commitment. He even extended the formal cabinet structures to include many consultations that under earlier prime ministers had been undertaken on an informal basis in the prime minister's office.

Consultation and control are not by any means mutually exclusive. Prime ministers do not have to choose between collective or individual styles of decision-making. It is as possible to dominate through consulting cabinet as through ignoring it, perhaps even more so. It is more time-consuming; but it may also be more effective. Cabinet discussion has political advantages as well as policy benefits. Fraser's use of cabinet illustrates how he was able to maximise his own influence without bypassing the cabinet.

A prime minister has to decide *how* cabinet should be used. How often will cabinet meet, how much should it consider, how long should debate last, how far should consensus be sought, in what terms should policies be discussed, how widely should decisions be circulated? Since cabinet is made up of powerful and ambitious individuals, they need to be managed and handled with care. Only the prime minister has the power and authority to manage. He needs skill. This chapter is therefore concerned to describe the *process* of cabinet decision-making. It illustrates the precept, espoused publicly by the Treasury, that 'control over *how* a thing is decided is very close to control over *what is decided*'.

Setting the arrangements

The importance of process is illustrated most dramatically by the control exerted by the prime minister over the proceedings and arrangements of cabinet. No meeting can be held without his or her approval; no submission will be listed; no decision will be circulated. The term 'cabinet' refers to the meetings of the full ministry, the members of cabinet, or any committee of ministers. Because the middle of these three was designated 'the cabinet' does not mean that its conclusions have any greater status than a sub-committee which has the authority to make decisions. All are part of the 'cabinet system'. Where decisions are made and who participated in which committee are the prime minister's responsibility; he or she determines the schedule of cabinet meetings, the particular arena (either full cabinet or a cabinet committee) where a submission will be taken and the agenda for each such meeting. The way this process was adjusted illustrates Fraser's style of running government and the power it gave him.

The cabinet agenda for each week was gradually put together in the ten days before the meetings. PMC maintained a record of submissions outstanding and sent a proposed schedule of meetings and agenda to the prime minister the week before they were due to be held. Full cabinets met at a standard time in the cabinet room in Parliament House – usually Tuesday mornings; the additional committee meetings would be fitted around parliamentary sittings and the timetables of busy and senior ministers. Occasionally, as an exercise in public relations, cabinet would meet in other capital cities.

The submissions were listed on the agenda according to the seniority of the ministers presenting them. It was the only sensible way of organising material. Officials in PMC were not in a position to decide that one submission was more important than another; and the political costs for a prime minister labelling them as of greater or lesser significance would be high. So although a review of cabinet procedures in 1981 proposed that items be listed in order of importance, that plan was never implemented. Of course, the prime minister did not have to take the submissions in the order listed, and often did not. The submissions were required to be lodged with the Cabinet Office ten days before the minister wanted them discussed. The intention of the ten-day rule was to allow circulation of the submissions in sufficient time for ministers to read them. Only the prime minister could waive the rule and permit quicker listing; ministers therefore had to approach him to ask for special consideration.

Two sets of examples illustrate the way the choices were made. Each proposed schedule included the week's cabinet and committees. For instance, on 11 September 1978, PMC proposed:

Tuesday 19 September	Legislation committee	9.00
	Cabinet	10.00 (7 items)
Wednesday 20 September	General Administrative	4.15 (2 items)
Thursday 21 September	Machinery of Government	2.30 (4 items)
then	Intelligence and Security	(2 items)
then	Monetary Policy	

Two weeks later on 29 September PMC proposed:

Monday 9 October	Ad hoc (Industrial Relations)	2.30
	Ad hoc (Parliament House)	5.00
	Cabinet	8.00
Tuesday 10 October	Legislation committee	9.00
	Cabinet	9.30
	Machinery of Government	4.15
then	Monetary Policy and Ad hoc (Uranium)	
Wednesday 11 October	General Administrative	4.15
Thursday 12 October	Reserved for ad hoc committees	

Each schedule therefore included standing and ad hoc committees that ran on, one after the other, until the business was completed. The details were liable to change. As crises emerged, or if the business was not completed, the meetings would be reconvened in the afternoon or the late evening.

Each proposed timetable was accompanied by a list of the submissions and a set of letters from ministers asking for special treatment. Then the negotiations between Fraser and his ministers began. For instance, Senator Carrick wanted to waive the ten-day rule to allow a report on study leave at universities to be considered quickly, arguing that the prime minister had asked him to bring it to cabinet. On PMC's advice, Fraser said no. However he allowed a submission from Street to be listed and, on Anthony's request, postponed a discussion of the common fund. Fraser added a discussion of interest rates to the Monetary Policy committee agenda. There were seven items listed 'under-the-line' (that is, items to be discussed without a formal submission); four of them were the prime minister's. By the end of the week three of these items had not been taken.

On 9 October PMC suggested the next week's program:

Tuesday 17 October	Legislation committee	9.00
	Cabinet	9.30
	Foreign Affairs and Defence then Uranium (if required)	4.15
Wednesday 18 October	General Administrative	4.15
Thursday 19 October	Monetary Policy	2.15
	Foreign Affairs and Defence if required	

On 10 October Fraser said he wanted a cabinet meeting on the Monday, and a full ministry meeting on the Tuesday to discuss the new Parliament House. PMC proposed a special cabinet meeting to discuss a report from the Uranium committee; Fraser decreed that it should be taken on top of the list on Tuesday. Street wanted a submission on wage indexation taken by cabinet, even though it had only been lodged on 13 October; PMC thought the timing would not give ministers enough time to consider it; Fraser sent it to the Wages Policy committee for a first review, and it was then to go to cabinet.

The schedule could become congested. On 3 December 1981 PMC warned of cabinet's heavy program for the last week of the year because it had to consider defence and academic pay, the AUSSAT satellite and the motor vehicles plan; there was a need for discussions with officials on future economic prospects; the Foreign Affairs and Defence committee had to review the Williamstown dockyards, B52 flights and the purchase of an aircraft carrier. There was a long list for the General Administrative committee, the so-called 'second eleven' of junior ministers which dealt, preferably expeditiously, with those minor items that required cabinet approval but were not so sensitive or important that they needed the attention of senior ministers. Both the Review of Commonwealth Functions (RCF) and New Parliament House committees needed to meet. To fit this rush business into the few days, the Cabinet Office proposed:

Tuesday 15 December	New Parliament House committee	8.45
	Cabinet: discussion with officials on economic prospects	9.00
	Cabinet	11.30–1
	Cabinet followed by Foreign Affairs and Defence, Co-ordination and Monetary Policy if required	2.00 onwards,
	General Administrative and RCF to continue into the evening	
Wednesday 16 December	Cabinet or General Administrative as necessary.	

The prime minister approved the program; the full cabinet was to consider fifteen items, if all the bids to waive the ten-day rule were accepted. Fraser agreed to list two items and deferred two; in three of the four cases he rejected a departmental recommendation. He required that the decision to purchase an aircraft carrier should be taken by cabinet, not by the Foreign Affairs and Defence committee, if an extension of the deadline could not be obtained from the British government. On 14 December three further items were listed, and a request by Lynch to waive the ten-day rule was accepted. Cabinet eventually had 22 items. As it was the last meeting of the year, the agenda reflected a desire to clear the decks of outstanding business.

These three brief descriptions illustrate the prime minister's influence on the scheduling and content of cabinet meetings. But Fraser always had to take account of a range of pressures. The interests of senior ministers were important. Doug Anthony in particular had the right to ask for special treatment. In April 1982, for instance, he asked that submissions on environmental protection in the Northern Territory and on LPG subsidies be postponed as he was away. The prime minister agreed but then forgot and cabinet made decisions. Anthony complained that they did not take into account key interests. The prime minister agreed to resubmit the decisions for reconsideration. As Yeend noted to the officials of the Cabinet Office, the prime minister overlooked – and Yeend did not remind him (because no one had reminded Yeend) – Anthony's request to be present. Fraser was not prepared to consider the submissions on the 1982 premiers' conference until Anthony's views were known.

Anthony could also add things to the agenda. One remarkable case occurred on 8 August 1978. A cabinet officer noted that he had been phoned at 1 a.m. by the departmental secretary. Anthony had rung the prime minister from the Philippines; he wanted urgent cabinet consideration of the Australia–Philippines nuclear safeguards agreement so it could be signed before he left Manila. Fraser told Anthony that cabinet would deal with the item within twelve hours. The official assumed that the cabinet meeting to be held in Sydney the next afternoon would be suitable. As it was a joint submission from the ministers for trade and foreign affairs and needed clearance from Peacock, then in Brisbane, he arranged for a courier to take a copy of the submission to Peacock on the first plane out of Canberra at 7.00 a.m. He was woken again at 2.00 a.m., to be told that as Anthony was leaving Manila at 1.00 p.m. next day, the cabinet at 2.30 p.m. was too late and new arrangements were necessary. At 7.30 a.m. it was agreed that a cabinet committee on budget presentation, to be held at 10.30 a.m., would be suitable, as the prime minister would be attending. At 10.10 a.m. the briefing note from PMC to the prime minister was sent across; at 10.20 a.m. the submission was cleared by Peacock. At

10.30 a.m. it was approved by the cabinet committee at its meeting in Sydney. That day, 8 August, was the occasion of the series of meetings over the resignation of Senator Withers. Cabinet approval in this instance was probably a formality; the agreement fitted within guidelines that had already been decided by cabinet and negotiated by officials. Nevertheless it was an impressive example of the influence of Doug Anthony and of the flexibility of what constituted 'cabinet'. However Anthony did not always get his way. In May 1982 he wanted cabinet to discuss IAC reports, while Lynch and Howard wanted them delayed so they could talk to Fraser before the cabinet discussion. Fraser agreed to the latter request.

Nor was Anthony the only senior minister whose interests were protected, even though he carried the greatest weight. Other senior ministers made similar requests. In April 1982 Howard as treasurer was to be away when the minister for communications hoped to bring forward five submissions on AUSSAT. He noted that it would be better if they awaited his return. Fraser agreed; he listed them for a week later than the minister, Ian Sinclair, wanted, in order that Howard could be there. Such a procedure was sensible as it allowed senior ministers to contribute to the debate. If the minister introducing the submission was away, Fraser had to decide whether an item should be delayed or whether the acting minister could present the case.

Fraser also protected areas in which he had a particular interest. He ordered, for instance, that a decision on federal assistance to Queensland for the Commonwealth Games 'was not, repeat not', to be considered in his absence. The Cabinet Office avoided listing items in which he had expressed a wish to be present or was known to have a personal interest. He was never totally out of touch; even when overseas he was informed (in lengthy cables) of the decisions made by cabinet and was provided with lists of decisions on his return. Officials often regarded committee decisions as tentative until Fraser approved them, even if they had formally been circulated.

Requests to waive the ten-day rule were considered individually. Even senior ministers did not always get their way. When Ian Sinclair wanted to bring four submissions and four memoranda about the Dix Committee to cabinet quickly, PMC was appalled, arguing that it was asking too much of ministers to get on top of important issues so fast. The ten-day rule was there for the convenience of ministers; whether the prime minister chose to apply it was a matter of judgement. Fraser generally went through the list provided by PMC, annotating with 'if possible', 'forget it', 'hold', 'Thursday', or 'not if it can be reasonably avoided'. Sometimes he seemed to be searching for excuses to justify decisions to bring items on quickly. In January 1982 PMC noted that Fraser had wanted a good reason to waive the rule for a submission on Olympic coverage. It indicated that as a deadline was approaching, the item had to be dealt with quickly. But Fraser usually insisted on the ten-day rule because it gave ministers more time to read and consider proposals.

At times Fraser became frustrated when submissions were too long or were lodged late and then he tried to tighten up the system. For instance in July 1979 he told Yeend that the Cabinet Office had all the necessary authority to send submissions back to departments. On 27 June 1980 he wrote to the secretary of PMC:

The handling of papers for this week's cabinet was unsatisfactory, to say the least.

Given the size of the Business List and the fact that it included many items which had to be considered for the Premiers' Conference this week, it was unacceptable to have papers and briefing notes coming in over the weekend and on Monday. This comment applies also to the Ad Hoc Committee (Budget) Decisions which required confirmation before the Premiers' Conference.

I am writing to all Ministers who have breached the 10-day rule for lodgement of Cabinet Submissions. In addition, I want you to make clear to Departmental Heads in a very firm and direct manner that such extensive breaches of the 10-day rule are not to occur again immediately before next year's Premiers' Conference, or indeed before any Cabinet.

The process of setting the agenda was designed to ensure that the routine business could be listed and dealt with, so as to leave time for important items. Fraser had to guard the system to an extent to allow other ministers the opportunity to read the submissions. A waiving of the ten-day rule was not a defeat for PMC; rather it was one of the routes available to have items considered by cabinet.

A similar approach was taken to under-the-line items – items considered without any formal submission being circulated in advance. Ministers often requested permission to bring urgent items forward. On some occasions they were accepted. Under-the-line items at a meeting in April 1982 included the terms of reference for a consultant's review on the selling of shares in TAA, support for Britain over the Falklands, and the funding of Aboriginal sacred sites. A month later cabinet discussed polling laws in the ACT, resident allowances for High Court judges, the upgrading of Launceston airport (relevant as a Tasmanian election was being held) and a parliamentary motion by Wilson Tuckey, a Western Australian backbencher, on waterfront labour. Other requests were rejected; when the attorney-general, Peter Durack, wanted to discuss legal aid under the line, he was told to wait until the submission he had been asked to bring forward was ready. Appointments were always taken under the line; they had to be cleared with the prime minister and with the senior minister of the state from which the appointee came before they were brought to cabinet. At times there might be a considerable number; the meeting of 8 December 1981 decided 33 positions, including membership of the National Gallery, the Electoral Office and the executive of CSIRO. No appointment was considered by cabinet until Fraser had agreed to the listing. He had an absolute veto.

This attention to detail was time-consuming, but vital to Fraser because of the information it provided and the control it gave him. He was not prepared to give it up. The initial draft of the report on cabinet procedures in 1978, written by Geoffrey Yeend, proposed that the powers to determine the agenda might be delegated to Lynch. It was not a serious suggestion and was intended as a gesture towards Lynch, because control over the agenda cannot easily be delegated. Only the prime minister can decide what should or should not be discussed. Says Fraser:

Every prime minister is going to say 'no' to that proposal. It's an important part of keeping in touch with ministers and it's an important part of knowing what's going on. If you delegated the job to somebody else the day would come when you went into cabinet not having read the papers beforehand and not knowing what was on the list.

As a senior official commented:

Lynch would have liked to have been chairman of cabinet, rather like the chairman of caucus. Purely on the grounds of cabinet administration, we were never keen on that because it was just a fifth wheel on the coach. If we thought for one moment that the decisions of the chairman of cabinet or the minister in charge of the cabinet agenda would automatically be endorsed by the prime minister, that would be fine. But they wouldn't be. You'd settle it with one and then have to go to the other.

Yet this control over the agenda was not used by Fraser to prevent a minister putting an item on the agenda. **No** minister recalls problems with having items listed; Fraser had experienced problems himself when a junior minister and was determined that the situation would not be repeated:

If a minister wanted the submission before cabinet, in my view he had a right to have it before cabinet and not some months or even weeks after the submission was in the list. In at least one administration I was in, if the prime minister didn't like the submission, he just didn't list it; it just never got discussed ... That is a hopeless way to run a government. So I just made up my mind, however much I like or dislike the submission, it will get on, it will get discussed and a decision will be taken on it.

Nevertheless, on the occasions when he was consulted before a minister put an item on the agenda or when he saw a submission, Fraser might ask that more work be done before it was deemed ready for cabinet discussion. In June 1980, for instance, he complained that the draft cabinet submission on contingency planning for vital services affected by strikes was inadequate. It did not advance the debate beyond the request for an interdepartmental committee report made thirteen months beforehand. Fraser spelt out a series of analyses he wanted completed and demanded a second report within two months. When the minister for the Australian Capital Territory lodged, at the request of cabinet, a report on alternative policies for the sale or lease of the Canberra bus service, Fraser sent it back, demanding more careful analysis. There was no point in wasting the time of cabinet with submissions that would not lead anywhere.

Indeed, far from items not being listed, the more common complaint was that too much was put on the agenda. However much of it was generated by ministers; Sir Arthur Tange argued that ministers should be quietly persuaded to take more on their shoulders. Some of the pressure was created by budget expenditure cuts that were always based on cabinet, not simply departmental, consideration. Many items were listed in response to requests by Fraser, who may have wanted to get proper discussion of a problem. Most submissions dealt with specific problems.

Occasionally Fraser sought broader discussions of the political situation. In May 1976 cabinet agreed to monitor the progress of election promises, but as a consolidated list quickly was overtaken by events, Fraser stopped work on it. However the theme recurred. In April 1977 he asked ministers to identify the more complex matters that were facing the country and sought submissions that could be considered by cabinet. For instance, he asked Anthony to prepare papers on energy and minerals questions, putting the Australian situation into an international perspective and relating the different parts of the problem. The discussions on these broad papers later led to some specific proposals. In November 1977 the ministry agreed to provide quarterly reports on all the significant achievements in their portfolio. In November 1980 Fraser again sought quarterly reports from ministers on the number of the 1977 electoral commitments that had or had not been fulfilled.

Meetings of the full ministry were sometimes held without a fixed agenda; the debate could range widely. In February 1979 the decision recorded that the ministry had noted the decision for an Australian contribution to the Namibia peace-keeping force; discussed the importance of parliament as a forum for the presentation and explanation of government policies; received a report on the prime minister's overseas trips and examined other issues such as the economy, technological change, the Indo-China conflict and refugees. In August the discussion concentrated on government procedures; it confirmed, for instance, the need for revenue matters to be discussed by a small group of ministers (thus legitimising existing practice) and reviewed parliamentary tactics. In May 1981 the ministry agreed to discuss policy and program priorities. That was the essence of meetings of the full ministry – general issues about the performance of the governments, assessments of policy areas but few specific decisions. The ministry meetings were to create a sense of involvement. It was part of a process of trying to maintain some direction and coherence, even if too general in its debates to go far.

The prime minister determined which non-cabinet ministers were able to attend cabinet meetings. Fraser rejected the practice in earlier coalition governments by which non-cabinet ministers were shuffled in and out of the room as their submissions were taken. He allowed non-cabinet ministers to stay after their submission had been taken. In March 1976 he agreed to a suggestion from Sinclair that co-opted ministers should be allowed to attend from the beginning of each cabinet meeting, instead of being called in for the one item for which they were co-opted. 'You were always able to attend meetings if you could find out when they were on', said one junior minister. Cabinet meetings usually consisted of many more than just the cabinet ministers; outer ministers often attended and officials were called in to explain options and submissions.

Even when Fraser could have ignored the cabinet process, he insisted on the forms being followed. For instance, when in Lusaka for the CHOGM meeting of 1979, he discovered that the Australian High Commission there only had temporary status. He wanted it made permanent as an indication of Australia's interest in and commitment to the area. He asked the secretary of PMC to ring around the ministers on the Foreign

Affairs and Defence committee; subject to cabinet approval, Fraser wanted to tell Kaunda personally that the post would be made permanent. At least two of the ministers, Lynch and Sinclair, were unhappy with the proposal, both because of the way it was being rushed through and because of the potential costs, but they acquiesced and a cabinet decision was duly recorded, even though no actual meeting was held. As part of the same process, foreign aid to Tanzania was increased by $1 million. When Fraser returned to Australia, PMC sent him copies of the decisions based on the telephone discussions with available ministers and suggested that, while the decisions gave all the appropriate authority for action, Fraser might like to mention them in cabinet.

If, therefore, it was possible to have decisions without meetings, so too could meetings come to authoritative conclusions without decisions being recorded. On 5 November 1977 a group of cabinet ministers (Fraser, Anthony, Lynch, Nixon, Withers and Street) decided to proceed with the establishment of an ethnic television service, but agreed that there would be no formal decision. Action was to be authorised by a record of the meeting. But, as the secretary to cabinet noted, it was still a meeting within the cabinet system; even if not included in the official register of cabinet decisions, the record of meeting was simply a cabinet decision in another form. The commitment to the ethnic television service was made in the policy speech on 21 November and included in the governor-general's speech on 21 February 1978.

Yet these occasions were exceptions: rare examples of the ultimate flexibility of the cabinet system. Fraser attributed great importance to the form of cabinet and the value of the collectivity. He regarded the process of cabinet decision as necessary, desirable and, above all, proper. Many papers were annotated with the comment 'To Cabinet' scrawled across them. Cabinet was to be the forum for discussion, even where it might be possible for action to be taken alone. One example can make the point. An official recalled the reaction to publication of a book containing some secret diplomatic documents:

CABINET

The wise heads would all say to you that he went out of his way to consult; he was really looking for consensus, almost to the point of exhausting the cabinet's system. I was often surprised at issues that I thought he could have settled either himself or by making one or two phone calls or checking with one or two ministers, where he would insist on a full cabinet. There was one notorious case for me at least. On a Friday night some librarian in Foreign Affairs had got the fly leaf in the book that Munster was about to release. The book had contained a lot of information which was very highly classified, cables and so on; the fly leaf description of what they had was sufficient to cause an alarm. The librarian reported to Peter Henderson [secretary of Foreign Affairs] and he spoke to Bill Pritchett in Defence and they both decided it was going to be a national catastrophe. They rang me to tell me about it at 6 p.m. on Friday night or something like that. I said, 'Well, why shouldn't we move to an injunction to stop publication. Get hold of Clarrie Harders [secretary of the Attorney General's department], seek his advice on whether we have an avenue. In the meantime I will talk to Malcolm Fraser and tell him what was happening and what we are up to'. I spoke to him and suggested that we should proceed to get an injunction. He said: 'Before you do anything you need to get hold of the cabinet; you should contact all of them'. Tracking down the cabinet on a Friday night by phone and checking through this issue was not easy. We found Doug Anthony in a restaurant down the South Coast at Milton; he was at the motel at Ulladulla, but he had gone to dinner; he hadn't said where but we worked out the best restaurant in the area – it was this seafood one that we all knew of. He was just amazed that we had found him. He felt that we had some spy following him around. But we tracked him down . . . and we got through them all eventually and the injunction was finally obtained at midnight.

The official also pointed out that the insistence on getting all other ministers involved created problems:

That sort of use of the cabinet – in the situation where there was very little time if they wanted to act but we needed to know what ministers wanted to do about it – is an illustration of the lengths that were involved. Yet even then there were risks of resentment. Ministers would say they were passing a view over the phone without seeing the papers, without having had time to think about it and this wasn't the proper way to take a cabinet decision. Now how do you draw the line? If he just consults the Foreign Affairs minister in that case and with his agreement takes action and gets an injunction, he will be criticised for not having used the cabinet process. If you have limited time to consult, then it has to be done by phone and he'll be criticised for short-cutting the procedure. Prime ministers can't win; that is the short answer.

Another illustration of the problem was Fraser's insistence on holding a meeting to discuss a Qantas strike, with three Western Australian ministers participating from Chaney's house in Perth.

At times indeed the meeting of cabinet seemed to epitomise the government in action. Even on holiday Fraser wanted to see some activity. Over December 1981 he was on official leave at Nareen while Doug Anthony, as acting prime minister, was ruling from his caravan on the Murwillumbah coast. Just before Christmas the Cabinet Office asked if there should be a cabinet meeting on 12 January; it recommended that, as there was little urgent business to be considered and few substantial items could be taken in the prime minister's absence, it might be better to hold everything over until 19 January. Besides, as many ministers were away, their items had to be held over too. Even though on holiday, Fraser insisted on being provided with a list of potential items on 24 December. He told the secretary of PMC on 26 December that a meeting should be held, as otherwise too much time would have elapsed without any sign of government activity. By 4 January there was still barely enough business – a mere eleven items, none crucial – to justify calling the ministers together. In a note to the deputy prime minister, with a copy to the prime minister, PMC listed the possible agenda. Determined to ensure that a meeting would be held, Fraser reacted by saying he was considering coming in from his holiday; if he was present all the items could be considered, so that no meeting would be needed on 19 January. He said he would ring Anthony. No meeting was held; Anthony clearly talked him out of it. But the desire to get on with business was typical.

This almost obsessive interest in the activity of cabinet

indicates Fraser's concern that it be seen as the centre of government activity. The consequence of this level of consultation was a massive workload. Cabinet met so often that ministers complained they spent too much time 'in the bunker'.

Although Fraser was relaxed about attendance, outside the formal schedule his organisation of cabinet was not always considerate. Committee meetings might be suddenly called, and adjourned meetings reconvened at little or no notice. Budd recalls:

Ministers were irritated at being summoned at a moment's notice. He would call together a cabinet or cabinet committee and adjourn it to 10.00 o'clock and then suddenly decide to start at 9.00 o'clock. They resented it. He lost goodwill because of the demands on ministers' time.

Meetings were called so suddenly and so often that, as Durack put it, 'there were always so many meetings going on and you were being summoned to this and that, you were never quite sure which meeting you were at!'. Sometimes Fraser would be late for cabinet, leaving twelve or so important people sitting there festering and grumbling. Running the timetable to suit the prime minister might be the chairman's prerogative, but it was not the best way to maintain cohesion or obtain the best contribution from its members.

The sheer statistics of the number of meetings held, submissions or memoranda lodged and decisions taken with or without a formal submission are impressive (see Table 4.1).

The Fraser cabinet took about 19 350 decisions. Some were important, others were not. Between 180 (in 1982) and 224 (in 1981) appointments came to cabinet for approval in any one year, a total of 836 positions between 1979 and the end of the government. It had 2446 meetings; many were held in sequence, one after the other. Some items came back to cabinet time and again. Between September 1977, when cabinet first considered a proposal from Kerry Packer to explore the prospects for a satellite, and October 1982, when it made its final decision, AUSSAT was considered by cabinet or one of its committees on *thirty-one* separate occasions, as ministers gradually dealt

Table 4.1: *Workload of the Fraser government*

		Meetings			Decisions	
	Ministry	Cabinet	Committees	Submission and/or memorandum	With submission	Without submission
1975 (December)	1	4	—	13	17	
1976	6	83	116	1000	2081	
1977	10	127	172	878	2357	
1978	8	162	257	1016	2955	
1979	15	97	324	1611	1917	1120
1980	11	70	226	1373	1577	868
1981	10	112	310	1719	2702*	1154*
1982	5	104	186	1281	1368	955
1983 (to March)	1	7	22	130	113	162
	67	766	1613	9021	19346	

*Decisions included 1007 by the Review of Commonwealth Function

Source: For 1975–78, there is a list of statistics in M1268/24. For 1979–83 the details are taken from the annual reports of the Department of Prime Minister and Cabinet and consolidated into figures for each year. The method of collection may not have been entirely consistent; the first list does not differentiate between decisions made with or without submissions nor the number of decisions that related to appointments

with the problems it created. Uranium was discussed at eight different meetings in July and August 1977 alone. This was either because the problems were intrinsically insoluble, or because they were so complicated that it needed several bites before ministers were able to understand the issues fully. Issues reach cabinet because they are complex; to take decisions at the first opportunity may be promoting expedition above understanding, and thereby ceding authority to the technicians. Nevertheless, for all the caveats with all the extenuating excuses, the amount of business undertaken by the Fraser government was immense.

Another indicator of the work is the time spent in meetings

(see Table 4.2). May to July are the budget months in which ministers are the hardest worked and the statistics include budget committees where only four or five ministers were present. Yet important decisions can only be taken by senior ministers, so the weight fell disproportionately on a few individuals – Fraser, Howard, Lynch, Nixon, Anthony. Further, for every hour spent in cabinet some time must be used for preparation: reading the documents, being briefed about the issues. So in May 1979, when there were on average two and a half meetings every day, and three and a half hours every day – or twenty-seven hours a week – were actually spent in meetings, the total load on those senior ministers was staggering, particularly when all the other functions of ministers – parliamentary, party and departmental – were added. 'In the bunker' was an apt phrase.

Table 4.2: *Time spent in meetings: selected months*

	Meetings	Hours
May 1978	63	85.05
June 1978	35	48
July 1978	43	98.42
January 1979	8	23.52
May 1979	78	107.36
June 1979	37	49
July 1979	51	67.58

Source: LC3263 Peacock Resignation.

Fraser, his ministers and his officials realised that problems were being created by the workload and there was constant research to reduce the pressure. Two reviews of cabinet procedures, in 1978 and 1981, were instituted. The first review, established by cabinet on 15 August 1978, was undertaken by Yeend and his deputy, Mike Codd. It examined the prospects of changing the rules on what came to cabinet, lengthening the ten-day rule, possibly altering the question-time procedures to put questions on set days for each minister, increasing spending discretion for ministers and linking senior and junior ministers in the administration of departments. A wide range of statistics was collected that documented the heavy workload. They showed, among other things, how many submissions dealt with appointments, and how many with items that cost less than half a million dollars.

Several methods of reducing the volume of business were suggested: that there be a prescribed expenditure level below which the minister for finance had authority to decide; that minor legislative matters go straight to the Legislation committee of cabinet; that the prime minister be assisted by another minister in cabinet procedures (Fraser put a line through that idea); that matters be settled as far as possible by correspondence. Ministers welcomed the discussion of items under the line, but felt that substantial policy proposals should still be made through submission. They also wanted to have strategic meetings without considering specific submissions, and a small 'leadership committee'.

The review recommended that all under-the-line items be cleared in advance with the prime minister, that appointments be cleared with senior ministers from the relevant state, that the minister for finance be allowed to approve expenditure on a program of not more than $500 000 in each of three years, that ministry meetings be held more often, that a 'leadership' committee (consisting of the leader and deputy leader of each coalition party and the leader of the government in the Senate) and cabinet committees for Industry and for General Policy be created. Fraser rejected two suggestions: that business lists and a list of cabinet submissions be circulated to permanent heads. This refusal was part of a desire to keep items as secret as possible.

Cabinet considered the report in December 1978. Fraser made clear that its discussions were not intended to lead to decisions, as it was his prerogative to determine which of the recommendations would be adopted. He demanded tighter control by the Cabinet Office of the flow of cabinet papers. In January he selected the title 'Co-ordination committee' in preference to leadership committee. The minister for finance was allowed to approve items up to $1 500 000 over three years and was to provide quarterly reports of approvals granted. Lynch could talk to ministers about the flow of cabinet papers (but not the specific agendas). Fraser vetoed the principle of allowing ministers assisting to attend cabinet committees as replacements for the substantive ministers. As Fraser reminded his ministry, in the last resort it was the ministers themselves who had to make the cabinet work effectively.

The second review in 1981 again emphasised the need for ministers to take decisions on their own and for submissions to be better digested. A cabinet decision on 1 December 1981 merely reiterated the need to keep items away from cabinet, suggested that items that breached the ten-day rule be listed at the end of the agenda and that items be listed in order of priority for discussion; it proposed that under-the-line items be taken at the end of the meetings. It seems that these reviews made little difference. The problem was not in the procedures – although changes could help – but in the pressure from above and below to have issues discussed by cabinet. Fraser saw cabinet discussion as necessary; the ministers thought them a useful self protection. The workload stayed high.

Arenas for discussion: the committee system

If Fraser did not keep items off the agenda, he did decide where they would be discussed: in full cabinet or in a cabinet committee. There were two types of cabinet committee: standing committees that dealt with the regular business of government and ad hoc committees that were established for specified purposes. Some standing committees met more often than others. The Economic committee, seen initially as the crucial forum for government strategy, only met fourteen times in the first two years before it was abolished. Fraser explained that, as most of the important decisions on the economy were taken in cabinet, the committee was not needed. The Legislation committee, responsible for vetting the final drafts of legislation before their presentation to parliament, met 127 times in the same period. Others, such as the Social Welfare, the Purchasing or the Machinery of Government committees, met rarely. Their authority to make final decisions depended on the importance of the issue. The Social Welfare committee was able to make final decisions, but they had to be cleared with the prime minister before being issued.

Ad hoc committees were established with particular terms of reference to consider troublesome or difficult issues such as uranium, AUSSAT and the new Parliament House. The Review of Commonwealth Functions was one of several ad hoc committees that undertook the detailed consideration of budget estimates or revenue decisions. These committees sometimes thrashed out options and then brought recommendations for action to cabinet. A few had the authority to make final decisions. Fraser decided all the terms of reference and the membership. Between July 1977 and July 1979, for instance, 1220 of the 6400 recorded cabinet decisions were made by ad hoc committees; 590 by budget committees, whose decisions were subject to ratification by cabinet; 136 by the Uranium committee that took any new policy issues to cabinet; 25 by the committee on the Williams report on education; 29 by the Crawford Industry Report committee; 33 by the New Parliament House committee. The range of subjects was broad.

Three standing committees were of particular importance. Foreign Affairs and Defence, and its later offshoot, the Intelligence and Security committee, made decisions on many issues of broad significance in relation to Africa, policy towards the great powers, defence procurement and Australia's role overseas. Its decisions were often not circulated to other ministers in cabinet.

The Monetary Policy committee and the Wages committee were created in 1977 to replace the Economic committee. The Monetary Policy committee was responsible for issues that had traditionally been kept isolated in the Treasury, or had been finally decided by the prime minister and the treasurer. It brought crucial economic decisions (on, for example, interest and exchange rates) into the cabinet arena, so that departments other than Treasury became involved in advice on economic policy. The Reserve Bank became more influential; so did PMC. Thus the Treasury's monopoly of economic information and advice was diminished and, as a PMC official put it,

Treasury was forced to become part of the normal advisory framework.

However the most significant committee, at least from the point of view of cabinet control and political decision-making, was the Co-ordination committee, created in 1979 at the behest of ministers after the 1978 cabinet review. Where the Co-ordination committee differed from the others was in its lack of a clear functional role. It had precursors in an informal committee of the party leaders that had been convened initially to consider the 1977 electoral redistribution and the percentage tolerance that would be acceptable and in the Planning and Co-ordination committee established in 1976 which rarely ever met. The Co-ordination committee's terms of reference stated that it should 'consider overall government strategy and priorities, and to deal with matters referred to by the Prime Minister'. In other words, it could discuss anything Fraser chose to take to it.

There was nothing sinister in the existence of a small inner group. All prime ministers are likely to be surrounded by a group of advisers and ministers whom they find compatible. These meetings are often labelled kitchen cabinets and have no official status. Fraser took many of those activities out of the prime minister's office and into the cabinet system. That meant that decisions had a formal weight. As a senior official explained:

Co-ordination committee was a testing ground for him to discuss a good range of political issues and tactics. Not everything in Co-ordination needed a decision. Most prime ministers have that sort of sounding board. Few of them have given it the designation of a cabinet committee.

The membership of the Co-ordination committee was initially only the leaders of the Liberal and the National parties in the House of Representatives, and the government leader in the Senate. But others were co-opted, depending on whom Fraser trusted and what was being discussed. In September 1979, when Sinclair resigned after being charged in a NSW court, he was replaced by Nixon as the second National party minister on the committee. Nixon's advice was highly regarded. When Sinclair returned to office in 1980, Nixon received a formal letter stating that Sinclair would rejoin the Co-ordination committee in Nixon's place. But Fraser added a personal note saying that he had agreed that Nixon be co-opted for all Co-ordination committee meetings until the election. In March 1980 Fraser and Lynch discussed the membership of the committee. While they decided to keep the official membership at five, Fraser instructed that Nixon be co-opted on most occasions and for most matters; he wanted the department to find the odd occasion when Nixon was not co-opted for the sake of appearances. The impression of a small membership was thus to be retained, but Fraser saw it as important that Nixon's advice continue to be available. During the 1980–83 parliament, as the committee became more involved in economic matters, Howard and Guilfoyle were often co-opted too.

The Co-ordination committee discussed a range of subjects. Some were political: the parliamentary program, four year terms and whether the speaker should be independent. Others were tactical: should ministers be allowed to appeal against decisions of a budget committee or against the imposition of a level of staff ceilings? Some were previews of items that came to cabinet: they were tossed around to guess their impact before being taken to full cabinet for discussion. Fraser says: 'If I was unsure how an issue should be handled, I might discuss it with the Co-ordination committee and then it would be decided by cabinet'.

Gradually the Co-ordination committee became the body responsible for revenue decisions (traditionally the province of a small inner group). In May 1979 it previewed the revenue options before the May statement. In August 1980 the Co-ordination committee spent two meetings looking at the priorities for government business in the next six months. The ministry then endorsed the report, the day after the second of the committee meetings. On 18 September 1980 it discussed proposals for the policy speech, with Fraser annotating each idea. The Co-ordination committee examined all the main budget papers in July 1981 before their consideration by cabinet and housing interest rates before the housing package of 1982.

Its agenda gave the impression of a wide-ranging committee that looked at anything that was significant or immediately topical.

The free-flowing style of the committee meant that the formal agenda bore no relation to what was discussed. The committee could start with a preliminary discussion of the budget and then roll on to other issues for which the responsible minister was not present. The committee became the place where the political agenda was exposed (often on the basis of flimsy information). It set priorities, commissioned work, developed options and ideas, and made a preliminary review of the political problems of the day. In November 1980 it asked for policy reviews on the length of parliamentary terms; commonwealth–state financial relations; income or indirect taxes; north–south relations; Radio Australia; the Makarrata (a proposed treaty between Aboriginal and White Australians); Agent Orange; nuclear safeguards, and poverty. Its influence could indeed be wide ranging. The meetings kept senior ministers informed about the prime minister's timetable and thinking.

Fraser was regarded at his best in the small meetings of this type. Brian Buckley, Lynch's press secretary and a frequent critic of Fraser, thought 'he excelled in those little Co-ordination committee and Expenditure Review rooms; that was where he could argue a case pleasantly over coffee, a great charmer.' This skill made him more effective still. Howard too recalls: 'he was at his best arguing a proposition around a table – that was probably his greatest strength – his knowledge, his strength, the authority of the position'. Small committees thus became very influential.

Partly as a consequence of its exclusive and privileged membership, the Co-ordination committee led to resentment among other ministers. When Andrew Peacock resigned in 1981, he claimed that the Co-ordination committee had been superimposed over the cabinet and its other committees; that when it discussed issues the responsible ministers were often not present, and that it was

in fact an extension of the Prime Minister's well-known lobbying of ministers before issues are brought to cabinet . . . when cabinet meets a significant number of ministers have already determined many matters concerning government strategy. In some cases, policy matters may have been decided. The decision of cabinet is a foregone conclusion and so collective wisdom of cabinet is aborted.

He objected that ministers were 'dismissed from the cabinet room' so the Co-ordination committee could meet. He argued that the Co-ordination committee 'is not just a kitchen cabinet; it is a formal structure crushing the cabinet system'.

Peacock's charges were denied by his colleagues in the debate that followed his resignation, but the material collected by PMC for Fraser's defence against the charges provided interesting insights into its role. From March 1979, when the committee was created, to March 1981, the committee made 463 decisions, of which 198 were circulated to Peacock. Of those 198, 94 were routine decisions of a kind that most prime minsters made unilaterally; they referred to parliamentary tactics, or commissioned papers for cabinet consideration; 75 were budget decisions in 1979 and 1980, when the Co-ordination committee became the small group reviewing revenue and expenditure; 29 were concerned with legislative priorities, policy reviews, staff ceilings and a range of particular issues – infrastructure borrowing, energy policy, subsidised housing – that were sometimes there as a matter of convenience, because cabinet had dispersed. In 1980 and 1981, the brief noted, only 14 of the 215 items that were considered in Co-ordination committee and in cabinet were considered first in the committee. There was only a substantive discussion of parliamentary superannuation, the length of the parliamentary term, broadcasting and television. In other instances the Co-ordination committee's discussion was sandwiched between two cabinet discussions of the same issues.

Two points are noticeable. First, not all ministers received all decisions of the Co-ordination committee, a point that will be taken up later; Peacock did not see more than 250 decisions. Second, the committee took up a wide range of issues for political reasons and for matters of convenience. Some of this may have been a cabinet preview, but not all was. One official described the committee as 'Fraser talking, us taking down decisions'. When the committee did make decisions, its members appreciated that they were expected to throw their weight behind those views and stick to them in cabinet. When it operated as an 'inner cabinet', it was the first of an expanding group of concentric circles. If the committee, consisting of the strongest ministers, had committed itself, Fraser had fewer qualms about asserting his views in cabinet as he knew that the leading members of the government were agreed.

The Co-ordination committee, like all other committees, is a 'partial' cabinet. It includes only a few ministers, has terms of reference (very general in this case) and has the authority to make decisions that will bind all other members of cabinet. Fraser used his committees extensively. That was necessary to get through the load of business; a committee structure is a vital part of a modern cabinet system. It also allowed the forum for discussion to be carefully chosen, with a select membership. Important decisions were taken by Foreign Affairs and Defence, by the Monetary Policy and by the Co-ordination committee, decisions that determined foreign policy, defence purchases, interest rates, wages policy and so on and on. Every one of these had the weight of a decision taken by full cabinet. They were *cabinet* decisions because the concept of 'cabinet' is more a description of a floating mélange of meetings than any precise institution with a set membership. A cabinet decision means that an item has been settled by some part of the cabinet system; it is enough to make it authoritative. Committees were an essential part of that system, a part that Fraser used with skill to get the business done.

Running the cabinet

Fraser went to cabinet well prepared. PMC gave him a brief on every submission and he sometimes went through the agenda with his staff to assist in clarifying his thoughts. He not only knew what problems were likely to be involved, but what their possible consequences were. He believed that cabinet should not take a decision if he had not considered fully any likely implication:

The prime minister has to be in a position in cabinet to know whether the decision that has been made is a sensible one or not. If a prime minister is not in that position, he is falling behind in his own work load. That doesn't mean to say you have got a violent interest in the subject yourself; it just means, if a decision of some importance is to be made, you want to know enough about it to be satisfied from your own knowledge that it is a sensible decision.

He therefore needed to give thought to every proposal to know that all questions have been asked and adequately answered.

He also ensured that as far as possible the important ministers understood issues. At times he asked his minister for finance to take a careful look at a proposal, fearing that the responsible minister did not understand all that was involved. The AUSSAT satellite was one of the more complex issues to face cabinet. Fraser asked Senator Guilfoyle to watch the issue closely and let him know if her department was worried, because he was not certain that the minister introducing the proposal understood all its ramifications. On other occasions Fraser asked the attorney-general to raise difficult legal questions in cabinet. If concerned about the implications of a submission, he might ask other ministers to take a close look.

He was renowned among his colleagues for lining up the numbers in advance. Lobbying in the coalition cabinet was strictly forbidden, but prime ministerial consultation was regarded as fairly usual. Lynch 'liked to know what my view was on any important issue he was taking to cabinet, which meant we discussed the issues right along the line', remembers Fraser. The Treasury also recalls that Lynch only argued 'until he got a whiff of the prime minister's direction'. Some ministers would preview an important item with the prime minister before the meeting. Fife discussed proposed changes to Sydney airport before he brought a submission to cabinet. Fraser wanted to know the details and the means by which the political problem would be handled. He would say, 'What you are doing I think is great, but we'll look at it when it's lodged!' However supportive, he would wait for briefs from PMC and Treasury. Fife argued that Fraser was never committed to the point where you could enter cabinet and say, 'I've got the prime minister locked into a submission!'

When he was minister for transport, Ralph Hunt talked to him about the Darwin–Alice Springs railway and took into account the general thrust of his views. The Bicentennial Roads program was another case:

I spent some time talking to him because I knew I'd run into opposition on it because it was intended to hypothecate revenue funds for a specific purpose, which was totally opposed to Treasury's view . . . We wrote into the legislation interesting policy decisions; all the states would have to put up on every project that 'this is a Commonwealth Bicentennial Project'. In fact Malcolm was so enthusiastic about that idea that he said 'I think we ought to make sure that Roads ministers wear a sandwich board that says "I'm a recipient of Bicentennial Roads Funding". It would be interesting to see Mr. Hinze in that situation; we'd need a helicopter to read it'.

Hunt thought that most ministers with a major project would have been unwise not to have talked to Fraser first.

Prime ministers need to have a broad appreciation of the directions cabinet is taking. Fraser could often guess on which side his colleagues would fall without having to discuss the specific items with them. Dealing with ministers on a regular basis meant that he had a fair estimate of who would support the leader and who would support the particular solutions. He says:

Henry Bolte used to say, 'don't let anything go into cabinet unless you know how you want it to come out. You've got to know the decision that's made is safe and will work'. That was good advice. I'd quite often not know how the numbers were going to go. But because I did a bit of work on the submission and I'd got briefed I wasn't all that often on the losing side in a cabinet discussion. If you're arguing with a bunch of people who are basically fairly pragmatic, if you've done your homework, you're likely to be on the winning side in an argument, not always, but more often than not.

On important topics, these calculations would be essential.

Fraser chaired all cabinet meetings in a very active fashion.

The atmosphere was formal. He was called 'Prime Minister' by his ministers. On many items the discussion was brusque. If Fraser thought an item was of little significance, he was inclined to push it through fast, without encouraging much discussion. If an issue was cut and dried, he would lead cabinet to a quick conclusion – and some ministers wanted to talk. If an agenda was of twenty items, only two would be of substance where proper argument should be developed. For the eighteen he seemed dominant in getting a quick conclusion and might go straight to the recommendations. It was not that he cared much what the result was, but time was needed for the more sensitive or substantial issues. Indeed on these minor items he might lose interest in the discussion. Mackellar recalls:

When ministers were putting a case, he'd turn aside, talk to other people and appear not to be listening. He was never known as a charming man and a lot thought he was rude. But it was not a calculated rudeness. His mind was working on so many areas he appeared rude when what he was doing was thinking about something entirely different and concentrating on that.

Yet for ministers to be talking to the back of his head while he talked to Doug Anthony was not encouraging.

However when items of importance or of interest to Fraser were discussed, then the atmosphere could become far more charged with tension. The cabinet spent much of its time on issues that were politically sensitive. Under-the-line items were taken first; for instance, a report on negotiations with the ACTU might lead to a broad hour-long discussion. (Or, less seriously, there might be a comment on the previous evening's episode of 'Yes Minister'.) On occasion under-the-line items led to discussions so lengthy that the substantive submissions were barely reached. (When the Hawke government was elected, the Cabinet Office persuaded the new prime minister to list the under-the-line items after the submissions; the submissions were dispatched first.)

Fraser's own interventions in a discussion were unpredictable, although, given his contribution on every item, he talked in total far more than any other minister. So much so that ministers and officials thought he was too interventionist to be seen as a good chairman (although cabinet is scarcely a normal committee). If he felt strongly, he might state his views early and explain why he held them; in a sense such a statement could be regarded as a challenge to other ministers to back him or not. Some ministers were always inclined to support the prime minister, but it was dangerous to assume that every question or statement was an accurate reflection of his views, because the process of cabinet was more a process of interrogation than formal debate. Fraser 'wanted to make sure that cabinet was fully exposed to the issues before taking a decision and I didn't want senior ministers to be jumped'. One minister complained that he was never given the opportunity to develop a case; as soon as he started to speak 'you had these questions rolling down the aisles like a bowling alley; if you let yourself be intimidated by that and went away speechless, it was your own fault'.

Senior ministers were unsympathetic; Sinclair has pointed out that the complainants often asked for it: 'they wanted to bring propositions up and have long discussions; there were interrogations because senior ministers were concerned about the outcome. It has always been that way and gives people the chance to show their mettle'. Fraser also thought that if ministers were a little nervous they would perform better: 'A minister who wanted to make his point needed to know enough to be able to answer the questions'. He argued that ministers could be expected to carry on the technical discussion in their own areas. Officials might be called in to provide more detailed technical information, but that did not release the requirement for the minister to be on top of his material. Senior ministers had the first right to questions: 'I don't think they were put in a hostile or acrimonious way, except perhaps when people got tired occasionally. It was a general seeking after the right solution'.

So the process was tough – and as brief as possible. It was a busy forum for making decisions, not an area for the judicious exposition of all the issues. Some ministers were treated more gently than others. Fraser was inclined to push and probe those whom he believed eventually might become senior; those who were never going to make it and had difficulty ever answering a question, were treated more gently. Public servants unused to cabinet ways might find it difficult. During a Telecom strike Jack Curtis, an engineer who was its managing director, was attacked in cabinet for actions that he regarded as proper industrial relations; his resignation was accepted some time afterwards. He was, noted an official:

a sacrificial lamb. Curtis was a fine old gentleman who did a good job running Telecom with 80,000 people and millions of dollars of investment. But I doubt he ever had anything in his background to prepare him for a cross-examination in the cabinet room by the prime minister with all the authority of the government.

The process of questioning sometimes led to ministers feeling they had a great victory. An official claimed:

If Fraser put his view early, ministers often thought he was decided because he'd come out with a challenge. But he was simply going on with the questioning style. If satisfied at the end, he would be happy to go along with the minister's submission. And the minister might think he had a stunning victory.

Indeed it was often dangerous to accept Fraser's view precisely because he might just be floating ideas. If his first hypothesis was accepted too quiescently, it just might not have had sufficient scrutiny. Ministers did change their views after Fraser spoke. In itself that is not surprising; ministers are meant to be influenced by the discussions they hear around the table. However one minister changed his opinions so often he was known as 'Mr 180 degrees' and lost all influence. The weight of ministers was important too; if Fraser, Anthony and Lynch were united, opposition was unlikely. There was a clear pecking order in cabinet.

Fraser's terse style – it was easy to tell if he was relaxed or not about an issue – led to charges that he bullied cabinet. His aggressive approach made it an easy charge to make. Even a close colleague like Nixon agrees in part: 'He tried to bully me as I opposed him at times. He would swing on me in cabinet with an angry look and say "What are you up to? What are you going crook about?"' But he never excluded ministers who wanted to speak. No minister recalls being prevente[...] speaking, although many thought some colleagues were [...] too scared to speak. A typical comment was: 'I was ne[...] stopped from saying something I wanted to say, either to hi[...] or to the cabinet. Never'.

However ministers were never certain how a submission would be received. Those who had duly consulted everyone before bringing a submission to cabinet may have been annoyed when they were questioned rather than given a soft ride; but that was always the way the cabinet process worked. The fact that departments and their ministers had agreed with the recommendation was no guarantee that cabinet would approve; problems that had not been recognised before could easily be identified in cabinet.

Summarising the discussion and announcing the decision were the prime minister's prerogatives. He could draw together the strands of the discussion, weigh the voices or postpone debate. His colleagues thought he was always ready to defer an item if he was not getting his own way. Ian Macphee remembers:

he would get ministers to withdraw submissions on the most curious pretexts; and ministers would do so rather than have the submissions rejected substantially. The ministers would talk to the PM after the meeting and the submission would come back in a different form – and with a greater chance of success.

One tactic was to ask for further information or another paper; it was, an official recalls, an alternative to saying we haven't reached a decision. This procedure was a useful tactic when Fraser was not gaining support.

Decisions were reached in several ways. Votes were not taken in the direct sense of a formal motion, but Fraser sometimes went round the table, asking ministers where they stood. It was not always easy to get views; sometimes he had to drag colleagues into expressing them. Fraser recalls:

I can remember one very senior minister. I tried to get him to give a view. He said: 'On the one hand, this; on the other hand, that!'

I said: 'Yes, but look, the numbers are evenly divided and it's an important issue. I would like to know, if you have got to make a decision, where you would come out.' 'On the one hand, this; on the other hand, that'. It took me about fourteen minutes to actually find out which side of the ground he was going to hit. I really struggled to make a minister give a view. If somebody said 'Look, I just haven't got a view', I can't have it, that's not doing your job. You have to have a view and to help in reaching a collective view.

Yet even when Fraser went round the table, his counting was often regarded as suspect. Nixon was reputed to have asked 'which way' when the prime minister stated one result. Killen grumbled that he must have counted the note-takers. There were also eight-six decisions, as they were called, which occurred when, on the basis of the views expressed, Fraser had stated, as the clear cabinet decision, the view of the minority – with which he agreed. The origin of the expression was the decision over the banning of sand mining on Fraser Island. One minister, on leaving the meeting, quietly told the prime minister he had changed his view. The final decision did not reflect the views expressed. But few were prepared to contest summaries of this type; most acknowledged such results were rare.

Numbers were often not in themselves enough. Fraser wanted more than a bare majority because of the importance of collective commitment. When everyone who wanted to speak had had their turn and there was a clear majority, cabinet would not pursue it further. If ministers were badly divided, then a decision might not stick and they all had to live with it and defend it. Fraser preferred to delay such decisions until there was greater support. He had a good notion of what could be pushed through and what needed to be reconsidered. He had to balance particular decisions against future cabinet cohesion. On important issues, therefore, a badly divided cabinet meant that the issue was likely to come back again and again. Durack reflected a widely-held view when he said:

He would persist. If he had a group of people against him in cabinet, he wouldn't just use the numbers, he would keep arguing; he would put it aside and come back to it at another meeting; then he would tend to try and get alliances together.

He was a collective chairman who went to extraordinary lengths to get ministers involved. He usually wasn't prepared to run with only a slight majority. His style may have appeared authoritarian, but he did not take decisions away from his ministers if they really wanted to participate.

When cabinet was divided, the process of making a decision was interminable. 'There seemed to be a paralysis of action', said Peter Baume. Even when consensus was achieved, it could be at the cost of innumerable meetings. Unwilling to have a badly divided cabinet, Fraser wanted to win the argument. At the very least he wanted acquiescence; he would have preferred agreement. When ministers disagreed and fought, the discussions went on and on. But if the issue was sensitive, Fraser would seldom close it off. 'He would do it by exhaustion; he knew what he wanted, but if he didn't have his colleagues on side, he kept them locked up until they caved in', said one cabinet official with only slight poetic licence.

There are also good political reasons. As one observer commented, the prime minister

has got to make the right decision for the country's sake, for the party's sake and in the end for his own sake. The hard facts of political life are that if the prime minister keeps getting rolled, his authority becomes weakened and that of the party becomes weakened and he'll fail rapidly.

Fraser was unable to recall any occasion where he cared and lost, although others pointed out that on some issues, like the Closer Economic Relations agreement with New Zealand, he was not favourably inclined, but chose not to fight it as Anthony strongly supported the plan.

Prime ministers have to live with and sell cabinet decisions. If they want something badly enough, most cabinet ministers are prepared to live with it. A senior official explains:

If prime ministers felt strongly, given their sense of politics, the decisions were likely to be supported by most of their colleagues. Even when senior ministers felt uneasy, in the end they gave their support because they felt, I think rightly, that the prime minister has got to sink or swim as the political leader of the government. In that sense, prime ministers do get their way. Ministers don't argue but have good will.

Chaney supported this view:

A prime minister has got a certain amount of room to move. He can take an unpopular stance on a limited number of issues. If he does it too much, he will exhaust his political capital.

However Fraser was often not prepared to use that power; he did not end debates by announcing where the government would stand. Withers 'can't ever remember Malcolm saying: "That is that and I brook no argument"'. He wouldn't override a cabinet majority against him; he would just wear it down because he wanted people with him. Jim Carlton strongly opposed Fraser's demands that Dennis Horgan, the treasurer of the Western Australian Liberal party, be required to stand down from official positions when named in tax evasion reports. Fraser could have excluded Carlton from the cabinet discussions because he was not a member of cabinet, but he brought him into the meetings because he knew his views and wanted to get his agreement.

At the end of a debate, some ministers did not know whether they had won or not, or what they had won. Decisions were often drawn from the recommendations of ministers, but occasionally there was a sting in the tail. When cabinet accepted the recommendations of the Coldham committee into defence forces pay, the decision noted that due to the magnitude of the additional costs ($260 million in a full year) they should be absorbed as far as possible in the Defence Five Year program, and so it required the minister for defence to bring forward a submission recommending commensurate savings in expenditure elsewhere in the department, an addendum not included in any of the briefing papers. The minister's public statement did not acknowledge this addition; indeed initially the department did not realise there was a rider to the decision that made the success in cabinet a Pyrrhic victory.

Decisions were written up by the Cabinet Office and often had to be extracted from the debate, since they were not based on formal motions. If the recommendations in the submission were accepted, they could be rephrased as a decision. If amendments were made, the Cabinet Office had to develop a coherent and consistent conclusion. One official, only half-jokingly, commented 'we record the decision ministers would have reached, if they had time to read their briefs and discuss the submissions at length'. Sometimes clauses not mentioned were added to make the decision logical. If any ministers objected the decisions could be reviewed.

Fraser could vet decisions before their circulation. For instance in October 1977 he wrote to Yeend:

You will be aware of my concern with the cabinet decision on Seas and Submerged Lands. I think it might be desirable if important cabinet decisions were not circulated without coming to me for clearance . . . I would be glad if you could examine the idea.

But that right was seldom exercised. When the Cabinet Office prepared a brief for Fraser after Peacock's resignation, it noted that only three or four times a year had the prime minister asked to clear decisions before circulation and that was usually when a decision was based on a discussion in cabinet rather than a submission.

In theory decisions were circulated to all ministers. In practice the distribution was often far more limited. Each decision had attached to it a list of ministers or officials to whom it should be sent. Often, for routine or non-controversial issues, that circulation list would include all ministers. Some were far more limited. When the budget ad hoc committee or the Review of Commonwealth Functions (RCF) committee made decisions, they were usually circulated only to members of the committee. Some of their decisions later came to the cabinet for ratification or endorsement, but when proposals were rejected by these committees the other members of cabinet were never informed. When issues were under discussion the interim decisions might only be given to a limited number of people. In February 1981 cabinet was considering the introduction of an indirect tax. When Lynch returned from overseas in the middle of the debate and asked for a briefing on the progress of the proposal, he was told by his department:

We have no idea at this stage what decisions, if any, cabinet might have taken on these various submissions in your absence abroad; access to the decisions has been limited to Mr Anthony, the Prime Minister and Mr Howard.

The department did its best to review the implications – working in semi-ignorance of the discussions could be difficult.

Fraser often changed, usually more restrictively, the list proposed by his officials. The decisions of ad hoc committees on, say, uranium, only went to the members. Revenue decisions, particularly in the budget, were given very limited circulation, often only to Fraser, the treasurer and one or two senior officials. The most limited circulation occurred while the tax evasion debate wracked the government; then cabinet argued at length over the way to deal with people holding commonwealth positions and named in the Costigan and McCabe–Lafranchi reports. The circulation of these decisions was *nil*. Obviously there were justifications; these issues were personal and sensitive at a time when gossip and rumour were rife. Yet they indicate the way in which a prime minister could use his position to control the flow of information.

Collective decisions or government by exhaustion?

Fraser always regarded cabinet as central to his government. He appreciated the political value of collective decisions. Former ministers point out that 'his speeches were always "the government has decided" or "cabinet has decided", it was never "I have decided!"' He would often emphasise that 'cabinet was unanimous'. He insisted that cabinet discuss and decide; every significant issue went to cabinet, sometimes time and again.

Yet even consultation created problems. The workload of

cabinet was large; the schedule was wearing. Ministers argued that the cost of consultations and meetings 'in the bunker' was government by exhaustion, with too many decisions made at late hours by tired ministers. Two reviews of cabinet procedures emphasised the need to reduce the workload of cabinet. It never happened.

Why? Partly because the growing interrelatedness of government business meant that there were more disputes to settle. Partly because ministers were rather too keen to bring items to cabinet, determined that they would get the collective support of cabinet; but also because items were considered at length. The repetition was an indication both of a search for certainty and of caution. Fraser 'roared like a lion but was pretty much a kitten in decision-making', said an official. Some of the workload was created by the cautious checking of options. Margaret Guilfoyle remembers that Chaney had cabinet approval three times to means test pensions for the over-70s, and then one decision not to because Fraser became nervous. Caution required constant reassessment, even if such a demeanour was rarely seen in public.

Fraser's imperatives kept cabinet busy too. His insistence that cabinet was the proper forum for decisions meant that he constantly demanded that submissions be prepared. He was *less* prepared than other leaders to determine issues outside the cabinet forum. Collective discussion gave power and legitimacy to decisions, at the cost of long long hours. The process of exhaustingly gaining consensus, or at least acquiescence, was seldom easy.

The insistence on consulting cabinet, combined with Fraser's impatience, put great pressure on ministers, pressure that made them tired and thus probably led to mistakes. It was not seen as necessary. One official noted: 'The moment Malcolm went away, you could almost feel everybody breathe a sigh of relief'. Doug Anthony's style was more relaxed, less interventionist and less impatient; cabinet meetings had a totally different atmosphere. Cabinet meetings tend to discuss sensitive issues; Fraser's determination to take all things there increased the difficulties cabinet must systematically face.

Fraser's style was not easy to cope with for those who lacked confidence. To be met with an aggressive range of questions prevented any free-ranging discussion; it may well have foreclosed options as debate concentrated on particular alternatives rather than divergent options or general perceptions. In part that is a natural consequence of any cabinet striving for solutions, but it was probably exacerbated in this instance by the prime minister's personality and some ministers who were not prepared to argue. At times, too, Fraser's drive to win arguments – not always so difficult against weaker ministers – might have meant that views were not expressed adequately. Strong ministers may have performed even better in the demanding atmosphere – if some thrived, others suffered.

Too much time, too many papers, too much consultation, too much interference in ministerial or departmental affairs. These are the readiest complaints. They are clearly accurate in that the cabinet was in constant session, but in each case a counter-argument can be launched. Cabinet ought to be involved; papers are needed for information; ministers complain if they are not consulted. Every cabinet has its share of weaker ministers and the prime minister needs to protect the government from their mistakes. It is a constant search for balance within the cabinet system. There are, claimed a senior official, 'institutional things that weigh against an efficient system. You can't even talk about an efficient system of government in the boardroom sense'. The contrary pressures remain too strong.

Less consultation may have led to less meetings but more complaints about lack of discussion and too much prime ministerial direction. It was probably the combination of the cabinet system and Fraser's style of running it that created some of the tension.

Indeed the activity of the Fraser cabinet indicates some of the dilemmas of cabinet government, and particularly for the prime minister. He or she needs to maintain some overview of what government is doing, but how much detail is required for that to be achieved? Political sensitivity or crisis can often be found in the aberrant detail. Fraser believed that he had to understand the detail to achieve the breadth of vision and cabinet therefore became deeply involved in many detailed discussions.

That indeed is part of the problem of collective responsibility. It was interpreted to mean that, as appropriate, ministers should be involved and often should express a view, even where their knowledge and interest might be limited. Uninterested ministers may well be loath to cross prime ministers on issues important to them and their support could be crucial even if uninformed. The former British minister, Edmund Dell, has condemned the process of involvement demanded by collective responsibility, arguing that it leads to bad decisions. Too many people without the proper knowledge become involved because cabinet government requires them to participate. He argued that it was preferable that a doctrine of collective purpose, centred around a determined prime minister, be adopted. Prime ministers would consult with the relevant ministers to determine the preferred lines of action. He considered that might lead to a more consistent direction. Under Fraser, government was collective; cabinet was involved in all important issues. But the collective purpose was imposed by the leader, the only person to stretch across the whole government in an active way.

The problem with the debate asserting that prime ministerial government has replaced cabinet government is that the two models are asserted as opposites, as though decision-making was either individual or collective. Fraser's activities prove that that is a false dichotomy. Everything went to cabinet; everything important was decided collectively; everyone was consulted – frequently and exhaustively. The cabinet process was used; the cabinet form adopted. Even decisions normally taken in the prime minister's office were brought within the cabinet system. Yet Fraser was still able to run the system. His retort that: 'Just because I consulted, it doesn't mean I didn't dominate' is illustrative. He used the levers of power through consultation and cabinet discussion. His success depended on the willingness and capacity of his colleagues to argue and sustain a case. Because Fraser's capacity was greater, his view prevailed most often.

CHAPTER 5

'DUCHESSING AND STRONGARMING'

THE PARTY LEADER

Prime ministers are party leaders. They hold power only as long as they retain the support of their party. They are elected by the members of the parliamentary party and can be removed if political fortunes decline. They must constantly be aware of the needs and views of those on whom their position depends. Members of parliament are therefore not merely sheep to be driven unquestioningly into the division lobbies. They need to be persuaded, satisfied, duchessed or overawed so that they will continue to follow the leader. Support cannot be taken for granted; it must be maintained.

In the Australian federal system, power in political parties is diffused. State divisions control resources: they select candidates and ensure the supply of money; they are the bodies to which branch members are affiliated. The federal party is little more than a coalition of state divisions, over which the federal organisation has limited control and prime ministers none at all. Prime ministers can influence the extra-parliamentary organisation, but cannot direct it. Nor can they afford to ignore it. Although the Liberal party grants to its leaders great independence of action in the selection of ministers, the development of policy and the selection of strategic directions, this deference is not extended to organisational matters. At the state level divisions retain both their organisational independence and insist on their rights to expound views on policies. State Liberal premiers, as heads of a government in their own right, claim as much right to speak for the Liberal party as prime ministers, and indeed may speak more authoritatively for local interests. Where the federal and state imperatives diverge, Liberal heads of government may take different sides. The Liberal party has no natural unity.

Fraser fully appreciated the importance of the Liberal party to his future; he accepted the principle that a good leader needed to maintain cohesion and solidarity within the party. A divided party was certain to lose. He was prepared to spend time and care in managing the government's image. He regularly attended the meetings of the parliamentary party, the federal council and the federal executive; he tried to fit into his schedule an address to each state council at least once a year. He consulted the party extensively, always prepared to argue his case, sometimes to listen. Each of these aspects of managing the party required effort. It was time-consuming but necessary because the party was responsible for selling the policy, providing feedback on local reactions to government and providing the personnel to fight electoral battles.

The parliamentary party

Backbenchers provide the numbers that keep the government in power and the leader in position, but they are not all as subservient and malleable as their public image suggests. Elected to parliament as party representatives, many will express their views frequently and strongly. Their support, so obvious on the floor of parliament, cannot be assumed. Fraser was well aware that these people had elected him. Since they could also unseat him, he knew he had to retain their support. Ignoring the backbench can lead to a divided and mutinous crew.

The geography of Parliament House meant that, while parliament was sitting, backbenchers could be in constant contact with the prime minister. They walked past the door to his suite of rooms on the way to the House of Representatives or the party room. They rubbed shoulders during divisions. They argued or listened in party meetings.

Backbenchers dealt with the prime minister both as individuals and as a group in party meetings. Fraser was always sensitive to backbench opinion, relying on the parliamentary whips and other colleagues to keep him informed about the swings of opinion or the mood of the parliamentary party. As ministerial colleague Michael Mackellar said:

He lived, breathed, slept politics. He was a numbers man, a real political animal; he loved it. He'd duchess people. He'd strongarm them. He'd get others to duchess them, others to strongarm them. He expected to know what was happening.

Individual backbenchers had reasonable access to Fraser. If they asked to see the prime minister, an appointment would generally be arranged within one or two days. The speed would depend on the importance of the subject and the regularity with which the requests were made. If the member was a frequent whinger, the private office might take rather longer to organise the appointment.

Fraser's reputation frightened some backbenchers off: many were overawed, unwilling or unable to enter a long debate with a forceful prime minister, but at least that reduced the number wanting to see him. If they weren't prepared to face him, then their concerns were not worth worrying about. Once there, as Kemp puts it, Fraser made a judgement: 'Do I cosset or can he take a battering?' The latter were held in higher regard.

Frequently backbenchers wrote notes to Fraser. Although compliments were welcome, sycophantic letters were just too transparent in their intentions. Often letters challenged him on policy issues: argumentative, blunt and direct. John Hyde, the leader of the 'dries', a group that developed coherence only in the last term of the Fraser government, had frequently written to the prime minister throughout the term of the government. In 1977 he complained about the inconsistency of the government's economic policy. After the 1980 election he argued that, as a sign of the government's firm intention to reduce expenditure, Fraser ought to set an example by cancelling a project to which he was known to be committed; he suggested that the Defence Forces Academy be stopped. (It wasn't.) When the Lowe by-election was being fought in 1982, Hyde proposed that no promises be made because they were not needed. Letters of this type either received a positive response, even if Fraser did not agree with the propositions, or Fraser called the member in to discuss the problem. He did not object to backbenchers challenging the government's policies in private, but he did strongly object when Hyde contacted several leading Liberals in the prime minister's electorate of Wannon, persuading them to ring Fraser to object to a particular economic decision. When Fraser realised he was at the receiving end of a campaign orchestrated by Hyde he was furious; he regarded it as improper to undermine a member in his own electorate and ticked Hyde off for his impertinence. Hyde merely saw it as an effective way to influence policy discussion while acknowledging that it was unusual. He kept pushing his views, on the grounds that backbenchers have few tools – but being boring was one of them.

Some members leaked, leading to strange exchanges. In March 1976 Chaney (in his capacity as party whip in the Senate) objected to the treatment of backbenchers. He wrote: 'the leaks which followed the last party meetings on the subjects of party leaks were contemptuous of the efforts made to stifle this activity'. But he argued that there was a need for change in the ways that party meetings were run. 'There is no need to stress the dangers of a number of people present being oncers [members likely to be defeated after one term]. They are all too acutely aware of the possibility.' Chaney later, as the leader of a delegation of chairmen of committees, asked that greater attention be paid to backbench views.

Backbenchers asked for a variety of things: a meeting of the party to discuss the US communications facility on the North West Cape; involvement of the party in considering legislation; no reintroduction of television licences; no early election in 1982; particular expenditure cuts; the appointment of a minister for federal affairs. Sometimes Fraser responded by letter, sometimes he defused the issue by calling the member for discussion, sometimes he sought a minister's opinion. Backbenchers were not isolated; Fraser listened.

He might back down. In the face of widespread party opposition he had stopped consideration of new television licences in January 1976. In March 1976 he saw government senators reject a proposal to remove funeral benefits. In December he dropped proposals to remove the staff-elected ABC commissioner. In those cases he realised that he could only push the backbench so far. It was difficult to get him to change his mind, but it did happen. 'He would argue and rage', said Peter Baume, 'but he would listen to a good case'.

Organised lobbying of the prime minister was rare. In May 1978 a group of backbenchers objected to the retrospective nature of the legislation to outlaw the Curran tax scheme in a co-ordinated series of letters. In the last three years the dries became better organised, deciding who would follow up which issue and who would ask questions at party meetings. They tried, claimed John Hyde, to organise their order of speaking to get around Fraser's tendency to call the speakers against a proposal early. When Doug Anthony publicly argued on 23 April 1981 that TAA should remain in government control before cabinet had considered the issue, several of the dries, particularly those from Western Australia, cabled and later wrote to Fraser demanding that he treat Anthony the same way as he had reacted to Barry Simon when he disagreed with government policy. When Fraser defended Anthony by stating that cabinet had not determined the issue of ownership, they claimed the issue was not now the future of TAA, but Anthony's breach of collective solidarity. So he called the critics in for a discussion, 'with at least one WA minister to be present'. In 1981, when the Western Australian dries were threatening to vote against the two-airline policy, the minister for transport, Ralph Hunt, wrote to Fraser asking him to speak to them. That was all part of the constant stream of advice and requests directed at the prime minister.

In his turn he maintained contact with the backbenchers. He used the available patronage to 'duchess' them. Most MPs would be invited to the Lodge for dinner two or three times a year – in a group made up of two or three ministers and seven or eight backbenchers. The private office kept a list to ensure that the prime minister rotated his invitations. These occasions may not always have provided an opportunity to talk about politics, but they created a feeling of participation. One participant noted that 'these royal command requests to have dinners at the Lodge were not always the most relaxed of occasions. Tamie used to save them. If Tamie was around everything was all right'. Fraser was not usually comfortable in a social situation, or in his element being thrown into great cocktail parties, but he was happy to hold forth in argument on whatever was on his mind. One minister thought he 'kept a number of backbenchers on a string, thinking they might receive the royal accolade one day. If you put it plain to people they are never going to receive the accolade, you are not going to have a very harmonious team!' Access, the feeling that influence was possible, was one means of trying to maintain support.

The party whips, responsible for maintaining the majority in parliament, acted as the link between the party and the prime minister. Deputy whip John Hodges explained:

The whip and his deputy are really the eyes and ears – if you like to use the words, the informer – of the prime minister. That not only applies to the backbench; it will apply with other members of the ministry. Any whip will advise the prime minister of any situation he believes is untoward or is developing towards a critical situation that may well jeopardise the government or the prime minister's position.

The whips would organise drinks with backbenchers, or drag Fraser into the dining room to eat with those he otherwise rarely saw. They also informed him when members failed to turn up to parliamentary divisions.

The whips would constantly be called into the prime minister's office to discuss the attitude of some MPs or the rapport between backbenchers and a particular minister: 'Are there complaints about him, is he conducting himself in a proper manner? It is part of the total process of the prime minister being well informed'. Since all leaders tend to be wary about attempts to replace them, the whips' services are essential for monitoring party members. They kept Fraser in touch with the feelings of individuals and groups.

Party meetings

Party meetings were a more formal mechanism for informing Fraser of backbench opinion. They were nearly always joint meetings, including both Liberal and National party members. When the Victorian backbencher, Roger Shipton, asked for a separate Liberal party meeting to discuss tax evasion, he was told, 'We don't do that sort of thing'. In these meetings ministers reported on government policy while backbenchers were able to put items on the agenda for general discussion. The agenda was drawn up by the party whips, but it was always cleared with the prime minister. He had the option to delay a debate, if he felt the subject was about to be discussed in cabinet or could lead to too many problems. In these very rare cases he would contact the member before deleting the item. The agenda of 2 May 1979 provides an example of a routine meeting. The list was divided into three sections: government business, private members' business, and reports. The first included bills, from Nixon, Howard, Newman and Fife; the second a range of topics to be discussed after the question time: sacred songs (requested by Hodgman); deposits on insurance (Archer); press conference (McMahon); post office closures (Hodges); taxation of subsidised rentals (Braithwaite) and the 1979 budget (Hyde). Then ministers reacted to the reports of parliamentary committees on oil pollution, Aboriginal reserves in Queensland, woodchips and annual reports.

At the party meetings Fraser sat at the front beside the minister making the report or responsible for answering the questions. He would intervene in discussions, and would not always accept the view of the minister. He could be 'heavy-handed' in the party room, but he did listen and he picked up nuances quickly. If there were serious complaints, he might suggest cabinet have another look, or ask a group of back-benchers to come and discuss them. Hodges recalls:

He wasn't so dogmatic and so brutal that he would impose his own views at all costs . . . He could be got to on some issues; but there were often issues where he was rock solid . . . He would be conciliatory to the extent that he would call a meeting of those dissenting backbenchers with the ministers or himself in his office and try to persuade the hard-nosed people to his view.

Fraser recognised the importance of the party room as a safety valve: 'It's an important vehicle for a private member because he ought to be able to feel free to say things within the party room that he may not want to say out of party loyalty in parliament'. Party meetings could be influential, but it was still difficult to force changes to the opinion of cabinet.

Fraser did not always leave the minister to speak alone. Staley recalls:

There was a party room debate on the ABC some months into my term of office as minister [for communications] and there was a great deal of attack. Malcolm whispered to me as the debate was going on, 'Tell them it's all the fault of management'. I said 'No, I can't do that'. 'It is', he said, 'It is. You tell them!' He put it very clearly. As I got up to sum up the debate, I said 'Yes, the problems of the ABC are significantly to do with management', but I then made the point that there was in the country an atmosphere which we in this government have to be deeply concerned about. That is that this government is seen to be out to destroy the ABC and as far as I'm concerned this has to come to an end. I developed that theme, and I could feel him seething beside me, absolutely seething.

Staley believes that this party debate and clear difference of opinion did begin to change the treatment of the ABC by the government.

Fraser always attended party meetings if he was available. He invariably summed up the debate. At times of crisis, claimed John Hodges:

One of his greatest strengths was his capacity to get to his feet and deliver a very telling and very convincing speech: This should be done and this is the position. He didn't have votes, but I've seen him get away with a decision that he wanted when there was probably a fairly angry and evenly divided party room.

He may have talked down, using the superior knowledge available to the cabinet, but backbenchers tended finally to accept his conclusion. 'After all he is the prime minister; you largely sink or swim by him', said one member. No minutes were kept; no votes were taken; the prime minister was the source of the final decisions.

In 1976 Fraser was faced with a backbench of around 100 members. Having for ten years experienced the frustrations of being an MP without any involvement in policy, he immediately asked a small group, under the chairmanship of Fred Chaney, to examine a possible party committee system. The committee met all day on 16 January. Tony Eggleton, one of its members, then offered to run through the draft proposals with Fraser, so that he could influence the final shape of the recommendations; Fraser accepted. The report recommended thirteen standing committees covering all portfolios, a Parliamentary Reform committee and an Electoral Tactics committee. The last was a development of an earlier Marginal Electorates committee; it was responsible for giving advice on extra-parliamentary and electoral tactics and monitoring public reaction to political events. Its membership was approved by the prime minister. The report also recommended the creation of a chairman's group to monitor the system. Fraser sent the report to cabinet where it was accepted.

The committee process required ministers to bring legislation to the party for its consent before it was introduced into parliament. Not all ministers were keen on the process. As Fraser recalls:

Some ministers thought it an aberration of the constitution to have to take legislation before a party committee before it went to parliament, but they knew that if they wanted this legislation they had to do it.

If ministers had not discussed legislation with the committees, they were often told to go back and consult. The system of committees was under constant review. In March 1976 an additional arts policy ad hoc committee was appointed. In May Chaney provided a report on the operation of the system. Another review took place when the new parliament met in 1978.

Fraser not only permitted the committees to review legislation but also used them to provide advice and opinion. In early 1977, in an attempt to gain a broad assessment of how the government was doing, Fraser asked ministers to consider areas of particular significance in their portfolios and, at the same time, asked the committee chairmen to provide an assessment of their committees' work. Eventually he got a series of papers filled with backbench views, perhaps as a counterbalance to those of ministers.

Other party groups constantly evaluated the government's progress on an ad hoc basis. In March 1976 Chaney wrote to Fraser arguing that the need for government to cut expenditure ought not to prevent it from implementing necessary reforms to which the party was committed. Chaney talked to Kemp and then convened a small group of senators and members (Peter Baume, Michael Baume, Missen, Hyde, Macphee and Wilson) to consider proposals that were cheap but necessary. The group held several meetings and then proposed a package that could 'help to project the government's concern for Australian social and cultural development, for disadvantaged groups in the community, and for equality of opportunity in important areas of human rights'. Its suggestions included administrative law, land rights and the promotion of initiatives in welfare and small business. Fraser discussed them with Chaney and Kemp and asked PMC for a report on their status by the end of the week. Many of the suggestions were later introduced, although the group's report was not necessarily the cause of action. Fraser was prepared to listen to the careful thoughts of concerned members.

The Tactics committee was the most directly political body. It was selected by the prime minister and reported to him. Its first chairman, Queensland MP Don Cameron, resigned after the 1977 election. He was replaced first by Chaney, then by Barry Simon. Its members included the party whips, at least one member from each state and Tony Eggleton from the party secretariat. The committee was intended to act as an early warning system, to keep in touch with grass roots opinion, and to maintain a constant campaign in the marginal electorates. It received regular reports from each state. A summary of each meeting was sent by the chairman to the prime minister, presenting the views of the committee on government proposals and electoral reactions. It could also act as a second line of defence if an argument had been lost in the party room but was still a matter of concern.

The range of topics for discussion was potentially exhaustive: on 24 May 1977 the committee's agenda included the referendum results and the prime minister's image; on 23 August the redistribution, the budget, uranium, industrial relations and tax sharing. After the 1977 election Fraser reactivated the committee and occasionally asked its members to undertake particular tasks. In August 1978, after the resignation of Withers as Senate leader, several senators had demanded the right to elect their own leader; Fraser asked Tactics committee chairman Barry Simon to canvass the proposition with a proportion of the Liberal members in the House of Representatives, primarily to provide a counterbalance to the senators. Of the thirty-seven asked, twenty-three opposed the idea of an election, and five thought it none of their business.

The advice of the committee to Fraser was often personal. In March 1976 it thought that he was 'engaging in overkill in preparing the ground for a responsible budget'. In November 1978 the committee felt it would be advantageous for the prime minister to be seen at more soccer matches (for the migrant vote), more national championships of minor sports like netball (for the youth vote), and at trotting, boxing and greyhound events (for the middle ground vote). Fraser promised to bear the proposals in mind when developing his 1979 program. In June 1979 a concerned committee had one item on the agenda: 'Promises, Promises'; and several meetings that year discussed how the prime minister could be seen as more trustworthy and credible; the committee even had a discussion with Fraser's speech-writers. In September 1980 it encouraged him to have an election as early as possible. Thus the Tactics committee acted as a constant link between the parliamentary party, the party secretariat, the grass roots and the prime minister.

Party policy committees could be useful to the government. Not only did they allow backbenchers to influence the cabinet, but a process of discussion and debate often allowed ministers to draw the party committee gradually towards their policy. Fraser remembers:

The best example of a committee of the party working was the arrangements on land rights in the Northern Territory. We had different extremes of opinion with the Country party and other Liberals, but a committee of both parties worked through the legislation and the proposals and came to a conclusion which I thought was quite respectable. If we'd tried to take a government decision and push that through in one party meeting, we'd have no hope. So there was a process of education and we got a unanimous recommendation at the committee – if not unanimous at least one they could support.

One instance where the party room was influential was when the government was considering a ban on the killing of whales. It can serve as a useful example of the way in which Fraser listened to party opinion. In August 1977 the anti-whaling group, Project Jonah, asked Fraser to receive a delegation to put their case; on the advice of his department he refused. Then backbencher Neil Brown interceded on the group's behalf, arguing that they had a persuasive case and constituted a very respectable group of people. When a second letter seeking a meeting arrived from Project Jonah, Fraser sought more information. The Department of Primary Industry was cool; the minister, Ian Sinclair, was strongly opposed; so was PMC. The private office was more cautious; it pointed to the wide public support for the anti-whaling campaign, and to a resolution against whaling passed at a recent federal Liberal council meeting. It thought it inadvisable to brush off the approach and proposed Fraser reply expressing sympathy with the principles of Project Jonah's campaign and surprise that they had not tried to meet Sinclair.

However by November 1977 an election campaign had

begun, with the anti-whaling lobby threatening an advertising campaign portraying the prime minister and the government as anti-conservationist. Fraser agreed to see the delegation, although his office thought he should warn it that the government did not appreciate threats of electoral retribution. When the delegation was introduced by Neil Brown, Fraser pre-empted discussion by telling the group that the government intended to establish an independent inquiry and would consult Project Jonah on its terms of reference. That left the delegation with little to say. In making conversation Fraser commented that his daughter Phoebe was a keen opponent of the killing of whales (hence the legend that his daughter had been the initiator of the proposal – a legend she does not endorse). Fraser objected to their claims that the government was not committed to protecting the environment and declared that it had proved its conservationist credentials after the decision to stop sand mining on Fraser Island.

With the election won, cabinet endorsed a Fraser submission in January 1978 to establish a commission, agreeing to consult the Western Australian premier about a person to head it. The report, presented in December 1978, supported protection of whales as wildlife and recommended zero catch limits. Cabinet accepted its recommendations and in January 1979 approved legislation to protect whales, using the authority of the offshore constitutional settlement that had accepted federal responsibility beyond the three-mile limit.

But then the party committees, led particularly by members from Western Australia where the only whaling station at Cheyne's Beach had been located, objected. The party room sent the legislation back for cabinet to reconsider the breadth of its application. Cabinet agreed to some changes, with the proviso that, if the party room again objected, the minister should bring it back to cabinet. The party room then opposed a clause that would have applied to Australian citizens worldwide; a third compromise was eventually accepted and passed.

Thus, an individual MP could play an important intermediary function, while the party committee monitored the legislation and kept pushing it back to cabinet until it was satisfied. The instance does show how party influence could be exerted.

Fraser needed help to manage the backbench. He was too busy to deal with every issue and he was aware of his tendency to be abrasive. So he used others to smooth the ruffled feathers. Anthony could be a calming influence, but Phillip Lynch, the deputy leader, was the most important. He was an ideal deputy – with no further personal ambitions but with a capacity to listen and defuse. Fraser may not always have taken him seriously in policy issues, but he appreciated how valuable he was in party terms. Backbenchers could use him as a conduit for complaints; ministers upset by a grilling could let out their frustrations. Although Lynch and Fraser never regained a close relationship after the election-time resignation in 1977, Lynch remained a dedicated party man, at his best in small groups, uncomplaining as he massaged the bruised egos of both ministers and backbenchers. In the Senate Reg Withers initially played a similar role. A man with Fraser's style needed someone to mollify the party on a regular basis, although he himself was capable of turning on the charm when he needed to persuade someone to his point of view. The decline in party morale after April 1982 occurred after the removal of Lynch from the deputy leadership and his withdrawal from the day-to-day management of party affairs; it was probably not entirely coincidental.

Party elections

Party elections for leadership were the most obvious occasion on which backbench support was needed. In the Liberal party the leader comes up for election after each poll, but the position can be declared vacant at any meeting. Only once was Fraser challenged – in 1982. There were three contests for the deputy leadership – in 1977, 1980 and 1982.

The deputy leadership is the one position in the party whose incumbent is not beholden to the party leader. Therefore, Fraser argues, the leader should be very careful about becoming involved in any contest. In 1977, while Lynch stood down, there was speculation that Fraser was sounding out colleagues about the promotion of Street to the deputyship. While the need for some planning was obvious, the activities, undertaken even while Lynch's financial affairs were under review, annoyed many in the party. However there was never a prospect of any other person having the numbers and when Lynch was cleared, Fraser made it apparent that he did not want Lynch opposed. In 1980 too, when Lynch was challenged by Peacock, Fraser was known to have wanted Lynch re-elected. The large vote that Peacock got was seen primarily as a warning to Fraser.

In 1982 Fraser's own position was threatened. Since Peacock's resignation in April 1981, a small group had constantly maintained lists of possible supporters for the occasion when a challenge eventuated. Their lists were often wildly inaccurate and optimistic, but they illustrated the persistence with which the Peacock camp was looking for the numbers and the opportunity. Particular members of the group were given responsibility to approach and persuade other members of the parliamentary party. A constant belief that others are plotting is common in politics. In this case it was justified. Eventually, when a challenge appeared inevitable, Fraser took the initiative.

Rumours had festered for months. While the CHOGM was being held in Melbourne a series of destabilising stories about Fraser's health hit the headlines. In March 1982 came the disasters of the Lowe by-election (after the resignation of Sir William McMahon) and the Victorian state election, both of which saw large swings against the government. Fraser decided to call on the fight. He and his supporters had no doubt that he would win; on 30 March the Senate whip had written that Peacock did not have the numbers. But a straight contest was the only way to end the rumour and speculation: Peacock was forced to declare his hand, knowing from the beginning that he could not win.

The certainty of success did not prevent Fraser from worrying about the result and trying to cover every eventuality. The whips were the main numbers men. Hodges recalls:

We physically had lists of members and ministers and we would go through it and put them in the 'certain' column, the 'doubtful' column and the 'certain for Peacock' column . . . We reported regularly to the prime minister. He was always edgy about these things.

Fraser relied on his senior and trusted ministerial colleagues and on the party whips to do all the lobbying. Their advice to Fraser was always at the heart of the tactics. The aim was not just to win, but to win overwhelmingly.

Most of cabinet had been locked in behind Fraser since Peacock resigned; the whips and other intermediaries talked to waverers. Impressions, not promises, were generated. Withers commented:

Some had been assured that there would be significant changes if he survived. He did nothing to discourage some high ambitions. They thought they were on a promise. They were never on a promise. Malcolm was never that stupid. He was always smart enough to allow people to draw their own inference, generally a wrong one. He was a good operator of people, a good manipulator and he knew he was dealing with some of the most selfish and egotistical people. And the suckers fell for it. They read into his words what wasn't there.

Colleague Tony Staley said:

It's often believed in politics that rewards are offered for services rendered; that's not true of the way Fraser did it. There's no way he would ever go around and say, 'If you support me in this issue, the back door will be open to you'. He hated making himself a hostage to fortune, a term he used quite often.

Yet backbenchers wanted Fraser to know they were supporting him. Victorian MP, Peter Falconer replied to Peacock's letter requesting support saying there was no need for a change, and sent a copy to Fraser. Wilson Tuckey complained to Dame Leonie Kramer, chairman of the ABC, that he had been listed as a Peacock supporter without being consulted – and again sent Fraser a copy. There was no point being on the winning side if it was not known. Even without such obvious tactics, the voting process itself could be a give-away. As one former minister recalled, we 'had to vote when Peacock is a long name and Fraser a short name. It's not hard to see'. Fraser won fairly easily, with fifty-four votes to twenty-seven, and yet the government never really recovered from the challenge because in trying to secure a safe and large majority, Fraser lost his deputy.

To what extent Lynch was pushed is unclear. He was certainly tired of politics and looking for a lighter load. As Andrew Hay explains: 'He felt he had had enough. Whereas previously he would have fought tooth and nail to keep himself up there, the doctors had given him sufficient warning that he was not a well bloke'. Lynch's letter to Fraser argued that he was willing to give way to a younger person (Lynch was just fifty), but was happy to stay as a member of cabinet. Significantly some earlier drafts had been more pointed. One comment later excised stated that he was 'confident my action in standing aside will assist in resolving current difficulties'. His decision may have helped. There are different opinions about whether he could have retained the position; the dries in the party wanted Howard as deputy and promised to throw their support behind Fraser if that were achieved. Fraser did not need that support to survive, but it added to the size of the majority. Fraser had been on the phone to the party whip and he knew that the numbers were slipping away from Lynch; but he did not intervene or try to persuade him to stay. One friend thought Lynch felt he had been needlessly left unsupported; he went quietly, but he was 'angry, red raw angry'. His decision to leave politics followed. Fraser's tendency to overkill, or to win by as much as possible, left Lynch as an important victim. The implications were to be dramatic; the surprising Liberal win in the by-election in his seat of Flinders in December 1982 was the catalyst that pushed Fraser into his decision to hold the general election of February 1983. A by-election might not have been held if Lynch had remained the deputy.

The party organisation

Fraser was careful in his dealings with the organisational wing of the party. He appreciated the need for the leader to act as a link between the government and those who provided the party with support. The federal party consisted of a secretariat, the national executive and the party conference. The federal secretariat consisted of a small number of professionals but it was influential because of one man, Tony Eggleton. Prior to the 1972 defeat, the secretariat had became run down. Ministers had become used to the advice of public servants; the party was then unable to provide similar support in opposition. Fraser was determined that there would be no repetition of that decline. He chose to ensure that the secretariat remained in the mainstream of political life – in anticipation of the party's eventual return to opposition.

Eggleton had a long record as assistant to prime ministers. He had worked for Harold Holt before moving to London on the staff of the Commonwealth Secretariat. Returning to Canberra in 1975, he had first headed Fraser's personal staff before shifting to the position as director of the Liberal party. Eggleton had long held Fraser in high regard. In 1971, after the resignation of Fraser and Gorton, Eggleton had encouraged a depressed Fraser by expressing his belief that he would one day become prime minister. The relationship stayed close.

The importance of the secretariat lay in its capacity to interact or 'tic-tac' with the private office and with the prime minister's department. Eggleton always had immediate access to Fraser. He acted as a conduit from the party, both officials and members. When the proposal to reintroduce TV licences was floated early in 1976, the party members kept the phones running hot. Eggleton passed on the gist of the messages; the government did not take up that option.

Eggleton helped prepare the briefings for question time. Each morning he would survey the newspapers to identify areas that might become politically sensitive; he would alert the private office so that it could get briefing notes from the department before the official briefing. Then he would assist in going through potential answers with Fraser. He could indicate problems for the party in the answers being prepared by officials. Eggleton was less concerned with policy than with party reaction, actual or potential. When Fraser asked him questions, 'it was not to ask my advice on how to run the country; it was to ask how did I think the party would react to this or that'. He discussed presentation of policies and electoral tactics,

Eggleton consistently sampled public opinion through

polls – he had close contacts with Gary Morgan. He also maintained links with all the divisional presidents. In 1976, for instance, he monitored the likely outcome of referendums on simultaneous elections and automatic double dissolutions. Fraser invited the state presidents to a dinner on 6 September 1976 at which the proposals, backed by Morgan's figures, were sprung on them. The state presidents counselled caution – and the referendums were not held until the next May. Eggleton acted as channel to the prime minister for as diverse characters as Talbot Duckmanton and John Kerr. His relationship with Fraser was strong enough for him to be able to comment on his treatment of others, particularly when it had been too rough. The federal secretariat linked the leader to other groups in the community and helped to channel alternative sources of opinion to him. Eggleton said of Fraser that in 1976:

he didn't want to depend totally on the bureaucrats, so he asked the party to set up a new group called the Economic Advisory Committee, consisting of representatives of different sections of industry. It would meet every couple of months with him and all the economic ministers to give a very frank assessment of the economy. We incorporated in the group four independent economists who had nothing to do with the party . . . Many of the problems which did develop on the economy were closely identified by this group a long time before they became a problem.

Yet gradually the difficulties of withstanding the pressures of the bureaucrats became greater; no occasional advisory system could provide the same continuity of advice as a department.

Fraser's commitment to party affairs was extensive; in retrospect he and his staff considered that too much time was given to the party. Eggleton advised him to attend at least one major council of the party in each state:

One of the first things we'd give to his private staff at the start of each year was the dates of all the major party meetings around Australia. So his book had then written into it this major meeting plan, plus the six meetings of the federal executive, and these economic advisory committees which were his own initiative.

Formal party business took about a month of Fraser's year. That figure does not take into account the additional informal soundings or the regular consultations with party officials. A month is a substantial commitment of scarce prime ministerial time.

The federal president of the party helped ensure the smooth collection of money and assisted Eggleton in putting the party view. Neither Sir John Atwell nor Jim Forbes, presidents for most of Fraser's term, was a public figure or played any policy role, but they were more inclined to debate issues with the prime minister in private than in the glare of the federal executive. Fraser's support was certainly important in the election of Forbes; the alternative was a nominee of the dissident Queensland/Western Australian branches. Forbes recalls that Fraser did not often contact him unless he had a clear objective:

He never rang just to have a chat. If he rang it was basically because he wanted something from you . . . He wanted to be able to say the federal president was on side!

The federal executive of the party met six times a year. Fraser attended almost all its meetings, and when he was unable to go he always sent his apologies. He saw the need to keep in contact with the state divisions, to ensure they remained in good order and were able to provide the necessary electoral support. When it appeared probable that Fraser would not be able to attend the full federal executive meeting in 1981, Eggleton tried to persuade him to change his mind. He feared a fragmented meeting because 'the main attraction for the federal executive is making their reports in your presence . . . and the feeling that the organisation's voice is being heard by the leadership'. Fraser understood these problems.

At federal executive meetings the state presidents each reported on their local situation, and then Fraser was meant to sum up and discuss the implications. In practice he was rarely so patient. Sometimes he entered the debate after each president had spoken. Federal president Jim Forbes thought these interventions were partly because the comments may have appeared ill-informed, 'but I suspect also to intimidate the later speakers'. Even so, he 'went to pains to have people onside or at least neutralised to the point where he knew people weren't likely to disapprove of what he was saying or doing'.

When the government was in dispute with one branch the discussion could get heated. Fraser always had an uneasy relationship with the Western Australian branch; it was partly a matter of personalities, but it exploded into open bitterness over the issue of tax evasion. The debates between Fraser and Ian Warner, the Western Australian president, became long and bitter as the two argued throughout one federal executive meeting. These debates emphasised the lack of power that a Liberal prime minister has over the party. He could argue and put a case with all the advantages of the weight of his office, his cabinet knowledge, and the strength of his personality, but he could not demand support.

The state divisions

Fraser could never control the state divisions; they remained as semi-autonomous fiefdoms. As former federal president, Jim Forbes, argues:

The Liberal party organisation has a weak federal structure; it is a loose confederation of autonomous divisions. So unless the parliamentary leader is prepared to take the initiative and work unceasingly to make it work, it doesn't and you get into trouble. Gorton and McMahon got themselves into trouble in that they were either not prepared or were unable to play this essential role, but Malcolm did.

Fraser worked hard at maintaining links with the state divisions and at persuading them to his point of view. He consulted the state presidents when it was suitable – and doubtless convenient.

However his influence was at best indirect and at times ineffective. When Vic Garland became high commissioner in London in 1980, Fraser encouraged Fred Chaney to stand for pre-selection in the vacated seat. He wanted to increase the talent in the House of Representatives and Chaney was widely seen as a potential leader. But Chaney was out of favour with the group who controlled the branch and lost the pre-selection to another senator. The support of the prime minister was seen as counterproductive – even as 'the kiss of death' – in a branch that was growing antagonistic to the government.

As the head of a coalition government, Fraser had an additional problem when he negotiated with Liberal state organisations who did not attach the same importance to the value of coalition. In Queensland the Liberals were the minority party in a coalition; and in Victoria they had governed alone for twenty years. Fraser, of necessity, became involved in disputes in both states. His view remained the same: 'As prime minister my first responsibility is to the preservation of the integrity of the federal coalition upon which the good government of Australia totally depends'. He frequently quoted the comment of Sir Robert Menzies, made at his retirement, that maintaining a stable coalition was one of his greatest contributions to Australian politics.

In Victoria a dispute occurred in the Gippsland electorate where the Liberals wanted to run a candidate in federal elections against National party minister Peter Nixon. The National and Liberal parties had signed agreements in 1975 and 1977 that they would not contest seats held by federal ministers. Arguing that as a consequence they were the only Liberals in Victoria unable to vote for a Liberal candidate, the Gippsland Liberals sought to implement a later state council decision to contest all seats. This revolt simmered for some time; Barry Simon, then the MHR for the neighbouring electorate of McMillan which he had won from a backbench National party MP in 1975, acted as the voice of Gippsland Liberals in Canberra. In August 1979 he sought and was given a chance for a 'frank discussion' with Fraser.

The local Liberals first attempted to get official endorsement in 1979. Faced with a vote at the state executive on 5 October, Fraser became directly involved in three days of intensive lobbying. Fraser, Street, Lynch and Eggleton called state executive members one by one into Fraser's Melbourne office and also talked to others, including Barry Simon (although

Simon had agreed not to advocate the Gippsland demand publicly). Fraser took a strong line, arguing that the move was a threat to the federal coalition. He also convened the state strategy committee and persuaded it to accept his view. By the time the state executive met, most of the party officials and state leaders were behind him and voted strongly for the prime minister's line.

But the Gippsland Liberals did not readily accept the decision, even after the National party had agreed on 12 October to stand by the non-aggression treaty; they threatened to run an independent Liberal. Fraser had to intervene again; he met two Liberal MLCs from the area in Melbourne on 7 October. On 17 October the two MLCs flew to Canberra for a second meeting with Fraser, Lynch and Street. On 18 October Fraser, party treasurer John Elliott, premier Dick Hamer and Lynch met Nixon and representatives of the National party to discuss possible solutions. Fraser had even obtained an opinion from a QC as to the power of the state executives or state council to prevent a contest; it concluded that only the state council had that right. But there was still no agreement from the local Liberals.

The final steps were taken at the state council meeting. On the prime minister's instructions, Lynch and John Bourchier, the party whip, wrote to the federal members from Victoria, telling them that Fraser wanted them at the state council. On 17 November the prime minister was the final speaker to the motion not to contest Gippsland. The hard work paid off, and the prime minister's views were accepted. The time committed to the issue illustrated the importance that Fraser gave to it – and to Peter Nixon.

In 1982 the issue erupted again. The National MLA for South Gippsland had switched to the Liberals and in the 1982 state election (where the parties were not in coalition) Anthony and Nixon had led a National campaign with fierce attacks on their former party colleague. He lost. The local Liberals demanded an apology from the National party leader and the right to run their own federal candidate. On 23 July a delegation from the local branches met Fraser and Street to put their case. In a lengthy and hard-hitting introductory statement Fraser explained that the government parties must stand together, and that if the local Liberal party chose to endorse a candidate, he would be forced to oppose him. Cabinet could not operate unless the coalition went into an election as a united government. He argued that the local party would do better to strengthen its branch network. The ensuing debate was tepid but Fraser restated his opinion a few weeks later at the state council. (As Nixon did not stand in 1983, the Liberals were able to stand a candidate after all. The National candidate won the seat again.)

Crucially, the prime minister came from Victoria. His involvement, with Lynch and Street at his shoulder, was the more acceptable because he was a local MP. In Queensland, where the battle was fought over the issue of separate senate tickets, Fraser could fight only through proxies. He could express his opinion, but not participate directly in decisions.

The Queensland Liberals were in an unusual position. They were the minority party as the consequence of a carefully manipulated electoral system and their declining electoral support. They wanted to become the dominant non-Labor force and, with the Labor party weak and divided, often saw the National party, nominally their coalition partner, as their real enemy. The Liberal party's difficulties were exacerbated by Eric Robinson, a cabinet minister in the Fraser government and at the same time the power behind the Queensland state Liberal presidents. John Hodges, a good friend of Robinson, thinks in retrospect that Robinson fomented some of the divisions, 'to keep himself in the forefront in Canberra, to make himself out to be vitally important to Fraser in Queensland'. It was a counter-productive approach. In 1979 he resigned for a week, telling colleagues that he was fed up with the way Fraser treated him and the Queensland Liberal party; and after the 1980 election he was offered a demotion to the outer ministry. The consequence of his erratic behaviour was an alienation of Fraser from both Robinson and the state division.

Fraser was always ambivalent towards the Queensland branch's demands for support. Llew Edwards recalls:

he was more prepared to try to find peace between Queensland and the federal government than trying to assist me as Liberal leader to defend our policies and our programs . . . I think he felt that the Liberal party was an ultimately lost cause; anyway he didn't see them as ever winning government, and therefore he wasn't interested in putting himself at risk with Joh.

Fraser endorses the view; the Liberals in Queensland were not prepared to do the organisational groundwork. Until they helped themselves, there was no point risking the stability of the coalition with purely symbolic gestures. The Liberals had few branches outside Brisbane or the larger cities; he drew a comparison with his own country seat of Wannon which had about thirty branches and three thousand members. He argued that when the Liberal party showed the willingness to spread their branch network, he would assist. As he wrote to the Queensland state president, John Herron, in October 1979 (after sending a draft of the letter to some Queensland ministers and members for comment):

I believe our overriding concern, as Liberals, must be to remain in government and to avoid taking action which would unnecessarily jeopardise our position. The practical reality is that the Liberal party is not able to govern on its own at the federal level. Crucial to our success is the continuance of the coalition, and this is particularly so with regard to Queensland, which has always returned a maximum number of anti-Labor senators.

Decisions about the state coalition, he publicly stated, were exclusively state matters, and neither the federal party nor parliamentarians should become involved. Also he realised the difficulties. On 16 July that year he had written to Robert Sparkes:

I appreciate your reservations about the Queensland division's decision to run a separate senate ticket at the next election. However this is a delicate matter for me. It is a matter for the Liberal party in Queensland to decide and it would be quite counterproductive for me to intervene.

This stance provided a contrast to his actions in Victoria.

Fraser approached most of his dealings with Queensland as head of a coalition federal government, dealing with a state coalition that was led by an unpredictable maverick. He was more concerned to manage those relationships than to promote exclusively the Liberal part of the coalition: if it required him to ring National party president, Sir Robert Sparkes, or to act through intermediaries like Peter Nixon and Russ Hinze, he was prepared to do so. Although Fraser continued to talk to state Liberal officials, he was never prepared to talk exclusively to them. That further alienated the Liberals, antagonised Robinson and made the battles, when they eventually occurred over separate Senate tickets, the more bitter.

The distance between federal and state parties became public in September and October 1979. The state council of the party met in Gympie and endorsed an earlier decision to run a separate ticket in the next Senate election. Fraser believed the lack of the branch infrastructure meant the Liberal party could not run a state-wide campaign, and feared that contests between the two parties could spread to the federal arena and destabilise the coalition there. Jim Killen, minister for defence, argued strongly on behalf of the prime minister that it was an electorally crazy tactic; he received a hostile reception and the prime minister's view got only a handful of votes. The Liberals stated that it was a party decision, duly and properly made, and that the state division had the right to make the decision. They felt that, as a Liberal, Fraser should come to Queensland and support the Liberal ticket, even against the National party.

Fraser was determined to have full support for his refusal to participate and got cabinet to endorse his position. On 17 June 1980, with an election looming, cabinet discussed the problems in Queensland and agreed that, irrespective of the party situation, the prime minister and ministers would campaign in support of their ministerial colleagues. The consequence of the split ticket in the 1980 election was that only one Liberal senator was elected in Queensland.

Fraser hoped that the policy would be changed at a council held at Chandler in 1982. Although he got more support this time, the Liberal party reaffirmed its decision. Fraser wrote to the president of the Queensland Liberal division, again in September 1982, regretting that Liberals in Queensland seemed more concerned with attacking the National party than developing policy or increasing membership – a concern which Edwards told Fraser he shared. The better judgement of Fraser was illustrated by the state election result of 1983. He never regained any popularity in the north, and the state Liberal party continued to decline.

Position without power

Prime ministers hold an important position in the party. They can persuade, encourage or dangle incentives in the face of Liberals. They can command only by the force of their personality and through the weight of their office. The Liberal party is too fragmented, too divided in its organisation and its culture to allow more. Where Fraser had frequent contacts with the parliamentary party, he was effective; but even there a third of the party was sufficiently disillusioned to vote against him. Where contacts were less frequent, his influence was more limited.

Fraser and his ministers were responsible for the development of policy; the Liberal organisation made no claim to be involved. But even then, state branches were prepared to dissociate themselves publicly from federal policy and to campaign for its change. Fraser could try to persuade them to accept federal policy, but could do no more.

The impression often given of parties as tight, monolithic organisations which use discipline to remove dissent and to give the leadership unchallenged authority is fallacious. The Liberal party was never monolithic nor even disciplined. Even as a prime minister who had led the party to three election victories, Fraser had to spend time duchessing the party leaders. His preparedness to do so was an indication of the importance he attached to maintaining coherence and unity and of the difficulty of achieving it. His efforts did not always succeed; the centrifugal forces were too great; state interests were given too much priority. The prime minister may be the leader of the federal party, but that position is not one of command.

CHAPTER 6

'THE HIGHEST AUTHORITATIVE SOURCE'

THE SALESMAN

As the leaders of their governments, prime ministers have greater responsibility for 'selling' governments than anyone else. A prime minister is recognisable, the subject of continual assessment by opinion polls, the spokesperson on television and other media, the figurehead of election campaigns. As the processes of Australian politics appear to become more presidentialised, prime ministers and their direct opponents are the most widely recognised federal politicians.

'Selling' the government takes place in several forums. In parliament prime ministers must defend the performance of their governments against the attacks of the opposition and explain what the government is achieving. Parliament may be partly theatre, a formal arena for legitimising and debating what has been decided elsewhere, but it is also crucial to the fortunes of a government because the image and reputation of ministers are shaped by their performance there. As governing is partly dependent on the communication of perceptions, parliament provides an important opportunity for presenting a case.

The media, electronic and print, commercial and the ABC,

are the second forum that needs to be mastered. Prime ministers must deal with the media at different levels. On a day-to-day basis the press gallery reports what governments do. Working with the politicians in the hothouse atmosphere of Parliament House the journalists often become fascinated with the intrigue and gossip that percolates around that building. They report, analyse, receive leaks and even invent stories. At a more rarified level are the editors and proprietors who require different treatment. Then there is the ABC, publicly funded but independent in the content of its programs. Since it matters to governments what the media say, prime ministers cannot ignore them; nor can they ever completely control them. The relationship between the press and politicians is forever based on a need for one another, yet it is also founded on suspicion, because journalists are looking for the stories that sell newspapers, and routine government decisions do not.

Prime ministers need to sell themselves continuously to the electors, their ultimate masters. The electoral impact of decisions, the perceptions provided by opinion polls of party performance and the gut feel for the political future, are constantly being reassessed, even when an election is not due. As prime ministers have the ability to choose election dates at times when they can maximise their support, that circumstance can change suddenly. Once elections are called, leaders still have to campaign to get the voters behind them on election day. Their future depends on electoral success. To argue that governments take decisions only to achieve re-election is simplistic, because it assumes that the results of decisions are so clear that their electoral impacts can be easily identified. Much of the time governments puzzle over the likely effect of their policies, therefore choices are rarely easy. The best solution is to be seen to be governing well. On the other hand, it is unlikely that any government will act in a way that it clearly perceives to be against its electoral interest. Being re-elected is a perfectly proper ambition. So governing is concerned with perceptions of the electorate's reactions. Selling the government constantly to that broad group is part of prime ministers' responsibility.

'Selling' the government therefore requires the prime minister to communicate with a number of constituencies, each demanding different skills. The constituencies – parliament, the press gallery, editors and proprietors, the ABC, and the electorate – are interconnected. Fraser was not comfortable in these larger arenas. His style was dogged; his determination to keep control of events and to maintain the initiative determined his relations with the media, and eventually undermined his reputation.

Parliament

Performances in parliament matter because the prime minister shows there the tip of the executive iceberg – to the opposition and to his backbenchers, and to the media. As Ian Sinclair, long-time leader of the House for the Fraser government, argues:

Parliament is important because you need to play to the aspirations and mood of your own party members as much as to somebody else. If you cannot satisfy them that you have the ability to stand up to the opposition, then it's pretty tough.

Fraser's view was similar:

If a political leader has a bad week in parliament, that reflects through in the commentaries, it reflects in the headlines. Even if it is theatre, that can be used to influence the way people think about events and people.

Fraser's performance was solid, aggressive and usually humourless. He appeared aloof, arrogant and determined – the familiar and constant public image. Initially he was up against Gough Whitlam, a brilliant parliamentarian, witty, articulate, capable of wounding with vicious shafts of ridicule and of inspiring and entertaining the House, but after 1975 a leader with declining support. Fraser could not have copied Whitlam's style and did not attempt to. Bill Hayden was an effective debater, with the occasional ability to show the government's weaknesses, but he was never master of the House, and never able to get the better of Fraser on a continuing basis.

Fraser could be an effective parliamentarian through the depth of his knowledge, the strong determination of his approach and his refusal to become openly concerned by the taunts of the opposition. Ken Begg, a former ABC TV reporter, comments that he had the necessary quality to 'stand to be hated':

He could cop abuse in the parliament. He could sit there with his big Easter Island face and cross his legs; and his leg would go up and down and they'd throw buckets of shit over him and he'd cop it. He'd get up and never made the mistake like Hawke does of getting emotional, at least on the surface, or over-respond. He'd say 'The honourable member may say that but his assumption is wrong', and sit down.

In parliament he restated his position doggedly; persuasion was by repetition.

Prime ministers do not speak very often in debate. A few pieces of legislation were introduced in Fraser's name – they covered subjects such as the Australia/Japan Foundation Bill, the Australian Heritage Commission Amendment Bill, the Advisory Council for Intergovernmental Relations Bill, the Public Service Bills or the Parliament House Construction Authority Bill. He made announcements about ministerial or administrative changes and explained – more often than he would have liked – the instances of alleged ministerial impropriety, announcing the decisions on those ministers' futures. He spoke on censure motions and usually on each May economic statement and each budget. He made several statements on the general world situation and on specific issues like the Sinai Force in which parliament was kept informed about developments; often he reported to the parliament on his return from overseas.

Because prime ministers do not speak often, every occasion is a performance, with backbenchers needing to be impressed, and with the leader on display. Fraser's performances were described as 'never fluent, but commanding' by a party whip; 'dour and not glossy' by Nixon. Sinclair regarded him as effective, but thought that he often spoke for too long. He would be well prepared, with the capacity to dominate the House as he drove determinedly onwards. He had the ability to end debates with a powerful performance. In late 1982 two issues – Nixon's involvement with the meat inspection scandal and Labor's attacks on the appointment of people involved in tax evasion, and specifically John Reid – were killed after Fraser's speeches on them.

In his attitude to the opposition Fraser was relentless, trying to discredit the Labor party and its leaders. When Whitlam's position seemed in doubt in March 1976, Fraser turned his attack on Hayden, potentially the next leader. With Labor, claimed a minister: 'he was not satisfied with a bloody nose, he stood on their throat'. Indeed he also had a reputation for overkill. Once a point had been made, a political victory taken, he tried to drive the lesson home. Claims Ralph Hunt: 'He certainly had the killer instinct. And when he killed he stood on the carcass'.

This parliamentary and political aggression, when added to the legacy of the 1975 crisis, meant that the atmosphere between the two parties was poisonous. The Labor party, decimated in two successive elections, saw Fraser as unfeeling and unscrupulous; they hated him with an unforgiving vigour. Looking across the chamber 'at that Easter Island visage was pure provocation' said one opposition member. They would, he went on, have regarded him as a 'cad and a bounder, except these words were too soft'. His demeanour was seen as 'haughty and contemptuous'. He provoked confrontation, but without the ability to reduce the tension with a quick quip.

Oppositions must make bricks out of straw, creating scandals and charges where they can, making them last for two days if they are lucky and longer if they can manage it. Fraser's tendency to allow ministerial crises to simmer helped the opposition's cause, because it kept issues on the front page. The Labor parliamentarians pursued him relentlessly, but seldom seemed to get on top of him in parliament, primarily because Fraser was usually unconcerned at their accusations. 'He was like a boxer who didn't seem to know when the punches should be hurting and he would just keep doggedly on and on', said a leading member of the opposition. Only occasionally was he rattled. He became furious when Hawke called him a liar and the speaker, Sir Billy Snedden, did not follow usual parliamentary practice and force a withdrawal. More often, when a censure motion was moved, he followed a prepared speech, attacking the opposition, defending the government and not worrying too much about any specific charges brought up at the time.

He left tactics primarily to the leader of the House, Ian Sinclair. When he spoke in the House he expected his backbenchers to be present and was annoyed when they were not. Assistant whip John Hodges recalls that usually Fraser spoke in parliament during 'prime-time, drive-home time'. He was usually given a call one or two minutes before he was due to speak so he did not waste time. 'Once', Hodges remembers,

he had been over his speech and he walked in ten minutes early. And of course there was virtually no one in the chamber. Every time the prime minister spoke, it was the whip's job to get the troops – ministers as well as backbenchers – in behind him. He came into the whip's office and ranted and raved that this is not good enough, John, get them in the House. We beeped everyone, but they wouldn't come in early. He came back into the whip's office and said 'What's going on, this isn't good enough, get them in here straight away'. He was obviously very toey.

Question time is the most obvious occasion when prime ministers are judged. Since questions could be asked without notice, Fraser had to be briefed on any item that came up. The volume of briefing notes had become immense in the previous two decades and the process of daily preparation more formalised. Each brief posed a potential question and a proposed answer; the compendium was well indexed so that the prime minister had rapid access to the relevant sections. The briefing was attended by members of the private office, by officials from PMC and by Eggleton. The group would anticipate questions, depending on what stories were running in the media or what problems were emerging, and:

we'd often have a discussion about the proposed reply; and Malcolm would kick it around and suddenly say 'What do you think, Tony?' or 'What do you think, Charlie?'

Forms of words would be assessed. Then the prime minister would determine what would be used. Dorothy Dixers, that is, questions from Fraser's own side that had been planted, were used to permit a planned attack on the opposition or a recitation of government successes. Some backbenchers wrote asking Fraser if he wanted a question; other questions were arranged by his staff. Half of question time was dedicated to questions from the government side.

Only the prime minister could adjust the notes in the briefing books to meet the demands of the question. Fraser was able to do so. Sometimes he took all the questions formally addressed to him; on other occasions, when he seemed to be taking too many questions, he would refer them to the responsible ministers to let them do a bit more of the work defending the government. He was at times, thought Sinclair, 'too long-winded, beating the drum' in his answers.

Even though Fraser never appeared comfortable in parliament, he did try to strengthen its role. In 1976 he proposed the establishment of a public expenditure committee. He did not wait for a parliamentary report on committees, but pushed ahead and insisted it be created. He then appointed to it several leading backbenchers. The committee never succeeded in changing the nature of parliamentary review, but was an example of Fraser's paradoxical approach: strengthening the institution in places, but determined to confront the opposition.

However parliament is bicameral and Fraser never felt he could rely on the Senate. Its actions had brought him to power in 1975, but within three months Liberal rebels in the Senate had defeated the proposal to abolish pensioners' funeral benefits and he could never be certain of the Senate's support. In 1978, when Withers was sacked, several senators asked that the right to elect their leader be returned to them. Fraser declined and appointed Carrick. After June 1981 Fraser lost control of the Senate when the Democrats won the balance of power.

Senators are all convinced that no prime minister can understand the peculiar demands of their chamber: the need to negotiate with Democrats, the standing orders, the different atmosphere. Nor do prime ministers readily accept the Senate's use of power. To Fraser the Senate became a source of frustration:

> The Senate seems to have taken to itself power not to oppose an adjustment to an existing tax as part of a budget but the power to oppose any new tax or modify any new tax. Its current practice is to distort every budget. I don't think they should have the power to reject a tax, but I don't mind them having power to reject a budget – as they pay the price.

He regarded the 'marauding power that the Senate now has' as very damaging.

Fraser was effective, not inspired, in parliamentary performance. He was never outperformed by his leading opponents, as his predecessors had been dominated by Whitlam. He was too well-informed, too well-prepared and too determined. Those characteristics reflect the public consensus: Sinclair believes he was seen as 'dour, remote and autocratic partly because of his parliamentary performance, rather than his performance in the party or cabinet rooms'.

The media

For Fraser, dealing with outsiders was never easy. His personal style and appearance – formal, stilted and seldom relaxed – meant that he found it hard to appear as persuasive in public as he could be in small groups. Respected he may have been, but the electorate did not warm to his public image.

Institutionally the media were hard to deal with. They were diverse and suspicious. The means of his coming to power soured relations with journalists in the press gallery, many of whom sympathised with Whitlam. The problem was spelt out to Fraser by Tony Eggleton in a note soon after the 1975 election:

Have you been able to find a moment to give some detailed and considered thought to policy on your own press relations in particular, and government information?

If we don't get this sorted out in a rational way fairly early in the piece, we could find ourselves getting off on the wrong foot. It would be politically unhelpful to get a reputation as a 'secretive' government. Conventional, responsible and low-profile, that's all fine; but not an attitude that our critics and opponents can distort as evasive and uncommunicative . . .

To my mind it is a political liability in this day and age for a government to be stuck with a reputation for undue secretiveness. There is no need for it. You can handle the press in a way that respects Parliamentary priorities, avoids unwanted headlines and yet still acknowledges the role of the media.

Getting media relations just right was a continuing problem. Successful governments may seem to be treated well, but with the hint of a story being leaked those good relations can quickly degenerate.

The party secretariat constantly provided advice on how to 'sell' the message; in 1976 it presented an initial proposal for the year ahead, one set of ideas for presenting the May package of economic measures and another for the budget. Fraser annotated each of the documents. To the suggestion that the party should bring Mrs Thatcher (then a newly elected leader of the opposition) out, he noted 'She isn't doing too well'. There was a decisive no to the idea of any advance briefing on the budget for key people like the president of the ACTU. The secretariat advice was on presentation, rather than content, of policy.

In August 1977 the secretariat arranged for a state-by-state media monitoring; the reports came from party employees or MHR's electorate assistants. The federal officials commented on the reports, particularly once an election seemed possible, providing Fraser with advice on tactics or highlighting potential actions. For example:

Pressure on dollar: Suggest PM continues to brand Hayden as irresponsible but without giving the media a chance to claim PM is pursuing a personal vendetta against Hayden – overkill could produce a sympathy reaction.

Wran is quoted as saying there will be no tax increases in the NSW budget. This might provide an opportunity in Question Time to underline the way in which the States are benefitting from the Federal Government's Federalism policy (11 October 1977).

Laurie Oakes and Brian Toohey have similar stories that Sir John Kerr is saying privately that he does not have to give approval for an early election. Stories are unsourced and are in accordance with ALP pressure designed to prevent an early election. Suggest no comment (14 October).

What a piece of disinformation that turned out to be! The advice was an exercise in determining political tactics; it measured every political opportunity. Yet advising Fraser on media relations was often difficult because he never regarded himself as accountable to the media. Dale Budd argues that Fraser used to 'pour scorn on public relations or communications programs. He only really made an effort to sell uranium mining. Too often he merely put out a one-page press statement'.

However Fraser encouraged his ministers to maintain regular contact with the media. When the Liberal party established a Communications Review committee in December 1976, Fraser gave ministers a series of instructions, encouraging them to 'seek informal meetings with editors and senior correspondents on their interstate visits' and suggesting the use of simpler and more timely announcements. Cabinet submissions were required to indicate public reactions to the proposals. At times the government attempted to introduce a systematic approach to 'promoting the government's policies'. In May 1978, after several discussions by a group of senior ministers, a Ministerial Public Information committee was established. It was chaired by Lynch and supported by a group of press secretaries, including Eggleton and Barnett, who worked from Parliament House to emphasise the committee's party political nature. Yeend refused to allow PMC to become involved. In September 1978 Fraser told Lynch that the government did not get full benefit from the sections in cabinet submissions that proposed the ways they could be presented. He asked Lynch to take special responsibility for examining submissions from the perspective of public relations. In March 1981 the committee was replaced by a cabinet Public Information committee; its terms of reference were 'to consider the public presentation of the government's policies and programs'. Its meetings took place on cabinet days a half-hour before the general cabinet; it usually considered reports from the Government Information Unit and went through the cabinet agenda to alert cabinet to issues on the list that required careful packaging. In April 1982 the PIC was replaced by a ministerial meeting on public communication, to be headed by the minister for administrative services. There was a constant search for the best method of dealing with public relations, but none of the committees seem to have had an impact on cabinet proceedings or improved media relations.

The press gallery

Relations between Fraser and the press gallery started out icily and they never really improved. One press officer commented that, as a consequence of 1975, 'whatever Fraser did was assumed to be wrong and evil'.

For the print media those suspicions were exacerbated by Eggleton's decision to split the print and electronic media during the 1975 election campaign. The electronic media, traditionally less critical because of its need to get a 30-second 'grab' to broadcast on the news, was given greater access. Press conferences, in which Fraser could be questioned in detail, with his answers available for analysis, were held less frequently – and only at his initiative.

Eggleton advised Fraser from the beginning to develop a 'media strategy' to deal with journalists. On 31 December 1975 he advised that 'although you are in a strong position politically, it would be a prudent investment in the future to establish a reasonable rapport with the Gallery'. He suggested non-attributable briefings for heads of bureaus, or even drinks at the Lodge ('Starting off the New Year with an olive branch!' was his comment). He also proposed some consideration for regular meetings. 'While there is absolutely no need to pander to the media with press conferences that are more value to them than to us, it would be undesirable to get a reputation for refusing to hold Canberra news conferences'.

Yet even by the end of January 1976 those complaints had begun because no press conferences had yet been held. The Eggleton plan to divide and rule was constantly disliked; in May 1977 the press journalists protested, and not for the first time, at 'the prime minister's selective use of the electronic media to get his message across'.

In the first two or three years, argues Ken Begg, Fraser

bluffed us; he had us very much under control. He set the agenda and we thrashed about trying to find out what exactly was happening. Then time wore him down and we increasingly set the agenda.

Press journalist Paul Kelly remembered the early days as having an atmosphere of repression: 'he didn't have to tell you anything; there was a tremendous feeling of secrecy'. When the government was well in control, it did not need the media. As its position deteriorated, so the need to sell its performances became more urgent. There was a constant jockeying as ministers tried to control the flow of information and determine the agenda and as journalists tried to break that hold. As the political contest became closer, the ability to limit information declined.

Prime ministers will always try to manage the press. The journalists explained Fraser's techniques; as Richard Carleton, from ABC current affairs TV, pointed out, he seldom had press conferences, he provided only half the story, he tried to split the electronic and print media. Michelle Grattan, chief political correspondent for the *Age* agrees with Carleton's analysis and adds that they were

fairly conventional well-known techniques. Any prime minister is difficult to deal with. The ones who appear not to be difficult are difficult to deal with because they're into seduction rather than browbeating. Fraser was a browbeater; his approach wasn't very subtle.

The senior journalists also disliked Fraser's gutter-stop interviews. As he arrived at Parliament House each morning, Fraser would be surrounded by journalists and cameras. The journalists saw their role as extracting some comment on whatever was the prevailing issue; they tried to get a female journalist in the prime minister's path to make him stop, or threw a question that would appeal to him. However, as usual the prime minister saw advantages in this too. He believed it was inappropriate to be seen walking away without answering and gutter stops also were occasions to get messages across. Sometimes he would stay until someone asked the right question and he could make his point. These exchanges were quickly transcribed and made available to the print media. The great advantage of the system was that the timing and context were largely in Fraser's hands. (By contrast, when Hawke made it clear that he would not answer any questions in that situation, the stops ended abruptly.)

Television interviews were often preferred by the government because they allowed a message to be sent direct. But even then, Ken Begg argues, Fraser was 'a master of not revealing very much, stonewalling, or making you seem unreasonable because you asked these questions'. He would redefine every question and answer it in his own terms. He might talk at length, though without providing that 30-second grab that was suitable for a news broadcast. An aggressive style of interviewing Fraser was often counter-productive as a means of getting useful information. In some circumstances he could perform well. He did pay attention to presentation. Eggleton found a producer who was able to teach him a technique of talking to a camera, but generally Fraser was much better when he was not scripted or required to talk for a precise time. Interviews were seen as preferable to formal presentations, even though an established interviewer like Carleton did not think he was any more comfortable at the end of his term than at the beginning.

Access to Fraser was not a problem; most leading journalists were able to obtain an interview, particularly for individual discussions that were to provide the basis of an article. Questions were not required in advance and particular topics were seldom banned. When Fraser travelled around Australia or overseas, access became much easier. Either some journalists would be called up to the front of the plane or Fraser would come back and discuss off the record whatever was on his mind. Paul Kelly recalls:

When he came back from the regional CHOGRM in Delhi in 1980, Lee Kuan Yew came back in Fraser's plane. As soon as we took off, Lee came straight down the back of the plane and started talking to the Australian journalists and Malcolm came straight after him and the two of them were talking with us for three or four hours; it was very interesting, asking Lee questions about Australian economic policy and protection policy, and Lee answering it and attacking it and then saying to Malcolm, 'Well, what do you think? Don't you agree?'

At night, when Fraser moved around Australia, the leading correspondents arranged a dinner with him where the discussion might range around all topics. He had views on everything and was likely to talk about whatever was on his mind; Paul Kelly again recalls:

Whether it was past experiences, what he thought of overseas leaders, uranium, the exchange rate; you would be able to build up a very clear, documented book of what Malcolm thought. In the last parliament, when he was going ahead with retrospective tax legislation, he would talk very frankly and critically about the Liberal party. That is why he was so interesting.

Fraser was not an easy person to talk to on casual matters - 'a crippled conversationalist' was one description; nor did he discuss personalities or other gossip with the press. But he was always prepared to argue about policy, where he was far more comfortable. He did not merely express his views but listened to those of the press. Part of the exercise was to ensure that the press understood the lines of thinking of the government, as the discussions were often genuine explorations of policy issues.

Yet the journalists retained a suspicion of what Fraser was trying to achieve, not so much from the policy comments themselves, but from the feeling that they were not always told the whole story. Few are prepared to recall instances where they were directly told lies (the one exception that they mention was the election speculation in August 1982), but they felt that they were not always given all the truth, and believed that Fraser had a great facility to redefine history. He was regarded as being flexible, although the press office stopped using the word because it was seen as a euphemism for liar. Richard Carleton commented that 'Malcolm wouldn't tell you anything, let alone lie'. The press office might steer people towards possible stories or interpretations and then allow them to draw conclusions. There was a thin line between being misled and lied to; several thought they were deliberately left to draw the wrong conclusions. Max Walsh, at the time editor of the *Australian Financial Review*, suggests that Fraser could be

slippery; he allowed impressions to be put around because they suited him; even though he had no intention of taking that action. He would use innuendo to leave an impression – Medibank being a classic – use a form of words that any reasonable person would take to mean something, and then Malcolm would say 'you didn't understand what I meant'. Disinformation I think it is, but he was careful not to be caught out in a blatant lie.

However the greatest problem was that the lack of trust, embedded since the crisis of 1975, never entirely dissipated. To Peter Bowers of the *Sydney Morning Herald*, he was

The quintessential manipulative politician . . . it always made you suspicious of him . . . you'd say 'what's this bugger really up to, what's he really going to do, is there something that he's not telling me?'

Because of his reputation, journalists always assumed there was. His relations with them were such that, as one adviser put it, 'even when he was telling the truth, people thought he was lying'.

Journalists were aware that the prime minister read their stories. Fraser would sometimes ring up to argue the merits of a case or to dispute the interpretation put on a story. He might browbeat them, or call them in for a discussion. Paul Kelly remembers an occasion:

Michelle [Grattan] and I were sitting next to each other in the press section on one of those trips where he had one of his big trade initiatives. She had basically written that it was a pretty useless exercise. We were just taking off somewhere in North America and I looked up and saw Fraser lurching down the aisle; the plane was at an impossible angle and Fraser should have still been in his seat. But he'd obviously just read what Michelle had written and he leant over me and said, 'Can't you give an Australian prime minister any credit for trying to do the best for his country?' He could be very aggressive if you got stuck into him.

His ministers also recall his occasional sensitivity to press reports. One was woken early in the morning to be asked how the government should consider some editorial (when most thought editorials were read only by politicians and other journalists). But Fraser was trying to solve problems; his approach was 'how do we fix this up; what's the problem; very anxious to help you through, not just browbeat'. The call was an indication of his desire to be in control, to know the answers.

Leaks were often of concern too. The most famous was the leaking of the full 1980 budget to Laurie Oakes of the *Sun*, attributed by most of Oakes's colleagues to Lynch's office as a means of distracting attention from an IAC report on footwear and textiles. Fraser exonerated Lynch, and believed that the leak probably came from the Treasury, because the wording indicated it was a particular draft that had not been outside the Treasury or the treasurer's office. Howard instructed the department to hold an inquiry, but finally had to tell Fraser it had been unable to find the culprit. Fraser's view was correct. A Treasury officer had given the draft to the office of the leader of the opposition which had then passed it on to Oakes.

Fraser was angry at the frequent leaking of government information to the press and constantly, and usually unsuccessfully, sought to close the holes. Ministers like Guilfoyle recall the determination with which he pursued leaks – although without any great expectation of finding the culprit. For instance, when a foreign affairs report appeared in the *National Times* in May 1976, Fraser wrote to Peacock: 'I would be grateful if you could let me know how Mr. Toohey got the information, assuming of course it is correct'. (The request had been toned down from the more peremptory 'How did he get it?' in the draft.) But it was not always done directly. Peter Bowers, political reporter for the *Sydney Morning Herald*, recalls one occasion:

The fact that Tony Street and Malcolm had a row in cabinet was fairly significant and what they had a row over, according to the story I wrote, was that Malcolm had made Lynch head of a cabinet sub-committee on industrial relations which was Tony's portfolio. What gave this story a lot of credence was that I actually had got hold of the cabinet paper and got the official number of the cabinet decision which is very hard to get, and it gave a real authentic look to the whole story, gave it a lot of credibility . . . well this upset Malcolm no end, so he had me down within an hour . . . and he was in one of his towering bloody rages, and sat me down, and literally physically stood over me. I'm sitting down here and Malcolm's operating at another level, pacing up and down in front of me, saying, 'you've got it wrong Bowers, you've got this completely wrong'. I thought 'he's got upset because I said his little mate, they've had an argument', I wrote 'he's only got one friend' or something. After a while, he pulled a letter out of his pocket and said, 'I want to read you this letter, Bowers' and the letter said, 'Dear PM, I don't know who gave Bowers that story, I certainly didn't'. And, of course, that letter was from a member of Tony Street's staff and I can say now as Tony Street is no longer in parliament and this fellow is now out in private enterprise somewhere, that he was the one and the very same person who gave me the story. So Malcolm read this out to me and said, 'what do you say about that Bowers?' I said, 'PM if you don't mind I won't say anything'. 'No, you can't can you?' I said, 'Yes, I could, I might well say a lot about that letter, I might well deny it or you may pull another letter out of your pocket which you probably have and you'll read that letter out and I'll deny that and you'll pull a third letter out and read it to me and in the end you'll pull out a letter that I can't deny – so if you don't mind we won't start down that track'. He said, 'well I just want you to know that you have been sold a pup'. I said, 'well, what do you want me to do, do you want me to put in a correction?' 'No, no, no, no correction. I want you to know that you were sold a pup and were given false information'. I said, 'All right suppose I concede that'. He said, 'All right I just want you to know that'. Now it took me a while to see what Malcolm was about. This is what he was about . . . Malcolm knew who gave me the story, got this letter from him and read it out to me, not to embarrass me but to discredit the source of my information to make sure I never went back to him again, . . . so he wasn't putting me down, he was shutting up the leak and letting us both know he knew who it was and to that extent I never really did go back to that fellow again. I rang him up and said, 'Look I didn't dob you in, I understand why you wrote the letter and I understand why Malcolm read it out to me. But I didn't dob you in, so just keep your bloody head down if he has you back, because he's liable to have you back and say Bowers owned up that you were the leak' . . . He used to operate . . . in great detail. Maybe Malcolm would have liked me to admit who it was and he would have sacked him, but he didn't really expect it. But he wanted at once to shut up a leak, put him under a lot of heat, make him falsely deny it, and maybe in the process hope that he could incite me either to exposing him or feeling so put off by that person that you would never go back . . . I think it was very revealing of the Machiavellian way that bastard could operate. He was not just a Stone Age politician as he often seemed to be, going around with a club hitting people over the head with it and dragging them into his bloody particular political cave. There was much more to the devious bastard than that.

This story perhaps epitomises the style that journalists recall most: detailed personal involvement, and strident determination. For Fraser stopping the leak was far more important than gaining a retraction.

Whether Fraser himself 'leaked' depends often on the precise definition of the term. He would attack the opposition, but did not talk much, if ever, about the personalities of his ministers. Off-the-record briefings were common, with one given on the Great Wall of China leading to the description of a 'highest authoritative source'. But he often gave in public the same information as he had just discussed off the record. He tended to 'background in the prime ministerial sense, rather than leak'. When Peacock resigned, he spent a day calling in senior journalists one by one to provide his account of events. If journalists wanted to check stories with Fraser's colleagues, they often found the messages had been co-ordinated. Begg claims: 'You would go around the ministers and get the rehearsed line'. Unable to check, 'you have sometimes to go with what you have got; there would be nothing attributable and you go out on a limb and he could chop your legs off'.

One notable leak for which Fraser was responsible occurred after the premiers' conference of 1981. Fraser had asked Howard to avoid putting forward any specific figures to allow the commonwealth to take the offensive in reducing government spending. Fraser would explain that the infrastructure program had got out of hand while the treasurer would state that there was no hope of any more money. The cabinet agreed that to go beyond a 10 per cent increase in grants would be out of the question and left Fraser and Howard to work out the tactics and the amount that they would concede. Fraser and Howard were not pushed to the limit and were able to satisfy the states with a sum that was 1 per cent less. Then Fraser, whether keen for a win after the battering of the Peacock resignation a month before, or from a state of exhaustion after three hectic months, gave senior journalists a background briefing on the federal government's success. The consequence was outrage, particularly from the premiers. Although Howard took much of the blame initially, it soon became known that Fraser had been the architect of the ideas; he had been saying lightheartedly that he had 'decided to show how tough I could be', and he was eventually forced to meet the gallery. He then just 'lectured the camera'. Peter Bowers recalls:

Howard told me they had done them out of 1 per cent and I worked out how much that was. It was $80 million or something. I thought this'll be good for the next day. I was going to go back to Howard and say 'I hope Malcolm told you to release this or otherwise there is going to be hell to pay and he'll have your bloody hide'. But I never got the chance. The shit hit the fan with Charles Court and everyone saying they had been robbed and cheated and what a dreadful bastard Malcolm was. Malcolm wouldn't front and it was John Howard who carried the can. We told Howard 'We know who put you up to this'. So sure enough, Malcolm gets smoked out and we had a complete go-in . . . it wasn't enough for Malcolm to win; it was no good winning unless people knew about it.

It was in retrospect 'a foolish error of judgement', that tendency for overkill that tarnished victories by leaving the opponent not only defeated, but sour.

The pressures of the media and modern technology meant that Fraser, perhaps nostalgically, looked back on earlier days when life was more measured. He had been in the ambassador's office in Washington when Menzies gave a press conference:

He came in with an overcoat on, kept it on because he had a cold, took out a cigar, lit it and blew out a great tail of smoke. 'Now what do you fellows think you want to know?' 'Sir, you've just had confidential discussions with the President. Can you tell us about them?' 'Young man, you've answered your own question'. 'I don't understand you, sir?' 'Didn't you call those discussions confidential? Do you expect me to advise you of their substance before I've spoken to my colleagues in Australia?' 'Sir, is there any particular purpose in your being in the US at this time?' 'Do you expect me to tell you that before I've informed the Australian parliament?' 'Sir, is it correct that a decision has been made to send half a dozen Caribous to Vietnam?' 'The same applies, young man, if it were, I wouldn't be advising you at this point. Right, is there anything that you fellows want to learn?' Now, if you did that today you'd get headlines of all sorts of terrible kinds.

Indeed times are different. Constant pressure for comment requires constant briefing. Any prime minister will at times become uncomfortable with the probing and pressure of the media. Fraser was no exception.

The editors and proprietors

Fraser did not deal only with the press gallery. He believed that editors needed to be courted too. He held regular dinners for them at the Lodge, exchanging views, and naturally they were often impressed by the privilege of dinner with the prime minister. Most people, reluctantly or not, are. The conversations were often informative, moving widely across current issues but off the record. Max Walsh remembers one dinner of Fairfax editors he attended with Michael Davie of the *Age*; it was an

amazing night of give and take. Michael had never seen a prime minister being so frank about policies and things. He'd have a better recollection of it than I would, because I was hosing down the booze with Malcolm. He would engage in pretty heavy arguing; he'd take you up; it wasn't a case so much of exploring as of challenging.

Yet these evenings could also be hard work, unless Tamie was there. Max Walsh thought that

Tamie was a stupendous asset in these circumstances. Having dinner with Malcolm could be a pain; with Tamie present it's a pleasure and you realise that that of itself shows you that Malcolm does have redeeming qualities.

Once when a crisis was emerging during a dinner for editors – it was the night Robinson resigned – and Fraser mentioned it, Fred Brenchley of the *National Times* excused himself on a pretext and rushed to the nearest phone in the Lodge to ensure that his political correspondent had the story. She had, but the breach of the accepted rules made Fraser furious. Usually the confidences were maintained.

The purpose of the dinners was disputed. Fraser said they were a means of giving the opportunity to ask questions about government policy in a congenial atmosphere. That is probably all they were useful for. The notion that these dinners were helpful in controlling the media was stridently denied by working journalists. Indeed editorial control over the leading political journalists is at best occasional. Some journalists thought Fraser hoped to influence coverage, but did not appreciate the comparative freedom leading political journalists had. More important were the continuous links with editors, the better appreciation of what the government was doing.

Proprietors too were seen as important. Fraser sometimes wrote to Sir Warwick Fairfax, to discuss some policy issue. In July 1976 he sent Fairfax excerpts from several documents to emphasise that Fraser's views on détente were held by other Western leaders and proposed a discussion on his recent trip to China and Japan. He would ring James Fairfax (although the discussions were never passed on to editors). He listened to Kerry Packer, whose initial suggestion for a communications satellite eventually blossomed with government aid for AUSSAT. When he planned changes to the Broadcasting Act in 1976, he ensured that through Tony Eggleton he received notes from Kerry Packer on the proposed bill, including the complaint that the legislation put too much power in the hands of the minister, particularly a Labor minister who might be able to dictate to the commercial media. He then got Robinson's view on those comments. Before further changes to the Act were introduced in 1980, Fraser negotiated with Murdoch and met the *Herald and Weekly Times* directors to discuss the amendments. A special 'grandfather' clause was added in cabinet, without a submission, on 14 May 1981 to provide that licences held by people who were not Australian citizens at the time the Act was passed could still hold them. The tenor of relationship was not one of dependency, but of mutual support and advantage.

The Australian Broadcasting Commission

The ABC always had an authority born of its independence. It was funded by the government, yet not the spokesman of the government. Free from the restraints of advertising, the ABC could in theory report fearlessly and openly both the successes and the problems of the government. For much of the Fraser government, however, the ABC seemed under siege, short of funds and of staff, the victim of attacks and apparent boycotts and characterised by the government as a left-wing fiefdom. The problem of finding a balance between these pictures is one of the continuing dilemmas of the ABC (now a corporation).

Yet behind the scenes, the picture was one of accommodation rather than independence. In 1975 the government was committed to cutting expenditure, but the ABC was dominated by Whitlam appointees. The general manager, Talbot Duckmanton, used a circuitous route to send information to the prime minister by talking regularly to Tony Eggleton. In December 1975 Fraser asked Eggleton to sound Duckmanton out for ideas for future control of broadcasting; he reacted by proposing a Broadcasting Act to supervise all aspects of broadcasting and indicated his concern with the existence of the 'so-called community stations'.

In January he directly undermined his commissioners. Eggleton noted to Fraser:

Tal Duckmanton was rather shattered by the way in which the Commission rejected his advice about economies in the ABC. He says those Commission members determined to persevere with Labor programmes/projects 'caucused' prior to the meeting. In the face of this intransigence, Tal believes it would be unfortunate if the ABC's supplementary estimates went through unscathed! Cuts may cause him some administrative problems, but he accepts this as the only way to force economies on the Commission. He also wanted the Chairman's position filled, suggesting 'Harry Bland' as a possibility.

Sir Henry Bland was appointed in mid-1976.

This cosy relationship continued. In August 1976 Duckmanton asked Eggleton to ensure that Liberal complaints were not sent formally to the ABC because, if they were leaked and at some time later action was taken, the ABC might be accused of being political; he preferred a phone call. He also asked Liberal backbenchers to tone down their enthusiasm for Bland's clean-up of the ABC, for while he was glad to have a Liberal chairman, it would be as well for backbenchers not to claim him as such. Eggleton asked Fraser to 'flash a signal' in the party room.

The first crisis with the ABC was in November 1976 when the government sought to reconstruct the commission in order to remove the elected staff commissioner, Marius Webb, whose position had been created by the Whitlam government. Cabinet argued that a form of management–staff consultation was more appropriate than a single staff commissioner. It proposed a commission of nine, with each state represented and two women commissioners. Backbenchers, and particularly senators, strenuously objected. Duckmanton wavered, finally arguing that he could work with the staff nominee; he forecast trouble, which he would accept if the government was prepared to live with the disruption in the ABC. Fraser, unsure of the support he would get in the Senate, dropped the proposal. Then Bland, already upset by what he saw as unfair prime ministerial criticism of the ABC and now feeling betrayed, resigned. He had not, it seemed, received the whole-hearted support of his general manager, whose links to the prime minister must have made the chairman's position difficult.

Such links can partly explain why the ABC was internally renowned for the 'pre-emptive buckle'. Close relations with government, and particularly getting messages through to the prime minister, were one way of trying to mitigate the constant struggle for funds, albeit only a marginally successful way. The government was severe in its finances – the one direct control it could have – by refusing many requests for increases and requiring the ABC to absorb wage rises and price increases.

However, the government did stop short of directing the ABC in program matters and political journalists like Richard Carleton do not recall management ever 'instructing them on the way that stories should be covered'. Nor were journalists on the 'AM' or 'PM' radio programs unable to use their discretion. When Fraser indicated through his press secretary during the tax evasion scandals that he was ready to be interviewed, his offer was rejected because a tape of an earlier press conference was already being played. He had to wait until the next evening. ABC journalists were not too overawed or scared to assert their independent judgement.

Cabinet was able to instruct the ABC to close down the experimental 3ZZ community station in Melbourne because it had remained a separate item of expenditure and the minister had to approve the specific estimates. It did not go further. In April 1977 cabinet noted with obvious disapproval a report by 'This Day Tonight' that implied that the Queensland premier was as hostile to their government as he had been to Whitlam's. It asked the minister for post and telecommunications to prepare a paper examining whether ABC programs should be subject to the same controls as those of commercial broadcasters. The submission argued that either the ABC could set its own standards or legislation could provide for the community setting of standards; its preference was to defer the whole question until the inquiry by the Broadcasting Tribunal was complete. The immediate heat was off and the issue was not raised again.

Appointment of ABC commissioners was determined by cabinet. After 1976 they needed to appoint one commissioner from each state and, because of the system of rolling appointments, one or two vacancies occurred each year. All the nominees had to be approved by the prime minister before they were put to cabinet and even then cabinet did not always approve the minister's suggestion.

Cabinet had no formal participation in the appointment of the general manager after Duckmanton resigned in 1982, but the ABC board clearly wanted to be sure that its choice did not offend. Its chairman, Professor Leonie Kramer, met the prime minister on 29 July and explained the commission's preference out of the short-list of two. Fraser supported the choice and also told Kramer which commissioners he intended to appoint to the board of directors when the commission became a corporation. He strongly rejected the hint that the ABC should take over the SBS.

The ABC was under constant review – with the Green report and then the Dix report. Beneath that activity was an informal network designed to keep the prime minister informed. The ABC management was always conscious of its political masters; the journalists remained stridently independent.

Elections

The timing of elections is the prerogative of the prime minister. Fraser held two early elections: in 1977 and 1983. The process of decision in each case is instructive because it illustrates the range of consultation that Fraser undertook. Decisions in retrospect gain an air of inevitability that was far from evident at the time.

The 1977 election was held twelve months before the Fraser government's first term expired. It was not surprising that discussion of the possibility of an early election took place.

There had to be a separate half-Senate election by May 1978 and there is a widespread disinclination to hold separate half-Senate polls.

Lynch had indicated that the economic forecasts were so gloomy that perhaps Fraser should consider an early poll. So in July the secretariat prepared a brief summary of the past early elections and the reactions of governors-general to requests for early polls; it concluded that governors-general had always acceded to the requests. The secretariat commissioned a poll on perceptions of Fraser, asking how effective he was perceived to be across a range of issues. On 25 July a federal executive meeting of the state presidents discussed their preferences either for an early joint poll or a separate Senate election.

The climate of speculation grew in September. How much was directly attributable to Fraser was uncertain. Begg's view was: 'He would start the brush fire; he'd be the arsonist and later come up as the fireman and say that in order to end this great uncertainty I've got to have an election'.

On 4 October the contingency planning of the secretariat swung into action. Eggleton proposed to Fraser several steps: the ongoing monitoring of the 'pros and cons'; a detailed assessment of the political and economic climate; the preparation of a credible rationale for the governor-general and the public; initiatives to prepare the ground; and consultation with ministers. A separate paper canvassed the alternative dates for a half-Senate or joint election. The date had to allow for a three-week campaign, uninterrupted by school or public holidays, with the polling day not on a school holiday or a long weekend. The paper concluded that, because of Easter school holidays, only three days in the first half of the year were possible – 25 February, 4 March and 22 April. The first two were seen as too early because many school leavers might be looking for work. So the choice in October was narrowed to a mere three dates: 11 or 17 December, and 22 April.

The private office listed the pros and cons for an early election. The pros, according to John Rose on 11 October, included the possible economic deterioration of the economy, an unemployment rate that would be lower than in May, the fear of a change of Labor leader or loss of control of the Senate in a separate half-Senate poll. The case against an election emphasised the need for time to allow the economic policy to work and interest rates to fall. Rose thought the case against outweighed the advantages. David Barnett put it more personally:

one con that does not appear in this table is the personal price that the PM would pay. There is too ready a tendency to brand him as ruthless, opportunistic, calculating, etc . . . This line, rather than arguments about the danger of losing control of the Senate to Don Chipp or the need to reassure the business community, would be what was likely to present itself as the explanation for a government with a large majority going to the polls a year ahead of time.

On 14 October Eggleton reported that the state directors were cooling towards the idea of a December election; four were nervously in favour, while New South Wales and South Australia opposed. All had reservations because there was not a credible rationale or central 'gut' issue. All but Victoria, however, acknowledged that they were ready.

The private office reported on 18 October that the general feeling was for a May poll; if economic conditions were going to get better, they thought there was no need to suffer the personal cost of a poll. Yet Barnett had now shifted; he reported that the gallery was now accepting the idea of a December election. Some journalists told Barnett they thought the prime minister should go:

Even Michelle [Grattan] seems to be accepting the idea. I do not see reaction from the gallery today as presenting the same sort of difficulty as would have appeared a couple of weeks ago.

Robert Crichton-Brown, the party treasurer, reported the views of leading businessmen at functions in Sydney on 18 October and from Perth on 25 October; they were not always in favour. Other reports from business circles were fed in through Eggleton. The 'pros and cons' list was updated almost daily.

Some ministers had their doubts. Tony Staley argued that

there was no certainty that the government would be returned and that it would be portrayed as 'scared'; he preferred to wait. The secretariat discussed Staley's paper with David Kemp, political analyst Malcolm Mackerras and pollster Gary Morgan. Kemp and Mackerras were optimistic. Kemp was not certain, but Mackerras thought the coalition would probably win. The next day, 21 October, Eggleton reported that Gary Morgan was confident that, based on current trends, the government would win. To get some accuracy, Eggleton commissioned special telephone surveys in Sydney and Melbourne to establish attitudes to unemployment.

Others were letting their views become known. Eggleton sent this note to Fraser on 21 October, passing on a message from John Atwell, the federal president of the Liberal party:

JK

John Atwell telephoned this morning to say that he had received a phone call from JK, who is wondering what sort of timetable you have in mind over the next couple of weeks.

He stressed to John that the necessary document that you would take to Government House should be thoroughly prepared and should set out, with sufficient arguments, the reasons for the course of action proposed.

JK is proposing to leave Australia on 10 December, which he is hoping and assuming would be *the* day – if a December election is held.

While journalists argued that the governor-general might refuse to agree to an early election, Fraser had no doubts. He only had to present a case – *any case*, it seems – to satisfy the formal requirements in order to get the election the governor-general hoped would be held. The message made no difference; every governor-general has granted an election when requested and no one seriously doubted that Kerr would. But it did raise grave doubts about the propriety of the umpire informing the prime minister about the results of his decision before the case was presented, let alone doing so through the party apparatus.

The polls on 25 October were not encouraging, showing little shift in opinions; there was a decline in Fraser's approval rating from 40 per cent at the beginning of October to 33 per cent by 16 October; 79 per cent of respondents believed the government should go its full term. Nevertheless Fraser took the issue to cabinet, asking ministers in turn what they thought. He noted the responses: for December were Lynch, Withers, Robinson, Carrick, Guilfoyle, Peacock, Durack, Hunt, Garland, Macphee, Newman, Viner, Fife, Mackellar, McLeay and Killen – sixteen in all. Sinclair, Street, Cotton and Webster opted for May, Staley and Aderman wanted separate elections, with Staley writing later that he felt that 'the separate Senate course is ultimately the best course for *you* in a very personal sense'. But Fraser had the support if he wanted to go.

Yet the final decision was still not taken, even with power strikes affecting Victoria. Fraser drafted in his own hand a speech, announcing

it may be necessary to give the people the right to chose between the supremacy of parliament and industrial anarchy. However . . . that time has not yet come. That parliament will proceed with the orderly conduct of its business . . . We believe that high purpose will be best served by the continuation of this parliament.

Fraser seldom wrote the first draft of his statements and would not have bothered if his mind was finally made up. Indeed on 26 October three drafts were ready for use; one stated that there would be a half-Senate election in December but no early House of Representatives poll, the second was to end speculation by declaring that there would be no election in 1977, and the third announced the poll.

The third option was finally accepted and the 'thoroughly prepared' case sent to the governor-general on 26 October. The December election, it argued, could end speculation and uncertainty; it would also bring the elections back into line. The governor-general approved after, as he now claimed, 'having carefully considered your views as expressed at our discussion and as set out in your letter'. Thus the process of consultation, consideration and recommendation had been extensive before the final decision was tabled. Despite the sudden problems caused by Lynch's resignation, Fraser's judgement was vindicated by the return of the government with the loss of only one seat from its vast 1975 majority.

1982–83 provided a contrast. Initially, in July 1982, Fraser considered the possibility of an election in September, but it was not, he argues, widely discussed. Nevertheless the press ran a story which, in the view of several journalists, could be traced directly to Fraser's office. When he denied the discussion, the journalists bluntly did not believe him. It was, according to Michelle Grattan, the one occasion when she felt she had been lied to. Ken Begg also recalls:

that famous speculation where Anne Summers [of the *Australian Financial Review*] got a story for a September election. I can remember that day. Malcolm abused us, saying where do we get these stories from and how irresponsible we were. It came from him. It came from his office, and we were getting lectured publicly about it. That made it a little hard to stomach . . . We learned the channel from which it had come and that channel led straight back to the prime minister. So it was part of the game. I remember standing out there and asking questions and getting a lecture and thinking of the hypocrisy of it all.

Begg says that they went around their sources and felt that they were being deliberately misled.

Others understood that the decision was being considered. Anthony recalls that senior ministers were canvassing the possibility, with commodity prices and the drought getting worse. They had mixed feelings, but wanted to go while Hayden was there. Eggleton was more specific:

He was going to actually announce an election on the night of Hayden's response to the budget, but the same day he received a report on the Costigan Commission and he rang me at one o'clock in the morning to say – Tony, it's all off; I'm not going to do it.

Lynch was hoping to leave politics as he was already ill. On 25 August he prepared a draft letter to Fraser:

I wish to inform you of my decision not to contest the House of Representatives election which is to take place on 18 September and as a consequence of my intention to stand aside forthwith as Minister of Industry and Commerce . . . I wish you and our colleagues every success on 18 September and during the government's next term of office.

The letter was premature as the election was not held, but Lynch resigned anyway a month later.

In October Fraser again considered an election, arguing that as the Flinders by-election had to be held, it would be as well to have a general election before Hawke could replace Hayden as leader. This time the party was not ready. A meeting was held with a group of ministers in the cabinet room; then Fraser returned to his office to discuss it with Eggleton and Jim Forbes, the party president. They argued strongly against the proposal and Fraser backed down, only to see a result in the Flinders by-election caused by Lynch's resignation that suggested his political instincts might have been right (even though he was flat on his back in hospital for the duration of the campaign).

When Fraser returned to work in January he first told Eggleton that there would be no immediate election. Then he began to change his mind. He pointed out that many businessmen were concerned about the instability and uncertainty. Crucially, he feared that Hawke would replace Hayden as leader of the Labor party. He listed for Eggleton twelve good arguments for having an election. There was a need to endorse the mandate for the wages pause, a desire to avoid instability through electoral speculation(!), Labor was doing poorly, later in 1983 would be less practicable. In addition Fraser did not expect to be able to persuade premiers to extend the wages pause. No one said no. Fraser talked to Anthony, but argued that he had to go immediately. He talked with many of his other colleagues, but not in the way that really allowed debate. He rang his ministers more to inform them than to consult them. 'I've pulled the plug', he told one. This time his mind was made up far more firmly. When the Labor party managed to change leaders before Fraser saw the governor-general, the tactic rebounded. Eggleton did raise the issue of not having an election but Fraser thought it would be 'just too laughable'. He had to wear it.

Tony Staley believed that the decision was the consequence of 'wanting too much of a good thing; he could have called the election in January, but he left it to February because he wanted the Labor Party seething in turmoil and the unions in vehement opposition to the wages pause'. Fraser's sense of history told him Labor could not change leaders easily. For once his timing was wrong.

If 1977 was a process of general consultation and of collective agonising, 1983 was a determined individual in action. Everything thereafter went wrong – from Labor's bloodless coup, to the bushfires and the abysmal campaign – but it was *his* decision.

Campaigning

As we have seen, Fraser was never comfortable in his relationship with the electorate; he was seldom popular. Between 1979 and 1983, for instance, there was only one brief period, between October 1980 and March 1981 (during the election), when more people approved of his performance than disapproved. In mid-1979 and in April 1981 during the crisis over Peacock's resignation, his approval rating slipped below 30 per cent. But disapproval of the prime minister is not in itself cause to vote against the party.

The Liberal party was aware of the austere and distant image Fraser portrayed. In 1978, speaking for the Public Information committee, Lynch wanted Fraser to appear in more 'human situations', so he could present 'a more real and genuine image'. The Parliamentary Tactics committee constantly wanted him to soften his image.

He seldom did. On the campaign trail, Fraser's performance was similar to that in parliament – dogged, usually unruffled, pushing home the advantage by persistence and repetition. Election coverage has tended to concentrate more and more on the leaders, so that each day the prime minister provided either the first or the second item on the news; the process had developed to such an extent that the prime minister became almost solely responsible for presenting the government's case.

He could earn respect, yet not inspire. Dick Hamer believed

THE SALESMAN

He speaks forcefully; he is very intelligent; he is not on the other hand fiery; he doesn't excite people; what he generates is respect for his intellect, respect for his integrity, but not the sort of one-eyed football-fan response.

To Charles Court, he failed because

he didn't set them alight with a vision; a leader performs not by arithmetic, not by theories and economic philosophies, but very much with the heart, with a capacity to capture the spirit of a nation.

Peter Baume believed his speeches had too much detail, too little image.

The campaign was organised by the federal secretariat led by Tony Eggleton. At the onset he discussed with Fraser the itinerary and the advertising campaign. He persuaded Fraser to attend one or two meetings with the agency, so he could react to the directions of the campaign. Thereafter Eggleton travelled with Fraser and acted as the link with the advertising agencies. Fraser used to read every word of the press advertisements, while judging the television ones on the basis of the general impressions.

Fraser's schedule was invariably exhausting. Two examples, taken from the 1980 campaign, illustrate the pace.

Programme for Thursday, 2 October 1980
8.55 am Depart Kirribilli
9.00 am Talk-back with John Laws, 2UE (237 Miller Street, North Sydney) After conclusion, John Laws will introduce Stuart Lamb, owner of 2UE
10.10 am Depart
10.15 am Arrive 2SM for talk-back with John Tingle and George Moore (182 Blues Point Road)
11.00 am Depart
11.30 am Arrive Dimitri's Bistro (Cnr. Campbell and Riley Streets, Surry Hills) for launching of Larry Pickering's book 'A Decade of Pickering'
12.30 pm Depart – proceed to flight facilities
1.00 pm Takeoff Sydney – lunch in flight

2.15 pm	Arrive Brisbane (met by John Herron)
2.20 pm	News conference in Ansett terminal
3.00 pm	Depart
3.45 pm	Arrive TVQ-0 for interview with Haydn Sargent (Sir Samuel Griffith Drive, Mount Coottha)
approx. 4.05 pm	Depart
4.15 pm	Arrive QTQ-9 studios to pre-record interview with John Barton (Sir Samuel Griffith Drive)
5.00 pm	Depart
5.10 pm	Arrive Italo-Australian Centre (23 Foster Street, Newmarket)
	Met by: Mr Vince Dimaro – President
	Mr Joe Rinaudo – Patron and Senior Member
	Mr Peter Johnson, MP
	Mr Don Land, MLA
5.15 pm	Introduced to representatives of Italian community
5.30 pm	Welcomed by President and Patron
5.35 pm	Prime Minister speaks briefly
5.40 pm	Peter Johnson thanks Prime Minister
6.00 pm	Depart
6.10 pm	Arrive Lennons Hotel
7.50 pm	Depart Lennons
7.55 pm	Arrive Greek Community Centre
	Met by: Dr John Herron (Mr Anthony to be met by Sir Robert Sparkes if he wishes)
	Introduced to: Mr Alex Freeleagus (Greek Consul), Mr George Pipos (President) and other members
8.05 pm	Move upstairs, walk to dais through centre aisle from back of hall
	Short welcome from John Herron
	Mr Robinson speaks
	Mr Anthony speaks
	Prime Minister speaks
approx. 9.15 pm	Prime Minister departs hall
approx. 9.20 pm	Depart for hotel

Tuesday, 14 October 1980
8.30 am   John Knight and John Haslem (at the Lodge)
9.00 am   Record interview with Richard Carleton for 'Nationwide' – ABC studios
10.00 am   Depart
10.30 am   Record half-hour special with CTC-7, Aspinall Street, Watson (411 0000). To go to air Wednesday 15th. Panel consists of Doug Holden, Max Walsh and Peter Cole Adams
12 noon   Walk through Kingston shopping centre
12.25 pm   Depart
12.30 pm   National Press Club luncheon
2.45 pm   Depart Canberra
3.45 pm   Arrive Melbourne
4.30 pm   Record interview for 'Willesee at 7' at HSV studios, cnr. Dorcas and Wells Streets, Sth Melbourne (699 7777)
5.15 pm   Depart
7.35 pm   Depart Windsor
7.55 pm   Arrive Heidelberg Town Hall (front entrance) Met by: Mr John Miles (Rally Chairman)
7.55 pm   John Miles introduces stage party (which includes Margaret Guilfoyle, Neil Brown and Rosemary Kemp)
8.00 pm   John Miles introduces Bruce Skeggs, who introduces Rosemary Kemp
8.10 pm   Senator Guilfoyle speaks
8.15 pm   Prime Minister speaks
8.40 pm   Neil Brown briefly thanks Prime Minister
9.00 pm   Supper in Mayoral ante-room
9.15 pm   Depart
9.30 pm   Depart Essendon
10.45 pm   Arrive Sydney

Talk-back radio sessions were prominent. As the media analyst, Clem Lloyd, has explained:

The structure of the talk-back weights its effect in favour of the answering politician. He can ignore the question if he chooses, or reshape it to suit the answer he wants to give. There is little danger of hostile questions or follow-up questions from the invariably deferential hosts of the programs. Control can be exerted over the accuracy of material by reference to written notes and other aids without risk of detection by the vast listening audience.

Lloyd concluded that 'the medium was ideally suited for Fraser's remorseless didacticism, particularly on the tax issue' in 1977. Fraser could speak directly, without interruption or heckling. He was much more comfortable there than in public meetings.

The campaigns were inevitably kept flexible, because they tended to be interactive, as the two sides sparred. Politicians see what arguments can run and follow their instinct. Fraser rang Anthony every day, to ensure that the media were not able to extract contradictory statements from the two of them. In 1977 Fraser fought on Labor's ground of unemployment and taxation – and won. He capitalised quickly on Labor's disarray and on the poorly thought out proposal to introduce a pay-roll tax. The change of direction in the last week before the 1980 election, with its fear campaign about the capital gains tax, was mainly the work of the advertisers, with Fraser kept in touch with the decisions; it was based on last-minute research. The party divisions too were constantly sending advice on what should be done to counteract local media coverage or reports. When in 1977 the Daily Telegraph reported that New South Wales would vote Labor, the branch telexed:

PM should urgently contrive to say something favourable about Tooth's KB, Harbour Bridge, Sydney Opera House, or best of all, St. George's Leagues Club.

So much for a national campaign.

Policy was the prerogative of the prime minister. Fraser may have discussed it at a meeting of the Co-ordination committee or in cabinet, to see what colleagues thought should be included, but the final decisions were the responsibility of the leader alone. There were often later costs that had to be paid when promises could not be responsibly kept. The 'fistful of dollars' promise of 1977 was very effective. Electors were invited to ring a number to find out how much they would gain in tax rebates; thousands did so. Yet when the tax surcharge nine months later ripped it back, the government lost much of its tax credibility: a very costly mistake.

Fraser was seen by his party colleagues as an impressive campaigner – at least before 1983. He had a good sense of timing and a feel for what the community would take. He provided leadership because he knew what he wanted. He could walk into a room and dominate. That was the impact politicians liked.

The media saw him as effective but dull. Paul Kelly claimed he had

great stamina, courage, dogged, no wit, slow, no repartee at all, hopeless when heckled, a hectoring sort of style, no inspiration. But if you got him with the right question, you'd get a story.

Max Walsh put a similar impression in a better light:

He wasn't warm, he didn't arouse any affection in anybody's breast and was definitely dull. But by the same token, the Liberals were good at identifying the issues and he just hammered these; when you are in government the only way you can really campaign is to create fear of the alternatives, and he did that effectively.

There was admiration for his determination, even if it was never coloured by charisma or panache. He won three times, twice by massive margins, and once by turning around in the last week an election that many thought had been lost.

Never popular, never rating highly in the opinion polls, he was still a successful campaigner: until 1983. Then everything went wrong. As the election slipped away, Fraser became more strident and abrasive. His comment, that if Labor won it would be safer to put the money under the bed, was effectively ridiculed by Hawke; yet in earlier years, Max Walsh believes, it might have been more acceptable or at least passed without so much attention. His hectoring interview with a bank association representative, leaning on the latter to accept Fraser's proposition about the threats of Labor's policy, was an unedifying example of prime ministerial bullying. Opportunities slipped away. Paul Keating said he couldn't guarantee the accord would work, but before any political capital could be made, Peacock agreed that no one could ever guarantee a policy would work. Fraser's colleagues called the campaign a disaster, believing that his political instinct had deserted him, perhaps because he was tired and ill. Almost alone, Fraser fought on, as his colleagues seemed to duck for cover to dissociate themselves from the approaching disaster. Fraser still defends his tactics:

the 'money under the bed' comment was not too rough because it's just a graphic way of saying in my view the policies of the opposition are going to damage the fortunes of Australia; nobody will know how right or wrong I was in that because they haven't applied their policies as they were stating them.

Most others disagreed. Perhaps the election could not have been won – either in March or in December – but Hawke's accession to the Labor leadership, the bushfires and the electoral mood all worked against Fraser. As the swing emerged, he got tetchier and angrier. At the last Press Club lunch, he snapped back at the press, attacking them for their bias and constant opposition. However, on election night he conceded gracefully.

Why did Fraser lose? Eggleton's analysis directly after the defeat drew on extensive polling. The electorate, he argued, was disillusioned; it did not care about the government's achievements but was concerned about the future. It was looking for hope, for a light at the end of the tunnel, but did not think the Fraser government would improve or change. By contrast it found Hawke and the prices and incomes accord attractive. The issues that could help the government were fears of union power and doubts about Labor's economic competence. Fraser was seen by swinging voters as a 'father figure', and safer than Hawke.

The strategy had followed the poll findings. The evidence demanded a negative campaign. Nothing in the detailed sampling justified anything but a strong focus on union power and Labor irresponsibility. It would have been 'grossly irresponsible if we had let our hearts rule our heads' and only talked about the positives, said Eggleton, because Hawke had captured the high ground of 'hope' – and the advertising had to be redone to meet the challenge of Labor's new leader. The campaign accidents exacerbated what seemed to be an uphill battle. The timing had been wrong; Fraser's style – for rugged and hard times – no longer reflected the mood of the electorate.

The public image of Fraser was determined by his performance as a salesman. That stiff and strident figure, austere and remote, was instantly recognisable. It was unusual for him to relax. Yet he was an effective salesman; he won three elections; he remained prime minister for over seven years. These are the criteria of success, but he was never popular, seldom received public approval, was not trusted, and he was finally defeated by a man whose public adulation he found distasteful.

Yet the public saw only part of the man; if they assumed that the Fraser in cabinet was as remote as the salesman, they were wrong. For acting as salesman was the arena in which Fraser was the least accomplished. He could not generate trust and approval; he did generate recognition for his strength and determination. Popularity was less important than victory, but finally that, too, was lost.

CHAPTER 7

AXING OR TAXING

THE ART OF BUDGETING

Formulating a budget resembles completing a jigsaw. Not only do all the individual pieces have to fit into the whole, but the final pattern ought to be both coherent and logical. Particular expenditure decisions have to be collected into a general economic strategy. Eventually the result will be expressed in a single figure: the size of the deficit or surplus, which has in recent times become almost the sole criterion on which a budget is evaluated.

Budgets are the documents in which governments express their priorities, however implicitly. Choices are made between programs, and between levels of expenditure and other economic objectives. Decisions are based on assessments of how the economy will behave. Forecasts of inflation, the growth of average weekly earnings and other indicators are derived from econometric models to provide estimates of the likely costs of government programs and the probable increases in revenue.

For the ministers making the budget, several points need to be borne in mind about these figures. Economic instruments have uncertain impacts. As a secretary of the Treasury commented:

There were those who believed in econometric forecasting; it was held to be the ultimate in precision. So far as I'm concerned, it was all a lot of bullshit. The plain fact is we tried to thrust in the right direction, the right direction being the direction your hunches led you to adopt.

So also with budget forecasts. They can be no more than best guesstimates. As officials constantly remind their political masters, estimates made in January or February for a financial year that is to end in July eighteen months away can only be rough indicators. After the end of the financial year in June, the estimates may be more accurate, but can still never be precise. They depend on a range of factors, whether local, national or international, beyond the control of government. These figures are invariably interlocking. One inaccuracy – in estimating the rate of inflation or the growth of average weekly earnings – is likely to have ever-broadening implications for others. Each indicator helps to create an environment for spending and taxing. Each variation leads to a need for reassessment and change. If all the indicators at the last minute go in the wrong direction, then the government may be faced with a need to alter many of the details.

In economic policy-making analysts are not always agreed on the best strategy. Budgeting is a wicked problem; determining the definition of the difficulties may be crucial to the choice of solutions. Therefore ministers and advisers contest the description of economic conditions as readily as the solutions; the one leads to the other. Budgeting and economic management require continuous attention and constant renegotiation in an ever-changing world where pressures and problems grow and decline.

Yet there is no normal or finally established way of drawing up a budget. Officials may be in a continual search for better or more 'rational' methods of budget formulation, and improvements may be made in the calculation of the figures or the presentation of choices. Good procedures may make relevant and accurate information available and give senior ministers the time and settled environment to consider them. But in the end one stark fact remains: hard choices have to be made by senior ministers. As there is no precise answer to the problem of how much should be spent on any one policy area, those final choices have to be matters of judgement and value. Since they are likely to have a wide impact, the leaders of governments cannot delegate them to their juniors. No procedures, however sophisticated, can replace the need for decision.

In the budgetary process prime ministers can influence both process and policy. First, they decide the processes of decision-making: how the budget is made and by whom. These choices will provide opportunities for some (including themselves) to become involved, while excluding others. The procedures will reflect the structure of power sought by the leader.

Second, prime ministers can determine the extent to which a full appreciation of the economic situation is developed and can be instrumental in deciding the precise strategy, including what target is considered desirable. They can accept the figures offered by one adviser, or insist that they be analysed and challenged. The appropriate interpretation of the economic context is not always obvious; it is likely to be contested by different, often equally persuasive, interpretations of the available data. This will lead to fights over the advisory turf as departments dispute which can and should be listened to. For instance, when the cabinet changed the Treasury's assessment of the predicted growth of average weekly earnings from 10 to 10.5 per cent in 1977, acting on advice from other officials, the secretary of the Treasury reacted hostilely. In a scathing letter to his minister, he claimed that ministers had arbitrarily amended the estimates and that the deficit they had calculated understated the real figure. He ended:

The only question was what can be saved from the wreckage. To put it another way: the question now is not whether a good budget can be brought down; that question has largely been decided in the negative, but of whether the budget position which now seems in prospect can be brought back from one of disaster.

PMC advisers retorted that as precision in forecasts was impossible, Treasury could have provided a range of possibilities. 'No such indication is given; nor are policy options discussed in a dispassionate way. The papers are directed, from start to finish, to advocacy of the policies which the authors want to see pursued'. PMC argued that 'it would be entirely appropriate for ministers to decide that the budget estimates should be based on a larger assumed increase in average weekly earnings' and it would be 'an entirely unsatisfactory position if ministers were obliged to accept, as gospel, estimates of prospective taxation yields under existing legislation, prepared by the same people whose responsibility it is to put advice on economic policy'.

The dispute was about the openness of the advisory process. Treasury reacted not only because the initial figure for growth in average weekly earnings was its 'best guess', but because as a matter of principle it preferred to control all assessment of the future of the economy. Later that year economic assessments became known as 'rubbery', a phrase used by treasurer Lynch, perhaps in self-defence.

This chapter is concerned with examining the degree to which the economic policy of the Fraser years could be labelled as Fraser's own. It will take four examples: the first budget in 1976, the mid-term budget in 1979 (the only budget that did not follow or precede an election), the well-known 'razor gang' of 1981 and the final controversial budget of 1982. The account can provide only part of the picture, for discussions of the economy between Fraser and his treasurers were frequent. The economy underlay all policies and Fraser always consulted outside the cabinet system. There is no record of those discussions. Yet even a partial account will illustrate the extent to which Fraser determined outcomes by showing how he established the procedures to allow his colleagues to develop an appreciation of economic conditions; how he used parts of cabinet and ad hoc budget committees as the forums for discussion; how he limited the circulation of papers, constantly sought alternative opinions and directed analyses and submissions; and how he ensured that the treasurer did not maintain the monopoly on economic decision-making that had existed in earlier regimes. Budgeting is about detail; so is the process of control. Tedious though it may appear, to understand the politics of budgeting it is necessary to show how, day by day, meeting by meeting, Fraser influenced the results. Behind every meeting, in every submission, can be seen either his influence or the desire of others to influence him.

1976: The beginning

The Liberal electoral victory presented the government with an immediate challenge. Fraser had campaigned on the basis that the Liberals would provide more careful and responsible economic management than Whitlam and more electors had voted on the perceptions of economic competence than any other issue. Inflation was high, the growth in public expenditure had been rapid, unemployment had increased. The Hayden Labor budget of 1975 had tackled all these problems and had substantially reduced the rate of the growth of spending, but it had failed to erase from public memory earlier images of the Labor government. What Hayden had started as a matter of regrettable necessity, Fraser enthusiastically adopted as the central and desirable plank of his economic policy.

Fraser espoused an 'inflation first' strategy. He recalls:

It wasn't a question of putting inflation before unemployment which is always the cry and might have arisen sometimes as our way of putting it. But we were really saying: 'You are not going to cure unemployment by spending more money'.

Reining in the deficit was seen as the way of making room for growth and expansion in the private sector. At the same time the government had to develop policies in other sections of the economic jigsaw. Fraser had promised in the election to maintain wage indexation, introduce full tax indexation to 'keep governments honest' and maintain Medibank. Budgeting could not be divorced from these policies. The strategy was set, but the details still had to be determined. Cutting government spending is easy in global terms, but nearly every cut offends a client group and may have electoral implications. Governments need to maintain a balance: stopping spending suddenly might push the economy into recession.

Fraser also had to decide how the policy would be made. His treasurer was Philip Lynch, a good deputy but not an independent economic thinker. The Treasury, under the dual leadership of Sir Frederick Wheeler and John Stone, wanted to assert the economic primacy lost in 1974 and partly regained under Hayden. What influence the prime minister would play was yet to be determined.

So the new government had to decide how to make spending cuts, what to support in terms of tax and wage indexation, how to maintain its image of economic responsibility; all at the same time as contesting internal battles about the administrative processes of budgeting. Fraser was faced with the need constantly to balance the broad and the narrow, the economic and the industrial, the ideological and the electoral.

Fraser restated the basic principles of economic strategy in his first public speech after the 10 December elections. Addressing the Young Liberals on 5 January 1976, he argued that Australia had to escape from the handout mentality. His first priority was to get the deficit down by drastic reduction in spending. Reforms should be directed to helping individuals make their own choices; governments could not solve problems simply by spending money. Controlling expenditure and pulling in the deficit were to be the central objectives of government policy.

Behind the scenes the fight for bureaucratic control of the budget had already begun. The issue was whether the treasurer (and by extension the Treasury) was to regain almost exclusive influence over economic decisions. If they did, and the distribution of information could be restricted, then the capacity of the prime minister to influence the details would be diminished. On 16 December the Treasury circulated two draft papers, one on Immediate Measures and one on Machinery for Expenditure Restraint: Cabinet and Administrative Arrangements. They proposed that no new spending commitments be made without Treasury approval and suggested cabinet machinery which would strengthen the Treasury's position. PMC was concerned; the plan to give authority to the treasurer would cut across many of the prime minister's prerogatives. It asserted the prime minister's right to be consulted on all substantial items if they were not to be taken to cabinet, and told the Treasury that Fraser had not yet finalised the arrangements for cabinet, although he had indicated that the Economic committee would bear the responsibility for expenditure cuts. The proposals from the Treasury were reluctantly amended after a meeting of Fraser and Lynch. The incident illustrated that from the start Fraser was not prepared to leave the direction of economic management to his treasurer.

Fraser also took the initiative in indicating general directions. On 22 December he announced the appointment of the Administrative Review committee, headed by Sir Henry Bland, to find savings in the federal administration. On 23 December Fraser wrote to all ministers, emphasising that central to the economic and social strategy of government was its determination to rein in the growth of public spending. The government had to cut programs as well as administrative costs. Ministers were required to provide a list of potential savings by 16 January and to review all their programs, list them in order of priority and decide which could be terminated, by 23 January. In a second letter Fraser demanded cuts in administrative and overtime costs. Staff ceilings, based at Fraser's suggestion on total (that is, including those on leave) rather than operative staff, were also promulgated. Lynch then filled out the details, calling for the first year of forward estimates and submissions for any projects promised in the election to be prepared by 14 February. He reminded ministers that, because parliament had appropriated money for a program, it did not need to be spent. By the end of December Fraser was able to announce $6 million savings from freezes in public service recruitment and travel.

Fraser kept up the pressure on both ministers and officials. He said he wanted the Treasury's report on forward estimates completed by 19 February, a mere five days after they were due to be lodged by departments. One of his officials thought it was a timetable Treasury had no hope of meeting, but left it to the treasurer to tell the prime minister. On 12 January PMC prepared a draft letter to all ministers, urging them to 'do all possible' to meet the 16 January deadline for their examination of departmental proposals. Fraser changed the letter, telling his colleagues to 'make sure the deadline is met'. All ministers had replied by 20 January and their proposals were circulated only to members of the Economic committee.

This committee, meeting under Fraser's chairmanship, had reports categorised as 'easy savings', those regarded as 'hard', those the ministers canvassed but did not favour and 'others'. On 22 January the committee decided to put into effect all the cuts that ministers thought could be implemented without difficulty, for savings of $103 million; it required officials to re-examine other savings that ministers had not supported. The Economic committee also made forty specific program decisions the same day; many of these were based on comments made by the prime minister. It thought savings for that year of $384 million were possible. Discussions ranged from large to small items. It also reviewed new revenue measures; it decided for instance that in principle only first degrees should be free, although Treasury estimated that full fees would bring in $45 million from universities. (This action was deferred on 5 March.) Fraser also discussed the National Gallery's overseas purchases with its chairman, and arranged to stagger payments for a Modigliani statue over two years.

The budget was only one part of the economic strategy. Wages policy was also important in the reduction of inflation. On 21 January cabinet had to consider what submission it would make to the Arbitration Commission which was hearing the national wage case, as Fraser had stated Liberal support for the principles of wage indexation during the campaign. The minister for industrial relations argued that his submission aimed to achieve a rate of growth that was economically consistent with the government's policy, industrially practical and helpful for the development of a rational system of wage fixation. He wanted the decision about passing on the rise in the CPI to wage earners considered separately from a productivity case and a full review of the system. Treasury wanted them all considered together, with a wage increase more limited than the CPI; PMC supported Treasury but was wary of too tough a line. On 22 January cabinet accepted Street's recommendation to support the full application of the CPI and to separate that step from a full review of the system. The decision was seen publicly as a defeat for Fraser. A week later, when the CPI quarterly increase of 5.6 per cent was announced, cabinet changed its mind. Fraser had already directed that the decision supporting full indexation be reconsidered by a committee of officials and then brought back to cabinet. The committee now recommended that the commonwealth submission emphasise the link between wages and inflation and urge the commission to use its own judgement in determining rises, rather than just follow indexation guidelines. If the government wanted to advocate a figure, the officials thought 5 per cent (a round, if not scientific, figure) would be an appropriate upper limit. On 30 January cabinet noted the rise in the CPI with concern and that the wage indexation guidelines did not stipulate automatic adjustments. While committed to the principles of wage indexation, cabinet agreed that its overriding duty was to reduce unemployment. It decided to support only half the increase in the CPI and argued that indexed figures should not include price rises caused by increases in indirect taxation. It stated that any rises should be tied to a review of the Prices Justification Tribunal – a body which Fraser had promised to abolish in the election, but which now became a bargaining counter in the negotiations with unions. Fraser's initiative had clawed cabinet back, but at some cost to the credibility of the electoral promises. The decision still did not satisfy the employers. According to employers' spokesman George Polites, any decision to support the concept of indexation – whether of wages or tax scales – was wrong.

The battle for savings continued. On 3 February the Economic committee made cuts to twenty-seven programs and Fraser was able to announce that the government had reduced spending by $300 million during the current financial year, although acknowledging that he would have liked the figure to be larger. He still hoped to begin the introduction of tax indexation in 1976. On 5 February Fraser and Lynch reviewed all potential expenditure cuts. Lynch informed cabinet on 9 February that the estimated deficit stood at $4700 million and that $365 million had been saved to date. On 5 March Lynch reported that they had achieved three-quarters of the $10 million savings sought on overtime; Fraser agreed it was adequate. He was also prepared to accept the need to be flexible. As he said publicly:

Dogmatism must inevitably lead to bad government. Measures that seem appropriate at one stage can – sometimes indeed must – be superseded by new knowledge, new events. The crucial thing is not to lose sight of the fundamental objectives. Flexibility in pursuit of the nation's interests must never be allowed to degenerate into expediency.

He emphasised time and again that the first concern was to bring inflation under control. He was consciously preparing the country for bad news and a tough budget.

Several observers already thought the government's actions had been severe, perhaps too severe. Fraser recalls the secretary of the Treasury telling him and Lynch in mid-January that, as cuts would apply to less than half the financial year, they had already done enough and did not want to push the economy into recession; a similar warning had been given to the Labor treasurer. The Treasury do not recall the meeting. The Reserve Bank was for a time concerned that the rapid reduction of government expenditure could lead to problems. PMC advised on 3 February that there were dangers in going too fast in cutting expenditure. In March backbenchers in the Tactics committee expressed concern that the government was making too much of the need to reduce expenditure. The *Sydney Morning Herald* speculated that the budget would have to be 'even tougher than the government expected'. There was never total support for cuts.

Yet even at this stage some chinks in the armour had occurred. When the *Sydney Morning Herald* ran a story that the government would reintroduce television licences, the phones at the Liberal secretariat ran hot with complaints. Eggleton sent a note into cabinet telling Fraser of the reactions and the cabinet backed off. An initial decision to reintroduce tertiary education fees for second degrees was rescinded, in part in the face of the strong opposition of the minister. Maternity allowances were abolished on 2 February, but the minister for social security, Margaret Guilfoyle, persuaded the committee to rescind the decision so that the allowance could be considered by an Income Security Review committee. When Liberal senators crossed the floor to defeat the abolition of funeral benefits for pensioners – a small allowance that was expensive to administer – the cabinet reversed its decision rather than confront its backbenchers. Anthony argues that this Senate opposition was the main factor that prevented the government taking tough measures. Well-timed pressure could be effective even at the time of strongest intent.

In February the Economic committee asked Treasury for a submission on the state of the economy by 12 March. On 14 March Lynch discussed with Fraser the budget outlook drawn from the forward estimates and then told cabinet the deficit appeared likely to be $4844 million. He argued that there was a need to reduce expenditure by $2000 million. If more could be found, then the government would be better placed to introduce tax indexation, which ought to be linked with expenditure cuts. Lynch recommended that only after cuts were made could the scope for tax indexation be determined.

When the officials' report on the forward estimates was prepared, Fraser circulated the paper only to the four parliamentary leaders: himself, Lynch, Anthony and Sinclair. He discussed the options with Lynch on 21 April. On 29 April he included the National party leaders. On 3 May the paper was given to the Economic committee. On 7 May the general strategy – that the government could not spend its way out of an inflation-induced recession and there was a need to reduce the deficit as a proportion of Gross Domestic Product – was endorsed first by cabinet and then by the ministry. The circle of commitment was gradually expanded. The forward estimates showed, with tax unchanged, a deficit of $4800 million. From 7 to 9 May discussions were held with ministers, portfolio by portfolio. Fraser took a close interest, particularly in departments like Environment, Housing and Community Development, which implemented many of the initiatives of the Whitlam government. In March he had told the minister, Ivor Greenwood, that the forward estimates were far too high; now he encouraged him to push many of the programs back into general purpose grants to the states and local government.

Even while expenditure cuts were being considered, other reforms were contemplated by Fraser and by a group of backbenchers and members of the private office. On 27 April

Fraser wrote to ministers, pointing out that, although the first priority was to bring inflation under control, the government must also 'press through measures and programs of reform outside the economic area' which would be consistent with 'our political traditions of progressive and enlightened reforms'. He asked individual ministers to bring forward proposals and even made suggestions as to what they might be. Guilfoyle, for instance, was asked to consider the establishment of a social welfare consultative group, to identify welfare needs and to explore guaranteed minimum income proposals. Fraser did not want his government to be seen in an entirely negative light.

The introduction of family allowances (in place of child rebates) was one outcome. Ian Castles, a deputy secretary of PMC, had just completed an income security review. He proposed the abolition of tax rebates for children (of greatest value to the highest income earners and no use at all to those without incomes) and the introduction of a family allowance that was not means-tested. It would be paid to the mother and provided greater scope for savings. But even though the scheme was initially revenue-neutral – that is, the costs of the new program were the same as the savings achieved from the abolition of the old one – it was thought difficult to sell because it shifted expenditure from the revenue side (by the removal of tax concessions) to the outlay side. Once Fraser was persuaded of its merits, he became a strong advocate of the new scheme, but at first he only circulated the proposal to the parliamentary leaders.

Throughout the second week of May PMC and Treasury disputed what might be a viable outcome of the expenditure cutting and whether there was scope for the introduction of tax indexation. Treasury wanted a deficit of $2500–$3000 million; if all savings were made the deficit would be $2370. Full tax indexation would cost a further $1220 million. Treasury thought the government could introduce indexation of tax scales from 1 July and it might also index the tax rebates for dependants. But, it argued, the government should go no further – that is, it should not index the basic rebate of $540 introduced by the Hayden budget as a replacement for the series of deductions that taxpayers had previously had to claim. PMC thought

Treasury was too pessimistic, and recommended a bold measure: full indexation of scales, dependant rebates and basic rebates; there should be no differentiation between parts of a tax system. If the government accepted wage indexation, it should also accept tax indexation. The Treasury then recalculated its figures, not, it ingenuously stated, to question the clear intention of ministers that the risks should be taken, but to ensure that the decisions were taken with eyes fully open. It became a battle between highly divergent views, a battle to win the support of the prime minister.

Treasury did not shift from its basic view that a deficit of $3000 million was too high to keep any downward pressure on inflation or to reduce the government sector. It still advocated further cuts and a differentiation in tax rebates; full indexation would lead to a deficit of $3500 million. PMC emphasised that the forward estimates were only rough guides and liable to be inaccurate. They could be up to $1000 million out in either direction and were far too imprecise to justify stopping short of full indexation. PMC argued against the announcement of a precise budget deficit in the May statement; it preferred a comment that the deficit would be somewhere around $3000 million. The Reserve Bank also emphasised the need for an inflation-first strategy, with a preference for a deficit of about $2 billion. An ad hoc committee of cabinet postponed a decision.

At the end of a hectic week of briefings and decisions, some decisions – on family allowances – were taken but several crucial tax issues were left undecided: what should be indexed and how (including whether indexation should include or exclude the impact of indirect tax), and when the package should be introduced. PMC and Treasury summarised in charts the impact of the four main measures: indexation, abolition of child rebates, family allowances and the changes to the Medibank levy. The paper illustrated how the new schemes would produce winners and losers; those who would lose most were single taxpayers without dependants.

Over the weekend Treasury tried again to change Fraser's mind. (Cabinet decisions can only be recommitted for further consideration if the prime minister agrees.) On Friday 14 May,

Lynch wrote a personal letter to Fraser at Nareen, although the style of writing and argument was that of senior Treasury officers. Lynch commented that he was deeply troubled and wanted to make a final appeal. He claimed that in opposition they had emphasised three points: expenditure was too high and governments should get out of people's pockets; the deficit pumped liquidity into the economy; tax indexation was needed to choke off the inflationary growth of revenue. Yet, he claimed, the May statement could not be reconciled with any of those elements and would put the government's credibility at risk. The government had done well in its search for savings, but now proposed to add $725 million of new expenditure. The deficit would still be $3000 million. There were dangers of 'locking in' expenditure if the general rebate were indexed as well as the basic rates. The trade-off between family allowance and tax indexation was too complex to sell. Lynch argued that he did not oppose family allowances, but was not in favour of their introduction at this moment. He thought the package could maintain the government's reputation without the allowance which could be introduced later in October. He knew Fraser considered the family allowances question as settled but suggested it be reopened. It wasn't. Fraser did not appreciate the lecture; he was angry at the attempt to reopen the cabinet's decision.

Early in the next week cabinet finally made the crucial decisions on tax indexation. They reflected Fraser's victory over the Treasury. Ministers had to decide whether a bold package of changes was worth the risks. The ad hoc committee decided on full indexation of all tax rates. The level of indexation was to be based on the CPI for the twelve months ending in March although it decided to exclude the impact of indirect taxation on CPI. The decision was circulated only to Lynch and Guilfoyle, two members of the committee, before it was announced.

On 17 May Fraser gave an address to the nation; he emphasised the need for the government to live within its means, but said that the choice did not exclude the capacity to introduce reforms. He foreshadowed more substantial tax indexation measures than any observers had predicted, and support for families through a new system of family allowances.

Cabinet agreed that the treasurer's speech should explain the government's philosophy in relation to Medibank, family allowances and tax indexation and emphasise that the government's main objective was a reduction in the inflation caused by governmental overspending and unreasonable wage pressures. On 18 May the ministry was briefed on the contents of the treasurer's statement; ministers were required to prepare individual statements, emphasising the size of the cuts in their portfolios and the fact that the disadvantaged and needy had been protected. Ministers were not to indicate publicly that any items would be reconsidered. The text of each statement had to be cleared with the prime minister and treasurer. On 20 May the treasurer announced the cost-cutting results, as well as the reforms. He stated that $2600 million had been cut from spending, particularly in areas of urban and regional development and health. Although Lynch was reluctant to name a projected figure for the 1976–77 deficit, an estimate of around $2500 million to $3000 million was calculated by observers.

How did observers react? Generally with some admiration. The *Sydney Morning Herald* declared: 'Mr Fraser has displayed the mettle so many expected of him on December 13 . . . A deficit of this level is as low as could reasonably be hoped for'; while Peter Bowers referred to the 'savagery of the cuts'. The *Age* declared it was a 'remarkably enlightened and intelligent plan from a supposedly conservative government confronted with big economic problems'; it welcomed the reforms with some surprise. Family allowances were seen as 'one of the most important advances in social welfare since federation, giving direct and substantial aid to the poorest families in the community'.

The first round had been completed, but there was no relaxing of the pressure. In June Fraser and his colleagues met the National Employers Policy committee and their joint communiqué re-emphasised the need to fight inflation; it was seen as another indication that the August budget would be a 'horror'. Indeed this expectation began to worry the business groups. In the pre-budget discussions with ministers, both the Chamber of Commerce and the National Employers Policy committee warned against too much emphasis on cutting as it might lead to a lower level of economic activity and add to private sector costs. That line was often repeated by delegations which agreed with the need to cut, as long as it did not disadvantage the group concerned. Even the Victorian Liberal government took the unusual step of lodging a budget submission, arguing the need for selectivity in cutbacks; it led to a retort from Fraser that the Victorians accepted the government's objectives but were not prepared to make any contribution from their programs to achieving those objectives.

In early July Fraser demanded from PMC a summary of problems and indications of financial commitments. On 7 July, the ad hoc budget committee met to review the Treasury overview, which stated that the deficit might be as high as $3010 million; it decided to reopen 'agreed bids', that is, levels of program spending agreed between the Treasury and the spending department. (Only two bids were reduced.) The committee emphasised the need to maintain a strict line and for cost increases to be absorbed by departments. PMC agreed in substance with Treasury's proposals, but believed that after the May cuts there was a need to keep the recovery going; PMC thought Treasury underestimated the growth in average weekly earnings and questioned whether unemployment would indeed decline. Treasury preferred to contain inflation, halt increases in spending and encourage the private sector, and it claimed the ideal budget deficit was $2500 million, but would accept $2622 million. When the full cabinet met, it accepted the treasurer's proposal that no new policy initiatives be introduced without prior consultation with the prime minister and the treasurer. There were only nineteen disagreed bids, with only three of them for programs that cost more than $1 million. The Treasury's view was accepted on all but three of them. Cabinet agreed to avoid adding to estimates and to get the deficit as close as possible to $2500 million.

There were still some lengthy fights. Treasury had earlier opposed the introduction of a new scheme of stock valuation adjustment. Fraser then became thoroughly briefed on the issue and brought to the discussion several outside experts such as Professor Russell Mathews, to argue the case for change. His view prevailed. Staff ceilings were reviewed for the third time in eight months. Up to July the cuts had been 1.3 per cent. Fraser asked for options to bring the total to 3 per cent. The ad hoc committee asked whether it could reduce ceilings without affecting services and eventually agreed on a further 2 per cent cut, details of which were finally sent to Fraser on 8 August.

Gradually the pre-budget message was changed. From being a tough budget, it was presented as a means of restoring confidence, boosting business and continuing reform. Cabinet gave careful consideration to marketing the budget to the public. First, it would explain its philosophy to justify the government's strategy: beating inflation, no increase in indirect tax and family reforms. Then ministers would need to ward off opposition accusations about ignoring unemployment. In the budget speech Lynch announced an estimated deficit of $2608 million, with outlays rising by 11 per cent.

The budget was seen as consistent with fighting inflation. The *Financial Review* claimed unequivocally:

Let it be said first and without qualification that the budget is what we were led to expect from the election campaign and everything that has been said by the government in the intervening period has prepared the community for it. There is no misrepresentation here. It is the type of budget the Australian people voted in favour of nine months ago. It represents a commitment by the Liberal government to the values espoused by Mr Fraser.

Brian Toohey agreed that the government had 'largely kept faith with its electoral promises to restore the private sector to centre stage'. In the *Age* Ken Davidson agreed that the government 'had done nothing more and nothing less than it promised last election'. The government was criticised for its creative accounting, juggling some figures back into the previous year's deficit, and for its more grandiose statements about the creation of business confidence. However no contemporary observer commented that the budget represented a lost opportunity, that the government could have – or should have – cut harder.

Backbenchers have similar recollections. Neil Brown recalls:

No-one stood up and said: now is the time to take those difficult decisions; but I can remember twenty of them standing up and saying: don't touch the pensioners' funeral benefits.

Liberal critics have argued that Fraser should have cut harder and that he missed a great opportunity to rein in expenditure in 1976. The opposition criticised its harshness, but some of its spokespersons were prepared to concede in retrospect that Fraser had no alternative; indeed from a technical economic view he might have been tougher, but it would have been politically suicidal. The perception at the time was that the government was hard enough.

The 1976 budget raised doubts about the effectiveness of the advisory process. Fraser liked to ensure that he was never the captive of one line of advice. He insisted on the availability of several sources of economic expertise and wanted all information shared – at least with him. But he had great difficulty achieving it. On 12 June 1976 Fraser wrote to the treasurer, asking for notes on the economy prepared by the Reserve Bank to be forwarded to him on a regular basis. He believed too that as prime minister it was appropriate that he receive the substance and the detail of the Treasury's economic forecasts. He reminded Lynch that in February the Economic committee had asked for regular reports on the economy and that the Treasury should now give effect to that decision. He annotated the formal letter: 'It is essential that this information and the Bank reports be available to my department'. Yet it was easier to ask than succeed. A month later PMC complained that it still had problems in obtaining the information from Treasury necessary to brief Fraser. So on 5 July he sent the same request again; the Treasury agreed to provide only 'a more succinct and up-to-date document' but none of the assumptions on which its calculations were based. His permanent head talked to the secretary of Treasury, but without result. On 12 July Fraser demanded the required information by the next day; he argued to Lynch:

it is not possible to have a situation in which any department of state is prepared to deny the prime minister or his department information that is necessary for advice to the prime minister. I know the position the Treasury is adopting is not a new position. It has, as I understand it, been traditional but it is not one that I believe you and I can accept in the interests of good government.

Even so Fraser did not get what he wanted. In August he reminded Lynch again of the need for cabinet to receive quarterly forecasts. On 2 September Lynch promised to provide regular reports but not the details of the econometric forecasts. Fraser welcomed the commitment, but nothing happened. In September Fraser complained about the standard of economic advice from PMC.

The long fight with Treasury over the family allowances, stock adjustment valuation and information took its toll. Fraser became concerned that he was not as well informed as he should be on economic developments. In October he discovered there had been considerable decline in Australian financial reserves without Lynch or himself being informed. He wrote to Lynch:

I regard that omission as most serious. You and I both agree that a full and free flow of information is absolutely critical if we are to make appropriate decisions. I find the omission incomprehensible because I cannot believe that the secretary of the Treasury and the governor were not aware of the figure.

This long series of fights to ensure that information flowed at least to the prime minister provided the background to the changes in the economic advisory machinery that started with the splitting of the Treasury. If Fraser was to play an active role in economic policy he needed alternative sources of advice. If Treasury obstructed, other channels would be created. The Treasury was split into two departments.

Yet he still did not get all he wanted. After the devaluation of the dollar in November, a group of officials, including the secretary of PMC, was established to 'manage' the float of the dollar after devaluation; Fraser once again asked Lynch why his permanent head was not provided with all the relevant information or decisions. A year later, on 18 October, he wrote to the treasurer:

I refer to the Reserve Bank document containing forecasts of the economy which appeared in the *National Times* while you were overseas.

Whilst I deplore the release of this document, the regular availability of the data and forecasts contained therein would be most useful. I am surprised to find that the Bank has been preparing, and circulating to its officers in Sydney and elsewhere, a report which provides the information which I unsuccessfully sought last year . . .

I do not regard it as satisfactory that I am denied, and my department is denied, access to such reports at the same time as they are widely circulated within the Bank and find their way into the Press in a context which is highly embarrassing to this Government.

I would be grateful if you would arrange for copies of the report on economic conditions and prospects which is circulated each month within the Reserve Bank to be supplied to me and my department.

In addition, I refer to the Reserve Bank's response to my recent request for its forecasts made early in 1977. What I particularly wanted was a full table corresponding to that on page 52 of the *National Times* and I should be pleased if this were sent to me.

A month later he was arguing that he had not yet received it.

However it should not be presumed that the Treasury was uninterested in what the prime minister thought. According to a former Treasury official,

The Treasury, as they did for most of the time I've been associated with them, tended to operate on the basis of influencing the prime minister if the treasurer is not a strong person in his own right.

Rather it was a matter of how information could be used to influence him. Fraser was not an easy man to control; but nor was he able to make a demand on the Treasury that was instantly obeyed. It illustrated the limitations of even a powerful prime minister, and the importance of process and of the control of information on the policies that are then adopted.

The 1976 budget demonstrated the weapons that Fraser used. Information was – as far as he could manage – to be shared at least with him. The Treasury was not to be the only economic adviser, with all the influence that such a monopoly provided. Fraser, however, kept the information limited to a small group who, because of position or portfolio, needed to know. He developed initiatives and drove them through several channels. He locked ever-expanding groups into acceptance of the basic directions. Procedures and information gave him the foundations on which to develop an economic policy; his attention to detail built on those foundations; his determination and drive took ministers with him. Yet even in 1976 his caution and his concern for electoral impacts were obvious.

The 1976 budget provided the model for future years; although the procedures were adapted constantly, the prime minister's close involvement was never to be reduced. Every budget was designed to allow the control he established in 1976 to be maintained.

1979: Routine

1979 was to be a year of consolidation, but also an opportunity to regain some lost reputation. In the 1977 election Fraser had promised electors a 'fistful of dollars' through tax cuts. In 1978 the government had introduced a tax surcharge of 1.5 per cent that collected only a small sum but undermined the credibility of the government as a party of lower taxes. Indexation had been half suspended too.

So the next budget, to be brought down without any election in sight, provided the government with a particular challenge: how could it continue to rein in the deficit and reduce government spending, while giving back to the voters the tax cuts that had been so suddenly clawed back? It was the classic choice between reducing the deficit by 'taxing or by axing', to use Senator Withers' colourful expression.

In 1979, as in previous years, Fraser first considered the procedures for making decisions. Ministers had spent many hours before the 1978 budget arguing over trivial amounts, rather than trying to fit programs into a broader perspective. Even if there can be no budgetary process that will satisfy everyone – for there are always inners and outers, winners and losers, in any allocation of resources – ministers were concerned to improve the process.

In November 1978, in conjunction with their review of the cabinet process, the secretary of PMC, Geoff Yeend, and his deputy, Mike Codd, completed a report on the forward estimates and the operations of budget cabinet. It was based on discussions with ministers who felt inadequately briefed on the overall economic forecast; they wanted greater knowledge of the economic parameters and more guidance on the likely spending limits in particular areas of activity. They spent too much time examining relatively small projects, rather than broader fundamental issues or priorities, and wanted new policy proposals and revenue options considered earlier. Some even saw merit in separating the expenditure budget and the revenue budget. Treasury and Finance, more sceptical perhaps, pointed out that senior ministers had sometimes chosen not to provide detailed briefings to their colleagues and that ministers had seldom made trade-offs between new and ongoing programs because they only focused on priorities 'in a crunch situation' where final decisions were needed. They opposed a split between the expenditure and revenue budgets because it would remove the discipline of equating increased expenditure with increased revenue.

On 12 December Fraser complained to cabinet that too many submissions were coming forward for cabinet to handle. He thought something more drastic than the Yeend report might be needed. On 14 December cabinet agreed that there was a need for briefings on the broad questions of economic policy, that new policy proposals should be forwarded by the end of February instead of early June, and that proposals for expenditure outside the forward estimate or budget context should be avoided; it also commissioned a paper on the budget outlook for cabinet in March.

On 19 January PMC circulated a paper on broad spending and revenue options requested by the prime minister, only to Fraser, Howard and Robinson. Set in the general context of a budget deficit of $4000 million if all programs were ongoing and based on work done in Finance and Treasury, it argued that for cuts to be found, programs would have to be abolished or curtailed. The list included reintroducing tertiary fees, modifying family allowances, selling government assets such as Qantas or Telecom, introducing a broad-based retail tax or a sales tax on wine. It argued that it was better to have some measures in place by 1 July, to gain twelve months' benefit. Fraser went through the proposed spending cuts, ticking some with approval, but complained that the paper was a collection of routine proposals rather than evidence of wide or deep perceptions.

On 27 February the report on the forward estimates, dealing only with ongoing programs, was completed. Ministers had been instructed by cabinet to take a personal interest and keep the estimates down; only half the estimates were endorsed by ministers. On 2 March Fraser discussed interest rates, the growth of monetary aggregates, budget deficits and options with five senior officers from PMC and with three from his own office. Arising from the meeting, Fraser asked for papers on interest rates, on a series of options on the coal and oil levies, company and personal tax, asset sales and limits on the depreciation on cars. He wanted further papers on revenue options. While the papers were to be prepared jointly with Treasury and Finance, he wanted a separate PMC note as well.

The same day Fraser met Howard and Robinson to settle the arrangements for the budget process. They decided the forward estimates were to be brought to cabinet on 13 March, with a covering paper pointing to areas of spending for review. An ad hoc budget committee, consisting of Lynch, Carrick, Nixon, Howard, Robinson and Viner, was to go through the reviews of expenditure commissioned by cabinet, and new policy proposals. Fraser, Howard and Robinson were to receive lists of the new proposals.

On 8 March, Michael Keating, the head of PMC's economic division, provided Fraser with his requested paper on budget options, emphasising that the figures were only approximate. On 9 March the treasurer's submission on the budgetary outlook estimated that the 1978–79 deficit had grown from $2812 million to $3240 million and the 1979–80 deficit was likely to be $4422 million. These figures represented an 11.5 per cent increase, and a 4 per cent rise in real terms; they included no new policy. The submission emphasised that permanent, rather than temporary measures were needed. The government could reduce outlays or increase tax, and probably could not fulfil the intention of reintroducing full tax indexation. Howard asked cabinet for broad areas where spending could be reviewed, and proposed, as arranged with Fraser, that the commissioned papers go first to the ad hoc committee. PMC proposed that the government hold outlays to a 9 per cent increase, requiring savings of $770 million. If it was to be held to 8 per cent growth, $1000 million in cuts would need to be found.

Cabinet delegated to the ad hoc committee the choice of areas in the forward estimates paper to be reviewed and asked it to scrutinise new policies too. It agreed that there would be no further reviews of defence, but identified particular areas such as payments to the states (where Fraser wanted a $400 million reduction), health insurance, and the sale of assets for careful consideration. The decision was only circulated to members of the committee, which annoyed the minister for health who wanted to know why he couldn't receive a copy of the full decision instead of the extract that related to his portfolio.

On 14 March Fraser explained to his department that he wanted a set of options to reduce expenditure by $1000 million. He also required regular briefs on the actions of the ad hoc committee. That meant more than being sent submissions, notes and decisions. He wanted to be consulted before each meeting and be given an account of its decisions afterwards; but he chose to meet Lynch, rather than the whole committee, to discuss how it would work. On 19 March the committee decided to go through the section of the forward estimates report which contained possible savings. On 20 March the full ministry decided that the object of the reviews was to limit growth in total expenditure to under 8 per cent and, desirably, close to 7 per cent. It was a figure, an official looking back on the process commented, that was pulled out of the air.

On 21 March another paper from PMC, prepared without consultation with other departments, analysed a range of proposals, including the introduction of provisional taxes, increases in income tax rates (in preference to deferral of indexation), the introduction of tertiary fees and cuts to expenditure. But the paper emphasised that some of these cuts would not even be supported by PMC. Fraser was also given three papers on the tax sharing arrangements with the states.

On 30 March Fraser met with Lynch, Howard and Robinson to decide how the committee would deal with each minister in turn. It was decided to meet in mid-April for its initial reviews, then on 4, 11, 14–18 May, 4–8 June and 28–29 June. In these discussions Fraser made it clear that the committee should take final decisions. Appeals to cabinet should be resisted. The whole purpose was to free cabinet from the need to debate expenditure programs in detail. New submissions were only to be circulated to the committee. In all these early preparations for the budget Fraser played a pivotal role, deciding who would meet, what analyses would be completed, what timetable would be met, and influencing the targets that were set.

PMC kept the prime minister in touch with the latest figuring. On 18 April PMC's Michael Keating summarised the progress, commenting that it might be possible to hold the increase in outlays to 8–9 per cent, with a possible deficit of $2357–2884 million after cuts. PMC also stressed the need for final decisions to be made on important items, particularly income tax, by 8 May, when Fraser was due to leave for Manila. It argued that $2000 million was a tight deficit, $2500 million was pretty tight, but not too bad for confidence, while anything higher than $2800 million would be seen politically as a failure of government policy.

In the first week of May Fraser decided that revenue decisions would be taken by the Co-ordination committee, with Howard and Robinson co-opted. In 1979 Co-ordination committee was at the centre of all the crucial decisions, particularly on tax. Expenditure decisions, effectively authorising the recommendations of the ad hoc committee, were to be made by full cabinet. The chief dilemma was the one that was always faced by the Fraser government: it espoused the economic goal of reducing the deficit and the political goal of reducing the tax burden. The two constantly jostled for precedence.

The crucial revenue decisions concerned income tax rates. The cabinet had five options: to increase the standard rate, to increase the tax payable by a fixed percentage (as in the surcharge), to suspend tax indexation for a year (sliding it), to pay indexation as a lump sum at the end of the year, or to suspend indexation adjustment to PAYE instalments. PMC did not favour indexation slide, and feared that the budget committee would not achieve its cuts; Carrick and Sinclair had already shown that they would be fighting hard against cuts. PMC advised Fraser not only on which of the 'bad news' options it preferred, but was concerned that he not 'be open to attacks on the grounds of sleight-of-hand, broken promises'. It argued that it would be better to bite the bullet; if commitments had to be broken, better to adjust the standard rate. Treasury argued that the government could continue the tax surcharge, suspend indexation for twelve months (although legislation would be required), or slide indexation. Co-ordination committee began its review of the revenue choices on 1 May and continued on 3 May. Cabinet had to maintain the severity of the proposed cuts and then determine the increase in personal tax. The size of the deficit would depend on how much was collected.

Co-ordination committee agreed to put off any decision; it would wait until 18 May for the final report of the ad hoc committee. To leave its option open, it instructed the commissioner of taxation to prepare legislation for a 1.5 per cent increase in the standard rate and for the sliding of indexation. On 15 May it began again, reconsidering the progress made by the ad hoc committee; it asked for a listing of decisions taken, portfolio by portfolio, with notes on how they should be implemented, and on which suggestions ran directly counter to explicit electoral commitments. The committee was reminded that some of the budget figures might be too optimistic; PMC now argued that there was a need to increase the standard rate from 32c to 34c. On 15 May PMC still supported a deficit of $2500 million, but the private office thought $2500 million too high in relation to expectations. The crude oil levy might raise $68 million. As an adviser had written some months earlier, even given the unsophisticated views about budget deficits, it did not seem credible that a deficit of $2900 million rather than $2800 million would be seen as a mistake; yet perceptions were an important constraint, and it took time to reduce the attention given to arithmetic measures like the deficit which had little meaning. By this stage the press was speculating that the surcharge would be maintained and tax indexation suspended. Both had severe implications; to keep the first or postpone reinstatement of the second would be clear breaches of promises.

On 21 May Co-ordination committee and then cabinet met in lengthy discussions. The next day Co-ordination committee finally decided to continue the effective rates, (i.e. not to remove the surcharge, and not to index the taxation scales) and to increase the oil level to parity prices. The committee agreed that the treasurer would explain that the costs of removing the surcharge and/or introducing full indexation were too great and that the tax levels would be reviewed in the budget. This decision overturned a tentative decision of the committee, made earlier that day, to increase permanently the standard rates of income tax by 2c to 34c, 48c and 62c in each dollar.

On 24 May the Co-ordination committee discussed the text of the treasurer's speech. Its expenditure and revenue packages were put to cabinet, then to the full ministry. The briefing note to the prime minister emphasised how the government was inhibited by commitments; the need for savings followed from the ministry's decision to limit growth to 7–8 per cent. The ad hoc committee had kept it to 8.3 per cent, but slippage had to be avoided. The deficit could not be reduced without decisions on revenue. Cabinet agreed. Fraser had been concerned about leaks and had asked that the reading available for ministers in the cabinet room relate only to those matters to be announced later that week; he did not want to circulate all the decisions of the ad hoc committee. Indeed copies of the decisions of cabinet and Co-ordination committee were often circulated only to Fraser, Howard, Robinson, Stone and the relevant minister. Fraser cut out proposals for wider circulation. Only when Nixon wrote to Fraser asking that decisions needing action be circulated to permanent heads did Fraser allow it.

Fraser was deeply involved in this process of discussion. While he did not attend the meetings of the ad hoc committee, he received regular notes from PMC. When the media speculated about changes to the provisions for income security, after

Guilfoyle had fought hard against possible cuts, Fraser discussed the implications of the stories with Howard, Lynch, Sinclair and Guilfoyle. Only Sinclair wanted to ride out the fuss. Fraser dictated a note for ministers to use to allay fears. He was often recorded as saying that the government could not take away benefits given to electors; it was a critical constraint.

On 24 May Howard brought down a 'savage preliminary budget' that continued the income tax surcharge until 30 November, suspended tax indexation and cut health benefits. Howard warned that there was no prospect of the government being able both to drop the surcharge and grant full indexation in the budget. The economic situation required the change of policy. The press stated that the government had 'unashamedly dishonoured election promises in the name of responsible economic management'. Fraser tried to explain the change of direction, defending himself from charges of broken promises. He said the changes were 'a cross we have to bear. It's one that we built for ourselves', and he became more cautious about making specific economic predictions.

The backbenchers were beginning to organise around John Hyde and on 30 May that group insisted that more expenditure cuts should be made. There appeared a split between the axers and the taxers, with the former now arguing that greater cuts might have been made earlier in the government's term. (After the budget Fraser admitted that expenditure might have been cut more and earlier, but, as he said, you can't replay it.) As the deficit blew out to $700 million above the budget figure, the problem became more stark. In principle Fraser would have liked to reintroduce tax indexation; in practice the scrapping of the surcharge appeared preferable because it more obviously returned money to the taxpayer (even if the taxpayer in practice gained no more).

After a general discussion on 22 June, Fraser decided the structure of the budget cabinet. No bids settled by the ad hoc committee were to be referred to cabinet without the committee's agreement. Co-ordination committee was to meet on 13 July to look at the general strategy and revenue options; cabinet was to meet on 16 July to have an overview of the expenditure decisions; the ministry was to meet the next day. Then on 17 and 18 July cabinet was to consider specific expenditure decisions, on the basis of the ad hoc committee decisions. On 19 and 20 July Co-ordination committee would decide on revenue.

Yet by the end of June the tough line on appeals was beginning to come unstuck. The ministers argued successfully before the committee that they had the right to appeal and Lynch accepted that. Of the eight decisions listed for confirmation at one meeting, three (all Transport) were overturned and ministers were seeking to review the other five. On 5 July Nixon wrote to Fraser expressing concern about the ad hoc committee's decision on airport facilities. Fraser suggested that Nixon (a member of the committee) ask Lynch to review it. Other appeals followed. When some ministers wanted new items considered directly by budget cabinet, Fraser directed that they be put first to the ad hoc committee. The information on expenditure decisions remained limited. In earlier years, budget submissions had gone to all ministers. This year, because of the existence of the ad hoc committee, only Fraser and the committee members initially had copies.

On 11 July the ad hoc committee settled its final budget figuring. On 13 July Co-ordination committee was faced by five main Treasury submissions: Economic and Budget Strategy; Monetary Policy and the Budget; Private Sector Views; Budget Figuring; External Economic Outlook; there was also a Treasury memorandum on revenue options and another reviewing, and hoping to toughen, the ad hoc committee decisions. Treasury argued for a deficit of under $2000 million, claiming the government had a unique opportunity because of the spending cuts made in May, the income tax options left open and the windfall effects of the crude oil levy. At the outset the potential deficit was $2569 million; the treasurer recommended a deficit as low as possible. He argued that the overrun in the last two budgets had reduced the government's reputation and he saw it as important that the government not fritter away windfall gains made from rises in OPEC oil prices that had led to an estimated increase of $800 million over original estimates of revenue from the export parity oil levy. PMC agreed with the proposal to cut expenditure, but thought a deficit of $2500 million was acceptable. It doubted the accuracy of Treasury's growth figure and thought that it underestimated unemployment. To go below $2000 million was too low; by how much the government went under $2500 million was a matter of judgement. Emphasising the importance of restraining monetary growth, Treasury wanted a range of 9–11 per cent; PMC preferred it be not greater than 10 per cent. Whether a target or a range should be included in the budget was to be left to the prime minister and the treasurer. Once again ministers were quickly locked into the approach. The ad hoc committee and the Co-ordination committee reviewed the general economic strategy, which was then endorsed by cabinet on 16 July and by the ministry on 17 July. Then cabinet could return to detailed consideration of individual items.

In the next week Co-ordination committee examined revenue options. Its decisions were to be circulated only to Fraser, Howard, Stone and Castles, with a set in the cabinet room for consultation by other members of the committee and Robinson. On 19 July the latest figuring put the deficit at $2728 million. Memoranda ranged widely across the possible revenue options from preventing income tax avoidance to taxes on wine and gold. The committee decided that a projection of monetary growth, stated as a range, be included in the budget, with that range to be settled by Fraser, Anthony and Howard, or by Co-ordination committee after Fraser's return from Lusaka. (On 14 August Co-ordination committee left the decision to Fraser and Howard.) The committee restated the need for discipline in taking its final decisions on 23 and 24 July, accepting an estimated deficit of $2714 million and a growth in outlays of 9.5 per cent. The committee discussed the economic situation with Stone and Higgins from the Treasury and Visbord and Keating from PMC on 20 August.

The budget delivered on 21 August was interpreted by the press as an effort to restore business confidence and give short-term relief to taxpayers. It abolished the surcharge from 1 December but abandoned indexation – tying its reintroduction to wage restraint. It forecast a deficit of $2193 million, a third less than the previous year's. Outlays increased by 9.1 per cent. The deficit was brought down by an increase in receipts. The

Australian Financial Review declared that because the budget kept to the policies articulated by the prime minister on the hustings, it deserved a clean bill of health. The *Age* gave it the virtue of consistency, but thought it had gone for political impact rather than fiscal honesty. The *Sydney Morning Herald* reported it as a 'sad compromise between the rigours of economic responsibility and the government's desire to bolster its sagging popularity'. In the next two days Eric Risstrom of the Taxpayers' Association drove home the point by illustrating how much better off taxpayers would have been with full tax indexation, thus invalidating the government's view that indexation was too complex to sell. Howard acknowledged that the choice had been made principally on political grounds. That was another blow to the reputation of the government as a proponent of low tax. Fraser was not prepared to forecast a date for the reintroduction of tax indexation. His caution was a reaction to earlier charges of broken promises. Peter Bowers, in caustic fashion, illustrated the declining reputation of the Fraser government's economic management: 'That public commentators tend nowadays to view a Fraser gift horse as if it had halitosis is a measure of how the government's credibility has fallen'.

At the end of the process the Co-ordination committee declared itself satisfied with the procedures; it had not been too time-consuming and had passed without undue trauma. It wanted the same system repeated the next year, but preferred a discussion of political priorities earlier in the process. However, a PMC official was more sceptical:

I suspect that the major shortcoming of the present budget review process is that political priorities are only reflected in a most haphazard way. The review of expenditure is concerned with an enormous amount of detail . . . there is little or no attempt to tie the results together to give some overview of what the various individual cuts have meant for the redirection of the government's expenditure priorities. Ministers are concerned and want earlier discussion. This year they only made an early decision to limit increase to 7 or 8% – that figure was plucked from the blue.

The Review of Commonwealth Functions: ideology rampant?

The 1980 election was much more closely fought than the eventual Liberal majority of twenty-five suggested. On election day many Liberals expected the government to lose. Fraser then saw a need to act strongly in implementing the electoral commitment to reduce expenditure.

PMC recommended a major review of government activities. Its initial proposal was concerned not with the cost of programs, but with their existence. It suggested that a committee should identify functions which were not necessary or which could be more appropriately performed by the private sector, those that duplicated state activities, those that overlapped with other federal policies and those whose benefits did not justify the resources spent. The committee was to recommend which functions could be reduced, eliminated, transferred or altered to achieve a better division of responsibility between federal and state governments and the private sector. The committee was to report by mid-December, a mere six weeks away. It was to be a quick and ruthless pruning of programs.

On 3 November Co-ordination committee agreed that Lynch, Nixon, Howard and Guilfoyle should carry out the review; at Lynch's request Viner was added to the committee. Fraser made a public statement emphasising the importance of the review, but he altered the terms of reference by excising 'transferring' from the options, since the exercise was to cut expenditure. Transferring programs to state governments (with all the negotiations that required) would only have complicated the process. He cleared the final draft with Anthony.

Yet the timetable was never practicable. The intention was that the first meeting would be held on 11 November, meetings with ministers between 25 November and 4 December, with a final session on 11 December. That timetable soon began to slip. The committee decided on its procedures on 11 November; Lynch was to discuss the timetable with Fraser and any functions to undergo examination with both Fraser and Anthony. No other ministers were to be approached until all firm proposals were discussed with Fraser and Anthony too.

On 18 November Lynch agreed that the Review of

Commonwealth Functions (RCF) committee would not meet until 1 December. It would discuss with Fraser and Anthony on 4 December several 'threshold' questions, such as the philosophy behind the approach to each program, the scope for absorbing payments under section 96 of the constitution (which allowed tied grants to be made to the states) into the general revenue grants, and the option of selling government enterprises. TAA, Qantas and the Commonwealth Bank were all listed as possible sales. The committee also wanted to vary earlier electoral commitments, allowing it to abolish the Prices Justification Tribunal or the new procedures for administrative review. As PMC told Fraser, the committee wanted support for its approach to these major questions. Lynch was already asking for a symbolic early announcement of, say, the abolition of some twenty statutory authorities, to make an initial impact. The ministers were not much help, even though the review was endorsed by both the cabinet and the ministry on 9 December, and Lynch spoke to the backbench committees' chairman. By the time the RCF committee agreed to talk to ministers, the Christmas holidays had intervened. Some of them would not be available until mid-January.

On 15 December programs were put into four categories: those to be proposed for review, those discussed only in general terms, those that Anthony and Fraser wanted referred to them before any work was commissioned, and those just noted. Papers that had an impact on administrative arrangements would be referred to Fraser, who received full lists of all decisions. Some final drafts reflected discussions with him. Members of the prime minister's office argued that a more rigorous application of practices of efficiency, cost recovery and means testing be applied; Fraser responded that he had no view yet. There was much activity, reviewing of options and officials' papers. After years of cuts, there were few easy targets. Areas which had once been protected needed to be reopened. Ministers' views were sought, but few decisions were made.

Doubts were growing about the actual impact of the committee. On 31 December Lynch wrote to Fraser, concerned that the review might fall short of public expectations and the government's commitment to smaller government. As extensive publicity had been given to the review in the initial announcement and in the governor-general's speech, its outcome might be used as a yardstick of the government's performance. Lynch argued that the government and prime minister's reputation were at risk. He forecast that if all the options (except the more sensitive ones that were still to be discussed with Fraser) were taken up, savings would be 1–1.5 per cent of expenditure and 2 per cent in staff. The options were leading to rationalisation, rather than greater financial savings. Presentation would be vital. The list of sensitive items referred back to Fraser included the future of the Institute of Criminology, the Prices Justification Tribunal and the Industries Assistance Commission, and child care. Rejected options that could be opened included tertiary fees, the sale of assets and grants to states for government schools. Lynch asked for a discussion with Fraser before the planned meetings with ministers began on 8 January.

Meetings with ministers were organised for the second week of January and Fraser himself met the committee on 15 January to discuss the policy co-ordination role of PMC. By this time the date for completion had been put back to 17 February, when the final review was to be considered by Co-ordination committee or cabinet. Proposals were now put into a few categories; some awaited the prime minister's decision; others had been rejected as offering no real savings or raising too much potential criticism. The latter included the sale of OTC, the sale of shares in Telecom, TAA, and Qantas, grants to the states for tertiary education, and aged pensions.

Fraser went through the list item by item, annotating and proposing. Some he disposed of on the following lines: 'the government clothing factory: sell quickly, even at give away price'. 'Australia Post: haul back from monopoly position and get out of courier service'. 'Trade commissioner service: integrate with foreign affairs'. 'Kakadu: transfer to the NT administration with appropriate safeguards'. 'TAA: can we restrict non-airline activities without being accused of restricting their competitive ability'. 'Housing Loans Insurance Corporation: get rid of it'. Others he protected: women's refuges were to be kept in the federal health program; SBS was not to be changed as it would lead to accusations of broken promises; deferring the Australian Defence Forces Academy would not save money; the abolition of the Law Reform Commission couldn't be got through the Senate; hearing aids were to be left alone; the telephone interpreter service was not to be reduced. He opposed restricting the staffing of the Ombudsman as he saw him as an important administrative safety valve. Fraser finalised decisions on around thirty programs.

In late January PMC began to consider how to present the findings. The head of the officials' support group thought that public expectations were still too high to let the government get away with a low-key announcement, and that the perceived success of the exercise would be increased if its announcement was coupled with the cuts in health expenditure. PMC recommended a parliamentary statement that explained the purpose of the review, the difficulties facing the government in making cuts and announcing some initial decisions. Lynch discussed the presentation with Fraser. Fraser also commissioned several review papers; they included the impact of a 1, 2 or 3 per cent cut to administrative expenditure, changes to the funding for tertiary education including the introduction of fees, major capital works, industry assistance, and Telecom and Australia Post.

In the first week of March Fraser met the RCF committee to review its recommendations to cabinet and to the prime minister in respect of administrative arrangements. It was planned that cabinet would consider the recommendations on 13 March. By 9 March the report was prepared, with most ministers provided only with the recommendations dealing with their portfolio. Fraser, Anthony and the RCF committee members received all the proposals, including details of the fallback options if cabinet objected to the initial proposals. When Fraser demanded to know what savings would be achieved, the Department of Finance reported that a tentative figure was $322 million in 1981–82 and $447 million in a full year. (A week later the figures were revised down to $274 and $352 million respectively.)

On 20 March PMC advised Fraser how the RCF proposals could best be handled. It emphasised that the RCF was not just about saving, but about absorbing programs into state revenue grants or opting out. PMC thought that cabinet could either consider only the main items, with the rest put off until the budget, or decide on and announce them all. It proposed that cabinet set aside 6 and 9 April to review the recommendations. Fraser agreed that the RCF be required to finish by the end of the week and that cabinet should meet on 30 March and make its announcements in conjunction with the health review. Not all ministers were finally slotted in to discuss their portfolios with the RCF until 3 and 6 April.

In the process of negotiating cuts Lynch was helpful because of his political skills. One official claims that Fraser

would know what was happening meeting by meeting. Before each meeting, he knew what was on the agenda and he also knew where they would come out at this end of the meeting. I'm not saying that he had a pre-determined attitude on every single item, but if it was significant he would tic-tac with Lynch. The Expenditure committee worked better when Lynch was head of it than when Howard was, because Lynch had a better relationship with the PM and was a much better politician with the rest of the administration. There is something about letting a minister down lightly. You may have to carve off his arm and his leg, but you give him a feather to fly with and let him down lightly. Lynch understood that. He got the result with the minimum of blood.

Fraser was never out of touch; he had the capacity to alter or change all decisions, especially on crucial matters.

The meeting of cabinet was finally rescheduled so that the proposals could be considered on 15 and 21 April. There were to be six papers: an overview from Lynch, a summary memorandum, a memorandum on legislative consequences, a list of general recommendations and a summary of related issues. In addition there was a separate note to the prime minister on three areas where recommendations had not been circulated: industry taxation concessions, the new Parliament House (the RCF had proposed that construction be abandoned), and a 2 per cent staff reduction. (The Public Service Board explained how a 3 per cent cut could be achieved but did not support the reductions because no functions had been identified for cutting.) Fraser did not want these items discussed in cabinet, but PMC thought it advisable to inform ministers of the decisions. Cabinet ministers received all but the last note; other ministers got the summary memorandum only.

On 15 April (the day Peacock resigned) a meeting of private staff, the Liberal secretariat, the government information unit and PMC considered the arrangements for the announcements. It chose 30 April, with the party room being informed of the details forty-five minutes before the announcement in parliament. PMC emphasised that the other education and health changes should be announced at the same time, otherwise the statement would be short of highlights.

Co-ordination committee reviewed the final details on 28 April, before Lynch reported to the ministry on the same day. It decided then not to take up the recommendation of the committee to stop construction of the new Parliament House, and also that if a minister wanted to review any decision, he or she had to approach the prime minister. The announcement was made on 30 April. All these final changes had been completed while the Peacock resignation wracked the government; staff in the Cabinet Office had been divided into teams – one to prepare the defence against Peacock, the other to service the RCF in its final weeks; both worked almost around the clock.

Over the next months the government tried to monitor the progress of the decisions. On 14 May an ad hoc committee was established as an RCF follow-up group; it included all the initial group except Nixon, who was added at Anthony's request a few months later. It checked constantly on staff savings (until it became impossible to work out what could be directly attributed to the RCF and what were the consequences of other decisions.) Fraser was briefed on particular items that concerned him, such as Australia Post's intentions to expand its courier service. By October the Cabinet Office reported that 74 per cent of the decisions had been implemented or were progressing, while the sale of assets would account for another 13 per cent. On 5 November and again on 11 December Fraser requested from all ministers progress reports that went through the different categories, explaining difficulties – such as getting legislation through the Senate. The Senate had blocked tertiary fees for second degrees and had subjected the sale of both Bendigo's ordnance factory and the Coburg clothing factory to Senate inquiries.

The RCF became a victim of its own high expectations. Announced as a major initiative, it became difficult to achieve the symbolic cuts. A member of the committee said: 'The truth is that we could not slash functions; that was the bottom line'. It degenerated more into an analysis of savings than a review of the need for functions or the problem of duplication. After two months much of the emphasis switched to presentation, to the symbolic gestures, to presentation.

1982: The finale

The 1982 budget has been regarded as the occasion when the Fraser government changed direction, relaxing its tight hold on public expenditure and allowing a blow-out of the deficit. It has been interpreted as an election budget, in which the Fraser government established the conditions for an early poll, and was reputed to ignore much of the advice presented by the Treasury. It contained the most controversial and contested budget strategy of the Fraser years.

The 1982 budget was formulated in a year of almost constant crisis, with a demoralised government and a prime minister under siege. Cabinet reeled from crisis to crisis. In March the Lowe by-election and the Victorian state election were lost. In April Peacock contested the leadership and two ministers resigned over the farcical TV affair. For two months attention switched to the Labor leadership contest, but in July and August, while the details of the budget were being worked out, there were constant rumours of an early election. In September the government was shaken by the reports of the Costigan inquiry and the splits in the Liberal party over tax evasion. The furore over the damming of the Franklin gradually increased in intensity. Only in November did some peace seem to fall, when Fraser was in hospital recovering from a back operation. While there he managed to orchestrate the wages pause.

At the same time the economy deteriorated. The international recession bit deeper; unemployment rose; the drought became severe. There were internal disputes about the nature of the economic problems and the viability of the alternative solutions. 1982 was not a year when the budget could be constructed even in semi-tranquillity. The strain showed.

Fraser tried to reduce the pressure on senior ministers by, for the first time, not appointing a budget committee to consider bids in April and May. A review of cabinet procedures had emphasised yet again the heavy workload of ministers, so on 3 December 1981 cabinet decided that the minister for finance should discuss spending proposals in 'bilateral' discussions with ministers, acting within the general context of targets and priorities established by cabinet. The bilateral discussions were to run from March to May and only then would a cabinet budget committee examine the more difficult items.

Debate about the general economic situation began immediately. In November 1981 Guilfoyle, the minister for finance, had alerted Fraser to a drift in the deficit; she proposed that she and the treasurer prepare a submission for Co-ordination committee. On 15 December the cabinet had a broad-ranging discussion on the economic prospects at a meeting which was also attended by the permanent heads of Treasury, Finance, Trade and Resources, Industry and Commerce, National Development and Primary Industry, by the governor of the Reserve Bank, by the deputy secretary of PMC and by senior economic advisers from the offices of the prime minister and the treasurer. As a consequence Fraser asked his department to provide an immediate projection of the economy. The note, prepared without the advice of Finance, emphasised the projection's limitations: that it had to assume no policy changes, and that it depended critically on assumptions made about economic parameters such as growth in wages and prices. Within that range of uncertainty, it suggested the deficit for 1982–83 would rise from the predicted $146 million to $612 million as a consequence of a decline in receipts. It estimated the 1982–83 result as a $245 million surplus and suggested that there was limited scope for new spending or for tax concessions if a roughly balanced budget was to be obtained.

On 6 January a Treasury submission commented that, although there was still growth in domestic demand, it was significantly met by imports; that the increase in wages and reduction in standard working hours were adding to inflationary pressures. Receipts were $300 million lower than the budget estimates, while outlays were increased by post-budget decisions including the rises in academic and defence force salaries. It forecast a $700 million deficit. By 13 January a revised estimate from Finance had the deficit up to $1045 million. PMC argued on 14 January that growth was slowing in non-farm output and unemployment was rising, and that the main danger continued to be inflation, particularly wage-push inflation in the post-indexation period. They too forecast an increase in the deficit to $1 billion. Every adviser agreed that the strategy adopted in 1981 was coming apart, as the deficit expanded.

However if they agreed on what was happening, their preferred solutions diverged. A Treasury note, passed on to Fraser by Howard, projected and supported a 1982–83 surplus of $1190 million, based on 15 per cent increase in average weekly earnings, no new expenditure and continued restraint. Fraser's economic adviser, Cliff Walsh, was scathing. He declared that this comment was

vintage Treasury. In broad terms I think they are right about the need for tightening up on the fiscal side, but wrong with respect to money supply and interest rates. A lot of their argument is based on so-called 'confidence effects' which surely exist but I suspect are overstated.

Walsh complained that as usual Treasury and the Reserve Bank had retained a monopoly over information about the money supply and that he wanted to see the basis of their estimates. He concluded that Treasury advocacy for a domestic surplus of $1190 million was 'a point with which I have no sympathy in political terms and little in economic terms'. He thought the overall picture was bleak. PMC commented that their estimates, based on a 13 per cent increase in average weekly earnings, projected a $250 million surplus, and that the scope for tax cuts would depend on what size of deficit was considered appropriate. As a consequence of these notes and a discussion at Monetary Policy committee, Fraser asked the treasurer for a submission on the economic situation.

In the first week of February Guilfoyle sought Fraser's support for guidelines for the levels of increase in ongoing estimates, suggesting that they might be taken under-the-line in cabinet. Cabinet delegated to the minister for finance, in consultation with the prime minister and the treasurer, the responsibility to promulgate the guidelines. Guilfoyle proposed that for large programs, departments maintain existing general restraint, while for others, expenditure be contained to 1981–82 figures, plus 5 per cent. The prime minister agreed.

On 10 February the requested submission from the Treasury stated that, although growth was in line with forecasts, it was to a large extent being met by imports. The wages outlook was poor, and wage settlements would take the increase in average weekly earnings beyond the forecast; the deficit was now likely to be $1300 million. It proposed as the only feasible approach a tightening of policy and possibly an increase in interest rates. PMC disagreed. It argued that the Treasury's forecast was very pessimistic, leading to excessively harsh prescriptions. It accepted that the balance of payments had weakened, but claimed that tougher domestic policies were the correct response. It argued that the deficit was still small by historical and international standards. Treasury's submission was noted by the Monetary Policy committee on 15 February. Neither prescription was endorsed.

On 26 February Fraser informed cabinet of the budget timetable. Additional estimates were to be considered in the week of 15 March; the preliminary budget outlook would be considered by cabinet on 22 March; the bilaterals would take place in April and May; the budget committee would meet from 15 to 18 June and from 21 to 25 June; budget cabinet would meet between 13 and 23 July. Cabinet duly noted the dates and the need for ministers to be available for discussion.

On 3 March Fraser received his copy of the report on the forward estimates. On 11 March, with the assistance of a paper prepared by Finance, Fraser met Howard and Guilfoyle to discuss the options and decide which programs would be further analysed. PMC prepared lists of possible savings and of those programs that needed review in the bilaterals. It offered two packages: one saving $460 million and the other $650 million, so senior ministers could decide which target should be pursued. The ministers agreed on a list of cuts adding up to $606 million, to act as the basis for the bilateral negotiations. The record of this meeting was circulated only to the three ministers; Fraser removed Stone and Castles, the two departmental heads, from the circulation list; Howard complained that those Treasury and Finance officers had a need to know.

The media were already perceiving that differences over economic policy were splitting the Liberal party. The backbench Tactics committee opposed any early election and any change in economic policy, but supported tax cuts. The 'dries' in the party had gained strength and cohesion since the 1980 election. In an attempt to re-establish his government's appeal with the Victorian election looming, Fraser gave an address to the nation that stressed the continuity of policy.

On 22 March cabinet met for a preliminary discussion of the budget and new policy proposals just before the Victorian election. For security reasons, Fraser required that all submissions dealing with saving options and the budget review be circulated only at the beginning of the meeting and left on the table at the end. PMC recommended that the government aim for a reduction of $650 million in the present estimates, implying no real growth, and a 4 per cent reduction on average (but it proposed excluding public debt interest, pensions, defence and tax sharing, if these items were regarded as formally committed). Since a trade-off had to be made between expenditure growth, tax relief and reducing pressure on interest rates, restraint was appropriate, even if it was still premature to become committed to a detailed fiscal and monetary package. However PMC emphasised that after six years of weeding out easy options, the cuts would have to include some options that were previously rejected.

Cabinet, and a day later the full ministry, agreed on the need for firm fiscal and monetary policy, and the need for a saving of $650 million. Ministers encouraged themselves to make major savings in the bilateral discussions with the minister for finance.

Proposals for new policy, to be included only when essential and unavoidable, were also to be examined by the minister for finance. Cabinet thus set the framework and the savings targets. PMC then briefed Fraser on the economic choices: to tighten macro-economic policy to reduce expectations, activity and employment, (but as this would take time, it was preferable to go steadily, bearing down on inflation but still supporting economic growth); or direct intervention by trying to control wages through a social contract, an approach that was likely to flounder on its impracticality, not least the federal government's lack of constitutional power. In effect PMC argued that there was no real alternative to bearing down on inflation and to a small reduction in the deficit.

During these discussions the Peacock challenge dominated the political life of the leading members of cabinet. Although meetings continued, their real interest was elsewhere. While Fraser fought for his position, the treasurer contested the deputy leadership. The 'dries' were seen as a coherent group and their support assisted the election of John Howard as deputy leader. Budgeting took second place to politics. Responding to accusations of dominance, Fraser promised to hold a party room debate on the economy, but when it took place on 21 May no new ideas were presented. The backbenchers demanded tax cuts to improve their chances of electoral survival.

In April and May the minister for finance, Dame Margaret Guilfoyle, held bilateral discussions with ministers. Fraser received details of her progress. By 21 April some 97 items had been agreed, 28 were disagreed, 41 were to go straight to cabinet, 54 new proposals had been withdrawn and another 49 were still pending. By 25 May Guilfoyle had achieved savings of $353 million towards the required $650 million. On 27 May Guilfoyle formally reported, but asked for more time. Fraser refused to change the date of budget cabinet. At the same time he showed his interest in detail. On 31 May he argued that medical and marine research and astronomy should not be jeopardised by insufficient funds. On 11 June he annotated a list of disputed bids, saying that the proposed levels for the Australian Institute of Sport and the bicentennial were too tough. Referring to the AIS, Fraser said: 'If you want to hold the Australian flag high, put money into it. Dries see everything from an accountant's viewpoint. There are other issues that are important'. He agreed that the Arts Council should not get a general grant. PMC kept Fraser's office in touch with progress on the programs in which he had a particular interest: from the building program in the ACT to the purchasing policy of the National Gallery to the eradication of cattle disease in the Northern Territory.

The divisions were becoming public. At a meeting of the Economic Advisory committee Howard had argued for no deficit and Fraser wanted one big enough to fund tax cuts, mentioning a figure of $500 million. Critics argued that the government had for the first time thrown over its economic policy, with considerations of an expansionary budget to meet the demands of the recession. At the National Press Club on 6 June Fraser acknowledged that new pressures made a change of emphasis obvious, but said a change of emphasis was not a change of strategy. That line gained some support. The *Sydney Morning Herald* declared that the increase in the deficit would illustrate 'a departure from the policy of Reining in the Deficit'. It took the 'charitable view that even a compulsive belt-tightener like Fraser has too much common sense to allow the Treasury to persuade him that the appropriate response in recession is to screw down the economy'. Fraser started to warn that the government might not be able to afford tax cuts and that it might need to 'rouse the economy with more government spending'; he was starting to prepare the ground in his normal way for possible changes in policy in different economic circumstances.

In early June cabinet reviewed the general situation again. The main submissions lodged by the treasurer were on the Economic Policy Context (although PMC told Fraser it believed the treasurer did not agree with its conclusions) and on the budget outlook. The former was circulated to cabinet ministers; the other was received only in the cabinet room by everyone except the prime minister, the treasurer and the minister for finance, who had advance copies. The budget-overview submission proposed a modest overall surplus. It argued that the economy had slipped in the last few months, with the squeeze on profits constraining employment. As a result of continued recession, large increases in labour costs and high interest rates, there had been little growth in private consumer spending, no private business investment and still a higher level of inflation than in other countries. The submission insisted that there be no relaxation of policy; expenditure must be reduced and monetary growth restrained. In general PMC supported that line but it argued that existing figures implied no real increase in outlays and suggested that the assumptions made by the Treasury on receipts were unduly pessimistic. It thought that, given the signs of a slow-down, a small surplus would be difficult to accept and preferred a deficit somewhat smaller than that of 1981–82 (announced as $146 million but eventually blowing out to about $600 million). Fraser also received comments from Doug Anthony, then in Houston, who thought the Treasury's proposals too severe and that it was not prudent to be too tough. Anthony argued that the government should aim for a higher deficit and that it should not be too harsh on the states. Lynch, as minister for industry and commerce, was advised by his department that there were difficulties in pursuing the anti-inflationary policies at the expense of other goals. There were dangers in an over-valued dollar, no corporate tax relief and a reduction in government capital expenditure.

On 8 June cabinet reaffirmed the need for a firm economic setting and acknowledged that to maintain expenditure restraint it would need both to confirm the savings options recommended by the minister for finance and to find a further $170 million in savings. A budget committee was to examine the outstanding matters and make recommendations to budget cabinet where disagreements continued. Then cabinet also decided that, given the government's objective of personal income tax relief within a responsible budget outcome, the treasurer and minister for finance, in conjunction with the prime minister, should identify a limited number of savings options rejected in the past and consider the possibility of increased revenue from indirect taxation. On 22 June cabinet noted an oral report from the treasurer on the latest budget figures. In early July the budget committee of cabinet went through the bids that had not been settled in the bilaterals, and its decisions were incorporated into a cabinet memorandum. Co-ordination committee met on 13 and 14 July to consider the revenue prospects before the budget cabinet met; it asked officials to bring forward options for variations to income taxation rates. Fraser also asked for information on the status of all new policy proposals; they were categorised into those agreed in bilateral discussions, those withdrawn, those discussed and amended; the brief explained what the budget committee had decided. Fraser as usual had some specific views. His adviser, Cliff Walsh, told PMC that it was unrealistic to cut the freight equalisation scheme and that Fraser was growing uncomfortable about the furore over the Franklin and thought the government should be seen to be spending more on the environment. On 11 July the ministers' bids were for $489.3 million more than PMC supported and $630.2 million more than Finance recommended.

Discussions of the economic strategy had of course been continuous; in early July Fraser hosted a group of senior businessmen to lunch at the Lodge. Guests included John Elliott, John Utz, Sir Arvi Parbo and several leading bankers. After a lengthy discussion on the state of the economy Fraser went round the table asking each person what size of deficit they thought the government should bring down. According to one account every proposal was between $2000 and $3000 million, with a general tendency for the figure to be at the higher end of that range; another placed them all around $2000 million. Whichever is accurate, the businessmen proposed a very stimulatory budget. The lunch, recalls adviser Cliff Walsh, 'contained some pretty senior bankers and businessmen, some closely connected with the Liberal party, all of whom have forgotten the lunch and indeed attacked the budget afterwards'. Before budget cabinet, ministers met the permanent heads of departments with an economic interest, who like business were not supporting the Treasury's hard line.

By the time budget cabinet met, the Treasury's main submission, the Budget and Economic Policy, was pessimistic. The treasurer claimed that the economy had gone bad and forecasts were so dismal as to predict no growth. The problems were caused by wage pressures as well as international conditions. If Australia was to restore its own position it needed to restore industry profit by reining in wages. Howard agreed that there was an expectation of tax cuts, but said that the drastic decline in revenue meant there was no room for tax relief unless it was accommodated by a shift towards indirect tax. Since the deficit had been the centrepiece of the government's economic policy for the last six years and the symbol of its commitment to reduce the public sector, it would be seen as weakness if it were to be increased. The government needed to pay close attention to expectations. Howard then indicated where he and his department differed. He said the Treasury saw the need to be as close as possible to balance, or a deficit of not more than $500 million. The Reserve Bank agreed. Howard thought that a deficit between $1000 million and $1500 million would be the outer limit. He concluded with the comment that the most important commodity the government had was the community's belief in its capacity as a responsible manager. The budget was therefore not just about fine tuning, but also about political credibility.

PMC officials generally agreed with the range of deficit proposed by the treasurer; they estimated that as much as $1000 million of the increase in the deficit was the essentially mechanical effect of the economic slowdown. They saw a slightly higher deficit, up to $1900 million, as consistent with past economic policy. None of these deficit figures was large in itself; they were important only if perceived as heralding a shift in policy towards consistently larger deficits in the future and a decline in the government's commitment to fight inflation. PMC did not agree that the decline was as marked as the treasurer suggested, but accepted the need to resist wage rises. They also agreed that there was no scope for major tax concessions.

PMC also briefed Fraser separately. It acknowledged that the public sector would be difficult to prune. The proposed 1982–83 deficit was $1382 million, a consequence of lower receipts and higher outlays; but much of that could be attributed to the economic downturn. Any domestic improvement would require tax relief, but business was not in a position to pay more tax. Although there was a strong case for a 'neutral' deficit of around $1380 million, the government could loosen fiscal policy to give some support for a weakening economy. The 1981-82 settings had been too tight. The budget deficit could go to $1900 million, adding a $500 million fiscal stimulus. The risk of a high deficit would be a signal of a weakening of the government's commitment to reduce inflation. The politically safe range was between $1400 and $1900 million. By the beginning of budget cabinet no leading minister was in sympathy with the Treasury's hard line. The question was to what further extent the economy should be stimulated.

Cabinet discussed the economic strategy from 13 to 15 July. Fraser started with the argument that the government should bring down a budget with the largest deficit it judged prudent, given the perceived onset of recession and the attitude towards deficits of the financial market. Cabinet decided that, consistent with sound economic management, it would direct any increases in spending to areas of need while avoiding more general increases; any tax concessions would respond to current circumstances; and the government would aim at a small domestic surplus and an overall deficit of $2500 million or a little more. The full ministry endorsed the strategy the same day. If the cabinet endorsed all the budget committee decisions, the deficit would be only $1418 million. Cabinet also argued that Treasury's estimates of receipts were too pessimistic and asked for an estimate of unemployment; Treasury estimates were based on a figure of 400 000; but by budget cabinet the fear was that this figure would grow.

During the ensuing days running scoresheets were provided to the prime minister. For each disputed item cabinet had three figures: the department's bid and recommendations from Finance and PMC. By 19 July cabinet had made decisions that added between $295 million and $313 million to outlays. Sometimes ministers accepted the PMC figures; they were never harsher than Finance suggested. Indeed if all PMC figures had been accepted, only $126 million would have been added: Finance's proposals would have added a mere $11 million. Ministers were far more generous than their officials thought necessary. Fraser continued to take a detailed interest, annotating and recommending particular figures. By the close of business on 20 July, with a further $334 million allocated, the deficit was estimated in the range of $1993 million to $2010 million – or, if as Fraser instructed, $350 million revenue from the fuel levy was added – between $1643 million and $1660 million.

Then the climate changed. Howard and Fraser had a private meeting where Howard's misgivings were strongly expressed. Two senior officers of the Treasury, led by David Morgan (but not including the secretary, who chose not to attend) strongly argued to cabinet on 20 July that the strategy was dangerous. They stood firm in the face of tough questioning by Fraser who 'used every trick, side-flanking, chopping off at the knees', says one observer That performance helped to turn the debate around. On 21 July cabinet decided to review all decisions taken up to the close of business on 20 July and again to reduce expenditure; this review was to be completed by the next day. Then, unsatisfied by the detailed proposals, cabinet made cuts across the board. It decided a reduction to the equivalent of 3 per cent was to be applied to all portfolios except Defence, and that each portfolio should also make a 3 per cent cut in non-salary, administrative and operational expenditure. The deficit was calculated to be between $1393 and $1779 million. On 28 July cabinet expressed its determination to hold the budget to outlays. The process had been exhausting; long meetings, bitter arguments, changes in direction, strained nerves, were all present in the most hard fought budget of the government.

While these expenditure reviews were being considered, Co-ordination committee considered revenue. Several packages illustrating possible income tax changes were prepared for the committee by the taxation commissioner. The most notable was an estimate of the amounts that could be secured from the payment of overdue income tax. Although a general review of the tax legislation had not been completed, cabinet asked for some immediate figures. The commissioner suggested that something like $2220 million of income tax was overdue, of which about $1000 million represented unpaid income tax from people who had participated in blatant, artificial or contrived tax avoidance schemes. The 10 per cent penalty, introduced in 1922 when interest rates were 6 per cent, was inadequate and encouraged the delaying of payments. The best alternative was to increase the penalty to 20 per cent or even 25 per cent. How much would be recouped was a matter of some conjecture. The commissioner of taxation argued that the 1982-83 budget had been calculated on the assumption that outstanding tax at 30 June 1983 would be $2130 million, excluding companies that had been stripped of untaxed profits. Of that, $380 million was clearly owed after the use of blatant tax avoidance schemes. A new penalty might collect half that amount: $190 million. Further, possibly a third of the $645 million tax in assessment schemes still under dispute might be collected, to yield $215 million. Of the $900 million owed by taxpayers not involved in avoidance schemes, and either disputed or not, new penalty rates might drag in, say, a third of the disputed and half the undisputed amounts: $360 million. The total, he estimated, would be $765 million. The submission recommended a 20 per cent penalty. A second memorandum offered alternative schemes that would draw in amounts ranging from $455 million to $660 million.

In a decision circulated only to Stone and the commissioner of taxation, cabinet decided to increase the penalty rate to 20 per cent, to apply it to all amounts outstanding two months after the decision was enacted and to decrease the discretion available to the commissioner of taxation. It noted that the measures were estimated to yield $615 million in 1982-83. The figure chosen was deliberately less than the $765 million estimated in the commissioner's submission, because that figure, as all figures in these calculations inevitably were, could be no more than an educated guess of what might be recouped. Yet in revenue terms it was crucial in bringing the deficit back to its final estimate of $1698 million; it provided 'the black hole' of revenue. Ministers might not have accepted the solutions provided by officials, but in all their calculations they did accept their figuring and their predictions.

While cabinet was meeting, election speculation was rife as journalists wrote that the budget was being designed for electoral purposes. The rumours, carefully stoked from the top according to journalists, led to an air of expectancy.

Attempts to influence the outcome did not end with budget cabinet. Some matters, like the level of duty on motor spirit, were left for final decision by the prime minister, deputy prime minister and treasurer. In early August, while the prime minister was overseas, the Treasury tried to reopen the budget, pointing out that already the estimated deficit had grown by $126 million. Some costs, such as the salaries of staff to collect tax avoided, had been forgotten; decisions on indirect tax would increase the CPI and hence outlays; it claimed that although the deficit in 1982–83 would be $1824 million, in 1983–84 it would be $4204 million, an increase from 1.1 per cent of GDP to 2.3 per cent. PMC was sceptical. Although acknowledging that it was hard to find out what was going on, much of the change was due to a miscalculation by Treasury who had badly underestimated both the increase in the unemployed and the percentage of these unemployed who were family income earners and hence recipients of unemployment benefits. The miscalculation blew out the deficit quickly. PMC warned the prime minister that the treasurer might try to restore the domestic surplus to the figure ministers had in mind at the beginning of budget cabinet, and that Treasury might be planning even more; as it was too late for expenditure cuts, it would mean more revenue proposals. Any differences were eventually settled in a meeting between Fraser and the treasurer.

On 17 August Fraser explained to the full ministry the philosophy behind the budget strategy, paying particular attention to likely criticism in the government parties of elements of the proposed legislation against tax avoidance. Ministers were exhorted to emphasise the justice of the legislation and the importance of not retreating from it. The budget provided tax cuts for the standard rate, from 32 to 30 per cent and raised the top cut-off point. Outlays grew by 13.9 per cent and the deficit was estimated at $1674 million. Family allowances for the first two children were lifted by 50 per cent. Concessions were made to several groups in the community, including small investors, small business and families.

The budget was regarded sceptically. The *Financial Review* argued that the budget was 'not a credible exercise and can only be understood as a preparation for an election campaign'. It was scathing about the Tax Office's estimates. The *Age* saw it as a budget for an election: 'a clever blend of economic responsibility, social concern and political cynicism'. The tax cuts would mostly be recouped by inflation and other charges. The consensus was that the government had dumped its economic strategy. For the first time in seven years it was budgeting for a deficit that was higher than in the previous year in order to offset the deepening depression. Fraser argued that there was no change of strategy, just a change of instruments.

Was it seen as an election budget by participants? Some ministers thought so; Guilfoyle noted that Fraser was initially ready to hand money away. She remembers:

in the last budget he was opposing what the Treasury and Finance wanted and giving more money all around the place. That was a last desperate throw at the last election. He also believed that the economy was so depleted that it would be unforgivable if we went without expanding through the government.

Chaney had argued for increased expenditure on public works earlier in the year, and then suddenly the atmosphere changed. Ministers were unused to an easy fiscal climate after years of rigour.

Other advisers were not convinced. In December 1982 PMC described it as a neutral budget or perhaps as a mildly stimulatory one. Cliff Walsh had long argued that the 1981 budget had been too tough and that the expanded deficit was not inconsistent with the way that Fraser had been going. Another adviser thought the basic problem was that the Treasury had not got its forecasts right, especially about unemployment, and its advice was received with some scepticism. As for it being an election budget:

Would you seriously go to an election with a budget you knew was going to fall apart or you suspected would. It was the greatest dog's breakfast budget I've ever seen, bits and pieces of everything. There wasn't any strategy.

But the greatest criticism was about perceptions. Howard argues that if a government in trouble, having preached a certain line for five or six years, suddenly runs in the opposite direction, it loses credibility. Fraser defends the increase in expenditure:

When we put out those increases, there was some evidence that Australia was going into a downturn and I have never believed that counter-cyclical finance was wrong if your budget was under control and ours was.

Besides, he argues, the Treasury's figures were wrong; no one in Treasury had any understanding of the depth or implications of the rural drought.

The reputation of the budget was destroyed by the speed with which the figures came apart. The Treasury was still defending its projections on budget night. When Hayden claimed that the figures on the recoupment of tax were rubbery, the Treasury told Howard that they did not seem overly optimistic. It admitted that the relationship between unemployment and unemployment beneficiaries was uncertain, but claimed that, even if the employment forecast was optimistic, it was not unreasonably so. In September Guilfoyle told ministers that the deficit had gone beyond $2000 million. By October the deficit had blown out again, as Howard announced the growth of unemployment to 460 000 (rather than the budget estimate of 395 000). The Monetary committee noted the additional expenditure in drought relief of $356 million and an increase in $200 million of unemployment benefits, both of which also led to declines in receipts. The estimated gain from action against 'bottom of the harbour' tax evasion schemes was reduced by $155 million. By 10 November the deficit had grown by $1674 million. On 6 December the overrun had grown to $2051 million, leaving a deficit of $3725 million, because the economy had weakened much faster than expected, owing to needs for drought relief, higher unemployment (now $603 million), slower employment growth (down by $446 million), and weaker economic conditions leading to reduced sales tax, import and excise ($354 million). It had been these pressures that led to the proposal for a wages pause.

The budgetary system: an assessment

These accounts provide detailed case studies of four sets of different circumstances over seven years. They indicate the style with which Fraser approached budget-making, although they cannot possibly encompass all the discussions Fraser had. There can be no way of doing that for the records do not exist. Economic management was an ever-present topic to be discussed all the time. Fraser and his treasurers would receive regular briefs on economic conditions; they would discuss problems almost daily. None of this constant monitoring and direction can be easily captured. Nevertheless several factors were common, even though the procedures altered from year to year.

Economic policy became far more the responsibility of the cabinet system than under any previous prime minister. The cabinet consideration of the broad picture in March, the review of expenditure proposals by the ad hoc budget committees, the discussions on strategy and disagreed bids by budget cabinet, the choices of revenue options by a small group: decisions were all made in one or other part of the cabinet system. Ministers were always looking for a way to increase their participation in the broad discussions without being overwhelmed by detail. 'The system changed every year,' recalls a PMC official, 'as people tried to find a simple way of doing a hard job. There is no simple way'. Tough decisions eventually had to be referred to Fraser and his senior colleagues. According to one economic adviser: 'All ministers had their opportunity. Fraser didn't prevent his ministers having their say'. Decisions were not made unilaterally. Nor were the treasurer or the Treasury allowed to maintain a monopoly of all the information, although the Treasury maintained a constant fight to limit the access of others. Even in 1981 it wanted to cancel the interdepartmental taskforce on economic strategy because of its 'heavy workload'! Fraser was not impressed. He always saw the need for economic data to be shared – at least with him.

Fraser still controlled the processes and the detailed direction of economic policy and the choice of who had access to what within that cabinet process. Usually after consultations with senior colleagues, he decided the budget procedures and timetables. He determined who was to receive which submissions and to whom decisions were circulated. He directed which submissions were tabled at the beginning of a cabinet meeting and then collected at the end. He chose the members of the ad hoc budget committees and decided which group would make the revenue choices. These procedures could be justified. Limiting the spread of information reduced the dangers of leaks. The full cabinet could not discuss every expenditure item; it would have become impossibly bogged down in detail. Revenue decisions had traditionally been made by small groups because of the need for confidentiality. It meant that the actual decision makers were few. Guilfoyle claimed that ministers thought they were participating fully in the budget process, whereas in fact they were concerned only with expenditure decisions.

Fraser's control over the circulation of information meant that he could determine outcomes by the gradual extension of those involved. Strategy might first be discussed with one or two senior colleagues, then by the Co-ordination committee. Then, often in quick succession, it would be put to cabinet and the ministry. Strategic decisions were often expressed in general terms. At the top of the cabinet table Fraser was provided with constantly updated scoresheets, giving him estimates of the broad picture which he could then choose to share with his senior colleagues or the whole cabinet.

Control over details and directions of economic policy was also firmly in the hands of the prime minister. He ensured that he was well briefed, both on the general economic picture and on the details of expenditure decisions. He went through the disagreed bids, advocating more or less – decisions that sometimes closed the discussion. Often the effect was to soften the cuts proposed by his budget committees. Peter Nixon recalls:

We put up a lot more things than were formally accepted. Very often the prime minister wouldn't accept them because he was a very polished practitioner of the art of politics. He would make political judgements that he thought were necessary. He would have cabinet support because they were hard options. There were certainly things he could have won that we put up to him that he didn't want to win and he'd give you a good reason why these weren't sensible.

Fraser saved the Australian Defence Force Academy and possibly the new Parliament House from the razor gang. He overturned a proposal to axe an official history of the Malayan emergency and the Vietnam war. 'Vital' was his annotation; he saw it as a commitment to those who had served in the two spheres. He increased expenditure on the Australian Institute of Sport and maintained expenditure on the National Gallery to ensure that it would open on time. His influence on the details of spending was thus considerable. It was easy in March, when broad figures were needed, for him to say 'chop everything' in pursuit of a predetermined target, but then the problems of cuts in particular programs, with their impact on groups in the community, would be brought to his attention.

Budgeting was a continuous process, as the assessment of one year's deficit ran into consideration of the next year's possible outcomes. In the early months figures for possible deficits were largely guesstimates, almost back-of-the-envelope calculations of what might be required to maintain growth and the government's reputation. Business confidence, that intangible target of all governments, is not ensured by any specific figure. The difference between a deficit of $2100 million and $1700 million may be insignificant in economic and historical terms, but crucial to a government in that the latter is regarded as symbolically reasonable and the former as irresponsibly high. From March to July the government was constantly assessing and reassessing what that figure should be.

Fraser never hesitated to ask for more and more details. He would write to the governor of the Reserve Bank, asking him to elaborate on arguments put earlier: how long should the government wait for the private sector to recover of its own volition? what were the characteristics of monetary conditions necessary to provide adequate support for wages policy? was there a need for change in the rate of expansion of the money supply? (to take three examples from a letter of 26 July 1977). He was always prepared to carry on the argument, too. If he thought the bank had not directly answered the precise question, he would ask it again, or ask for clarification if the information was not adequate. When people he met complained that their overdraft limits had been cut, Fraser dictated a note asking for reports from PMC and the bank, and required them to be ready by the time his plane landed at Kalgoorlie airport.

He would also get comment or second opinions on official advice. He would expect PMC comment on all Treasury papers, and would sometimes send PMC's economic analysis over to the Treasury for review. The economists in his office would discuss issues with him directly. No one could ever be sure to whom he had spoken, what he had asked and what he had been told. It created tension, but Fraser remained at the centre of the process.

The advisers did not always agree. The Treasury's prescriptions were generally more severe than those of PMC; the latter argued that they were more in tune with political reality and appreciated where cuts could be made. The Treasury developed the reputation for using a variety of tactics in the hope of pulling back the deficit. Whether accurate or not – and it is not accepted by Treasury – their recommendations were often treated as though they were ambit claims. Their general attitude was regarded as Jesuitical: 'The Treasury view was that if you didn't do all of what they wanted, you were totally sinful', says Fraser.

Fraser was personally involved in all economic decisions, but how expert was he in understanding the implications? He did not necessarily satisfy all economists. One adviser commented:

He had a low level of economic literacy; he had a practically oriented view of the value of the exchange rates and interest rates but no perception of the adjustment process and policy mixes. He didn't have a picture or a model of a box in his own head that fitted things together. He knew some things didn't work and some things did work.

But public servants, more used to dealing with generalists, were usually more polite. Said one:

Fraser was economically literate in the sense that he could pass the exam, but no original thinker. He would understand the arguments and if you tried to mislead, he would be able to pick a hole in the arguments.

Others agreed with reservations:

He was very bright, so he could catch on very quickly. The difficulty was that he didn't follow a system; he would swing around . . . He didn't have a consistent approach.

He was said to have appreciated the main relationships in the economy, even if at times he had unreal expectations about the capacity of business to react just because he wanted it to. While constantly trying to rein in the deficit, he still believed in state action; he wanted to solve problems. In that sense he was in economic terms a conservative in the mould of Menzies, rather than a member of the radical right who distrusted state intervention. He always believed the state could play a constructive role.

To what effect? Some myths have been created since Fraser's defeat or even before. One is that 1976 was the great missed opportunity when spending could have been cut back; that idea was beginning to develop by 1979. Yet even then it was with the wisdom of hindsight. The press in 1976 argued that Fraser delivered what he promised. Ministers recall that no one wanted to push harder, and most feared that the strategy might stop the economy in its tracks anyway. All advisers, including the Treasury, recommended that the deficit be around the range that was finally accepted. The public was conscious primarily of the government's cuts. In the context of 1976 expectations and knowledge, everyone thought that Fraser delivered.

In the broad picture, too, Fraser had succeeded in reining in the deficit and slowing the growth of spending. Any broad figures can be misleading, as expenditure programs may be shifted in accounting terms from year to year and even off the budget. However the impact of that general approach, the measuring stick against which the government deserves to be judged, can be easily seen.

Table 7.1: *Federal government expenditure*

	Outlays as % of GDP	Receipts as % of GDP	Public Sector Borrowing Requirement %
1973–74	23.8	23.3	0.5
1974–75	28.9	24.8	4.1
1975–76	30.0	25.1	4.9
1976–77	29.0	25.7	3.3
1977–78	29.6	25.9	3.7
1978–79	28.4	25.0	3.4
1979–80	27.7	25.9	1.8
1980–81	27.8	26.9	0.9
1981–82	28.0	27.6	0.4

In two years, 1976–77 and 1979–80, there was a real decline in expenditure. The deficit was gradually brought down, even if in the last years at the expense of a growth in tax receipts – until the problems of the recession. The commitment to tax indexation, so fervently espoused as a means of keeping governments honest, was eventually dropped when it got into the 'too hard' basket. Symbolic tax cuts could give as a matter of government generosity what taxpayers would have received under indexation as a matter of right. Political impact triumphed over ideological commitment. Whether 1982 was a blow-out of the deficit in an attempt to win an election or counter-cyclical pump-priming in the face of recession and drought – and it was probably trying to keep options open – was a matter of interpretation.

In the individual programs, Fraser was often not harsh. Always an advocate of the proposition that governments can't take benefits away because of the political reactions, he was often softer than colleagues. He at times looked beyond the immediate demands for economy. Whether future generations consider the new Parliament House as a monument to extravagance or a great building, and the Australian Defence Force Academy as a defence benefit, Fraser did not allow them to be the victims of immediate requirements for cuts.

Yet even if he can be criticised for not being as tough as his image, Fraser did change the terms of economic debate. He governed at a time when the debate about the effect of different economic instruments was continuous and unresolved, when snake-oil merchant solutions were prevalent and when no country seemed certain about how it could control its economy. Yet the economic approaches of the Labor governments that preceded and followed him could be and were substantially different partly because Fraser had talked down public expectations. Responsible economic management became the synonym for good government, the foundation without which no party could get elected. Fraser's public commitment to reining in the state pre-dated similar strong campaigns in Britain and the USA by Thatcher and Reagan. His rhetoric at least blazed a trail. His lengthy, and not always successful, efforts showed how hard it was to fulfil those expectations.

CHAPTER 8

TREATING WITH BANDITS

THE FEDERALIST

P rime ministers in a federal system share power with state premiers. The commonwealth parliament's powers are nominally restricted by the constitution to an enumerated list; therefore the federal government must use a limited range of powers, some directly granted, some indirectly gained through judicial interpretation or financial pressure. Federal governments have, for instance, used their external affairs power to protect the environment and their financial hegemony to control tertiary education, although neither the environment nor education is directly allocated to the federal government. At times its constitutional authority may be questionable, but no other government wants to challenge its decisions. The policy outcomes of the Australian federal system are therefore a combination of legal restraints and political compromises. They can be explained not merely by what governments have the legal authority to do, but by what the political implications might be where authority is disputed or applied through the use of shared powers.

Managing the federal system is a time-consuming but necessary function for every prime minister. State premiers, as heads of sub-national units, often demand to be treated as heads of government, corresponding exclusively with the prime minister. They require meetings and promises. They are perceived to wield great political power. State premiers took much of the credit for the political destruction of Gorton and Whitlam. Even if that reputation was much exaggerated, the image of power, even of local invulnerability, had an impact on federal choices of political strategy.

Premiers are power-brokers within political parties at the state level; they often have electoral influence in the state. Federal and state parties are irrevocably intertwined. Liberal premiers deal with the prime minister not only in their capacity as the head of government, but also as local party leaders through the federal MPs from their state, because the latter depend for their future party selection on state support and may be caught between the demands of federal policy and state interests. Premiers live in the state capitals, near the centre of power for the local party; prime ministers usually have no direct influence in party divisions outside their own state. It is easier for the former to maintain a constant influence on party matters and at times to consolidate support for the state's interests.

Prime ministers must deal with premiers on the daily business of administration and policy-making, sometimes harmoniously, sometimes in an atmosphere of confrontation. These bilateral relations must be maintained simultaneously with six state premiers and one territorial chief minister, all with their own problems. At the same time prime ministers must deal with the premiers as a group, at Loan Council or at premiers' conferences, where they must sell federal policy, persuade the premiers to accept national solutions, or impose financial policies. The general process is time-consuming, sensitive, fraught with political danger and eventually open only to compromises. Federal governments are always faced with the dilemma: they may have the capacity for direct action, but what will the implications be in other policy areas?

For Fraser there were particular problems, partly ideological, partly personal. They were ideological because of the government's public commitment to 'new federalism', a policy designed to reduce federal intervention in detailed state government activity. The Whitlam government had made extensive use of section 96 grants, that is, grants to states that were tied to particular programs and often demanding some state financial commitments. The federal government had been able to redirect state priorities. The Fraser government argued that this interference was excessive. The Liberal platform stated not only that some capacity to raise income tax should be returned to the states, but also that there should be a new style of co-operation between the federal and state governments. Fraser therefore came into office with a public commitment to a new co-operative deal.

Second, the problems were related to personalities. He was faced by state premiers who were either ideologically opposed, like Neville Wran in New South Wales, or who had a very limited view of national goals. Sir Charles Court in Western Australia and Joh Bjelke-Petersen in Queensland regarded the progress of their states as the equivalent of national success. John Carrick, minister assisting the prime minister in federal affairs, commented 'Premiers don't believe in federalism; they believe in states' rights'. Court and Bjelke-Petersen were populists, working with the belief that their opposition had helped to destroy the Whitlam government and that they could repeat the performance if necessary. Neither was slow to give advice; Sir Charles Court in particular unleashed a stream of letters and telexes to Fraser, providing comment on both federal and state business. Between June and October 1979, for instance, PMC's register listed twenty-three letters from Court, relating to everything from the Ord River, the Trade Practices Act, the Seas and Submerged Lands Act, abattoir inspection fees, tax concessions, to migratory birds and Antarctic seals. The answers required advice from over fifteen different departments, and every one had to be cleared and signed by Fraser. Every reply had the prospect of starting new correspondence. Even when the federal government was in dispute with another state, Court was likely to rush off a note, usually proposing that states should be left to their own devices. Fraser described him, almost affectionately, as 'a wonderful bandit; it was the state first, last and forever'. Dealing with loquacious prima donnas could be a trial for all prime ministers.

Fraser found both Court and Bjelke-Petersen difficult to deal with because they approached politics with the certainty of the true believers. They were often unpredictable. One official claims: 'Fraser saw himself playing by the rules, whereas Joh and Court never played by the rules'. Fraser therefore used a variety of tactics to deal with these local barons. He also started with the basic premise that he did not want confrontation with the states. 'It's not only destructive to your own party and party relations, it doesn't achieve anything!' Almost all the time he preferred to negotiate.

State premiers were not averse to exerting pressure on the federal members of their party. Court often reminded Fraser that federal members were strongly opposed to his legislation on tax evasion. Lindsay Thompson as Victorian premier summoned all federal Liberal members to a meeting; Fraser agreed that Guilfoyle should attend to allow the ministry to learn what was said. Whenever there was a state election – and that was two or three times a year – the federal cabinet had to be careful not to undermine the local division's chance; in 1979 John Carrick was asked to monitor all legislation to ensure it did not contain unexpected problems that would have an impact on the NSW election result. The federal members could not often afford to upset either the local machine which might influence preselection, or the prime minister on whom their ministerial aspirations depended. They were caught in a political vice.

Fraser's methods can be understood best by examining particular cases where the federal and state governments clearly had overlapping powers: in Aboriginal matters, in the ratification and implementation of international treaties over seas and submerged lands, and world heritage. In the former the referendum of 1967 had given the federal government the power to legislate for Aboriginal affairs, but the states retained the substantive administrative responsibility. In the case of international treaties the federal government's power was less certain. A High Court decision in November 1975 had declared as valid the legislation that gave the federal government jurisdiction below the low water mark. Whether the High Court would take a wider interpretation of the external affairs power and allow its application to all treaties – particularly on environmental issues – was not yet proved. In the case of the Seas and Submerged Lands Act, Fraser had to deal with the premiers as a group at premiers conferences; in the other cases he was often negotiating with coalition premiers, notionally on the same side in political life. That it was so difficult to reach compromise illustrated both the degree to which a federal system creates incompatible interests at different levels of government and the necessity for prime ministers to consider the broader implications of the exercise of power. That Fraser did not choose to use the full powers in either case is typical of the style of his approach to federal relations.

Aboriginal affairs in Queensland: compromise with Joh

During the Fraser years, Queensland premier Sir Joh Bjelke-Petersen was at the height of his power. Sly, ruthless and revelling in the reputation of a Whitlam-destroyer, he ran the Queensland cabinet in his own style – with little attention to collective decision-making or Westminster traditions of behaviour. Dealing with Queensland meant dealing with Joh. That meant that relations were often unpredictable and never straightforward. A brief survey of the different tactics that were adopted provides insight into some of the relationships and difficulties that face any federal government which has to deal with independent and self-interested state barons.

Fraser would occasionally deal directly; he did have the ability to persuade Bjelke-Petersen individually. Llew Edwards recalls:

He would get Joh up to the Lodge and butter him up. He was absolutely unbelievable. That was one side of Fraser – he was the warmest and happiest man when he was buttering Joh up. He really had that ability to kid to Joh, to tell him how wonderful he was and yet not to ingratiate himself. He would do it in such a way that Joh felt proud of the prime minister taking notice of him.

Fraser thought Bjelke-Petersen was 'quiet, affable, doesn't raise his voice; he can be very determined and not always relevant to the particular discussion'. The problem was that Bjelke-

Petersen did not always abide by those decisions and, more often, he had to be persuaded in Brisbane, rather than in personal meetings at the Lodge. No prime minister is likely to risk his prestige by constant and fruitless negotiations with intractable premiers.

Fraser often worked through federal intermediaries or emissaries sent to Queensland as as though to negotiate with a foreign power. Nixon was, as usual, the most common of the troubleshooters. He would be called in when Joh was refusing to talk. Nixon commented that 'the time he spent negotiating with Queensland was mind-boggling':

I found the technique for handling Joh. I would ring him up and say, 'Joh we've got this problem'. Joh says: 'Peter, Peter, don't talk to me . . . I don't want to hear from you, Peter, Peter . . . tell Malcolm he's wasting his time'. I'd say 'Joh, Malcolm thinks I should come up and have a yarn with you'. 'No, Peter, Peter, it's a waste of time, you are wasting your time'. (He always called me Peter, Peter, and still does.) I would say: 'Joh, we can't leave it there. It's quite obvious that I've got to see you to see if we can't find a solution to this problem'. 'Don't want to talk to you Peter, Peter' and I'd say, 'Thanks Joh, goodbye', and we'd hang up. Then I would go about my business; I would ring Russ Hinze; and whatever else there is about Russ Hinze let me tell you that he had the most astute brain in the Queensland cabinet. He had all the other faults we know about, but he's very astute and what's more trustworthy. He was a very sensible bloke when it came to policy issues. He and Bob Sparkes were the two keys that I worked with. If it was a Bob versus Joh situation then I'd leave Bob out and go through Russ and I'd say 'Look Russ' – and they'd be issues that had nothing to do with Russ Hinze, they'd be Charles Porter's [Queensland's minister for Aboriginal and Island Affairs] or somebody else's – so I'd say to Russ, 'Look Russ, we've got to get this fixed. We can't let this go on, this is ridiculous'. So I'd explain it to Russ and he would comprehend what the feds were about and I'd say 'and I want to get to Joh'. And so if I couldn't get to Joh myself, Russ would get me to Joh or Bob Sparkes would get me to Joh. I had a variety of ways of getting to Joh and we'd set up these meetings and we'd talk these things through. There'd be heaps of meetings, sometimes it would go on and on endlessly.

One Liberal, John Moore, claims Nixon was trusted, 'because Nicko didn't owe anyone anything; he was an independent guy and he used to stick it into Petersen as much as anybody else'. Occasionally Nixon and Anthony were used in tandem – using the hard man and the conciliator routine.

Emissaries would be changed to achieve federal ends. One issue that required immediate attention was the boundary between Australia and Papua New Guinea in the Torres Strait. It went very close to the PNG shore. Islands in the Torres Strait were part of Queensland, so the approval of the Queensland government was required for the renegotiation because the federal government could not change the state's boundaries unilaterally. Cabinet first agreed on its position on the Torres Strait on 26 February 1976 and Anthony began the negotiations with Bjelke-Petersen. In May 1976 after a lengthy meeting between Anthony and Bjelke-Petersen, a settlement was reached; and it was also decided to make the announcement on a Saturday morning, just before the first race, so that it would get little attention. After the announcement, Bjelke-Petersen reneged, with the cry that he would not concede one inch of Queensland. Then he refused to meet Anthony again. Such inconsistencies made negotiations difficult. It took two further years and a change of negotiator. Andrew Peacock, as minister for foreign affairs, was finally successful on the same terms as Anthony had negotiated.

Sometimes Fraser sent a senior official of PMC, Alan Griffith, who became known as the 'ambassador to Queensland'. Griffith advised on the best means of bringing Bjelke-Petersen to agreement on a range of issues – Aboriginal affairs, land rights, funding for the Commonwealth Games. The advice was sensible, politically sensitive and direct. One note, dealing with Aboriginal affairs, provides the tone:

The Premier ranged over a wide number of areas not connected with Aboriginal matters . . . In the wash-up he thought the leasehold idea 'sensible' but he would like to kick it around a bit with his colleagues. At this point I suggested that Dr Edwards become involved and he agreed. Shann [head of the Queensland Premier's Department] is now seizing on this development to give Dr

Edwards much more command over the internal processing of the matter.

Overall the developments so far are positive. I am not too sanguine on the Premier's commitment to the word 'sensible' but we have now entrenched our basic minimum commitment into the Queensland system without abrasive eruptions and there is now scope for us to use Dr Edwards as a channel for matters of detail.

When federal negotiators were unsuccessful, Fraser used state politicians as channels to Queensland centres of power. Fraser would seek the advice of Llew Edwards, the deputy premier and the leader of the Liberal party in the last years of the coalition government. He often proposed that federal ministers of Aboriginal affairs dealt through Edwards because he was more sympathetic. He rang Edwards about the suitability of applicants for the Gold Coast casino. The process could work both ways. In one note in February 1982 to Fraser, his private secretary told him:

Senator Baume [minister for Aboriginal affairs] spoke to me earlier today. He had spoken to Dr Edwards who suggested to him that it would be helpful during your meeting with Premier Bjelke-Petersen tomorrow if you were to ask the Premier how the Aboriginal land matter is going. Apparently the Queensland cabinet may have decided on a land package during today and Edwards feels that if you raise the topic with the Premier, he may lock himself into a commitment on the subject.

Yet Edwards was not in the same party as Joh, and could not always, in the view of federal officials, get his way: 'utterly agreeable, could never deliver' was one overly harsh judgement. But he was regarded as reliable and would at least try.

Fraser himself, like Nixon, sometimes worked through members of the National party, particularly through the only two men who were regarded as powers in their own right, Sir Robert Sparkes, the president of the Queensland National party, and state minister Russ Hinze. Fraser recalls one occasion during the negotiations on Aurukun:

Joh and Charlie Porter came down with Russ Hinze. Joh would say something that was a little bit receptive to some of the points of view that the Commonwealth was putting – not too receptive, mind you, but not being totally negative. Charlie Porter would say: 'Well, Mr Premier, if that's the attitude you're going to take, if you are going to allow these Commonwealth people to run over you like that, I'm not even going to stay here. I thought we came down here to fight for Queensland, and for Queensland's rights and you're going to give it all away without a fight. I don't know what I'm doing in your government Mr Premier.' And Joh says: 'Oh, Charlie, come on Charlie, you've got me wrong Charlie. No Charlie, I'm much tougher than you on these people'. That would go on for about ten minutes and we'd just sit back. At the end Russ Hinze would say: 'Gentlemen, I think we are here to talk about this problem or that problem'. None of the Commonwealth people could have done it. Russ always got it back to something that made sense . . . Russ is an extraordinary negotiator and without him being there we would never have got an agreement.

Hinze had an ability to reduce issues to fundamentals.

Behind the scenes Sparkes often disagreed with the premier. He co-operated with Fraser over the 1977 referenda for changes to the constitution which the premier opposed – sending Fraser copies of the circulars he sent to party members. Fraser would ring or write to him to discuss issues that affected the two governments. Fraser always maintained alternative channels and different options. He was also cautious of being outflanked. When Fraser was invited to the opening of the Comalco smelter in Gladstone, his staff warned that Bjelke-Petersen might 'steal the show'. Prime ministers and premiers are competitors.

The tactics were nearly always similar. Maintain contacts, keep negotiating, try not to foreclose options, leave escape routes. The essence of the strategy was to move the state gradually in a preferred direction, but without ever totally alienating it. One typical, and highly public, occasion was the negotiation between federal and state governments over the fate of the Aboriginal settlements of Aurukun and Mornington Island. Fraser orchestrated the federal campaign; he selected delegates, decided what concessions would be made and how the federal policy would be best applied.

Aurukun and Mornington Island are two remote Aboriginal settlements in Queensland. In 1975 they were administered as a reserve by the Uniting Church in Queensland. Relations between the local community at Aurukun and the Queensland government were strained even before the Fraser government came to office because, during the distraction of the 1975 election, the Queensland government had pushed through the Aurukun Association Agreement Act. The Act allowed bauxite mining to take place without Aboriginal approval; it replaced an earlier agreement that had referred only to prospecting. Fraser wrote to Bjelke-Petersen on 9 and 22 December 1975, asking for clarification of the bill's intention.

At Fraser's instruction the new minister for Aboriginal affairs, Ian Viner, flew to Aurukun to consult the local community. He reported that, contrary to earlier promises, neither the Queensland government nor the company had negotiated with the community and that there was nothing in the Act to benefit or protect the interests of the local community. The Queensland government's actions did not conform to coalition policy or to established practice in the Northern Territory. The commonwealth provided funds to the community; therefore the federal government ought to be involved in any future plans for it. Initially it only asked the premier for a reply. One finally arrived on 11 February, but was of little help because it provided no new information.

Viner then presented a submission to cabinet, repeating his view that the government would be in an intolerable position if it refused to take any action. His preferred options were to persuade the Queensland government to defer the agreement until satisfactory negotiations with the Aborigines took place and to enter direct communications with the community, although he raised the possibility of refusing export licences for the bauxite. On 2 March cabinet was more cautious; it suggested that the reply to Bjelke-Petersen should draw attention to the lack of consultation, refer to the commonwealth's constitutional responsibility for Aboriginal affairs, and state that federal ministers were prepared to discuss the issue with their state counterparts. Fraser's letter of 5 March emphasised these points. He told Bjelke-Petersen that the foreign-owned companies would be subject to foreign investment guidelines, and requested that no action be taken until the commonwealth was satisfied that Aboriginal interests had been protected. Fraser reminded the deputy prime minister to take up with the Queensland minister the foreign investment guidelines. Bjelke-Petersen responded to Fraser that 'it would appear that the centralist policies of the Whitlam government are either deliberately or inadvertently being maintained by Canberra'. It was very easy to get the premier in an aggressive mood.

Bjelke-Petersen was scarcely co-operative. Fraser had discussed with him the proposal that representatives of the Aurukun community meet the premier and federal minister to discuss the commonwealth interest in the development. Bjelke-Petersen stated that he had no intention of varying the agreement. When Fraser sent a telex to remind Bjelke-Petersen that Viner and Nixon were available in either Canberra or Brisbane, the premier responded that there was nothing to be gained by meeting because the Aurukun community had taken out an injunction to prevent mining. When the injunction was upheld by the Queensland Supreme Court, the premier appealed to the Privy Council, threatening that if necessary the state would take over the Aurukun reserve. The federal government watched for two years as these events unfolded. Fraser was kept informed, responding without any sympathy to complaints from Bjelke-Petersen about new federal legislation that established Aboriginal councils and associations, and about the accusations that federal officials were fomenting land rights activity.

When the Privy Council upheld the Queensland government's appeal in March 1978, the confrontation suddenly erupted. The government had to react to Queensland actions. The Queensland government had regarded the church's policy towards the reserves as opposed to state government policy, and argued that the community at Aurukun wanted the reserve taken over by the state. It proposed to do so on 31 March. At Mornington Island the community had been given no notice until the decision was taken. Both communities sought commonwealth assistance. A cabinet submission, lodged on 21 March 1978, was designed to ensure the community could manage its own affairs. It proposed either non-legislative solutions, including the compulsory acquisition of the reserves, or legislative steps including possibly the provision that Aboriginal affairs in Queensland were a federal responsibility. The submission had been developed in consultation with other departments; PMC had suggested that the most profitable strategy would be a series of steps, gradually turning up the heat. The submission recommended initially persuading the Queensland minister not to proceed and approving direct financial aid to the reserve. It proposed legislation that would strengthen the communities' self-management opportunities. PMC advised that the government present its action as entirely based on a commitment to Aboriginal self-management. To introduce discussion of land rights or cutback of funds and/or anticipate legislative acquisition would only muddy the waters.

Fraser urgently 'called the submission on' and cabinet confirmed the minister's recommendations. It supported the community but it decided not to publicly mention compulsory acquisition or the prospect of offsetting the cost of acquisition by reductions in tax reimbursement to the state. Cabinet was acting in the public glare, with a torrent of letters and telegrams, all demanding commonwealth intervention, being sent to Fraser from the Uniting Church and other leading figures.

Nixon and Viner went to Brisbane to discuss the issue with the state, but no meeting took place. The Queensland government ingenuously declared it didn't know they were there. On 24 March Fraser wrote a carefully worded letter to Bjelke-Petersen, stating that the cabinet held the view that the Aborigines on reserves should be allowed to manage their own affairs, regretting that no meeting had taken place and hoping for and recommending another meeting on 29 March.

Fraser directed the activity of presenting his government's policy. He proposed that Viner go on television, and received daily reports on the TV coverage and on other developments. Sir Charles Court tried to exert pressure, arguing that he didn't know the facts, but he was concerned at the way the commonwealth was acting and asked for the policy to be rethought. On several occasions on 27 March Fraser's staff sought answers to his demands for detail from the Department of Aboriginal Affairs. On 28 March Fraser telexed Bjelke-Petersen to confirm that Nixon and Viner were again available for discussion in Brisbane or Canberra. Bjelke-Petersen finally agreed to talk the next day. Fraser established an ad hoc committee of ministers to review developments and report to cabinet. At the same time he was told that the Aurukun community wanted an injunction issued to stop the takeover; Aboriginal affairs and Attorney-General's officials discussed contingency plans if the talks broke down.

Initially, however, an agreement appeared to have been reached after Nixon and Viner met Queensland ministers on 29 March. Management was to be shared with the Uniting Church and the community, as long as that was acceptable to those two bodies, and the state would consult the commonwealth in the preparation of legislation. Bjelke-Petersen then reneged and, in breach of the discussion, announced that he would go ahead anyway, regardless of federal views. But neither the communities nor the Uniting Church were agreeable. In the rapidly changing environment Viner recommended, in a hastily prepared submission, that legislation for acquisition be immediately introduced, although he argued that the reserves should only be acquired after a specific decision of cabinet. Treasury thought it would be unprecedented to offset the cost of compulsory acquisition against tax reimbursements to the state. PMC proposed a cooling-off period, giving Queensland the option of amending its legislation. It appreciated that it might be harder to sell, but thought it preferable to confrontation, as long as the federal government made it clear that the commonwealth would not be overridden and that it must agree fully with the terms of Queensland legislation.

On 3 April cabinet agreed to introduce legislation to free the reserves from discriminatory legal practices and accepted acquisition in principle if it was needed, but cabinet was to be advised before legislation was proclaimed. Bjelke-Petersen, Porter and Court were to be notified before the press conference; as were Sparkes, Yvonne McComb (president of the state Liberal party) and the president of the Uniting Church. Sir Charles Court remained unimpressed, seeing in the decision a reduction of state independence, even though Fraser assured him that the legislation would apply only to Queensland.

Bjelke-Petersen reacted angrily. Although he had no details of the federal legislation, he declared that the management and continuation of the reserves was a matter for the states; he claimed dissatisfaction on the reserves was fomented by outsiders. Fraser replied by insisting that the federal government was acting on the basis of authentic expressions of the wishes of the people and sought a meeting between Viner and Porter. The ad hoc committee began to consider what options were available if Queensland abolished the reserves or changed their status. In the meantime it continued with its plans; the new Bill, the Aboriginal and Torres Strait Islanders (Queensland Reserves and Community Self-Management) Bill, was explained to the party room on 5 April.

On 7 April, cabinet was told that Queensland had changed the reserves to crown land, taking the land outside the terms of the federal legislation. Cabinet agreed to examine the options and to consult with the Uniting Church; the prime minister was to seek early discussions. Bjelke-Petersen responded by accusing Fraser of breaching the ministers' agreements, and of introducing confrontationist legislation that attempted to take over state rights and even citizens. He declared that his ministers were too busy to meet, and told Fraser to leave Aboriginal affairs to the state government.

Cabinet met to review the impasse. A submission presented three options: talks; legislation to reserve the local rights of Aborigines as of 5 April (before the Queensland government's decision), which would entail some acquisition; legislation to guarantee Aboriginal rights in Queensland. The minister recommended merely that cabinet consider the options. He did not say which position he preferred. PMC supported the second option, which fell short of full acquisition because it would keep the attention on Aboriginal self-management and away from land and mineral rights. Cabinet decided to continue talking. Nixon was to arrange a meeting with Queensland ministers, with the primary objective of securing Aboriginal rights at least at a minimum level. If Queensland did not agree, acquisition would be the fall-back position, although the Queensland ministers were not to be told that in advance. Fraser proposed a form of words that emphasised that the federal obligation to the Aboriginal people was inviolate. Nixon reported the same day that Bjelke-Petersen had agreed to a ministerial meeting and then a premier–prime ministerial meeting on 11 April. Then Bjelke-Petersen himself rang to propose that he and Fraser be in from the start and that his cabinet felt he should not come unless Fraser was involved. As Dale Budd noted: 'He sounded amiable and made some other remarks about wanting to solve the problem and not wanting more confrontation. He mentioned that at some time in the future you would want to be campaigning together'. By the end of the call he was prepared to withdraw the demand that Fraser and he should be in the meeting from the beginning.

Cabinet laid down conditions for agreement – that Aboriginal rights be protected, that the Aborigines have rights of self-management, that mineral rights remain with the crown, and that an agreement in writing was required. It agreed too that its objective was the creation of a local council authority based on the old reserve and holding a special lease. After lengthy meetings a joint announcement by Fraser and Bjelke-Petersen on 11 April appeared to settle the issue. Cabinet then established negotiating principles to guide the following discussions with the Queensland ministers; they proposed that Aboriginal rights were inviolate and needed to be protected by an adequate form of title, that self-management should be ensured, and that prospectors required permission for entry to the reserve. The next week Viner went to Brisbane to negotiate the form of the committee needed to support the local councils. The federal government wanted further consultation with the Aborigines; Queensland did not. In particular the federal government wanted a long lease and the guarantee of traditional rights, and opposed the advisory councils having statutory powers.

Viner had little success. The draft of the Queensland Local Government (Aboriginal Lands) Bill did not satisfy any of the federal conditions; indeed the Queensland government had made little effort to reach agreement. The advisory councils were to assist the minister and there was little protection for the leases. The Department of Aboriginal Affairs argued that the Act should be modified or rejected; PMC supported a continuation of negotiation. Cabinet told its ad hoc committee to examine the legislation and to seek clarification of its meaning. Fraser contacted Bjelke-Petersen to seek a further meeting.

The local communities were losing faith. They sent telegrams urging Fraser to reject the new state legislation. In a two-hour meeting with the leaders of the Aurukun community, Fraser assured them that the government would stand by them but, insisted Fraser, while it was easy to pass commonwealth legislation, it would only bring about years of court actions and therefore legislation should only be used as a last resort. The community was unimpressed and, in an open letter, declared that they had lost faith in the federal government and were 'totally disillusioned with you and your government as an ally'.

On 4 May Viner and Nixon had further talks with Hinze, minister for local government in Queensland, and the points in dispute – terms of lease, role of advisory committees, rights of entry – were discussed. The discussions were at last productive. When the legislation was introduced into the Queensland parliament, cabinet noted that it agreed substantially with commonwealth requirements and that Hinze had indicated a willingness to review it in a few months.

However the federal officials had to maintain a continuing interest in the administration of the reserves. When in August Hinze was reported as threatening to remove forcibly from the areas all those he termed 'drop-outs', Fraser promised an outraged Senator Bonner that the federal government would stand by its commitments. Cabinet again considered what action it could take when it discovered state officials were handling all the money and that little authority had really been delegated to the community. It recommended that, if the control of the Queensland Department of Aboriginal and Island Affairs (DAIA) was not rescinded, the federal government should make direct grants to the communities. As PMC noted, the real question was whether there was a partnership; it would be preferable if the Department of Local Government, not DAIA, ran the councils. Cabinet agreed in principle to introduce direct grants and authorised the minister to meet Hinze.

On 13 August cabinet noted that Queensland had agreed to direct funds to the communities through the Local Government

Department and that the premier would visit the communities. But there were still problems because the Mornington community had incensed Bjelke-Petersen by refusing to talk to him. There was a danger that the local councils would be dissolved; cabinet agreed to send PMC's Alan Griffith to negotiate and gradually a settlement was reached. In November when the department of Aboriginal affairs argued that the commonwealth should acquire the territory, regardless of the political disadvantages, PMC officers told them that they could not advise the prime minister on those lines as 'it was our job primarily to keep the prime minister out of trouble'; but when shire clerks were appointed and suitable leases proposed, the urgency declined.

Almost immediately other problems emerged. As a response to the Queensland government's proposed takeover of Aurukun the federal government passed the Aboriginal and Torres Strait Islanders (Queensland Reserves and Communities Self-Management) Act. In September 1978 four communities asked Viner to bring them under commonwealth legislation. One of those communities was Yarrabah, which asked again to be brought under federal legislation in January and whose case was the subject of discussions at the Lodge between Fraser, Bjelke-Petersen, Chaney and Porter on 14 February 1979. Several advisers carried on negotiations for months. Griffith was sent to negotiate and told to use the skills of Llew Edwards as he had the reputation of a moderate; he talked directly with Bjelke-Petersen.

The new minister for Aboriginal affairs, Fred Chaney, took the brunt of the negotiations, after an initial meeting between Fraser and Bjelke-Petersen. Chaney met Edwards on 20 April and sent a report to Fraser; he anticipated that he would need to meet Bjelke-Petersen, Hinze and Porter. On 30 May he met Edwards and Porter for five hours and feared as a consequence that the commonwealth might be put in a position where it had to override Queensland policy. As a compromise Edwards proposed a joint delegation of federal and state ministers meet the Yarrabah council; Chaney agreed to work from the same list of negotiating principles as guided discussions with Queensland over Aurukun. Then the Queensland ministers dropped out, and Chaney went alone. He wanted Fraser to negotiate directly with Bjelke-Petersen, while Griffith talked to Edwards. The link was useful because by this time relations between Porter and Chaney were too bad to make any useful progress, with Porter accusing Chaney of setting a collision course and arguing that further talks would be inimical to any progress.

By October it was still unsettled. Chaney met Edwards again on 18 October and wanted to fulfil the undertaking to visit Yarrabah made a month earlier when Edwards was invited to attend. He wanted Yarrabah to gain a long-term lease, with an incorporated community council as managing authority. Edwards agreed to take the proposal to the Queensland cabinet. Chaney and Edwards met again on 28 October in preparation for a meeting between Anthony, as acting prime minister, and Bjelke-Petersen. Anthony was provided with a résumé of the premier's likely arguments, a series of talking points and a discussion of options. Griffith advised that Bjelke-Petersen's position had little support within his cabinet, but that he took a strong stand as a tactic to inhibit any challenge; therefore 'anger might be tactical'.

Federal cabinet became involved for the first time in the negotiations over Yarrabah. The submission confirmed a preference for a settlement with Queensland, with legislation to be used as a fall-back position. Cabinet agreed the same day as the submission was lodged, but when Anthony declared that the purpose of the talks was to secure a negotiated settlement that met the commonwealth's policy commitment to self-management, Bjelke-Petersen telexed that the Queensland cabinet had agreed discussions could not begin from any preferred unilateral position and proposed they be cancelled. After an assurance that the commonwealth was not rigid in its attitudes, the meeting was held and Yarrabah was placed under an incorporated community council.

The running sore of Aboriginal lands indicated Fraser's preferred tactics. He was kept informed all the time. Cabinet determined the negotiating principles and tactics. A range of intermediaries was used, both state and federal. Although the ministers for Aboriginal affairs might have proposed federal intervention for purchase and acquisition, cabinet always pulled back from confrontations that were irrevocable or unnecessary. Negotiation, with the threat of action, was preferred as the recalcitrant Queensland government was pushed in the right direction. As Fraser wrote to Viner in August 1977 when he finally settled another issue:

I commend your approach to finding a solution to outstanding differences with Queensland and agree that more can be achieved through discussion than public confrontation.

Was it effective? Fraser believed it was the only responsible strategy:

We could have asserted our power and secured their future, but there would then be two warring administrations and it would have made sensible resolutions almost impossible. They're dependent on the state for education, health, all sorts of services which they are equipped to provide and we're not. That's one path and I would be really fearful of the consequences. The other path was for us to be resolute and to extract everything we can possibly extract that's reasonable from the Queensland government. It would also be difficult, but it would enable you to preserve a relationship with the Queensland government.

Several advisers thought so too:

If he had taken them on over Aurukun, the outcome for the Aborigines might have been a damn sight worse. The federal government might have won the battle, but the Aborigines would have suffered as a consequence of the war.

Where power was shared, confrontation was not regarded as useful. It would lead to internal problems for the federal and state National parties; it would spill over into other policy areas; it would set positions in concrete and make later negotiation difficult. The power to act may have been there, but Fraser's preference was not to use that authority. Federalism required negotiation.

Multilateral negotiations: the ebb and flow of seashore federalism

Throughout the 1970s authority over the territory beyond the low-water mark had been disputed between federal and state governments. The question was where the boundaries of the state ended: at the low-water mark or at the three-mile limit of the territorial seas? When John Gorton was prime minister, the federal government had asserted its authority beyond the low-water mark. The constitutionality of any legislation was important, not only because it would determine which government could exert control over the Great Barrier Reef and oil exploration, but also because it had clear administrative implications. Any piers or harbour-works that extended beyond the low-water mark could be under federal authority.

In December 1975 the High Court upheld the constitutionality of the Seas and Submerged Lands Act 1973 which meant that the federal government had legislative authority over territory below the low-water mark. Some solution was obviously needed to reduce the political contradictions that could emerge. Indeed the problems of which level of government should make the decisions occurred almost immediately. The federal minister for transport, Peter Nixon, wanted to extend the application of the Navigation Acts to ensure that it was applied uniformly in all waters under federal jurisdiction, particularly in respect to oil exploration. Sir Charles Court immediately asked that it be discussed at a premiers' conference. Fraser asked the attorney-general, Robert Ellicott, for a brief on its implications. However it never came to cabinet because the premiers' conference decided to refer the problem to the conference of attorneys-general.

Several issues had to be determined. What was administratively feasible and sensible? How could the ambitions and demands of the state premiers be made consistent with the decision of the High Court? What legislative route was best to implement any agreement? The states wanted returned to them what they believed they had had before – authority to the three-mile limit. The issue became an important touchstone for the genuineness of Fraser's 'new federalism'. The final problem for him was that any agreement needed to be accepted by all the premiers. It was not enough to reach settlement with them one by one; multilateral negotiations, consummated at premiers' conferences, were necessary.

The evaluation of the High Court decision by the conference of attorneys-general took time. The March meeting set up working parties which reported in May. The attorneys-general then sent their views to the states for consideration. Not until late September 1976 did cabinet's Economic committee finally demand that a submission identify the areas that needed fixing. The subjects were offshore mining, shipping and navigation, ports, fisheries, marine parks and marine pollution. The submission noted that the states believed the commonwealth should take no steps to control offshore activity and that Western Australia wanted to extend the state limits. Cabinet agreed to regard the High Court's decision as the final settlement of the general issue of sovereignty, but accepted that other areas should be subject to negotiation. Fraser wrote to the premiers stating that the commonwealth could not legally accede to the request to extend the limits of the states, but wanted to resolve the practical issues that arose out of that decision.

Submissions on transport, marine pollution and offshore oil were brought to cabinet in December. The submission on offshore oil argued that, although full commonwealth control would have advantages, it would create too many problems. Its preference was for commonwealth legislation to be administered by the states. Cabinet accepted these arrangements for marine pollution and navigation, but Court and Bjelke-Petersen objected to such a strategy for offshore mining. Fraser asked Nixon to withdraw the submission and establish a taskforce to develop a consensus view; he gave him a week, a time Nixon regarded as inadequate. Indeed, it took much longer.

On 22 March 1977 Ellicott and the solicitor general lodged a memorandum, in response to Fraser's request for an opinion on the minimum powers that the commonwealth must retain in the national interest and on the alternative methods that could be adopted to achieve that share. The opinion offered several options, including constitutional amendment, mirror or complementary legislation by federal and state parliaments, delegation to joint authorities, commonwealth legislation administered by the states, or use of section 51(xxxviii) of the constitution. The opinion questioned whether constitutional change could extend the state boundaries. (Section 51(xxxviii) gave the parliament power to make laws in respect to 'the exercise within the Commonwealth, at the request or with the concurrence of the Parliaments of all the States directly concerned, of any power which can at the establishment of this constitution be exercised only by the Parliament of the United Kingdom or by the 'Federal Council of Australasia'. It is a residual and unspecific clause that was rarely used.)

Fraser asked officials to consolidate the opinions of the law officers and the officials' taskforce. He then wanted to devote a whole day of cabinet to the offshore settlement because of its importance. Fraser argued as a basic position that the commonwealth should not be using the High Court judgement as a means of intruding into functions that were the responsibility of the states. He proposed that the federal government's direct role should be confined to the minimum of areas in which in the national interest it was reasonable, rational and economic for it to be involved. In a letter to ministers he regretted that some departments were pursuing a centralist policy that was contrary to the government's federalism policy.

By July 1977 the options had shrunk to four: the use of section 51(xxxviii), commonwealth delegation of authority, commonwealth legislation and administration, or commonwealth legislation and state administration. The cabinet selected different strategies for different problems: complementary legislation for shipping, a joint authority or the status quo for fisheries, and a grant of powers to the states for marine ports. For offshore mining it initially proposed a joint authority, but the states wanted to extend not merely their powers but also the state boundaries to the three-mile (or even the twelve-mile) limits. The attorney-general was asked to review for cabinet the options for extending state boundaries, fisheries and mining rights. (Actually cabinet did not mention state limits, but the Cabinet Office added it to the decision because it was necessary to provide the context for the others.)

Amendments to the Seas and Submerged Lands Act were the main item on the agenda of the premiers' conference held in October 1977. In a letter to the premiers Fraser canvassed the approach spelt out to officials in April. Premiers listed the range of problems created by the High Court decision, particularly in regard to fisheries, offshore mining and marine parks. All the premiers wanted territorial waters 'returned' to the states, with constant debate on what was included as a 'territorial water': a three- or twelve-mile limit.

Fraser was not prepared to go too far. When asked if he would commit his government to the return of the territorial waters to the states he responded:

As to a firm commitment, whatever comes from here I have to take back to my own cabinet. However, Mr. Anthony and Mr. Lynch are here and I suppose we have a reasonable chance of getting something through the cabinet.

The premiers' conference agreed to the general proposition that day-to-day control should be handed back to the states. As Fraser constantly reminded the premiers when they niggled, the High Court decision gave the federal government the power. If it had not wanted to negotiate, the item would not have been on the agenda.

The details were sent to the state and federal attorneys-general for discussion. They met on 7–8 April 1978 to discuss the options. The state attorneys thought section 123 (which allowed the federal government to increase the territorial limits of the state if the parliament and the majority of electors agreed) could extend over the sea; federal officials did not. They were not certain that section 51(xxxviii) would work but thought the legal difficulties did not outweigh its advantages. Unilateral commonwealth law was inconceivable, and UK legislation was possible but only if all else failed. It was accepted that there was merit in expanding the powers, rather than the boundaries, as the latter would need legislation and a referendum in each state. Section 51(xxxviii) seemed the most attractive route.

The cabinet submission of 7 June 1978 took as given the premiers' conference decision of October 1977 that territorial seas be the responsibility of the states and that the limits or powers of each state be extended without affecting the commonwealth's international responsibilities. While acknowledging that the use of section 128 – a national referendum – was most secure, it appreciated the problems; it also accepted that a request to Britain for legislation to be passed through the British parliament would be unacceptable. It recommended the use of section 51(xxxviii) and the extension of powers but not the territorial limits of the states. To use section 51(xxxviii) required the commonwealth and state governments to pass complementary legislation.

Fraser wrote to the attorney-general, Peter Durack, in May 1978 that while he was overseas, 'I will be relying on you to maintain the commonwealth's general posture'. On 8 June cabinet, in Fraser's absence, queried whether legislation based on section 51(xxxviii) could be unilaterally repealed, and postponed discussion. Cabinet was raising basic questions: did the commonwealth wish to change the legal balance permanently; was a referendum preferable; was section 51(xxxviii) irreversible? Cabinet wanted to move carefully as the states were demanding an extension of limits and powers to the twelve-mile limit, with constitutionally watertight amendment processes. Durack was obviously concerned about the tenor of the debate; he argued that Fraser should be present at the next discussion because it had implications for federal-state relations and particularly for the prime minister's personal relations with the premiers. Durack rang Fraser, who asked for more details to be sent to Singapore.

The additional information sought by cabinet indicated the dangers. Of the seven legal opinions sought, five thought section 51(xxxviii) legislation could be unilaterally repealed by the commonwealth without the states being consulted, although the attorney-general argued that it would be politically difficult. It was regarded as doubtful whether the UK parliament would agree to legislate unless other options were tried, although some states were coming round to preferring that option. Durack still favoured using section 51(xxxviii). So did PMC. Its advice suggested that cabinet should not endorse a position contradictory to that espoused by the 1977 premiers' conference as that might allow premiers to reopen the issue. With Fraser back, cabinet's objections were overcome and Durack's proposals were accepted as the basis of the commonwealth position for the premiers' conference. The powers, not the boundaries, of the state would be extended to the three-mile limit and ministers were authorised to agree to the use of section 51(xxxviii) if that mechanism was the choice of the states.

Events at the premiers' conference of 22-23 June 1978 emphasised the strong position of the prime minister. The premiers doubted whether the use of section 51(xxxviii) would be effective and now preferred to ask the British parliament to legislate. Even Labor premiers agreed. The Tasmanian Labor premier had approached the British Foreign and Commonwealth Office and been told that there was no problem at the British end if all the states agreed. Don Dunstan commented that there was every chance of getting agreement for a British bill. 'Any other way would invite either a political exercise which is extremely doubtful in the result or a legal exercise' that was equally doubtful. He acknowledged that it was unusual for someone from his side of politics to accept the colonial ties so easily, but thought UK legislation would assist in getting rid of one area of colonial ties. Wran stated:

No one cares how we give effect to what are fundamental objectives we are agreed upon . . . The only issue is how to do it in a way which will be legally binding and least subject to challenge in the courts.

Court and Bjelke-Petersen wanted the same route. Victorian premier, Dick Hamer, was alone in believing that an appeal to the British parliament should be a last resort.

Fraser however was adamant. 'If we were a colony I would not mind, but we are not a colony' he retorted when the acting premier of Tasmania, Neil Batt, agreed with Wran's stand. He stated 'I do not know that the commonwealth is prepared to ask the UK to solve a problem which I think we are quite capable of solving. I find it basically offensive'. He emphasised that the conference was talking about an area where the commonwealth had sole constitutional authority. In any arrangements the commonwealth was giving away power, rights and responsibilities, or at least sharing them.

Fraser used the weight of the collective cabinet decision to restrict the subjects under discussion to those he wanted. When the premiers predictably sought to extend the limits to twelve miles, Fraser replied: 'I have no authority to agree to anything other than three miles'. The conference eventually accepted a resolution drafted by Hamer that agreed to use section 51(xxxviii), amendments to the Seas and Submerged Lands Act and assignment of powers to the states. The motion was agreed: 'I think it will give us peace in our time', cracked Joh optimistically. Yet at times the ever-increasing demands of the states sorely tried Fraser's patience:

Medcalf (WA minister for federal affairs): There is no doubt whatever that your government has made a tremendous effort.
Fraser: I would like to see some recognition of that occasionally.

Fraser was also not averse to drawing on the premiers as allies. Once the general principles appeared accepted, he asked the premiers to bring their influence to bear on the senators from their states, to ensure that the legislation would get through. The constant problem of getting legislation through the Senate often emerged in premiers' conference discussions.

Senior ministers still had doubts. Fraser discussed the use of section 51(xxxviii) with leading colleagues on 28 June. Durack thought it appropriate. Howard expressed the widespread doubts of cabinet; he reminded the group that the constitution should not be changed, however inadvertently, without a referendum. If section 51(xxxviii) was irreversible, cabinet was likely to be opposed to its use. Anthony agreed that the correct answer would be a referendum, but considered it out of the question as it would probably fail. He thought the best solution would be federal legislation and assignment to the states, but was not as opposed as most members of cabinet to the use of section 51(xxxviii) as a last resort. Carrick agreed with Anthony. Fraser thought it would be 'a bugger of a job' to get an amendment to the constitution agreed to.

On 17 July Fraser wrote to the premiers confirming the

extension of powers and control over offshore mining to the three-mile limit, to be achieved by legislation using section 51(xxxviii). He sent the attorney-general a list of items that needed to be completed. It appeared that the main issue was settled, but then the premiers began to have second thoughts. Doug Lowe in Tasmania said he reserved the right to raise the extension of state power to twelve miles if the commonwealth proclaimed a twelve-mile territorial sea. Then, led by Court, they again demanded an approach to Britain. In December 1978 Court asked Fraser to reconsider UK legislation. He claimed that section 51(xxxviii) would not solve the problem, while the UK would provide an easy alternative. He said his state did not object to the use of the UK, particularly when the alternative left open the prospect of 'having to rely on the philosophical views of Mr Justice Murphy in order to find reasons for bolstering the use of section 51(xxxviii)'. This break in the ranks caused problems because the use of section 51(xxxviii) required all the states to agree to request the federal parliament to legislate. The commonwealth could easily legislate on its own, but then there was a danger of later repeal. If section 51(xxxviii) were not to be adopted, there were only two options: UK legislation or a referendum. Cabinet had discussed but not accepted the idea of an approach to the UK in June 1978, on the grounds that it was inappropriate to ask the UK to fix Australia's domestic problems. On 17 April 1979 cabinet decided that if the states did not agree to use section 51(xxxviii) Durack should explore whether the states would agree to unilateral commonwealth legislation and the vesting of proprietary rights in the states. Cabinet declared that it was not prepared to approach the UK or to hold a referendum under section 128. The states were in effect being told to accept the federal offer for complementary legislation or to be faced with unilateral federal legislation.

Nevertheless the states still tried to improve their deal. The state attorneys-general did not want a clause expressly declaring that nothing in the bills derogate from any power of the commonwealth, and wanted more than the three miles if a twelve-mile territorial sea was declared. On 7 June 1979 Bjelke-Petersen took the same line as Court. He argued that the bills were inadequate and hoped that the governments would not follow a course 'that is legally and practically unsound because of what is basically a political aversion to another means that does not suffer the same defects'. Cabinet decided on 12 June to persuade the states to keep the clause protecting commonwealth powers and the three-mile limit. It agreed to put the remaining issues in one package, including a clause that reserved the commonwealth's reserve plenary power to legislate. But no decision was finally made on offshore mining, as negotiations were needed with Court. Cabinet noted that Fraser and Durack would discuss it before the premiers' conference.

Fraser stood firm at the 1979 premiers' conference. He pointed out to the premiers that the federal government did not have to use section 51(xxxviii). It could simply amend the Seas and Submerged Lands legislation; indeed this had been the easiest preferred tactic, but had changed because of states' wishes. He would certainly not concede on the issue of an approach to Britain which he declared 'offensive':

Court: We hope you can settle something permanently. I am taking it that you have said categorically on behalf of the commonwealth government that you are not prepared to follow the safest route, which is under the United Kingdom legislation.
Bjelke-Petersen: I think he will.
Fraser: I do not have any authority to do so. The word 'offensive' is not mine; Cabinet finds it offensive and does not want to do it.

Fraser was interpreting cabinet's mood. The appeal to cabinet as a source of legitimacy was not uncommon. On another issue – a proposal for a study of the remaining links with Westminster – Fraser agreed without any commitment to its outcome. 'I for one do not have the authority to do so. It is not the Fraser view; it is the cabinet view'.

As the other states gradually accepted the federal approach, Bjelke-Petersen and Court became isolated. Fraser constantly kept the debate moving, trying to get agreement and refusing to refer anything substantial back to the officials. Eventually some minor concessions were given to Court and agreement was finally reached. It was necessary, claimed Neville Wran at the end of the 1979 discussions, to

> recognise the historic nature of the decision that has been made. We would want to compliment you Mr Prime Minister for the role you have played in what to my mind has been the best illustration of co-operative federalism in the last three years.

After the premiers' conference Fraser was kept informed with two-monthly reports as the negotiations ground on to success. When progress with legislation in some states was slow, he wrote encouraging the premiers to maintain their commitment.

It was a telling illustration of how 'co-operative' co-operative federalism sometimes was. The federal government entered negotiation as a political choice; constitutionally the High Court had declared that its exercise of power under the Seas and Submerged Lands Act was legitimate. Fraser and his cabinet made decisions on what was desirable: no derogation of federal power, no extension of state boundaries, no appeal to the British parliament. Fraser used those decisions as non-negotiable conditions. In order to have the administrative responsibility up to the three-mile limit, the state governments had to acquiesce, even though five of the six preferred a different means of solving the problem.

Yet to reach that conclusion and to satisfy the premiers was a drawn-out, time-consuming and repetitive process, as premiers fought for greater authority. Because the solution required legislation in every state parliament, they could not be bought off one by one. There was no great difference between Labor and Liberal/National party premiers, although Dick Hamer was perhaps the most amenable to the federal position. Premiers pursue the interests of their states and prime ministers need to negotiate or to supervise the activities of their colleagues. The prime minister's relations with the premiers are always important.

External affairs and south-west Tasmania: 'Damned if you do, damned if you don't'

How widely the federal government's powers can be applied is a matter of interpretation by the High Court, which determines whether particular federal acts are legitimately within its constitutional powers. The clause that has in recent years caused the greatest controversy is section 51(xxix) which gives the federal government powers to legislate for external affairs. The question in dispute in the last fifty years was whether that clause gave the federal government the authority to pass laws to implement any treaties of which Australia was a signatory, and particularly those which had an impact on areas where the federal government otherwise had no jurisdiction, areas such as the environment. The full scope of this power was unknown when Fraser came to power as federal governments had been reluctant to use this provision to override state legislation. However it had become controversial when the Whitlam government passed several laws which relied on its authority, including the Racial Discrimination Act and the National Parks and Wildlife Act.

Fraser did not believe that the federal government should use the external affairs power as a means of enforcing its will on a state. He saw this extension of federal power as largely inconsistent with the federal compact and certainly as inconsistent with the policy of new federalism adopted by his government. Yet to maintain that stand had political costs, because it required the federal government to stand by without intervening when the external affairs power was known, or at least expected, to give the government the power to act.

The issue first emerged in February 1977. In a routine briefing for question time Fraser was told that land had been acquired by the Whitlam government at Towra Point 'for commonwealth purposes' under the National Parks and Wildlife Conservation Act; it was to be used for the conservation of birds. The acquisition was being challenged in court by the New South Wales government, with the argument turning on the term 'for commonwealth purposes'. The external affairs power had not yet been mentioned, but if necessary, the commonwealth intended to use as a second line of defence that Australia had obligations under the agreement between Australia and Japan for the protection of migratory birds and birds in danger of extinction, and for their environments. The brief also suggested that to implement the agreement the commonwealth had the power to acquire the land.

Fraser reacted hostilely. He said it was the government's view that it could not use the external affairs power and yet the advice was just what Court was constantly complaining about – the government could put something in a treaty and that then gave it the power to do whatever necessary to fulfil its obligations under that treaty. Fraser said he was not convinced that 'federal clauses' were inappropriate for Australian circumstances and asked for a paper on federalism and federal clauses. (Federal clauses recognised the division of powers in a federation and allowed the central authority to ratify a treaty on the basis that it was required to use its best endeavours to have the treaty implemented by its constituent parts.) The same day he took the issue without submission to the Foreign Affairs and Defence committee which endorsed his view and asked for a submission on the inclusion of federal clauses in treaties and the implication of treaty obligations in federal-state relations. In preparation for the premiers' conference of April, cabinet also asked for a paper examining the problems arising from attempts to use treaties to extend federal powers. At the April 1977 premiers' conference the premiers agreed that use of the external affairs power was a threat; Court wanted the inclusion of federal clauses as a matter of routine.

Despite a general review of the impact of federal clauses and the establishment of a process of negotiation before treaties that impinged on state responsibilities were signed, the states did not achieve their purpose of limiting the external affairs power. However, while Fraser was not prepared to restrict commonwealth power, in the practice of federalism he was not necessarily prepared to exercise it. In one case where the external affairs power could have been used, south-west Tasmania, he insisted on a process of consultation or self-exclusion.

The building of dams in the wilderness of south-west

Tasmania had been a matter of controversy for a decade. The Hydro-Electric Commission (HEC) of Tasmania had a program of dam construction in the wilderness and it had a powerful voice in Tasmanian politics. In 1973 it had flooded the unique Lake Pedder. In the 1980s it proposed to dam the Franklin River. In justification of its dams, the HEC provided projections of electricity usage in Tasmania that were based on unstated (and often wildly optimistic) assumptions.

Conservationists were determined to save the Franklin from the HEC and published alternative economic assessments that challenged the HEC's electricity forecasts. Yet the majority of the Tasmanian parliament, conscious of a need for development and employment, saw the program of the HEC as necessary and desirable. The question for the conservationists was tactical. If the state government would not stop the dam, pressure could be brought on the federal government. This option became more relevant when the state requested that the south-west wilderness be nominated by the federal government for World Heritage listing; that proposition might give the federal government power under the external affairs power to implement the World Heritage conventions and protect the area. The World Heritage convention argued that, when actions were within the legislative competence of the central authority of a federation, the obligations of the central government were the same as those of unitary states. Yet Fraser regarded such an action as opposed to his policy of federalism and did not want to become involved.

The dispute gradually widened, with pressure growing on the federal government to intervene. Initially the Tasmanian government wanted aid in developing the area; the federal government assisted in conducting a detailed resources survey of the region. But in 1979 Fraser insisted in correspondence to the Tasmanian Wilderness Society that 'land use and management, including power generation, are essentially matters for the state government'. He never shifted, although the federal government did support the establishment of a national park. Fraser wrote to Labor state premier, Doug Lowe, on 17 April 1980:

I find it somewhat surprising to discover that you have not suggested that the South-West Tasmanian area – one of the few remaining temperate wilderness areas in the world – could merit consideration for nomination for the World Heritage List. I would appreciate knowing your views on the possibility of nomination.

Lowe tried to protect state interests; he wrote to Fraser on 26 August 1980 that there 'is a clear understanding . . . that the matter of power development in Tasmania is one for the decision of my government'. Once that was settled, on 8 December 1980 Lowe decided to nominate the south-west national park for inclusion in the World Heritage list and asked the federal government to forward the proposal. Fraser promised to carry out the listing procedures with all possible despatch. But when in January 1981 Tasmania sought financial assistance to manage the south-west, Fraser delayed a decision until the resources survey was completed. He was kept informed – he wanted, for instance, an assessment of where Tasmanian MPs stood – but he did not become directly involved. On 18 September 1981, the minister for home affairs, Ian Wilson, brought a submission to federal cabinet to discuss commonwealth involvement in developing a national park. The submission argued that as the state proposal for a national park could collapse, the cabinet needed to be prepared to react, depending on the result of the dams referendum. It had supported the World Heritage nomination and would need to take account of its responsibilities under the World Heritage Convention Act. The options ran from doing nothing to running its own inquiry. The minister favoured the inquiry, but most departments thought it more appropriate to do nothing. Cabinet merely acknowledged that hydro-electricity development was a state matter and that no action was required. On 22 September Doug Lowe finally submitted the official nomination for the World Heritage List and Fraser forwarded it to Paris.

In November 1981 the state government held a referendum to ask Tasmanians which dam they preferred; the voters were not given the option of 'no dam'. Although 33 per cent of the electorate wrote 'no dams' onto the ballot, a majority still opted for the Franklin or the alternative Olga dam. The conservationists had lost their battle at the state level.

Fraser wanted it to remain a state concern. When asked to comment on a statement by Robin Gray, leader of the state Liberal opposition, that the federal government would not prevent the funding of the dam, he told his press secretary 'No comment. Keep out of it'. However he was inexorably drawn in. He eventually saw Gray on 17 February, 1982, although he ensured that the resulting press statement was first approved by the senior federal minister from Tasmania, Kevin Newman. The chairman of the Heritage Commission advocated the protection of the environment; the Tasmanian Wilderness Society met Fraser to explain its position. In June the Wilderness Society unsuccessfully tried to obtain a High Court injunction to restrain the Loan Council from providing funds to Tasmania – an application that cabinet noted. On 28 June the commonwealth could stay out no longer. Gray, by then Tasmanian premier, asked Fraser to withdraw the application to the World Heritage Commission; he did not want to be bound by the decisions of his predecessors and was determined to avoid a situation where Tasmania's sovereignty or autonomy was diminished. Fraser was informed that, although the listing could be withdrawn, such a decision would lead to criticism because the commonwealth had responsibilities under the convention. Fraser decided to make no decision until the UNESCO ambassador, Ralph Slatyer, had been consulted. Slatyer advised that there was no precedent for withdrawal. PMC suggested three reactions to Gray's request: to refuse to withdraw; to commence discussions with the Tasmanian government; to try to defer the UNESCO decision on its listing. Fraser ticked the first option and told Gray that withdrawal would create legal and political problems. He personally believed the listing must proceed, even if it might be delayed, because by identifying the area as part of its natural heritage Australia, as party to the convention, had incurred conservation responsibility for the area.

In the meantime public opinion was mobilising. Some thousands of letters demanded commonwealth action. Cabinet had to react and on 10 August noted that, while the state governments were responsible for land use decisions, the commonwealth had an interest in the UNESCO convention and that it would not withdraw the nomination. It also observed that Tasmania might not need the additional power and that it might be preferable to postpone the building of the dam. It decided to ask for a detailed submission for consideration the next week.

The submission questioned the estimates developed by the Hydro Electric Commission and, assuming the nomination would not be withdrawn, argued that the commonwealth could retain its stance of non-involvement; it could alter the nominated boundaries to remove the affected areas; it could make a strong statement in opposition to the dam; or it could offer financial assistance to the state to meet the costs of achieving equivalent power elsewhere. The minister preferred the last, but PMC and Finance were both concerned about the open-ended commitment while Treasury still opposed any intervention. PMC put the position clearly: the issue was essentially whether the costs of persuading the Tasmanian government to turn to an alternative source of power would be justified by the wider environmental benefits. Cabinet endorsed Fraser's decision not to withdraw the nomination, and sent the minister for foreign affairs, Tony Street, the attorney-general, Peter Durack, and Wilson to discuss options with Gray. Gray predictably objected strongly to the potential use of commonwealth power and threatened to go direct to UNESCO.

Advice to Fraser pointed out that Australia had identified south-west Tasmania as suitable for listing and could not undo it. Tasmania's 'sovereign' powers were subject to any valid commonwealth legislation. In practical terms this also meant being subject to financial incentives or disincentives. It would be inconsistent to allow a state to go direct to a UN organisation. The legal advice from the Attorney-General's Department went further: the commonwealth was obliged to act to protect south-west Tasmania and its clear constitutional powers prevented it from relying on a federal clause as an excuse for inaction. Fraser asked for amplification of the points, to be done as soon as possible, but not in a way that would disrupt work on the Costigan inquiry into tax evasion which was dominating the activities of the Attorney-General's Department. Several issues, all out of control, were coming to a head at the same time.

The state and federal officials met with ministers on 6 September. Then a further submission re-emphasised that as the commonwealth had the power if it wished to use it, it could not be excused under the federal clause in the World Heritage convention, saying that land use and conservation traditionally lay with the state. The government had the external affairs power and could use section 96 grants. Whether the federal clause of the convention required the government to legislate or merely to 'recommend' action to Tasmania was seen as arguable. Given its obligations (which did not include intervention regardless of its consequences) the government could renounce the convention, do nothing and be in breach of treaty obligations (which Foreign Affairs did not support), or take action to prevent the dam. The minister favoured the third, but pointed out that further discussions were due on 20 September. Gray also wanted to see Fraser, but Fraser preferred to postpone any meeting and told the senior federal minister from Tasmania, Kevin Newman, to inform Gray that any meeting was premature. Cabinet watched a slide display organised by the Heritage Commission and then decided to continue discussions, on the basis that the nomination would not be withdrawn. A week later it noted the reports of discussions, but asked that the prospects of a conditional listing be considered. On 29 October a submission agreed that a conditional listing might be possible; Australia could inform the World Heritage Commission of the conditions under which it would consent to its listing and acknowledge that it would be affected by the building of the dam. There remained a range of departmental views from Treasury's case for non-involvement to Foreign Affairs' concern with breaches of treaty obligations. The options seemed to be either to intervene and authorise an approach to Tasmania by persuasion or coercion, or to start justifying non-intervention.

With the commonwealth unbending, Gray then sought to have Tasmanian representation on the delegation to UNESCO, or even a separate Tasmanian delegation. Fraser, flat on his back in hospital, initially delayed the announcement of the delegation until after the Flinders by-election on 4 December; three officials, led by UNESCO ambassador Ralph Slatyer, were selected. Once the by-election was won, cabinet had to settle the delegation's strategy. Howard, as acting prime minister, phoned Fraser to argue that the majority in cabinet on 6 December wanted to spell out clearly that the final responsibility lay with the state. Fraser disagreed, saying the delegation should say as little as possible; the major objective was to get the listing registered, and just acknowledge that talks were being held with Tasmania. Slatyer agreed with the prime minister that the comments should be brief; the hearing was not the place to air constitutional problems. PMC advised the acting prime minister that the lengthy draft of instructions circulated by the attorney-general was too long and would, PMC tactfully suggested, be unacceptable to the prime minister. Fraser was also sent Slatyer's amended version. Cabinet finally endorsed the paper in the form that Fraser had approved. It agreed that any additional details would be brief. The Tasmanian deputy prime minister was added to the delegation. The decision excised references in an earlier draft to the Australian federal system and the government's non-interventionist approach. Even when he was absent, Fraser's views were vital. The decisions were endorsed a week later as cabinet prepared to defend its parliamentary statement declaring that the federal government would not intervene to stop the dam.

Yet Gray demanded more. He wanted statements proclaiming Tasmania's sovereignty and right to develop included in the submission. Fraser instructed that no reply be sent. When Gray rang to ask what the response to his telex was, Anthony tersely told him that there needed to be some give and take, that the commonwealth had agreed the dam would go ahead and the federal government would never have come this far if it had not been trying to accommodate Tasmania. The area was listed, but with the knowledge that a dam was planned. Australia was asked to take all possible measures to protect the integrity of the area.

However, the issue was still politically sensitive. In January PMC calculated that Fraser had received 21 000 letters opposing the HEC's schemes and only 65 in support. On 13 January Fraser told Gray that the commonwealth would not coerce

Tasmania, but it also could not ignore its international obligations and public pressure. He said that he accepted that the powers lay in state hands:

We do not intend, for example, to see the use of the external affairs power alter the balance of Commonwealth/State responsibility.

So he made an alternative offer of a modern, environmentally-clean, coal-fired power station, estimated at a cost of $500 million, and on 18 January, at a press conference in Hobart, Fraser argued that the dam should be delayed. But the offer was rejected by Tasmania. Under electoral pressure Fraser refused the use of international treaties to coerce Tasmania; he saw that use as unconstitutional and immoral. If Gray had accepted the offer, the alternative would also have been very expensive.

A need to negotiate?

In a federal system a prime minister's powers are limited. Even when powers clearly belong to the federal government, those powers cannot be exerted without any attention to the political consequences. When powers are held co-ordinate, the problems are magnified. Confrontation, particularly between governments of the same political colour, was seldom regarded as fruitful or desirable. Fraser never wanted to attack the premiers too publicly, or to get offside with the local barons. Negotiation, persuasion, gradually nudging them along where possible were preferred tactics. Indeed, for any prime minister who wanted to survive, it was probably the only feasible option.

Fraser was not an ardent centralist. Although he may have been determined to protect the rights of the federal government, he also moved out of policy areas where he could have exerted federal authority, but chose not to. The decision to negotiate an offshore settlement was administratively practical; the non-intervention in south-west Tasmania was politically costly. In both cases federal power was not used to the full. Nor was it in the dealing with Queensland over Aboriginal settlements. That the federal government had the authority was never doubted, but the ideological commitment to the concept of federalism and the political costs of confrontation were too influential. Fraser played by the rules, even if his opponents did not.

As a result he spent much of his time trying to pacify premiers or persuade them to adopt policy he regarded as suitable or necessary. Even when he was not prepared to concede, as on the appeal to Britain to pass legislation to extend the states' boundaries, he argued with the premiers until they gave in. He was at times prepared to use federal authority, but seldom to act unilaterally. In retrospect, indeed, he appears to have been soft on the premiers. He may have cut their funds, but not in a public attack.

Was it inevitable? Probably. Fraser was still attacked for eroding federalism, particularly by Court and Bjelke-Petersen, despite his willingness to concede to principles of federalism. His cutbacks in spending never were as severe on the states as on the federal government. Yet prime ministers cannot spend their time in constant confrontation. It is too time-consuming and politically too costly, particularly if those opponents belong to the same political party. Influence and persuasion are the necessary tools to make the federal system work. Fraser well understood that and worked hard to achieve some progress.

CHAPTER 9

'NOT WITHOUT HONOUR'

FOREIGN POLICY

Prime ministers often dominate their nation's foreign policy. In part the reasons are personal. Prime ministers appreciate the opportunity to influence the affairs of nations. Representing their country in the councils of the world's leaders can be intoxicating. For a middle power like Australia, direct influence may be limited, but all prime ministers have sought to maintain contacts with those foreign leaders with whom they have most in common.

The reasons for the dominance of the prime minister are also institutional. Whereas once prime ministers made occasional lengthy trips, being away from Australia for months at a time, the improvement in modern communications and the demands of the modern media have changed the expectations of the job. Frequent short trips have become normal, visiting two or more countries in a few days or a couple of weeks. Leaders are expected to attend summits or meet their national counterparts for bilateral discussions. International conferences have become annual events, at which Australia has to be represented at the highest level.

At these meetings prime ministers must be able to negotiate

on behalf of their countries. Authority has to be delegated from cabinet to the leader, for prime ministers can scarcely be repudiated by their cabinet without also being removed. To comment that it is necessary to gain cabinet approval may be a useful tactic; it is scarcely a necessity. In foreign policy prime ministers have greater freedom of action than in domestic matters, and can choose the degree to which they involve their cabinet colleagues in deciding the directions their foreign policy should take.

Contact by itself does not immediately turn into influence or power. That has to be achieved by dint of performance and persistence, and by an appreciation of what was possible. Fraser believed that Australia had a role to play. There was a need to recognise the limitations of Australia's position and, as Fraser put it, to 'exercise influence by the quality of what you say to your friends, your major trading partners or through associations like the Commonwealth'. He enjoyed foreign policy; Victorian premier Dick Hamer recalls: 'If you ever went to a dinner party, he was always into foreign affairs'.

As he became established, so he made more personal contacts among other national leaders. He kept in touch, constantly writing, informing, encouraging and cajoling. When he held discussions with a series of heads of government in 1982, for instance, he reported the results to several others. He wrote to Thatcher about meetings on the Pacific. His correspondence with Presidents Carter and Reagan became more personal as he developed the contacts: 'Dear President' becoming 'My dear Jimmy', or 'My dear Ron'. Advice was given on every issue, from nuclear safeguards to a reiteration of the need for freer trade. There is evidence that Fraser was well respected in international circles, with such unexpected friends as Michael Manley, the socialist prime minister of Jamaica and Menachim Begin of Israel.

It is difficult to describe the influence of prime ministers in broad issues, for many policies are continuous, beyond the term of any one leader. They are accepted, restated and widely supported. The centrality of the American alliance has been repeated by all governments. Relations with Japan are understood to be critical. Other themes may be more specific to one leader. Fraser constantly asserted his fears of Russian menace in the Pacific. His crusade against international tariffs led to frequent charges of internal inconsistency, even though Australia could not act alone in this area. To put each of these policies into context it is necessary to describe a wide range of events and there is naturally a consequent difficulty in clearly distinguishing cause and effect, or identifying Fraser's contribution to them. Or indeed of appreciating whether they have any identifiable outcomes. To find evidence of the impact of prime ministers, it is necessary to examine particular events. This chapter will therefore look at three controversial areas in which Fraser chose to participate on behalf of Australia. In the first he acted as a member of the Commonwealth; in the others as a middle-ranking ally of the USA. It looks simultaneously at two aspects: the impact Fraser had in deciding what Australian foreign policy would be, and his ability and style in negotiating with other leaders.

The Commonwealth: Zimbabwe and South Africa

Zimbabwe–Rhodesia was to be the focus of much attention in Fraser's first four years. A former British colony that had unilaterally declared itself independent in 1964, its small European minority, less than 5 per cent of the population, had monopolised all positions of power in the colony and had been fighting an escalating war against the Patriotic Front guerilla armies, led by Robert Mugabe and Joshua Nkomo. Zimbabwe was bordered by other states of the British Commonwealth, particularly Zambia, led by Kenneth Kaunda, and Tanzania under Julius Nyerere. Although it was recognised that the bringing of Zimbabwe to legal status and majority rule was a British responsibility, its geographical position ensured that it was always a matter of direct concern at meetings of the British Commonwealth Heads of Government meetings. So was the question of South Africa and sporting links with a régime that brought apartheid into sport. Where some countries, primarily New Zealand, were prepared to host South African teams, the African and Caribbean members of the Commonwealth wanted a sporting boycott and economic sanctions applied to

South Africa, as they already nominally were to Zimbabwe.

The Australian policy was by 1975 effectively bipartisan: long-standing opposition to apartheid and condemnation of the illegal régime in Zimbabwe. Both policies were based on a refusal to accept race as an indication of superiority or as the reason for political rights. Racism to Malcolm Fraser was abhorrent. Ian Macphee recalls Fraser saying: 'there are not many issues of conscience you can afford to have if you are to be a successful politician. Race is mine. I will never tolerate racism'. If Fraser was prepared to accept compromise on most issues, he did not on this one and his beliefs were reflected in his policies.

There have been many explanations proposed for Fraser's commitment to the support of African independence in Zimbabwe and South Africa. His colleagues suggested that he had reacted against racist South African neighbours in his youth, that he had close black African friends at Oxford, that as part of the post-Holocaust generation he grew up abhorring racism, or that with a Jewish mother he felt an outsider in the genteel establishment of the Victorian Western District.

Fraser denies all these explanations. The South African neighbours were charming; he had no close black friends at Oxford; he never felt an outsider in the Western District or was conscious of his mother's Jewishness. His strong anti-apartheid speech in the 1961 debate about South Africa's departure from the Commonwealth is cited as evidence of Fraser's long-standing commitment to the anti-apartheid cause. The speech in 1961 was made to provide full support for Menzies, who was reluctantly taking a stand. Indeed, Fraser is amused at the constant hunt for explanations or deep psychological reasons for his stand:

People have to find a reason, because they think that somebody that lives in Nareen and was educated at Melbourne Grammar and Oxford couldn't possibly have these views. So they look for some other explanation.

Indeed the reasons were more prosaic, but perhaps the more convincing as a consequence:

It's time and circumstance. I happened to be PM and at the first conference in London sport in South Africa was going to be high on the agenda. Rhodesia obviously was too . . . The issues were divisive ones for the Commonwealth and I believe the Commonwealth is worth preserving. I also thought, not in 1977 because Jim Callaghan was in the chair, but certainly at Lusaka, there was the possibility of total breach with Britain and a severe break in the Commonwealth if the problem wasn't handled well. So I was just there where these issues were on and inevitably became involved.

Both the official record and the memory of Andrew Peacock, foreign minister for the crucial period from 1975 to 1980, bear out this explanation.

In late 1976, in the last months of his term as secretary of state, changing circumstances forced Henry Kissinger to join the British in an attempt once again to bring Rhodesia back to legality. The issue was thus back on the agenda of the great powers. In January 1977 Fraser met Sonny Ramphal, the secretary-general of the Commonwealth, for the first time. On 10 February 1977, in a speech at Port Moresby, Fraser claimed: 'The Commonwealth is a microcosm of the international order. It should be used to make a real contribution to resolving the problems we face'. He also made clear his attitude towards Africa:

We have repeatedly said that the only way to resolve the Rhodesian situation is by a significant and early move to majority rule . . . So far as South Africa is concerned, Australia has stated its views on the policy of apartheid many times. It is a system that cannot and will not work.

These were long-standing party policies.

Tony Eggleton had played an important part in developing Fraser's appreciation of the Commonwealth. He had been a senior member of its London secretariat before his return to Australia in 1975 and was thus both well-connected and conscious of the potential uses of the Commonwealth. A Commonwealth Heads of Government Meeting (CHOGM) was due to be held in June 1977. In preparation for that meeting

Fraser responded at length to Ramphal's request for items to be discussed and sought to make contacts with other Commonwealth leaders; he wrote, for instance, to Datuk Hussein Onn, the Malaysian prime minister, proposing that the minister for foreign affairs, Andrew Peacock, visit to ensure an exchange of views. He held talks with the prime ministers of Western Samoa, Tonga and New Zealand.

There was a lengthy process of preparation and negotiation between departments before the minister for foreign affairs brought two submissions to cabinet. The first discussed the potential role of Australia in the region: the possibility of establishing an informal consultative arrangement in the Pacific, the offer to establish a regional office, the likely success (and problems) of a Commonwealth disputes committee. The second, more important submission, contained two basic papers, 'The Key Issues' and 'The Australian Strategy'. The key issues were identified as the changing power relations, the world's economic situation and prospects, southern Africa, Cyprus, the patterns and possibilities of regionalism and the Commonwealth's functional and economic co-operation. The submission acknowledged there was no identifiable strategic profile for the Commonwealth in great power matters, but wanted Australia to impress on other heads of government its concern at the Soviet lack of restraint in the competition for influence. The submission predicted that the conference's discussion on the world's economic situation would be based on the main themes of the final report of the Commonwealth Experts Group (the McIntyre report), with a proposal for the establishment of a common fund the likely point of contention.

However, the southern African issues – Rhodesia, Namibia and sport with South Africa – were the items that the African and Caribbean nations wanted to discuss most. The debate would depend on the progress of the UK and US initiatives in calling another conference on majority rule, initiatives that reflected Western concern at the opportunities provided for expanded Soviet influence by African reaction to the situation in Rhodesia and the policies in South Africa. Australia's interests would be best served by support for a peaceful settlement; it was seen as necessary to counter the tendency to see Australia as having an affinity with the whites in South Africa and to continue to demonstrate that the Australian denunciation of injustice and apartheid was genuine. New Zealand was the focus of criticism because of its sporting links with South Africa. The submission reported that the secretary-general was working on a communiqué that would be at once acceptable to New Zealand, Canada and the African members of the Commonwealth.

The submission on Australian strategy emphasised that, as Australia's record of participation in the Commonwealth had not been good, it should play an active, progressive but moderate role. It should support Western attempts to negotiate a transition to majority rule, while calling for patience and declining to support armed struggle. On sporting links with South Africa, Australia should support any formula that could receive widespread acceptance and make clear that Australia genuinely wanted to exert influence on South Africa. It was to be preferred that the formula should be supported by Muldoon, although Australia should be prepared to mediate on New Zealand's behalf by pointing to its creditable record on race relations.

On 4 May PMC recommended to the prime minister that the CHOGM submissions be circulated on 9 May and discussed in cabinet on 16 May. The prime minister's brief had to be completed by 19 May before the prime minister left for overseas. Fraser decided to move more quickly. He instructed that the two submissions were to be taken in the Foreign Affairs and Defence Committee (FAD) on 5 May, the following day. This decision speeded up the process and precluded any further consultation – a point that Treasury later complained about as it disapproved of the decisions to promote the common fund.

FAD endorsed both the main policy papers and thus established the general directions to be followed at CHOGM; it included the commitment to support a statement on sporting links with South Africa that was not extreme. Only two provisos were attached to the decision: a flexible approach was to be taken on the common fund, and the delegation was to use its discretion on the need for a working party on food security. The general thrust of the Australian strategy was not altered.

The decision was circulated to all ministers; it was to act as the basis for policy towards sporting links with South Africa and independence for Zimbabwe. Cabinet *was* consulted.

In London Fraser had the delegated authority to act. In the week before the conference he gave a major speech at the Royal Commonwealth Club. He emphasised there the role of the Commonwealth and the importance of some united action against South Africa. On the first day of the conference he published an article in the *Guardian*, arguing that the diversity in the Commonwealth was its greatest strength. He claimed that the Australian attitude on southern Africa was that 'there ought to be moves as early as possible towards majority rule in Zimbabwe'. Apartheid was a policy that 'cannot work. It cannot succeed'. The speech and the article took the press and many Commonwealth leaders by surprise. Observers had expected that the new Australian prime minister would be conservative; the views he expressed were not.

Fraser soon made personal contacts that were to be of later significance. Eggleton recalls his first impact:

He made some good interventions in the course of the first morning, about the strategy of warming relations with the Third World. I walked out to have my cup of morning tea and down this grand ornate staircase at Lancaster House came Malcolm. I just had to blink and look again, because there was Michael Manley with his arm around Malcolm, walking down the staircase. He had made a good impression at the start. He emerged from that meeting with a sudden international stature which was never quite appreciated in Australia.

Other links were formed with African leaders; Ramphal saw a convergence of views between Fraser, Malaysian prime minister Hussein Onn and Manley, an unusual combination that occurred because 'he was ready to be innovative, not in an ideological sense but on the basis of very practical hardheaded experience: his rejection of stereotype rules in North/South relations'. His outspoken attack of racism in southern Africa, his lead in the conference's condemnation of the behaviour of Uganda's Idi Amin and his espousal of a common fund all marked him as very different from the conservative Australian that heads of government had anticipated.

Yet Fraser was not yet seen as a central figure in the Commonwealth. The main achievement of the 1977 conference was the Gleneagles agreement – the declaration about sporting links with South Africa that was drafted at the prime ministers' weekend retreat at Gleneagles Hotel in Scotland. The communiqué was written by a small inner group. As New Zealand, the main source of problems, had to be included and as its prime minister, Robert Muldoon, effectively vetoed Fraser's presence by refusing to participate if Fraser was part of the group, Fraser was not directly involved. He enthusiastically supported the outcome.

He followed up his contacts after the conference, emphasising to African and Caribbean leaders Australian support for Gleneagles and commitment to the Commonwealth. He sent Kaunda a copy of the parliamentary speech of Sir Robert Menzies on 11 April 1961 in which he condemned apartheid and argued that it would end in ultimate conflict (it was a speech Fraser often incorporated in letters to his critics). Fraser explained that Australia would not accept any sporting team or individual representing South Africa, although he also pointed out that the Australian government would not prevent individuals from travelling abroad.

His appreciation of the African cause was heightened by his growing awareness of the problems that could be caused by too little co-operation by Western nations with the newly independent countries. Zambia had been forced to get arms from communist countries because of a western embargo. Fraser believed the best defence against communism was cooperation and assistance. Any other strategy was silly.

Fraser found the other heads of government often congenial. They helped one another; they were colleagues, not domestic rivals. They exchanged gifts. Fraser recalled during the interviews:

The cigars I was smoking last night were ones Fidel Castro gave to Forbes Burnham [prime minister of British Guyana], with Forbes Burnham's name on them. Forbes never smoked and when he found that I did he said 'I'll pass mine on to you'. Unfortunately Forbes is dead so I no longer get Castro cigars. Fidel takes the whole production from this tobaccory and gives them away to his friends.

After 1977 the Australian government had to decide its attitude to changing circumstances in Zimbabwe. First it had to react to the internal settlement that was to promote Bishop Muzorewa into the prime ministership. In March 1978 the Western Australian premier, Charles Court – as usual writing on any topic that interested him – expressed the hope that the federal government would support 'responsible black leaders', by which he meant Muzorewa. In May Fraser asked for a briefing for discussions with Court. He laid down the directions it was to take. It was to assert that the Patriotic Front was not communist, that all parties must be involved in any settlement, and that Australia supported the British-American efforts to broaden the base of the settlement.

In July a submission prepared for the Foreign Affairs and Defence committee argued that the internal settlement was not a blueprint for majority rule and regretted the lack of involvement by the Patriotic Front (the nationalist forces led by Robert Mugabe and Joshua Nkomo). It presented three alternatives: an expression of support for the settlement; a rejection of the settlement, but warily expressed in case it gained widespread internal support; and an argument that the UK-US proposals had the best chance of success and should be supported. The submission – and PMC – both recommended the third option, a line which Fraser had already expressed. Events moved so fast that the submission was not taken. When Ramphal requested Commonwealth support for a stand against the internal settlement, Fraser replied on 28 August:

In our view an agreement that does not represent a reasonable consensus is unlikely to result in a lasting and peaceful settlement. It is for this reason that Australia has supported the current efforts of the British and United States governments to broaden the basis of the agreement to include all shades of opinion in Zimbabwe, including the Patriotic Front.

In April 1979 the Australian position for CHOGM at Lusaka had to be determined in the context of an election in Zimbabwe to consolidate the internal settlement. Fraser had been briefed on the new constitution that assured whites with only 4 per cent of the vote and 28 out of 100 seats. The brief asked, and Fraser approvingly marked, how an election could be free if 90 per cent of the country was under martial law. Despite the government's opposition to the settlement, cabinet did agree to fund a delegation of MPs from the joint parliamentary committee on foreign affairs and defence, but baulked at sending an accompanying Foreign Affairs official.

Fraser was anxious that nothing Australia did should be allowed to erode its capacity to influence the African states. On 19 April he rang the head of Foreign Affairs (having tried to find Peacock) to discuss the difficulties in closing the Rhodesian Information Centre in Sydney and the composition of the parliamentary delegation to the elections. Fraser also annotated the drafts of the cabinet submission, prepared at his request, on CHOGM and South Africa, ticking the sections he approved, asking a series of questions. In particular he agreed that

We need to ensure that our reputation on South Africa remains high. We should not wish to be placed in a situation at Lusaka similar to that experienced by New Zealand in London. A poor showing at Lusaka could jeopardise our chances of hosting the 1981 CHOGM.

He agreed that 'our attitude to the proposition that the elections be declared "null and void" and that the government accord no recognition to the resulting administration' was the key issue. The submission was redrafted to take account of Fraser's views before it was presented on 30 April as a joint submission from Fraser and Peacock. FAD decided on 1 May that Australia should use its influence to support the Commonwealth's stand and instructed the foreign minister to arrange meetings with his counterparts in Britain, Canada, New Zealand and the United States at the OECD in June to press that view.

On 5 May Margaret Thatcher became British prime minister. She was noted for being sympathetic to the internal settlement. Her new foreign secretary, Lord Carrington, was not. Further, as a former British high commissioner in Canberra he was well known to Fraser. Carrington became the pivotal figure in the future negotiations. He had to maintain links with the front line states while nudging Thatcher – then largely inexperienced in international affairs – to a position that was more widely acceptable. Encouraged by Tony Eggleton, who had gone to London to assist in the Conservative election campaign, Fraser sought to help Carrington in his attempts to prevent Thatcher from locking Britain into support for Muzorewa or from lifting sanctions immediately as many of her backbenchers favoured. He sent Alan Griffith of PMC to express the Australian view and to find out what was happening. Griffith wrote to Fraser on 29 May that the British had a plan to take over legal authority and retain Muzorewa with some changes to the constitution. He said it had to be assumed that the plan had been discussed with the USA.

Some action was needed as this proposal would be entirely unacceptable to most Commonwealth countries. Fraser immediately drafted a letter to Thatcher, expressing his fears:

I am especially concerned that the Rhodesian issue could prove divisive at CHOGM. It has the potential to split the Commonwealth at a time when all the other signs have been pointing in the direction of enhanced Commonwealth harmony.

He emphasised the need to invite the Patriotic Front's leaders to all-party talks and claimed that the earlier election had not provided the answer. Fraser stressed the need for some form of new political process, but he also argued that the African leaders should not be allowed to think they would get everything their own way.

After the Australian high commissioner in London had talks with Carrington, he advised that the letter to Thatcher be delayed until Carrington had met the US secretary of state, Cyrus Vance. But Fraser demanded that the letter to Thatcher be sent immediately, to influence those talks or at least to avoid charges of 'me-tooism'. He also strengthened the draft of a letter from Peacock to Vance, arguing that recognition of the Muzorewa government could destroy the chances for unity in Africa.

In the next month diplomatic activity was constant. Fraser's role was, according to Ramphal, crucial. Because Pierre Trudeau had just lost power in Canada after twelve years in office and Thatcher had just won in Britain:

> Malcolm Fraser was the only leader from the older Commonwealth countries that could help us bridge the gap between the old and the new, between Africa and Britain. Again he found an ally in Michael Manley. They played very critical roles by being able to work together.

Fraser sought to develop support for the all-party discussions. He reassured Michael Manley that Thatcher was not likely to rush into support for the Rhodesian regime, and arranged to meet the day before the Lusaka conference opened. Fraser wrote to the new Canadian premier, Joe Clark, and replied to a thoughtful letter from Kaunda with two letters. He received reports of Peacock's discussions with Carrington on 16 June.

Fraser was provided with an additional opportunity to influence Thatcher during her visit to Australia. Her initial response on 5 June, later to be repeated in the Commons on 25 July, had been that her objective was to bring Rhodesia back to legality with the widest possible recognition. Just before her visit to Canberra in July 1979, Fraser took his proposals to cabinet. There was no submission, but cabinet approved briefings that emphasised the need to avoid a premature recognition of the recently elected government in view of the divisive nature of the settlement. Cabinet agreed that recognition of the new regime without adequate support from African nations, including the front line states, would not lead to a peaceful or stable solution. Armed with this resolution, Fraser had lengthy talks with Thatcher and seemed to make progress as she acknowledged privately that the Rhodesian constitution would have to be changed. Yet in a speech at the National Press Club, Thatcher reverted to her formal public position, claiming she was seeking Australia's support as a moderator to shift opinion towards the recognition of Muzorewa. Fraser disagreed and distanced himself from Thatcher's stand; Britain should not take Australian support for granted.

Fraser reported to cabinet the results of his discussions with Thatcher; he was less concerned about her public statements as her speech had been written in advance and did not reflect the concessions she had privately made. At the same time FAD endorsed a package of proposals that spelt out the general approach to be adopted at the meeting of CHOGM at Lusaka. Cabinet left details to the discretion of the prime minister and foreign minister. Fraser talked to Vance and they agreed on the need for further constitutional change. He asked advisers if they thought there was anyone else who should be approached. Australia was to act as a moderating influence. The Africans were suspicious of Thatcher, who wanted to 'wrongfoot' the Patriotic Front to show it up as obstructive. There was a need to illustrate that Fraser was not persuaded by Thatcher's stand. The brief recommended letters to Ramphal, Kaunda, Obasanjo (of Nigeria), Moi (prime minister of Kenya) and Julius Nyerere (of Tanzania) in addition to the letter to Manley that sought the chance of a chat before proceedings began. Fraser also rang Carrington to discuss progress, particularly as he had been told Carrington was exasperated by the African suspicion of British good faith and was warning that Britain would not give way to threats at Lusaka.

After several drafts Fraser approved the letters to Clark, Kaunda, Muldoon and Obasanjo, always keeping the British informed of what he was doing; he also phoned Manley, asking him to tell the frontline states that Thatcher might shift her ground, and received a detailed report from Peacock about his discussions with Carrington on 24 July. Before the conference Fraser visited Nigeria, whose president was seriously disenchanted with Britain but prepared to give Thatcher a chance, while Peacock went to Kenya and Tanzania; both visits were to ensure some unity of purpose at the conference. Peacock arranged for Fraser to meet Thatcher soon after arrival in Lusaka. The meeting would allow Fraser to report on his visit to Nigeria and to explain that Australia wanted general approval for a settlement, but had no specific plan of action. Much of the activity was personal, drawing on the links developed by Fraser and Peacock during the previous years. It was a constant greasing of the diplomatic wheels, maintaining a dialogue and an exchange of views and solutions.

At Lusaka it continued that way. A paper on tactics presented by Peacock laid out the proposed approach. Negotiations would be handled at head of government level, with time allowed for private consultations before the final meeting. The focus was to be on the elements of a settlement that allowed general recognition to follow. The objectives were to ensure that Britain continued to consult widely and to build on the progress that had been made. Australia should recognise British sensitivities and seek to 'jolly along' Mrs Thatcher in a way that could protect Australia's credentials as a mediator. There was a need to be careful of 'cornering' Britain or of igniting Thatcher's 'short fuse'. It was accepted that any settlement needed to be accepted by the African states.

On 29 July Peacock met the secretary of the Tanzanian ministry of foreign affairs to discover the current Tanzanian views, arguing that Australia wanted to help where it could. He passed these views on to Fraser. He also met Nyerere and then on 31 July Carrington. Carrington was cautious, suggesting that Thatcher would make a nice speech at the opening session on the Friday, but would not go much further than she had earlier in the Commons. He said Thatcher would in effect just be saying that she would be listening to views. Nyerere had been given a 'wink' to indicate that the British intended to return Rhodesia to legality and majority rule. However Carrington argued the African states were not entitled to any assurances because Rhodesia was a British responsibility. He wanted Fraser to talk to Thatcher very early in the proceedings. By 3 August Fraser had talked to Kaunda, Nyerere, Thatcher and Carrington, Manley and Ramphal, while Peacock had also seen Tekere, a leader of the Patriotic Front.

Fraser delivered an address at the opening ceremony. It had been carefully prepared, with an initial draft written as early as 25 June by foreign affairs adviser, Owen Harries. Fraser said:

No one at this meeting believes that a settlement is compatible with a constitutional situation in Salisbury which is tainted in any way with racialism. We are all in favour of majority rule – the majority rule which takes account of all the parties involved and which is reflected not only in elections but in the underlying structure of power and authority.

He emphasised the need for flexibility and took a very tough stand on racism: 'All oppression is repugnant, but there is an obscenity about oppression based on no more than the colour of a person's skin'.

The discussion on Zimbabwe started on 3 August, with speeches by Nyerere and Thatcher, with the latter making no reference to elections. On 4 August Fraser and Peacock first met Nyerere and then Thatcher and Carrington. Thatcher said she could not appear to be 'under direction' from the conference, but she needed to make some progress by the Conservative party conference in October. Fraser was acting in part as an intermediary for the front-line states, pressing their case and pointing out that Nyerere was now prepared to accept a British-appointed interim government. Thatcher was sceptical at Nyerere's desire for reference to elections in the communiqué, recalling the lack of elections in Tanzania. As the notes recording the discussion read: 'She checked the details of this, referring to a paper in her handbag: "the most secure place in Whitehall – my armoury".' Thatcher and Carrington refused to discuss interim or transitional arrangements; all they were prepared to discuss was the constitution. Thatcher was particularly concerned about her internal party difficulties. Fraser insisted on the need to take account of the African states' problems and argued that the front-line states, and particularly Nyerere, were trying to help. The meeting concluded with an exchange that epitomised the two approaches. Thatcher said it was imperative that the meeting adopt a communiqué that did not embarrass the United Kingdom in its forthcoming negotiations. Fraser accepted the point, but argued that it was also important for the front line states to have their own arguments for their constituencies, not least to enable them to handle the Patriotic Front.

On Saturday, an inner group – consisting of Thatcher and Carrington, the front-line leaders, Kaunda and Nyerere, Fraser, Manley and the Nigerian minister for foreign affairs – met to discuss the options. After a morning's discussion, Ramphal produced a draft communiqué that included nine basic points.

The process was laborious. Fraser annotated his copy with a range of amendments that were incorporated in the final draft (although how many were his suggestions is impossible to identify). At times he tried out forms of words. The intention was to persuade Thatcher that the internal settlement was not a solution. The main concession written into the final edition was a recognition that the supervision of the elections was a British responsibility. It also welcomed 'British government indications' that a conference would be appropriate, instead of stating blandly that a conference was required. In the final version, redrafted by Ramphal and British diplomat Sir Anthony Duff, Thatcher retained the formal rights of British sovereignty, while conceding the need for all-party conferences.

On the Sunday an acceptable draft was circulated to all heads of governments. Kaunda's covering letter suggested it be discussed the next morning: 'You will appreciate the importance of maintaining the confidentiality of the text meanwhile', he concluded. But the details were leaked to the Australian press by Fraser, Barnett and Eggleton. Eggleton and Barnett provided off-the-record briefings before Fraser provided background information to journalists. Barnett noted that the British journalists were resentful that they had received no details, but the Australian journalists were pleased because he had tipped them off that the communiqué was being put out. Eggleton went through the brief with them – indeed the press had never been kept better informed than on this trip, remembers Michelle Grattan.

One explanation of the leak was a desire for Fraser to take the credit, but Australian journalists were more pragmatic; Fraser, they thought, realised there was a need for Australian journalists to meet their domestic deadlines. Otherwise they would be merely repeating accounts in the British press a day later than necessary. A more Machiavellian explanation was that Fraser leaked the communiqué to ensure that Thatcher was not able to back out. Fraser agrees it had that effect, but he did not recall that it was as a deliberate strategy. The cleverness came with hindsight as it almost had an opposite effect. One

British journalist attended the Australian briefing and then asked Thatcher for confirmation. A furious Carrington sent a note to Thatcher (then in church listening to an anti-imperialist sermon) arguing that the whole settlement should be called off. Ramphal, sitting next to Thatcher, managed to persuade her to continue discussions.

The Australian delegation was due to hold a barbecue that evening. There was a constant round of talks, in the hope that there would be a final agreement to release the communiqué early. For a time it looked as though Thatcher would stay away, even though it had by then been agreed to meet all the heads of government there. Ramphal recalls:

She was going to make her point with Malcolm. She'd agreed with the decision. She'd agreed to stand by the text. She agreed to the process of the release at the barbecue but she'd be damned if she was going to Malcolm's barbecue.

Thatcher was eventually persuaded to attend by Carrington and Peacock and all the heads of government crammed into the small reception rooms. Kaunda told the gathering that it was necessary to endorse the communiqué immediately, as it had now become public. While Muldoon asked mischievously whether the leak should not be investigated (although everyone knew its source), the other heads of government agreed to release it immediately. Thatcher, claims one observer, 'never took her eyes off the tall Australian'. Fraser recalls: 'I wasn't looking at her that much; my attention was elsewhere'. The atmosphere was 'slightly tense'. The barbecue then took place. An angry Carrington snarled at Eggleton: 'Tony, you're very good at domestic politics, but I do wish you'd keep the hell out of international affairs!' In a later briefing Fraser was advised to distract attention from the Australian–British differences by focussing on the communiqué itself and emphasising that the special session had been anxious to announce details because rumours were rife and ill-informed.

The next morning as Fraser entered the conference room, he was applauded by the African leaders, who saw the leak as a brilliant ploy. Fraser continued to act as a mediator; when

Thatcher objected to a virulent anti-apartheid statement in the final communiqué, he helped to reach a compromise. Having won the main issue, the African leaders were prepared to concede on symbolic statements.

Fraser's role at Lusaka had been important. While Carrington must take the greatest credit for shifting Thatcher to a more conciliatory position, and Nyerere assisted in bringing the African states into the agreement, Fraser's links with the African and Caribbean leaders gave their position greater legitimacy and acceptability, and perhaps helped to sell the settlement to Thatcher's Conservative party.

After the delegates left Lusaka, the initiative was entirely with Britain. Fraser was determined to remain in touch. He congratulated Thatcher on moving fast on 15 August; exchanged letters with Nyerere about the latter's concern with white representation in early September; asked for regular intelligence assessments from the Office of National Assessments. On 4 October he demanded a report on British proposals, asking his advisers whether Australia should be getting other countries to endorse them; it was suggested that he use question time to state support, but that Britain preferred other states to keep on the sidelines, particularly as the front-line leaders, especially Nyerere, were active behind the scenes.

On 17 October two briefing notes spelt out options: letters to Thatcher or to Ramphal, official action or wait. Foreign Affairs advised waiting, but the offer to help, perhaps by a letter from Fraser to the front-line states, was sent to the British Foreign and Commonwealth Office. The British preferred Australia be kept in reserve, as it was tactfully put.

By 25 October, as discussions at Lancaster House turned to transitional arrangements, the possibility of a request to Australia for observers and personnel for the ceasefire force was raised. On 29 October Manley rang Fraser. On 30 October Fraser finally wrote to Thatcher, reasserting the principles of Lusaka and offering to involve Australia in ceasefire arrangements. Carrington wrote to Peacock complaining that it was hard to bear when friends seemed to be supporting the Patriotic Front. Thatcher responded in similar terms to Fraser, emphasising the need for Muzorewa to be included in the negotiations and that he would not accept ceasefire forces from countries that were supporting the Patriotic Front.

A frantic set of diplomatic exchanges followed. Kaunda wanted Australia to put pressure on Carrington. Fraser rang Canadian prime minister, Joe Clark; Peacock talked to the Canadian foreign secretary, Flora MacDonald, and the US secretary of state, Cyrus Vance. Ratu Mara of Fiji wanted to talk to Fraser about peace-keeping forces. Eventually on 8 November the British High Commission formally asked that Australia contribute forces to the ceasefire monitoring force; in Fraser's absence, cabinet agreed the same day, as long as a settlement was reached. In the meantime both Kaunda, on 10 November, and Nyerere, on 13 November, kept Fraser informed of the progress of negotiations, while Fraser's press office briefed Andrew Clark of the *National Times* on Fraser's activities.

On 20 and 21 November three submissions were lodged: on monitoring forces, on Commonwealth election observers, and on Australian interests. On 21 November the Foreign Affairs and Defence committee agreed to support the first two. Fraser was absent, but had cleared both recommendations before the committee considered them. Fraser had also approved the parliamentary statement attached to the third submission. He made several changes to the text that had been faxed to Nareen; the changes greatly strengthened the text.

On 6 December, as the final settlement was almost complete, it was suggested to Fraser that he give a comprehensive press release setting the agreement in context and announcing the final decision to send a monitoring force, that senior officers give a press briefing, and that congratulations be sent to Thatcher. Fraser agreed and also decided that the lifting of sanctions would be included in his statement, rather than in a separate press release from the foreign affairs minister. These preparations were completed by 18 December.

In January Nyerere complained to Fraser about the presence of South African troops in Zimbabwe, and suggested that a heads of government meeting be convened. Fraser responded that the position had not yet deteriorated to that extent and he agreed to consult with the British, even though he also knew from his own intelligence sources and the group of Australian observers that the British were not being entirely frank about the people responsible for some of the outrages. Kaunda both wrote to and rang Fraser to express concern.

All these issues were discussed at a lunch in London with Thatcher and Carrington on 4 February 1980. Carrington argued that Mugabe's forces were the greatest threat to the election, but thought that, of the eighty seats, Nkomo would get thirty with the others split between Muzorewa and Mugabe; Muzorewa should not be counted out because as a bishop he had the women's vote. The best solution for Britain was a Nkomo–Muzorewa alliance. The British were deeply suspicious of Nyerere. When Fraser offered to speak to him, Thatcher quickly agreed and Carrington commented that it might be worth telling Nyerere that he should not wreck the Lancaster House agreement.

Fraser duly contacted both Kaunda and Nyerere on 12 and 15 February. Then on 18 February he was approached again by the British High Commission, asking him to use his good offices with Kaunda and Nyerere to persuade them to influence Mugabe to reduce infringements of the ceasefire. Both said they have tried and would influence Mugabe, but thought the problems came from elsewhere. Fraser told the British high commissioner the details of the discussions and wrote to Thatcher on 25 February encouraging her to re-establish personal links with the leaders of the front-line states; he said he did not believe that Kaunda and Nyerere had become irretrievably partisan, but they could be influential in the months after the election. He also wrote to Kaunda and Nyerere, urging them not to take any actions that might put the settlement at risk or that might threaten the elections. Fraser also rang both men just before the election.

The election was a triumph for Mugabe, who won a clear majority of seats. Fraser was keen to assist and a week later waived the ten-day rule to allow a high commission to be established in Zimbabwe. Fraser attended the independence ceremonies and was determined to assist the new state. When he met the newly appointed high commissioner-designate on 8 May, Fraser told him that if the proposed $5 million aid for

1980–1982 was not adequate, it should be brought to his attention – he believed $5 million over two years was not enough. When a cable from Salisbury proposed an increase, Fraser ordered it be doubled to $10 million. He announced the first $5 million while in Salisbury. When Australian Development Aid Bureau was informed of Fraser's views, it asked the next year for a further doubling to $20 million – a committed prime minister was too good to miss. Further, Fraser believed that his part in the settlement was important as an indication of Australian independence. He told the high commissioner-designate that the Zimbabwe settlement showed that the British had learnt that they had to ask for Australian support, not simply presume they had it. In earlier years they had once asked for support without even making it clear what they wanted it for.

The camaraderie of the Commonwealth leadership was to be important later in ensuring that there was no boycott of the Brisbane Commonwealth Games in 1982. Burnham and others said 'our job is to protect our friends'. Llew Edwards was also conscious of the importance of Fraser's contacts; he believed that Fraser's standing was primarily responsible for the lack of any reactions to demands for a boycott. Fraser certainly was continually briefed on the likelihood of any problems.

The Commonwealth is indeed a strange group. The countries have nothing in common except their former links with Britain and the English language. But Commonwealth meetings gave Fraser insights into problems and perspectives that might otherwise have been closed to him. Because he developed a sympathy with Manley, Kaunda, Nyerere and Burnham, he could appreciate far better the north–south issues which divided the world. Among his colleagues in the Commonwealth he was readily accepted as an 'eminent person'.

Within his cabinet his policy was supported, but not strongly so by many ministers. The National party ministers did not agree with its emphasis but did not regard Africa as sufficiently vital to Australian interests to be worth a dispute in cabinet. Most ministers agreed that in a few areas the prime minister could run his own policy; Zimbabwe and South Africa were such cases. Some consistently agreed, particularly the foreign minister, Andrew Peacock; others kept quiet. In the party room, where the disquiet was more open and where many backbenchers supported the whites in southern Africa, Fraser could be more abrupt. Ian Macphee recalls: 'He would give the opponents a respectable modicum of time in which to put their views, but when he curtailed debate, he did so in words which unmistakenly meant "That's the policy; it will not be altered".' But Fraser constantly wrote letters to backbenchers and party members explaining and justifying the government's policy. His continuing reaction to party opposition reflects the strength of his commitment:

The attitude to South Africa was long standing party policy. What they mightn't have liked about it was the higher profile I gave it. Since the sanctions element has entered the debate, a lot of them would not have agreed with that. Well, too bad. That's their view and I've got a different one.

As prime minister he was able to determine the policy with minimal cabinet opposition.

The Sinai: multinational peacekeeping force

If Fraser was able to act as a mediator on Zimbabwe within the confines of the Commonwealth, he was in a weaker position when dealing as a middle-sized power with the superpowers. Yet he continued to exert what influence he could apply.

In the 1979 Camp David Accord, President Carter persuaded Egyptian president Anwar Sadat and Israeli prime minister Menachim Begin to continue negotiations towards a peace treaty. One central feature of the agreement was that Israel would withdraw its troops and settlements from the Sinai which it had occupied since the 1967 war. In support of the agreement, Carter promised that he would arrange for a multinational peacekeeping force to be stationed in the Sinai. For the Israelis, this force was an absolute condition of withdrawal. Although both Egypt and the US had a preference for a peacekeeping force under United Nations auspices, they accepted that, even if they gained the required nine votes in the Security Council (and there were doubts about that), the Soviet Union would veto its establishment. Nor would the General Assembly approve the force; all the other Arab nations had condemned the accord because it made no provision for a Palestinian state. The alternative was a force sponsored by the US, but also containing contributions, however symbolic in size, from other nations. It was important that the contributing nations were acceptable to the signatories of Camp David and were seen as internationally respectable by the West.

Australia was always near the top of the list of favoured countries because it was an ally of the US, without a high profile in the Middle East and acceptable to both Israel and Egypt. Throughout 1981 Australia was encouraged to commit itself firmly to provide a contribution. Because few other countries, particularly not Canada, Britain or the other EC nations, were keen to contribute, Australia was placed in a pivotal position. From the US view, her agreement might encourage others to participate. From the Australian view, there was a belief that Australia would only contribute if it was part of a wider respectable group. It was on this fence that Fraser sat poised throughout the lengthy debate.

The first stories about the invitation to participate in the multinational force (MNF) emerged from a report in an Israeli paper in February 1981. The counsellor at the US embassy agreed that Australia was head of everyone's list. Fraser asked for a briefing. He was told that the US was exploring the UN option and had made no request so far. Fraser then demanded that a submission be prepared urgently for the Foreign Affairs and Defence (FAD) committee four days later; it was circulated only at the meeting.

The Foreign Affairs submission to FAD explained the background. A UN force was unlikely to be approved; Australia (together with Canada, Sweden, Argentina, Brazil and Panama) was on the list of potential contributors to a US-sponsored force. When a request did come, a rapid response would be needed so it would be prudent to anticipate the request and formulate a position. The submission canvassed the arguments for and against; they were arguments that were to recur throughout the year. In favour was the view that a contribution would be a visible and appreciated demonstration of support for US peacemaking in the Middle East; Australia had strongly endorsed Camp David; if the MNF was to be effective it might lead to concessions on the West Bank or Gaza; Australia strongly supported peacekeeping efforts (although in the past under UN auspices). The arguments against were also strong. There was a risk of identifying Australia with other US actions in the Middle East over which they were not consulted; there was no time limit; involvement might affect trade with Arab countries and make Australia appear as a client state of the US; if Sadat fell, hostilities could recommence and lead to MNF casualties. The submission concluded that the main argument in favour was to illustrate to the US that Australia was a reliable ally; but that it might be against Australia's national interest. It proposed two options: decide in principle to respond positively, or take steps to discourage a formal approach. It recommended the latter. FAD agreed; while Tony Street, the foreign minister, was in the US, he should indicate that, while wanting to be helpful, Australia would only participate in UN peacekeeping forces.

The US was not so easily discouraged. Despite the Australian reluctance, an informal message was delivered from Al Haig, the US secretary of state, to Street. It emphasised that the US, Egypt and Israel were preparing a list of possible countries, although he was only informally approaching Australia and Canada. He was conscious of Australia's domestic and trade problems, but hoped Australia would be a vital element in maintaining peace. He asked that the message be kept confidential. Doug Anthony, in Egypt to discuss uranium sales, was approached by the Egyptian minister for defence. Street discussed the invitation with Fraser and then summarised the views in a further memorandum. He argued that a UN force was impossible and that the trade implications were difficult to assess (Australian exports to the area were $940 million); he thought that if the invitation came from Israel and Egypt there might be advantages in participation. He offered several options: an interim reply to Haig, that Australia wait and see what emerged from Israeli–US–Egypt negotiations on the size of the force, send a request for further information, or make an in-principle agreement to participate. PMC believed that, as Australia was to be a 'main partner', ministers should agree in principle to participate. On 2 April FAD tentatively began to mute its opposition but made no decision; it asked for a report from a joint Foreign Affairs–Defence officials committee.

While the report was being compiled, Street was in contact with the Canadian foreign secretary, Mark McGuigan, who wanted to ensure that Canada's UN peacekeeping credentials were maintained, and Lord Carrington, who commented that Israel would not accept a British or major West European contribution. New Zealand also indicated reservations and preferred not to be asked.

The officials' report of 13 April proposed five choices: a straight no; participation only if UN-sponsored (which it acknowledged couldn't happen); a reserved position (depending on the position of other countries, a formal invitation from Egypt and Israel, clarification of size and command details, and a further attempt to get European participation); a statement of willingness to participate, subject to being satisfied in relation to the issues listed under the third option; or agreement subject to details like timespan. Most of the committee proposed the third option; Yeend thought the fourth preferable because, if the US assumed Australia would eventually agree, it was better to strengthen the bargaining position rather than play coy and ask questions. They all agreed that Street should write to Haig asking for clarification.

Unfortunately the next FAD meeting did not reach the item and so Street, expecting a formal invitation from Haig, asked Fraser for authority to send the letter without FAD consideration. Yeend protested that, even though the letter did not commit Australia, it would be the wrong time to make a unilateral decision. So Street discussed it with Fraser and Lynch, who asked the Cabinet Office to clear the letter with FAD members; their approval was duly recorded as a cabinet decision. The letter did not commit Australia; it emphasised support for Camp David, but explained that the government needed to know what others had in mind. Before Australia would agree to participate, it needed assurances of others' participation, and not just countries from the Western club; it hoped Haig would persuade Israel to accept European involvement. It sought specific assurances about the command structure, size, time limits and financial arrangements. The leading members of cabinet were divided. Fraser believed that as an ally Australia needed to support the US. Anthony, as minister for trade, was more nervous; he was concerned about the impact on Australian trade with the Arab countries and could see no reason for Australia getting involved, particularly if European countries were not, because it had no direct strategic interest in the region.

Haig replied on 19 May. He reinforced the informal messages by emphasising the need to prevent the Soviets from vetoing a legitimate peacekeeping operation. A detailed paper answered many of the Australian queries. The Defence committee was still not satisfied and wanted more information about the intentions of others. It suggested that Street should talk to the prime minister, because it assumed – correctly – that Fraser wanted Australia to participate. On 25 May Street discussed the invitation with Fraser; it was important to reach some decision because Fraser was to meet Haig at an ANZUS gathering on 30 June. They decided that Street would make a statement to the House on 26 May, indicating that, although Australia was favourably disposed, it had made no decision yet. A lengthy debate emphasised the strong opposition to the proposal from the Labor party.

On 23 June, a few days in advance of Fraser's meeting with Haig, FAD discussed it again; there were still two main points of contention: the composition of the force and the lack of progress with the implementation of the Camp David accord between Israel and Egypt, particularly over Palestinian autonomy. Fraser had been told that the Canadians were disposed against participation because it was not a UN force or geographically balanced. Canadian support for Sadat was stopping it from making an outright refusal. FAD decided that while overseas Fraser would convey to Trudeau and Reagan the committee's view. It wanted Trudeau to defer a final decision until he had talked to Fraser and then to adopt a common approach. In Britain Carrington was to be approached again, while Fraser was to make clear to Reagan not to expect an early decision.

On 27 June, Haig got agreement from Israel and Egypt on

the structure of the force. He assured Street that he did not think the Arab nations would impose any sanctions. But it was clear that Britain had no desire to be asked. New Zealand, Italy and Holland were still cool about participation.

Australia therefore took one small step further. On 22 July it noted the importance the US placed on Australian participation and agreed that, in future discussions with Thatcher and Trudeau, Fraser would indicate that, if they participated, Australia would give close consideration to participation. On 17 August Fraser reported the results of his personal diplomacy, but no progress on the crucial issues. He had discussed the issue with Trudeau, Reagan, Thatcher, Mitterrand and then Sadat; and was constantly asking that any Israeli veto of Britain (a veto the Israelis denied) be lifted. To Sadat he also expressed concern about trade sanctions (a week later he received a message from Sadat that the US would arrange everything with the Saudis). PMC official Alan Griffith also talked to a representative of the PLO. The Israelis agreed on 26 August that Britain could be approached, but that move was not popular in London.

Fraser was regularly briefed on the developing situation, with the Office of National Assessments providing papers on 'Is Begin genuine re the Peace Process?' and analyses of the PLO. On 25 August FAD discussed the issue again, emphasising in a message to Washington the need for Britain to be invited and expressing again a concern with trade – not so much with the Saudis as with Iran and Iraq.

There, for two months, the negotiations stalled. Fraser explained the difficulties:

There were a lot of sensitivities. Doug was worried about trade. Everyone was worried by everything. It was one of those issues where I just couldn't see the circumstances in which we would be able to make a positive decision.

In a party meeting participation was opposed primarily by John Spender, who argued that Israel would withdraw anyway and that there were dangers of an open-ended commitment, and by Andrew Peacock (now a backbencher) who said he had shifted from support to opposition because Australia had taken too long in making up its mind and had therefore lost any advantage with the US. In the meantime Britain prevaricated, France thought it might cause problems, New Zealand feared that it would threaten its live sheep trade and Canada didn't want to be invited.

Then Sadat's assassination changed all the circumstances. At Sadat's funeral, Doug Anthony discussed the MNF with Haig, McGuigan, Carrington and Colombo (Italy). Haig put sustained pressure on Britain, but Carrington thought participation would undermine the EC initiative to negotiate a Middle East settlement. He also wanted some tangible evidence such as a commitment from Israel for no more settlements on the West Bank. Reagan was to ring Thatcher to exert more pressure. The Egyptian foreign minister arranged to meet Anthony to try to persuade him. Canada was rethinking its position. Anthony had gradually come round. He now feared instability in Egypt and saw good reasons for Australia to win credit by committing troops to the peacekeeping force. He was able to speak strongly at the funeral, knowing that Fraser was in agreement. Haig also wrote to Street emphasising that the most substantial support for Mubarak, Sadat's successor, would be the formation of the MNF. At CHOGM in Melbourne Fraser had discussions with Thatcher, Trudeau and Muldoon. The Israeli ambassador called to say that a negative reply would be a rejection of Sadat's achievement and a turning away from the peace process.

Fraser demanded action. He had discussed the possibility of listing the submission with Anthony and was kept in contact with the discussions in Cairo. He required a memo on the Sinai force that evening – 9 October. It was not to be distributed at all before the meeting and was to be collected at the end. All information was to have the minimum possible circulation. The memorandum traversed the options, and acknowledged that it did not know what the impact on trade would be. Despite the rushed preparation on 9 October, cabinet did not make a decision until 12 October. It noted the messages from Reagan and Haig and agreed that Fraser would tell the US that Australia would participate if Britain and Canada did, noting that European participation would be crucial. It also added some additional conditions: the force to be there for a limited time, the contingent commander to have reserve orders in case he received orders contrary to the agreed purposes, a request for an assurance that there were no links with the proposed US rapid deployment force. It was agreed that there would be no publicity while awaiting reactions. Only three copies of the decision were made. Fraser wrote to Reagan in those terms and told Thatcher and Trudeau of his decision. Fraser sent an additional covering note to Reagan inviting him to use Australian willingness to participate in the negotiations with Thatcher and Trudeau.

The Canadians were glad that Australia agreed to participate, but showed no anxiety to change their stand. Thatcher was tied up in the Conservative conference. Carrington told Haig he would discuss it with the EC – he felt Britain had been put on a 'nasty hook'. However his stance was changing, perhaps as a consequence of Reagan's call to Thatcher and her declared willingness to help. Haig hoped Thatcher would prevail. The US reaction to Fraser's message was appreciative but cautious – Haig hoped Australia would stay loose in its precise terms, although he was not happy about the interlocking vetoes. To the American ambassador Fraser emphasised that the contingent decision was meant to be positive and to make it easier for Reagan to use his persuasive powers.

No public announcement was made as Australia waited for the responses of other nations. The danger of leaks was ever-present and, as parliamentary questions continued, the prime minister was left in a difficult position: could he admit yet to a firm, if conditional, decision? On 20 October Fraser stated that Australia's decision on participation would await decisions to be made by other governments. While technically correct, this could be open to misinterpretation. Yeend thought the risks too great and advised a parliamentary statement, but there was a need to tell Britain, Canada and the US before an announcement was made.

On 21 October FAD agreed that a public statement to parliament was needed, a decision approved by cabinet on 22 October, the day the announcement was made. The day before the government had been told that the EC had decided in principle to participate, leaving the terms and rationale to be worked out by the three countries concerned. Neither Britain nor Canada was enthusiastic about their participation being nominated as a condition for Australia's involvment. The US wanted an element of flexibility left in the statement as to which countries would be involved but Haig did give a commitment on the rapid deployment force. The Australian ambassador in Washington, in the light of a phone call from Fraser, still could not give any assurance; Fraser justified the contingent process as a means of putting pressure on the Canadians, though he conceded that he felt sure cabinet would accept France as an alternative to Canada. The conditions were also designed to assist in gaining domestic acceptance. Fraser states: 'We quite deliberately put the conditions in as a protection for ourselves in political terms. It was more defensible and it wasn't a universally popular position'.

On 22 October cabinet indeed agreed that France could be an alternative to Canada and Fraser announced the government's decision. He was accused of having single-handedly determined foreign policy. The opposition, concerned about possible casualties, condemned the decision. Hayden claimed in parliament the 'single-minded obsessiveness of the prime minister had bluffed and bullied a concession from his colleagues'. On 27 October, in a decision of which there were only two copies, cabinet noted that as the UK, France, Italy and the Netherlands had agreed to participate, it would confirm Australia's participation.

Thereafter it was a matter of waiting while the EC, and primarily Britain, negotiated with an intransigent Israeli prime minister, Menachim Begin. Begin had not made it easy for his allies. While negotiations were continuing for the creation of the MNF, Israel bombed the Iraqi nuclear facility, invaded Lebanon and then in December annexed the Golan Heights. It never seemed remotely possible that progress on Palestinian autonomy, the second strand of the Camp David accord, would be achieved.

Fraser was kept in touch but could do little. FAD could note progress – or the lack of it – while planning for the contingent continued. When Fraser was told that Begin might veto EC participation, he wrote to Reagan emphasising what a disaster it would be. He also enquired whether it would be useful for him to ring Begin. However Begin broke his thigh and was hospitalised; so Fraser wrote instead. He said that if European participation was vetoed, then the MNF would be destroyed and there would be no basis for Australian participation. Fraser also met the leaders of Australian Jewry and encouraged them to put pressure on Begin. Begin replied truculently a month later that Israel was not going to negotiate with the PLO or allow a Palestinian state to be established; he claimed that Carter had never expected it to. But Begin did say he liked the ANZACs because they had played with Jewish children and had a habit of being 'very unkind' to British officers.

The remaining details concerned the arrangements for the contingent; eventually *HMAS Tobruk* sailed while the final legal details were being fixed; the process was not completed until 15 March. The Sinai force never became involved in the problems that its opponents, both in the Liberal party and more vociferously in the Labor opposition, had warned of. The Israeli settlers withdrew from the Sinai; peace was kept. No trade sanctions were imposed. Indeed the force's tenure was extended once by the Labor government. Gradually, over a period of months, Fraser had drawn his colleagues, particularly Anthony, into the commitment. But he was not prepared to go it alone; he would neither commit Australia without international agreement, nor commit himself until he knew he had the necessary support in cabinet.

The Olympic boycott

While the final negotiations for the 1980 election were taking place in Zimbabwe, Russia invaded Afghanistan. The Soviet ambassador travelled to Nareen to explain the action as a response to an appeal for help; Fraser declared it was unacceptable and morally wrong. He discussed possible responses with his colleagues, including reactions to the trade embargo announced by President Carter. On 8 January cabinet met, with a submission from Peacock. It explored the commercial, cultural and scientific links with the USSR, recommending the continuation of scientific exchanges (from which Australia benefited) but curtailing other connections. On the Olympics, due to be held in Moscow in 1980, it thought it only worth supporting a move of the games from Moscow if Australia could act in good company. Peacock was reported as opposing the suspension of wheat sales and holding the view that an Olympic boycott was a matter for sporting bodies.

Cabinet took a stiffer line on 9 January, suspending scientific collaboration and agreeing to enter no new wheat contracts (as long as other countries maintained an embargo). On the Olympics, cabinet agreed to wait for the views of other nations since it was an international, not bilateral, event. It noted that the Soviets would use the games as propaganda, and it would be preferable if they were not held in Moscow. No decision was taken, but cabinet agreed that the Olympics might be split between several venues. Fraser denied that cabinet had buckled to National party pressure by refusing to ban all wheat sales – there was no point in taking actions from which Australia alone would suffer, as it would from a unilateral wheat ban. Diplomats were quietly sounding out national views on a boycott, while Fraser supported publicly a proposal that the games go permanently to Greece.

On 19 January Fraser announced that he would visit Carter and Thatcher to support – or strengthen – Carter's stand. He discussed the options with the Japanese prime minister, while Peacock visited India, Pakistan and several ASEAN countries. Fraser was supporting the notion of a boycott. By cabinet's next discussion, on 22 January, Fraser had received a letter from Carter, saying he could not support US participation in the games and that he would ask the US Olympic Committee to seek to cancel or transfer the games, or if that failed, not to participate. He asked Fraser to do the same with the Australian Olympic Federation (AOF). Thatcher had also written to her Olympic Committee asking for the games to be moved. Support for the boycott was growing. Cabinet agreed to support Carter and for Fraser to write to Syd Grange, chairman of the Australian Olympic Committee.

In his letter to Grange, Fraser argued that opposition to the invasion could be expressed tellingly by an effective boycott.

He asked the Australian Olympic Committee (AOC) to tell the International Olympic Committee that, if the Soviets did not withdraw from Afghanistan, the games should be transferred or cancelled. He agreed to give the grant of $500 000 that cabinet had approved on 12 January to the AOC (although cabinet also determined a week later that the money should not be used to send competitors to Moscow). The US embassy asked whether part or all the games could be held in Melbourne. PMC took a few confidential soundings and concluded that Australia could handle only a limited number of events and that it would probably not be in the country's best interests.

Ellicott, as minister for home affairs and with a responsibility for sport, now took up much of the running from Peacock. He met the Australian Olympic Federation which opposed any transfer of the games from Moscow, because they claimed the games were a single entity. Fraser annotated his brief with the comment that they were already broken down with the Winter Olympics. Anthony said it was unrealistic for the Australian team to expect to go to Moscow. Grange noted publicly on 31 January that the government had not directly asked the Australian Olympic Committee to boycott the games. He stated that, if the government said 'don't go', the AOC wouldn't.

On 29 January Fraser departed for Washington and then Europe to see Thatcher, Giscard d'Estaing and Helmut Schmidt, and then back to Washington. He carried a proposal, supported by Thatcher, that the US should convene a steering group, to meet on 12 and 13 February, to consider the next steps. Ellicott initially sought a delay, but Fraser replied that events were moving on and there was a determination that the Olympic teams should stay away. The steering committee included the US, Canada, Britain, the Netherlands and Australia.

On 12 February cabinet received a report on the prime minister's trip and hardened its stand. Fraser and Ellicott were to meet the Australian Olympic Federation, requesting it to ensure that no Australian team went, but cabinet reaffirmed that it would not restrict passports. On 13 February Fraser addressed the nation on television, justifying government support for the boycott. On 15 February he and Ellicott met the executive of the AOF and were told it required a full conference to make a decision and that the next such meeting would be on 19 April. Fraser reasserted that politics and sport were inevitably tangled because the Soviets would make propaganda out of the games. He quoted the official USSR handbook on the games that claimed their presence in Moscow was 'a general recognition of the historical importance and the correctness of the foreign political course of our country, of the enormous services of the Soviet Union in the struggle for peace'. Fraser also telegraphed the leading officials of each sport. It was accepted that there was a need to keep pressure on the AOF, but differences about tactics emerged. As prime ministerial adviser Alan Jones wrote to the head of the Government Information Unit:

We must massage the AOF, keep them onside, encourage them and embrace them so that they come around to our thinking. Anything that suggests at this stage that we are dictating to them may affect the decision that they make in April.

But such a gentle approach was not the style of his employer, even though it may have been good advice.

In the meantime the cables traffic intensified as the steering group frantically both sought alternative sites for the games and encouraged other countries to join its activities. As the former possibility became more remote, so the desirability of joining declined. The US even decided not to host the meetings of the steering groups; they were transferred to Geneva where they were to alternate between the British and American embassies, so that even their actual US sponsorship could be 'clouded'. Governments were awaiting decisions of national Olympic committees. The British committee was to decide on 4 March (but it postponed a decision), the Americans on 11 April. A constant 'scorecard' was maintained, with reports of the failure of EC foreign ministers to reach an agreed position leading Foreign Affairs to take a pessimistic view of an effective boycott.

On 4 March an ad hoc cabinet committee established to monitor the situation decided that the next steering group meeting should have ministerial representation and committed $3 million to host the hockey and shooting competitions. On 5 March Fraser wrote to Thatcher, Carter, Schmidt and Trudeau emphasising that it was important that the boycott succeed and proposing ministerial representation at the steering group meetings as cabinet had approved; he also rang Thatcher. However most leaders wanted the steering group maintained only at official level. Ellicott was to visit other countries to maintain high level discussions. Thatcher responded that they must 'keep the pressure up' and that she would send the minister of state in the Foreign and Commonwealth Office to the steering group. Trudeau, who had just returned to office after eight months of opposition, welcomed Ellicott's visit, but did not commit the government. Ellicott reported that Canada was cautious but that there had been little contact between Canada and the US over the boycott; he asked Fraser to suggest to Carter some direct discussions. Fraser wrote again to Carter, proposing that he ring Trudeau.

The steering group met in Geneva on 19 March and identified several alternative sites, but agreed that governments should not be seen to be taking too prominent a role in organising them. It did not want them to appear as the 'Alternative Games' or 'Free World Games'. On 25 March Ellicott reported to cabinet on his discussions in Ottawa, Washington, London, Bonn and Geneva. Cabinet agreed that, if asked, the minister would tell parliament that the boycott was likely to be effective. A week later it agreed to compensate the Yachting Federation for any shortfall as a consequence of its decision to withdraw from the games and compete in alternative world class events.

As the Australian government awaited the decision of the AOF, due on 19 April, Fraser continued to restate his position, condemning Soviet tactics and atrocities in Afghanistan. At the same time the boycott campaign seemed to falter. The British Olympic Committee rejected its government's request to boycott the games and decided to send a team. The US thought the prospects of alternative games were dead. In West Germany the government opposed the Games. In Australia public opinion began to drift, as even conservative premiers like Bjelke-Petersen withdrew support. Fraser became more determined;

on 1 April he stated: 'The government has a policy. It will continue to pursue it because of the much larger issues which are specifically areas of government responsibility'.

The Olympic boycott was harder to sell because the government had not added a trade boycott to bans on cultural, scientific and sporting exchange. Fraser argued that the government would stay with concerted action because there was no point in imposing unilateral trade boycotts when others would fill the gap. 'There's no point in taking measures that will only hurt Australians'. The issue had been effectively muddled because wool exports continued. Not everyone was prepared to accept the different circumstances, particularly with unsubstantiated rumours of wool from Nareen being shipped to Russia.

Before leaving Canberra to attend Zimbabwe's independence celebrations, Fraser sent telegrams to the delegates at the AOF to the effect that it was in Australian interests not to send a team and that he expected them to support the US Olympic Committee. (The latter had decided on 14 April that, as the president had declared national security was at stake, it would not send a team.) Fraser claimed it was 'not in the interests of national security' to go to Moscow. He made his telegram public and insisted that Anthony, as acting prime minister, Peacock and Ellicott, attend the AOF meeting, addressing the executive one day and the plenary session the next. The AOF decided to defer the vote to let the AOF see what happened elsewhere, although some AOF members thought Fraser's tactics intimidating. Fraser welcomed the move.

In the last week of April the West German and Canadian Olympic committees joined the boycott and Fraser stated that he would be very surprised if the AOF decided to go. He suggested on 29 April to Carter, Thatcher, Giscard d'Estaing and Schmidt that they should all meet to ensure a unity of purpose. He told Muldoon and Trudeau of his proposal, asking Trudeau for his active support. In the week before the final decision, there was constant pressure on the AOF. Cabinet decided that it did not want to see the viability of the AOF threatened and privately told the AOF that it would make funds available for travel to other international events.

On 23 May the AOC voted by six votes to five to send a team. Fraser reacted angrily: 'I pray that those Olympians who do go to Moscow will not pay the price that many of those who went to the Berlin Olympics paid once the War started in 1939'. He argued that an effective boycott was in place: the AOF 'had an opportunity to contribute to that paramount objective by placing Australia first. It is with profound regret that they did not take that opportunity'. He asked them all to think again.

Cabinet agreed to maintain the pressure on individuals and sporting bodies, although the Co-ordination committee decided that the prime minister should not withdraw as AOF patron at that stage. Fraser also had the unpleasant task of informing those leaders in whose support he had constantly written that the AOC had voted to go to Moscow. He told Thatcher, Trudeau, Carter and Schmidt:

We remain firmly of the view that an Australian team should not participate in the Moscow Games and I and my ministers shall do all that we can to persuade the Executive to reconsider its position. We shall also call upon individual sporting bodies and sportsmen and women to make their own decisions not to participate in the Moscow Games.

Fraser wrote strong letters to members of the AOF, arguing that the country was isolated from its neighbours. 'Let me put it to you personally, and through you to the executive, that Australia, as an independent nation with an unqualified record in defence of liberty and the right to be free, has a bounden duty to support other free and independent nations'. Even though he, Anthony, Peacock and Ellicott met the executive on 19 June to try to persuade it to reconsider, it didn't and the team went, although several leading competitors, such as Raelene Boyle and Tracey Wickham, did withdraw.

Throughout the campaign, PMC had carefully monitored public reactions, as indicated by letters to the prime minister and reactions to various speeches. They had run strongly in favour of the boycott at first, but by the time of the AOC's decision, the balance of opinion had turned against the government.

When competitors won medals, Fraser was put in an awkward position. A member of his staff recalls the problem:

Michelle Ford, I think, won a gold medal. I got the call at home from the press. 'What's the comment of the PM?' This is at 5 o'clock in the morning; one of the afternoon papers rang me. 'Right, I'll be back to you'. I rang the PM at the Lodge and he said 'What does Yeend think?'. So I rang Yeend and he said 'Send a congratulatory message. He's got to send a congratulatory message; after all, she is an Australian'. I rang a couple of other people; similar sort of view. I rang him back and I said 'these are the views'. 'Uh, I'll think about it'. I said, 'Look, the Melbourne Herald want a statement straight away and no doubt others will too as the news becomes clearer'. 'I'll think about it'. Finally, at 6 or 7 that night we got an answer and he sent a fairly guarded message. I got a number of calls during the day wanting other people's views, Tamie's views and all over the place . . . He could see a principle being pushed aside if he was to go ahead after having vigorously opposed them going; but at the end of the day it was a political decision only.

Eventually Fraser sent telegrams to all medal winners; the one to the swimming relay team, the 'Mean Machine', said:

You know I did not and do not approve of Australia being represented at these Olympic Games. I do want to say however that your performance in the relay was a truly great sporting achievement. My personal congratulations.

Fraser remained single-minded. Throughout the campaign he was constantly kept informed about international developments, about commitments from other countries, and about likely decisions. He went to AOF meetings informed about the background and careers of the people he would meet.

The campaign was perhaps a case of a collective decision being tougher than any of the individuals' views. Three ministers were concerned: Fraser, Peacock and Ellicott. Peacock played a minor role. Tired of long years of travel, he was content to let Ellicott take the international running. Nor was he strongly in favour of the boycott. He remembered:

I was privately opposed to the boycott. We had an initial informal cabinet discussion and we had strong requests from the Americans. I was arguing against the boycott privately before we got our formal paper to the cabinet. I then conceived that I wasn't going to go to the wall on this and I publicly supported it . . . but I started with great reluctance.

But then in retrospect neither of the other two were keen. Ellicott claimed:

When the matter of the Olympic boycott came before cabinet and the decision was made to support President Carter in relation to it, that was a near to unanimous view. I may have been the only one who wasn't overly happy about it. I took the view that before they used the sports people for political purposes, they should be prepared to take initiatives in other areas such as trade. Anyhow it went through cabinet. I had to pick it up and it was my responsibility. I then pursued a fairly vigorous approach.

But he argues that his heart was never in his advocacy.

Fraser's comment was that he was uneasy; further, 'it was a very hard sell job, partly because of the attitude of the Labor party', but he did not see it as a defeat. 'People didn't like the policy, but I think by and large more people would have respected the government for sticking with it'. He was concerned at the time whether the policy was durable and likely to succeed. But the crucial point was the need to support the American line in this great power dispute. Being an American ally had responsibilities. In cases like the Olympic boycott Australia had to act as part of a co-ordinated Western bloc, as most of the leaders were advocating a boycott. Even if Fraser entered the campaign with misgivings about its effectiveness, it was more important that Australia give full support as part of its international obligations. Therefore although Fraser's campaign failed domestically when the AOF voted to go to Moscow, it could be justified in international terms as an ally paying its proper dues.

Perhaps the doubters were right. The boycott may have reduced the appeal of the games; it did not force the Soviets out of Afghanistan. That occurred after eight dogged years of resistance by the Mudjahadeen. Yet solidarity, not direct impact, was the driving force of the policy.

Fraser and foreign policy

The three events described in this chapter were perhaps mere episodes, but each was important because it reflected the way in which Fraser became involved, and in each case there was some outcome towards which he worked. As a consequence they can perhaps be explained more readily than broader continuous campaigns where the capacity of Australia was limited and could not be so clearly focused: the American alliance, the campaign to reduce tariffs, the concentration on the Soviet threat. In each of these Australia had to act on several fronts at once, and it is less easy to isolate results and identify the means adopted. Yet they probably still fit the same pattern of decision-making with Fraser playing a dominant role, as the more specific events described here.

Fraser liked to develop and use personal connections. He developed close links with African and other national leaders. His correspondence became more personal as he knew them better. Fraser tried hard, if eventually unsuccessfully, to have Australia invited to join the Group of Seven (the meetings of the leading Western nations) because he had ambitions for the role that Australia, and he himself, might play. At times those roles were appreciated – by all but the British at Lusaka. At times they seemed to grate on his allies – his conditional commitment to Sinai was not welcomed by either of the sides he was trying to influence. However in foreign, as in domestic, policy Fraser was an activist and clearly exploited the position of prime minister.

How much freedom he had depended on what other forces were in play. If little domestic participation was involved, there were few restrictions. Cabinet – or at least FAD – approved the policy towards South Africa and Zimbabwe – as it approved or endorsed every foreign affairs decision. In that case Fraser ran without continuing internal support. Many of his own party and even his ministers did not share the strength of his commitment, but were prepared to let him run. In the Sinai force, he needed some domestic support because Australian troops were to be committed. There was a process of educating colleagues and the public, connected to ensuring that there was an international effort; it took time. The Olympic boycott required decisions from bodies over which the government did not have control. Despite the vigour with which Fraser pursued the boycott internationally, in this case he could not deliver his own country; but he did perform as an ally.

It is not surprising that Fraser enjoyed foreign policy and the opportunity to argue in the north–south debate. Foreign leaders have been prepared to pay tributes in print to his influence in foreign policy that have seldom been acknowledged domestically. Andrew Peacock believed Fraser 'had a rounded view of the world, its strengths and its weaknesses. he saw moral issues and strategic issues'. Coral Bell has concluded that Fraser's foreign policy

had been one of substituting rather complex balancings for rather simplistic loyalties. The balancing, for instance, of economic dissatisfactions against strategic loyalties, the American alliance against Third World connections . . . The issues on which Australian policy took stands at variance with those of the United States and Britain . . . were quite fundamental.

She comments that Fraser had made himself such an earnest advocate of Third World causes that Washington 'heaved a sigh of relief' that Hawke was not going to emulate Fraser's fervour.

Fraser's actions in foreign policy provide both different perspectives on his reputation and illustrations of how an activist prime minister, working on behalf of his country, can negotiate with few constraints. He fits the model of a strong leader, acting primarily in terms of his conception of the national interest and clearly enjoying the freedom provided in international forums. He was conscious of the limited influence a middle power like Australia has, but sought to maximise that influence.

CHAPTER 10

DECISIONS, DECISIONS

The prime minister's participation in the development of policy depended on his interest. It was a consequence as much of a policy's political sensitivity as of its intrinsic importance. Fraser of course liked to know something about almost everything. He was seldom relaxed about issues, particularly not those that were likely to damage the government's reputation or have a widespread impact. To some issues he brought preconceived ideas, but even then he was prepared to argue the merits of his case – be they political, presentational, tactical or even moral. As long as he retained an interest – and that was usually while the policy was controversial – he was deeply involved in the detail.

A series of cases – all seen as sensitive and important at the time – can illustrate the point. They show a prime minister in action and usually in control, a prime minister pushing for results and using the available sources of power to achieve a satisfactory result, a prime minister who always sought to understand the ramifications of complex and sensitive issues. They were selected because in each instance the prime minister had to face strong opposition, either inside or outside his party, and because they were all of great public interest. The cases are the decision to export uranium: a matter of presentation and public education; the decision to establish and implement the Campbell report: a shift towards deregulation; the campaign to oppose a 35 hour week: a struggle fought without the sanctions of federal power; and the battle against tax evasion: a message both moral and public. Each case illustrates different facets of political style, as well as similarities; each shows both the power and the limitations of the prime minister's position.

Uranium: a matter of presentation

The mining and export of uranium was one of the most controversial issues of the late 1970s, an issue which nationally divided the two major parties and always threatened to become the electoral focus for campaigns. When the Fraser government entered office, it had to decide to what extent existing or new contracts for uranium exports would be honoured and on what conditions. Any decision was likely to be put under scrutiny and to invite outraged opposition. It was anticipated that a decision to export would have important economic implications (although the initial forecast was over-optimistic). Therefore the policy on uranium, finally announced on 23 August 1977, was the result of one of the most careful and protracted debates of the Fraser government.

The Whitlam government had established a royal commission, headed by Mr Justice Fox, to examine the environmental and social impact of the Ranger uranium mine in the Northern Territory. In January 1976 Fox asked the new government what its attitude to safeguards was. Inevitably all decisions on uranium were to be intermingled with the treatment of the Fox inquiry.

The minister responsible, Doug Anthony, had no doubts about the desirability of exports. He publicly supported the change of policy and planned to visit Japan to discuss contracts. He wanted to move as fast as possible, making the government's intention to mine and export uranium clear. The party policy stated that the 'mining and export of uranium oxide for commercially viable deposits will be permitted', although it acknowledged that there would be some regulations for marketing and that export would have to be consistent with Australian obligations under the nuclear non-proliferation treaty.

Anthony immediately brought two submissions to cabinet. The first asked cabinet to endorse a press statement that expressed general support for uranium development and expounded the government's intentions on overseas ownership and marketing; the second examined the possibility of the Australian Industry Development Corporation taking up financial involvement in Ranger now held by the government through the Australian Atomic Energy Commission, because government policy was not to get directly involved in mineral development. Ranger was becoming impatient of delay. So too, Anthony argued, was he.

Anthony's initial press statement was in places so specific that it could have pre-empted many decisions that cabinet would have to make. It was redrafted by PMC, probably in consultation with Fraser, to exclude details of foreign ownership requirements and other commitments. On 30 January cabinet noted that several submissions on safeguards, marketing and general development would be brought to cabinet. Anthony's press statement on 2 February merely indicated that the government was giving urgent consideration to aspects of uranium development, including the legislative basis for mining, royalty rates and marketing arrangements. He accepted that uranium was a 'unique material for which governments recognise that special arrangements must be made'. Anthony emphasised that private enterprise, not the Atomic Energy Commission, would be responsible for future uranium exploration.

In the next two months, ministers and officials prepared the required submissions. The royal commissioner, Mr Justice Fox, first refused to rush his report and then adjourned his inquiry on 18 March while waiting for the government's decision. He called for a statement of the government's policy towards marketing, safeguards and the role of the Atomic Energy Commission. The government was committed to both the free enterprise exploitation of uranium and to government intervention to ensure controlled exploration and development. One submission examined the need for a safeguards policy. Brought to cabinet by Anthony and Peacock, it proposed that safeguards be required to be consistent with non-proliferation treaty obligations and exports be conditional on arrangements agreed between Australia and the country purchasing the uranium. A second submission recommended that Mary Kathleen, Ranger and Queensland Mines be allowed to proceed with development, subject to finalising all necessary procedures concerned with environmental and Aboriginal interests. Both submissions were first sent to an official taskforce; its report was considered by the officials committee of the Economic committee, representing PMC, Treasury, Trade and Employment and Industrial Relations. However the officials could not agree; instead of providing a paper on the terms of production and marketing, they decided to brief ministers individually.

On 22 March cabinet postponed the decision for a week, while officials re-examined the issues, but it decided not to brief Fox yet on the state of play. On 30 March the cabinet played safe. It decided that, pending the outcome of the inquiry, its decisions would only be indicative and would not represent a final position. It agreed to the establishment of a marketing scheme, initial production quotas, and price guidelines. On safeguards it agreed to most of the recommendations for bilateral treaties that would ensure security, peaceful use and no reprocessing, and it established missions to examine the problems of drawing up bilateral agreements. But it was again stated that these decisions did not represent a final position, although the minister would indicate to Fox the state of the government's thinking.

Fraser told parliament that the government had not taken any decisions that would pre-empt the Fox inquiry and that it had provided the information to Fox that he had requested. Anthony said that the government wanted the development conducted 'in an orderly manner'. The broad directions may have been decided; the details were left in abeyance.

The government wanted to export uranium, subject to safeguards. It was not prepared to do so while the inquiry was under way, because of possible reactions. Rather than rushing ahead immediately it chose the cautious route. In so doing, it tied itself irrevocably to the wheels of Fox's inquiry; it became dependent on it in terms of conditions and timing. For twelve months it could do little but wait, while always assuming mining would go ahead. In June Anthony prepared a paper for the prime minister, indicating that he would announce abroad that the government wished to honour its commitments and that he was confident it would do so, but was awaiting the Fox report. He even stated that he had no great apprehension at exporting uranium to the Soviet Union, as long as it was in accord with international rules and regulations. Fraser also talked to Trudeau about safeguards, in the hope of developing a unified policy with Canada.

The position was difficult to sustain because the government knew what it wanted to do, and was merely awaiting the report's legitimation. When Fraser visited Japan, the briefing note reflected the position. It proposed that he state publicly that Australian governments had given assurances that existing approved contracts would be met and he did not qualify that position. The brief suggested that he privately indicate confidence that contracts would be honoured, but that he was inhibited from public comment because of the agreement not to make any official decision until Fox reported. It stated that Australia would meet delivery dates, but asked for understanding as the matter required careful handling.

In November 1976 the first Fox report was released. It argued that the hazards of mining and milling uranium, if properly regulated and controlled, were not so great as to justify a decision not to develop Australia's uranium mines. It concluded that the dangers were sufficiently serious to restrict the expansion of mining. The government was able to interpret the report in a way that it found useful. It contended that the report accepted that uranium was potentially dangerous, but on balance argued that mining and export were desirable, subject to proper controls and strict regulations. There should be no sales to countries that had not signed the Nuclear Non-Proliferation Treaty (NPT) and a national energy policy should be developed. However it was only an interim report, dealing with broad aspects and international considerations. A more detailed, second report was to look at local and national considerations, including the impact of mining on Aboriginal land rights and the environment. Nevertheless the first report was accepted by the government as giving sufficient support for mining for it to announce that it would be developing policy while Fox worked on the second report.

In November Street held discussions with ACTU president, Bob Hawke, and reported that Hawke felt he could secure union agreements to export uranium for existing contracts if the country of destination had ratified the NPT and processing was regarded as safe; the unions had an open mind on future contracts. The Labor caucus too agreed that existing contracts should be honoured. In December the cabinet agreed to allow the Mary Kathleen mine to proceed, but it did not want a parliamentary vote until the second Fox report was received.

Fraser maintained a constant interest, particularly where he thought that Australia's stand could influence others. He exchanged informal messages with Trudeau, wrote to President Carter, and tabled the correspondence. In March Anthony reaffirmed his strong support for the speeded-up development of mining.

Then in May 1977 an intensive three-month consideration of the issues began. On 2 May Fraser declared that Australia had a global responsibility at a time of energy shortage but promised that exports would take place only 'with the most stringent and comprehensive safeguards and strictly for peaceful non-military purposes'. First the cabinet analysed in detail the problem of safeguards. It was presented with four submissions, lodged on 12 May; one dealt with general issues; the others with International Atomic Energy Authority (IAEA) safeguards, with bilateral agreements and with the selection of eligible countries. They were considered quickly, both because Anthony wanted an early decision and because Fraser wanted to make a statement on 24 May, before he went overseas.

The prime minister put the four submissions on the cabinet agenda at the last minute on 16 May. Although no final conclusions were made, ministers agreed that the statement should be tougher, and should have an international flavour; it should not be seen to pre-empt Fox's report but could announce his future role as ambassador-at-large. Cabinet still wanted more details on the precise implications of the NPT and on IAEA safeguards and an educated guess on French intentions.

The further details were lodged in a submission on 20 May. Fraser stated publicly that he wanted a final decision within a day or two of the receipt of Fox's report, because it would allow him to support Carter's recent statements on nuclear development; but his office discounted the possibility of such a quick decision. On 23 May cabinet finally endorsed the main safeguard proposals and approved the revised statement by the prime minister, with final details to be settled by Fraser, in conjunction with Anthony, Peacock and the attorney-general. On 24 May Fraser announced government policy on safeguards in the House, but he emphasised that the decision did not pre-empt any findings of the Fox report. Rather it was to establish a framework within which policy could be developed. He declined to promise that the House would have an opportunity to debate the report before a decision was made.

The second Fox report was released on 25 May. It recommended the development of legally enforceable obligations for those countries to whom exports went, sequential development of mines and the establishment of marketing authorities to police the development. While clearing the way for development, it was far from unequivocal about the advantages. As Fox himself said 'The report does not lend itself to green light or red light summaries'. Before leaving the country Fraser said no decision would be made before he returned. Yet, when he spoke to the Italian prime minister on 30 May, he was able to forecast confidently that Australia would soon be able to resume exports.

Fraser was kept in close touch with the developing debate. Anthony rang him to report on the cabinet discussion on 2 June, when it was decided to send groups of officials to Europe to examine safeguards and markets. Anthony noted that Fraser's insistence on some action had been accepted by cabinet and hoped that, while eschewing any suggestion of blackmail, Fraser would remind the EEC what a large supplier Australia was. On 3 June Fraser reported to cabinet that his talks with British prime minister James Callaghan had been satisfactory as the UK was interested in substantial purchases of Australian uranium. He emphasised the need to be ready to talk about safeguards and to demonstrate to the EEC that Australia was ready to press ahead. PMC was to prepare a general paper for the prime minister to use in discussions of Australian mineral policy, to be cleared with Anthony. Anthony agreed with Fraser for the need for a decision to export 'in principle', preferably before the ALP conference in Perth where the export of uranium was obviously going to be a divisive issue. Anthony wanted to issue a broad statement that the Ranger report had been received, that the general issues were considered, that Australia was ready to proceed immediately and on a large scale, and that Ranger, Yeelirrie and Narbalek were to commence immediately. Anthony was still the man in a hurry, although Fraser also anticipated that the government would make its decision in July, and continued to emphasise that the decision had *not* been made.

On 8 June Anthony and Yeend discussed the timing of the decision, because speculation was growing. Fraser was reported in the *Age* as having decided unilaterally in Britain that the decision would be taken in July; he wanted it after the premiers' conference. Fraser was concerned that the press understand that cabinet, not he, had decided the timing and he asked Yeend to emphasise the point to Anthony; he had already tried. Anthony wanted it before the ALP conference, leaving a week or so in early July. Fox had his own opinion; he told PMC he wanted the prime minister to take a statesmanlike view, balancing cost against ethical and international considerations and always emphasising the complexity of the issues involved.

When Fraser returned to Australia the discussion recommenced. PMC's proposed strategy was clear; the clamour from the community would be in direct proportion to the gap between the Fox recommendations and the government's decisions. So Fox would be the key, and there would be a need for careful presentation of the government's decision. It was preferable to start with Fox's proposals and then explain when or if the government was moving away from them. Barnett concurred. He reported that a public relations committee, consisting of representatives from PMC and the prime minister's office, had met Eggleton to discuss the presentation of the policy. All of them preferred a single consolidated decision and argued that it should not be rushed just so that it could be made before Fraser's mid-July Press Club speech. They thought this speech could prepare the ground for a complex decision, canvass the international implications, attack the opposition for failing to face the problem and reassure the community that the decisions would be proper and responsible. A series of separate decisions would appear to be reacting to the media. Fraser, perhaps typically, was unconcerned; he did not see why the main decision – that Australia would export – could not be taken the next Tuesday. Carmody and Yeend persuaded him to relax the deadline.

Thirteen submissions supported by reports from the overseas missions on markets and safeguards and from meetings of heads of departments, were discussed by cabinet over two days, on 12 and 13 July. There were reports on fundamental issues, Aboriginal issues, national parks and land use, environmental protection, future developments, memoranda of understanding, legislative considerations, royalties, and the creation of a uranium advisory council. The issues all interlocked. The previous week the ALP conference had decided to ban the mining and export of uranium until adequate safeguards had been developed. Uranium mining was quickly becoming an issue that clearly divided the parties. Fraser attacked the change of policy of the ALP at a Press Club lunch on 13 July, maintaining still that the government had yet to make a decision. His speech emphasised the problems of uranium mining and appreciated why people were concerned.

Cabinet still had not come to a conclusion, but it identified those issues where it had a preferred position. Its call for several more papers bore all the hallmarks of a prime minister not yet satisfied in his own mind. He particularly wanted to understand the way that safeguards could be implemented. Cabinet was also concerned that the opponents of mining were receiving all the attention and established an officials' committee to look at the public presentation and the desirability of parliamentary debate. The cabinet's request reflected Eggleton's emphasis on the need to plan the different stages of announcement. The need for attention to the public presentation of the policy was created by the growing organisation of the anti-uranium movement, with large protest marches and publicity about the dangers of mining. The final decision had to be taken in the atmosphere created by this campaigning.

Four more submissions were lodged between 26 and 31 July, and Fox was consulted both about the government's proposals and the ALP's new platform. On 1 and 2 August cabinet returned to the task, even though it could only indicate its 'preferred position' because any final approval was still subject to the environmental protection legislation. Cabinet accepted proposals on administrative arrangements and uranium enrichment, but asked for yet another paper on safeguards so that ministers could effectively deal with questions or counter-assertions about the dangers of processing. Ministers also wanted a model bilateral agreement prepared and an explanation of how compliance would be verified. These four submissions were lodged on 12 August and discussed on 15 and 16 August. Cabinet approved the safeguard arrangements and accepted the need for a uniform code of regulation and control for the nuclear industry.

In the same week a group of senior ministers agreed that an ad hoc committee on the presentation of the uranium policy should decide on which areas the government should concentrate and whether it was appropriate to bring in experts from overseas. Nixon was asked to chair the committee but it met only once before the decision was made.

On 23 August cabinet finally authorised the uranium package. The procedure was unusual, both because of the complexity of the issues and the constant eye for public presentation. On 18 August, after cabinet's endorsement of the final papers, PMC circulated to the five main departments a draft cabinet decision some forty-five pages long that consolidated all the earlier discussions. The decision was in four parts; the first acknowledged the two Ranger reports, and noted that an exemption from the environmental protection requirements had been granted. It agreed in principle that uranium mining should proceed, subject to environmental and nuclear safeguard controls, and it agreed to endorse the Ranger findings unless there were compelling reasons to the contrary. The second part endorsed the general findings of the first report. The third went through each of the specific recommendations in the second Ranger report; and the last one added some general conclusions.

Between the first draft and the final submission, a few cosmetic changes were made. Whereas the first had occasionally stated bluntly that cabinet did not accept some findings of the Fox report, the final wording emphasised that, whereas cabinet endorsed the thrust of Ranger, the actual timing and development of uranium mines might be different from those he proposed.

Cabinet accepted the long and complicated draft with only minor changes. It was not prepared to decide in what order or when other mines would be developed (thus failing to accept the Fox recommendation that provided a planned sequence of development); it required them to satisfy environmental and developmental requirements and to negotiate successfully with the Aborigines (for whom lands rights legislation had been passed in 1976). It added a proviso that it would need assurances from the nuclear weapon states that they would not divert uranium for military purposes, and it noted (at Anthony's request) that the infrastructure for mining should be in place before Aboriginal land claims were granted. In a state of exhaustion cabinet also agreed that Fraser should announce the forty-eight-page decision in parliament on 25 August. His speech emphasised the degree to which the government had followed the Fox proposals.

Then the emphasis turned to justification and to implementation. When one member of the Fox inquiry indicated the differences between the decision and the report, Fraser was involved in planning a press statement to meet the implied dissent by emphasising the degree to which the government *had* agreed with the report. The ad hoc committee met on 7 September to plan the program and had its general approach approved by cabinet. Over the next week it approved a three-pronged attack: ministerial speeches, the circulation of public material, and the invitation of independent experts. It met several times and approved an information booklet which was carefully prepared to present the best case. The word 'cancer', for instance, was not allowed to be used in discussions of radiation effects. According to one official, the uranium decision was the 'first time there had been a professional job in the presentation of decisions'.

Also important were the industrial relations problems. The ACTU declared that it would give the government two months to hold a national referendum. The government refused to accept external directions and rejected the proposal, but Fraser had established a taskforce to recommend how the government should overcome any industrial disruption if it decided to export uranium. The taskforce acknowledged that as the unions, particularly the transport unions, were registered in Queensland or New South Wales, they might be difficult to control. It argued for an early meeting with Hawke. Fraser was also provided with a schedule of the timing of shipments and the movements of uranium from the Mary Kathleen or government stockpiles.

On 4 October cabinet decided to assist where proper requests for early shipment were made by purchasers, but preferred to continue a dialogue, with Street keeping in touch with Hawke. Cabinet did decide that when officials canvassed the options for breaking the strikes, they should not include intervention by the defence forces (as a media story had suggested). The minister for defence was instructed to develop contingency plans so that the government had the option of involving the services, but that planning was not to be made public. Street continued discussions with Hawke, although the 1977 election interrupted any easy relationship.

In early 1978 Mary Kathleen faced threats of strikes as the unions were awaiting a vote of the rank and file over the handling of uranium. The company refused to confirm their shipping bookings unless the government guaranteed them; but the government could not, as Anthony publicly stated. Cabinet initially asked for plans if the ACTU bans continued, but then decided to wait, as it assumed Hawke wanted to honour existing contracts. When the union branches voted in favour of fulfilling existing contracts, the immediate pressure was relieved. Fraser was thereafter provided with regular lists of shipments.

The problems facing the miners were by no means over, as

all the details had to be fixed. Anthony took a submission to cabinet in March, complaining that the process was too complex and slow. Cabinet duly told everyone to speed up and established an ad hoc committee under Anthony's chairmanship to keep it moving. The framework had been established; the details were to be left primarily to Anthony and Viner. These were often crucial; they included negotiations with the Aborigines and monitoring of environmental controls. Without Fraser's overriding and detailed interests, some of the principles fought for in cabinet appear to have been forgotten, as the Ranger Aborigines were at times bullied into submission and agreement in a way that was not consistent with Fraser's aspirations.

In February 1979, when a note detailing changes in the shipping schedules was sent to Fraser, it was returned with the comment that the prime minister thought it could have gone to another minister. While it may have been important enough once, it was not so now. Prime ministers only have time for items of political and national sensitivity. By 1979 uranium was off the immediate agenda.

The uranium case is a clear example where Fraser set and maintained the strategy. If Anthony had been given the freedom to act, uranium would have been exported immediately; he thought the delay for eighteen months unnecessary and, in terms of markets missed, expensive. Fraser was more cautious, more environmentally aware, more concerned about Aboriginal rights; he was also most conscious of the potential public response. He therefore restrained his most powerful lieutenant, set the timetable, oversaw the presentation of the case, insisted that cabinet examine all the implications with care and some understanding. He rejected the easy solutions – that could have been made, ironically, when opposition was still disorganised – and followed a more considered and lengthy path. He wanted, claimed a close observer, 'a domestic and international position that was unassailable'. Even though he was always convinced that uranium should be exported, he wanted the options properly considered. The timetable, the process and the outcome were all carefully orchestrated.

The 35-hour week: the politics of impotence

The federal government must become involved in wages policy because of the broad economic implications of any changes. Yet it has limited power to influence those changes. The constitution provides the government with the authority to legislate for the conciliation and arbitration of industrial disputes, a power that is exercised through the Federal Conciliation and Arbitration Commission. However it is a federal power that is shared with the states, so wage claimants may often play off one level of court against another.

The confrontation with trade unions over wage changes was continuous during the Fraser years, but since the government did not have direct powers over prices or wages, it could only rely on persuasion – of employers, unions and the courts. Therefore when the metal trades unions began a mobilisation campaign to reduce the working week to 35 hours in 1980, the government had to react.

In June 1980 the ACTU voted to instruct the metal trades unions to call off the campaign, but the metal trades determined to continue. Cabinet decided to keep the campaign under review, and approved an ominous and threatening press release from the ministers for industry and commerce and for business and consumer affairs. The statement of 16 July regretted that some companies were giving in to the campaign and threatened that any companies who entered sweetheart deals with unions would be referred to the Prices Justification Tribunal (PJT) and have all prices frozen, or have their tariff referred to the Industries Assistance Commission (IAC), with the prospect of reduced protection emerging from the inquiry. It also said government would take such deals into account when awarding government contracts.

The cabinet established a taskforce to review the deals that were under way before 16 July and at the prime minister's insistence its proposals were incorporated into a formal submission. It recommended that cabinet agree that the 16 July statement should not apply to long-standing arrangements or to deals reached before that date. It wanted cabinet merely to monitor change and maintain a low-key approach. PMC proposed a stronger reaction, wanting the tobacco industry referred to the PJT as an example to inhibit employers' acquiescence. Cabinet took the soft route recommended by the minister for industrial relations.

In November a report requested by cabinet on the progress of the campaign indicated that some firms were under constant pressure and seemed likely to capitulate. Cabinet was offered several options: to take strong action by opposing any change, perhaps by referring the companies to the PJT; to act without interfering in the bargaining and arbitration process; to induce a test case; to present a submission to the Arbitration Commission; or to slow down the process by accepting a limited form of productivity bargaining. The department continued to recommend caution, both because direct action might threaten the indexation system, and because the only realistic goal was to slow down the process as the federal government had no direct power over wages and conditions of work outside its own employees. But the submission assumed (as PMC noted) that no comment accepting the inevitability of the change would be made publicly. Cabinet duly agreed to encourage resistance, while accepting that referral to the PJT would only be used with discretion. It really had no choice, for it had no power to do anything else. Cabinet thus adopted a public stance of threatening, not the unions, but its own traditional supporters.

When the metal trades unions recommenced their campaign in February 1981, cabinet noted that the new minister for industrial relations, Andrew Peacock, would announce the government's opposition to shorter hours when the case was heard before the commission. In late February unions considered strike action in support of shorter hours, while the case was being argued before the Arbitration Commission. A cabinet submission lodged on 6 March reported that the ACTU campaign had had some success, as the chemical, brewing, glass and aluminium industries were entering into productivity agreements. Besides, as 36 per cent of the workforce already worked less than 40 hours a week, flow-ons were hard to resist. The submission offered four options: to continue current tactics of public opposition, referrals to the PJT, on the lines of the government's involvement in the chemical and aluminium cases, or through intervention in the metal trades case before the commission on 2 March; a stronger position with automatic penalties; forcing a test case, which might prove dangerous if it failed; or adopting a lower profile and accepting the inevitability of shorter hours. The submission did not recommend the last alternative but thought there might be a time when the cost of resistance outweighed the losses caused by the shorter week. The minister recommended a continuation of the campaign, again using PJT referrals but only with discretion. On 12 March cabinet agreed to continue the extensive publicity campaign, with a parliamentary statement, a letter to all premiers and consultation with employers. Fraser and the public information committee agreed to meet with the Confederation of Australian Industry (CAI).

The government was working closely with industry leaders, encouraging the Metal Trades Industry Association (MTIA) in their refusal to join an ACTU working party on shorter hours. But industry was not so convinced of its own position. While the MTIA had rejected the ACTU offer, the majority of its members did not accept the decision without question. They wanted a strong government reaction, including an appeal to the responsibility of industries not directly affected by the campaign to support their colleagues by not withdrawing orders, and some innovative government proposals, such as the deferral of tax payments for companies under siege.

The cabinet committee of public information planned a publicity campaign of newspaper advertising and public statements, while cabinet considered possible deterrents, including the use of tax powers and the possible amendment of the Conciliation and Arbitration Act to place the question of hours outside the commission's jurisdiction. A budget of $200 000 was approved for the campaign, to be met by additional appropriations to the Department of Industry and Commerce. Fraser constantly attempted to get the message across; he told a businessmen's breakfast on 18 March:

The Federal Government has made decisions to make sure the Australian community will fully understand the costs of a 35-hour week. Trade unions that press for a 35-hour week are pressing for higher unemployment, reduced sales of Australian-made goods and reduced activity in this country.

Other ministers sustained the campaign.

Yet the increasingly frenetic round of cabinet meetings was unable to disguise the reality that the government had limited powers, especially over what was in effect private bargaining. When Fraser met the MTIA delegates on 23 March, he acknowledged the point. He said that a large part of the government's position was rhetoric and he asked the delegates whether there was anything more substantial they wanted the government to do. He mentioned that the government might be able to use its constitutional power over corporations or take commonwealth employees outside the Arbitration Commission, but regretted that really the government's only weapon was the money supply. He also acknowledged the government's powerlessness. 'He emphasised the need for the government to do something so horrendous it will never be employed. The objective would be to make discussion between employers and unions on shorter hours totally impossible.' Although it might be possible to defer tax, there were not many other alternatives. The government was bluffing. It had to. The MTIA was concerned that all the punitive measures were being aimed at companies rather than at unions.

In the last week of March the dispute reached a crisis, with ICI painted as the villain of the melodrama. On 24 March the commission ratified a 35-hour agreement at the Altona chemical plant. The ACTU saw it as an example of successful productivity bargaining, the government as a catalyst for a flow-on. Cabinet agreed that it was prepared to give special treatment to firms holding out by ensuring they got paid promptly and even considered deferral of tax payments. Fraser also telexed the premiers asking for support and suggesting the problems of the campaign be listed at the premiers' conference. On 26 March Peacock announced the array of government proposals to parliament, mostly repeating what Fraser had said the day before. But then the *Financial Review* of 25 March reported that ICI had agreed to begin negotiations with the Chemical Workers Union for a gradual reduction in working hours as long as a number of conditions were met, including the offsetting of costs with productivity increases.

The government's reaction was immediate and strong – perhaps overreacting when it seemed that the story was only half-true. On 27 March Fraser held two meetings with two officials from ICI. A note to Fraser listed the main directors of ICI and mentioned that the year before the company had argued strongly against a referral of the chemical industry to the IAC because it wanted to complete its new investment plans first. Clearly tariff referral could be a major pressure point. In the first meeting ICI denied that it was negotiating for a 35-hour week, but was dealing with agreements as they came up on a site-by-site basis. Fraser said that if the company announced publicly that it was not negotiating for shorter hours that might be a factor in deciding whether a reference to the IAC went forward. He also foreshadowed other possible responses, including a punitive tax rate in the range of 75–80 cents for companies that did negotiate. Later that day he met the managing director, Dennis Cordner, who continued to deny negotiations ever taking place. Fraser asked: 'How can we hold out if ICI caves in?' Cordner was prepared to release a statement, but feared that ICI's investment program, particularly in the Sydney suburb of Botany, might be in jeopardy. Fraser hoped the punitive tax rate would make it impossible to negotiate shorter hours. He wanted to pull ICI into line and for it to deny that discussions of hours were on the table. Cordner duly announced in public that ICI was not negotiating shorter hours, while Lynch announced more proposals to assist firms that contested the issue.

PMC warned that the government should be careful. Although it was constitutionally possible to remove working hours from the commission, the state courts could fill the gap. The punitive tax might be constitutional, but would be messy. It was difficult to isolate companies through the IAC. Indeed there was no group of measures which could be used effectively without undesirable results.

On 29 March the prime minister strongly attacked the 35-hour week campaign. The chairman of ICI, Milton Bridgland, responded that it was damaging and disappointing that, having perceived the threat of the 35-hour week, the government elected to threaten publicly a company which had resisted the campaign. He denied the story in the *Financial Review* of 25 March which had begun the crisis and concluded: 'Our incentive to resist unrealistic demands is not increased by threats from government'. Since eighteen months earlier ICI had been promised a moratorium of IAC inquiries until 1984, it felt badly treated. On 31 March ICI suspended $900 million of investment in New South Wales; the *Age* reported that the decision was a response to possible federal government retaliation and that NSW premier Neville Wran had been so advised by telex.

Co-ordination committee discussed the ICI response the same Tuesday and noted the report that new projects would be suspended because of action contemplated by the government; it agreed that a strong response was called for by the prime minister. First, Fraser discussed the problems on the phone with Bridgland and then asked him to come to Parliament House where Fraser, Lynch, Peacock and Kemp held a long and bitter discussion with him. Fraser brought to bear the full weight of his position, his harrowing aggressive style and his argumentative vigour. The tenor of the discussion became tense as Fraser and Bridgland began by arguing about the statement ICI had put out the previous Friday, but which had received little notice. Bridgland argued that ICI had no choice but to suspend investment, given what appeared to be a serious threat to their tariff protection: 'Not a threat, a statement of fact', retorted Fraser. Bridgland was pushed into admitting that a 35-hour week might jeopardise all investment in Australia and attacked for not keeping Fraser informed at the same time as Wran. 'I would like to thank you for your courtesy', he was told sarcastically. Fraser accused Bridgland of 'quite deliberately playing politics between Wran and the federal government' and reminded ICI how dependent it was on the Australian government. Fraser proposed that ICI take out a full page advertisement in the *Melbourne Herald* to rebut accusations. Bridgland in turn accused Fraser of threatening the chemical industry (even though not by name). Fraser constantly pointed out that ICI's British owners would need to know what was being done. As he put it in masterly understatement, the communications between ICI and Wran do not 'really put me in a good mood to try and be helpful'. Fraser wanted a 'good hard statement knocking Wran'. He finally told a clearly rattled Bridgland:

You make out I'm a western American gunslinger out to prove a point and western American gunslingers didn't live very long. The courteous thing would have been to come back to Sir Phillip Lynch, Andrew Peacock or myself; but you chose quite deliberately to do it through the media and Neville Wran.

On that acrimonious note the discussion ended; but did it have any real impact?

The intention of Co-ordination committee, which met both before and after the meeting, was to force ICI to issue a statement that it had not negotiated and would not negotiate with unions, and that it would continue with all planned development projects. The Co-ordination committee decided that if it was not satisfied it would resume discussion of the reference of the chemical industry to the IAC. Fraser reported to Co-ordination committee that ICI had agreed to the proposed statement. Cabinet decided that the prime minister would welcome the statement and say that the government was not referring the chemical industry to the IAC, conditional on the strong opposition of the company to reduced working hours. A joint press release, drafted by Bridgland and the ministers and issued on 1 April, stated that 'any concession to a shorter working week at this time would certainly jeopardise the company's investment plans' and that it was 'strongly opposed' to a reduction in working hours. It regretted any misunderstandings. The government agreed to withdraw the reference of the chemical industry to the IAC. A compromise was reached, but its long term impact was probably minimal. ICI was pushed into a tentative reinterpretation of its position, but the shift to shorter hours was barely delayed. Ayres's conclusion that Fraser 'stemmed the tide towards a 35-hour week singlehandedly' is clearly an overstatement. Fraser did not have the constitutional power.

The campaign was continued on other fronts. Fraser and other ministers met the ACTU on 1 April, when Cliff Dolan warned that the government was negating the normal process of negotiation and conciliation. Dolan appreciated that there could not be a general move to 35 hours, but pointed out that the commission had approved productivity bargaining. Fraser and Dolan agreed to meet regularly to discuss proposals. On 9 April the ministers met the CAI and MTIA. Employers' spokesman George Polites said he had doubts about any broad inquiry unless the push to shorter hours was stopped while the inquiry was held. He appreciated that, given the government's powers, it had gone as far as it could, and he also pointed out that while business was still resisting, survival might eventually require it to give in. Fraser promised to be supportive.

Fraser, Lynch and Viner met the MTIA again on 13 May. They were told that MTIA members had been critical of the organisation's failure to negotiate a phased-in reduction of hours. The MTIA wanted the government to use the Industrial Relations Bureau (IRB) to prosecute and fine unions acting outside awards; Fraser was prepared to support action, but did not want to use the IRB. The MTIA and officials then co-operated in drafting a paper that discounted penal options and emergency legislation, but agreed to include a bans clause. Cabinet agreed to insert the bans if the MTIA formally asked for it.

Yet gradually, one by one, companies and industries conceded shorter hours. Fraser asked for a brief providing details of shorter hours negotiated in four ship repair companies in Victoria. It led to a prolonged discussion (indicated by the tattered corners and Vegemite-stained paper) and a request for a cabinet submission. On 3 June a cabinet ad hoc committee agreed to reaffirm its policy, but decided not to pursue the withdrawal of tax or export incentives. The line was gradually weakening, as the Department of Industrial Relations had forecast months before.

In October the MTIA reported that it had conceded 38 hours, with many firms on even shorter hours, but it also acknowledged that it might have done better to negotiate a general reduction to 38 hours rather than deal piecemeal. It was disenchanted with government support and was looking for industrial peace. In November Alcoa claimed that the federal government had failed to honour its promise of assistance to oppose shorter hours; in May it had asked for a deferral of company tax to offset future costs; the treasurer had refused. ICI told the minister that the demands for 38 hours would have to go to the full bench.

In April 1982 a cabinet submission proposed that the government policy of absolute opposition to shorter hours be amended to allow orderly discussion with the ACTU as the government position was impossible to sustain. Fraser was not about to give ground and cabinet decided that the policy of opposition to a general reduction in standard hours be maintained. While it might be necessary to respond to some claims, there was to be no indication of any general approval for negotiations. By then the battle was lost.

The government's attempt to thwart the campaign for the 35-hour week was doomed from the beginning. The lack of federal power meant it could not prevent change. Yet Fraser saw the reduction in hours as economically undesirable and fought it bitterly, while many in his cabinet wanted to concede. The events showed him at times at his worst: hectoring, browbeating, using the prestige of his office to force others into changing their minds. He did not accept that some industries had to give way to maintain production. But crucially here was a case where, even though the power was elsewhere, the prime minister felt he had to be involved. Action was required for political credibility. In politics a lack of power does not excuse inaction. Whether the tactics were right may be debateable; but he had no choice of weapons.

Deregulation and the Campbell inquiry

Whether the Fraser government began the deregulatory trend in Australia, and if so who was responsible, has been a subject of dispute. Several steps were taken. There were moves to change the methods of sale of Treasury bonds and to release state statutory authorities from the controls of the Loan Council. In 1980 the government deregulated the inward deposit rate of bank funds. It also allowed the banks to merge. The most obvious example of deregulation was the inquiry into the

Australian financial system, which has had a dramatic impact on the economic development of Australia.

In the 1975 policy speech Fraser promised: 'there will be a comprehensive examination of ways in which the efficiency of the Australian Capital Market can be improved with special reference to the availability of finance for the expansion of small business investment'. Nothing was done while Lynch was treasurer. During the 1977 election campaign, when speaking to the Securities Institute, Fraser answered a query on the prospects for an inquiry by stating that it would start next year. In January 1978 Eddie Visbord of PMC and John Rose, a member of Fraser's private staff, discussed the proposal on a flight from Melbourne to Canberra and Rose wrote a paper proposing an inquiry to cover the management of tap issues, the auctioning of securities, foreign exchange, foreign investment guidelines, banking and the role of the Reserve Bank. He argued that, 'provided a group of six good people could be persuaded to do a lot of work to produce a high grade report', he would recommend a general capital market inquiry. The paper was revised in consultation with PMC; it suggested an inquiry into the adequacy and efficiency of the capital formation process and into the relationship between the government's monetary policy objectives and its desire for improvement in the efficiency of capital markets. It proposed particularly an examination of the appropriateness of the Reserve Bank's role. The paper was sent to Fraser on 8 February. The next day the Monetary Policy committee noted the commitment in the 1975 policy speech and agreed that Treasury and the Reserve Bank report on a possible form of inquiry by 16 February.

Two weeks later, on 24 February, the Monetary Policy committee agreed to proceed with an independent, non-judicial inquiry into the Australian capital market with powers to review the existing institutional framework including the position of the Reserve Bank. The treasurer was asked to bring proposals for the terms of reference, membership and support arrangements to the next meeting of the committee.

On 1 March Howard wrote to ask for a two- or three-week delay. Fraser was prepared to accept the need for time to approach people to serve, but saw no reason not to discuss the terms of reference immediately. It still took longer. On 5 May Monetary Policy committee noted that the treasurer would bring forward a submission in the next week – it was trying to push action along. On 14 July it agreed in principle – for the second time – to the inquiry; one set of terms of reference (largely the one finally accepted) was tabled, but Monetary Policy committee asked for a series of options by the next meeting. On 21 July a paper was circulated, presenting options from a one-line term of reference to a very detailed description. PMC proposed that foreign exchange and the short term money market be included in the inquiry's ambit. The terms of reference first tabled on 14 July were adopted, with PMC's changes added. The treasurer was asked to suggest names for the inquiry.

On 26 October Howard wrote to Fraser with a list of possible names and they were approved by cabinet the same day. One change was made in January, with the prime minister's agreement. The establishment of the Campbell inquiry was announced on 18 January 1979.

From the proposal until the establishment a year had elapsed. Many committees of inquiry have been created more quickly, but in part the delay was understandable. Howard had just become treasurer; he had to bring down a tough budget, pulling back many of the tax handouts promised in the election by adding the tax surcharge and half suspending tax indexation; the minister for finance was stood down for much of the budgetary process so that Howard had to carry both portfolios. Amid the pressures of the need for immediate decisions, the creation of the inquiry was not the highest priority. The Treasury does not recall being given any oral hurry-ups or deadlines, so it was constantly pushed aside until Howard and his economic adviser, John Hewson, who between them determined the members of the committee, could give it sufficient attention. It was not seen as a matter of urgency.

Fraser and Howard maintained a continuing interest in the progress of the inquiry. On 11 June 1979 they met Campbell, who claimed that the inquiry was in good shape, but that it was unlikely that it could report by June 1980. Campbell also had refused to produce an interim report on building societies. The ministers and Campbell then discussed the government's interest rate policy.

Thereafter the existence of the inquiry sometimes acted as an encouragement to delay decisions. Twice in 1980 Monetary Policy committee reconsidered foreign exchange controls in the context of the report. In November 1980 it thought it inappropriate to remove the controls on bank interest rates before consideration of the report. It also postponed consideration of tax provisions in July 1981 and the tender system for the sale of Treasury bonds in October.

In November 1981 the report was finally delivered. PMC feared that if Treasury monopolised all advice, it would be the one body advising on its own and the Reserve Bank's future; that seemed undesirable. At Yeend's suggestion the report was circulated to ministers, but it was made clear that there would be no rushed decisions on such a complex document. Cabinet simply agreed to the statement that the treasurer would make when tabling the report. Submissions based on the report did not come to cabinet until January 1982. The problem was caused by the coherence of the report. Both PMC and Treasury advised care. They emphasised the quality of the report, but pointed out that it was integrated and therefore it was not possible to pull out a few plums; there were many proposals of what should be done, but not much advice on how to do it. For instance, there were no specific proposals on how to choose the limited number of foreign banks. Implementation of the report would be 'a long slog'. There were to be no sudden decisions. Indeed there was care to ensure that cabinet did not take any precipitous decision; it was to be a gradual response. In particular PMC argued that the proposal to deregulate housing interest rates should not become too visible or the whole package might be threatened.

A taskforce considered whether there should be one package or individual issues; it thought it preferable that ministers were not presented with 'in principle' decisions on issues like the deregulation of interest rates, unless they rejected them outright; it decided therefore to emphasise the interdependence of the recommendations, with an initial package coming to cabinet in February, and with other sections to be introduced at Loan Council and in the 1982 budget. Howard approved this strategy:

> I took the view that the only way you would get substantial progress because of the deep-seated opposition was in fact to do it bit by bit. We decided we would never make a definitive statement or give a definitive response because that would force the government to take specific decisions on particular issues.

By pushing along bit by bit he hoped to build up momentum.

Fraser decided that Monetary Policy committee would be the most suitable forum to consider the report. The taskforce included officials from PMC, the Reserve Bank, Treasury and both John Hewson and John Rose. There were disputes within the taskforce about the entry of foreign banks – Treasury wanted greater controls; Hewson and the Reserve Bank wanted fewer – and whether the draft papers should reflect the taskforce's or Treasury's views. They were told by Hewson that the treasurer expected differences of opinion reflected in the papers.

In late January cabinet simply noted a paper on public sector financing and the fact that the taskforce would be bringing forward papers in the coming months. The response did not have to be 'all or nothing', but it was crucial that the government be seen to be making a serious and thoughtful response. Monetary Policy committee did ask particularly if the taskforce could produce a paper on increasing investment in housing; it was introduced rapidly in the shadow of the March 1982 Victorian state election.

By May many of the taskforce papers were prepared. To give time for ministers to consider them it was proposed that cabinet discussions be held on 22 and 28 June. But first Howard was not ready to proceed and then Anthony could not attend, so the dates were pushed back to a preliminary discussion on 29 June and substantive decisions on 8 July.

By the end of June the submissions were finally ready. The submission on monetary policy and interest rates thought the process of gradual change should be continued, but argued that the financial system needed time to digest changes; therefore it did not recommend any particular changes at that time. The submission on banks agreed unrestricted entry was not desirable, and recommended that ministers agree the existing policy be eased, decide on the number of licences and conditions and ask for further papers. Howard's submission followed the view expressed in the taskforce by PMC, Rose and Hewson. It supported the entry of foreign banks, and rejected the Treasury and Reserve Bank view that didn't want even an in-principle decision until the implications were examined. A month earlier the Australian Bankers Association had expressed deep concern that a cabinet decision might lead to a premature entry of foreign banks before existing banks had adjusted to the new competitive situation. On exchange rates PMC wanted controls relaxed as soon as possible; Treasury and the Reserve Bank thought the existing controls were reasonably effective. Howard's submission endorsed the view that some government intervention in the exchange process was warranted and argued that the government should act carefully. It did not argue for floating the dollar, probably because Howard knew it would not be approved and did not want to lose an important submission and perhaps thereby all momentum. The submissions did not adopt all the deregulatory proposals of Campbell.

In the briefs to the prime minister, PMC argued for in principle support for the entry of foreign banks, no further change to interest rate controls and a gradual move to the thorough dismantling of exchange controls (in which they argued that Howard was closer to Rose and Hewson than to the Treasury). On 28 July cabinet agreed to continue moving flexibly towards deregulation, but in an evolutionary rather than a dramatic manner. It said it was disposed to the entry of foreign banks and asked for papers looking at suitable conditions.

Three months later Fraser asked what progress had been made on the entry of foreign banks. PMC proposed that he talk to Howard before the issue came to cabinet, or at least to get broad agreement with him on the conditions. On 1 November Fraser wrote to Howard asking him to bring forward a submission on foreign banks in the new year; he was told by PMC that the submission was with the treasurer. It was lodged in December; it recommended in principle agreement to the entry of up to eight foreign banks and proposed questions of Australian equity, the range of services and the geographical spread be considered. In January Howard argued that Australian banks now had no objection if foreign entry was on equal terms. On 13 January cabinet agreed to up to ten banks and accepted the treasurer's criteria. It had been fourteen months since the report had been delivered.

Why so long? It is too simple an explanation to blame Howard alone; the Peacock leadership challenge, a tough budget debate, the furore over tax evasion, were all time-consuming, particularly for the new deputy leader who had increasingly become the government's troubleshooter, the voice of a beleaguered government. The report was complex and integrated. Importantly, Treasury was opposed. According to one adviser: 'Every single deregulatory measure through to the floating of the Australian dollar and the licensing of new banks was opposed by either Treasury or the Reserve Bank, every single one of them'. The government was not prepared to act in the face of Treasury's opposition and was not confident that the Treasury would implement enthusiastically a policy it opposed. Fraser argues that on 'these sorts of technical, but infinitely important decisions, we believed that in the end we at least had to have its acquiescence'.

It is speculative to argue that greater push – from Fraser or Howard – might have speeded the process up. It probably would have. Some progress was made, such as the decision to allow foreign banks in. Other deregulatory decisions had been taken; indeed no submission on Campbell was rejected. A decision to float the exchange rate would almost certainly not have been made, as Fraser did – and still does – oppose such deregulation. Nevertheless, more than most investigations, the Campbell inquiry has established the terms of the debate from the 1980s.

However the case does illustrtate certain limitations on the prime minister's position. Deregulation was complex, technical and uncertain. If the relevant department was opposed to change, it was difficult to use other channels. For whatever reason – other commitments, lack of interest, fear of defeat –

no one tried to push along the implementation of the report with the energy shown in other areas, and no other group had the capacity to do it either.

Tax avoidance: confronting your allies

Tax policy dogged the Fraser government. Tax cuts were often promised; their delivery was less frequent. Tax indexation was promised in the 1975 election, 'to keep governments honest', introduced in full in May 1976, and then piece by piece dropped as the difficulties in cutting expenditure made it too hard to sustain. The main issue of the 1977 election was the 'fistful of dollars' which had just been given in tax cuts; yet in 1978 a tax surcharge was imposed that effectively pulled back any benefits the electors had gained.

Indirect tax, as an alternative source of revenue to income tax, was analysed in several submissions to cabinet after the 1977 victory and again after the 1980 poll. A general services tax was proposed, but the taxation commissioner advised that a services or value added tax would take over two years to implement. The political problems of introducing a tax which would have its maximum impact just before the next election were seen as too great for a cautious government and it decided not to act. Howard publicly announced that there would be no changes and effectively moved the item off the agenda for the remainder of the term of office.

Yet the issue that finally destabilised the government was not the amount the wage and salary earner had to pay – although that was always the unspoken agenda. It was the revelation that too many people were not paying their share at all. For the rich, it seemed, any payment of tax was increasingly voluntary. By 1982 the issue culminated in a debate when Fraser confronted his allies in the Liberal party.

There was nothing new about efforts to end tax evasion. Problems in the tax law had been evident since the mid-1970s and the government had attempted to close off one loophole after another. On 11 July 1977 Fraser received a paper analysing tax evasion schemes from outside the bureaucracy and asked officials for comments. On 19 July the Tax Office advised that there was a need to move against specific schemes, because the High Court had made tax avoidance easy and respectable by its interpretation of the legislation. It argued that the government's well known reluctance to enact corrective legislation that was retrospective assisted those planning the schemes; this 'emotion-charged issue of retrospectivity' meant that any clever new tax dodge was likely to have two to three years' currency. The Tax Office effectively spelt out the challenge: it wanted to overhaul section 260 of the Tax Act because its broad provisions had been read down by the court, and to couple this change with specific counter-measures against evasion. The commissioner also warned that 'in my experience it would never be wise to count on additional revenue from anti-avoidance legislation'. The treasurer agreed to take these issues up with the commissioner of taxation, with Fraser to be kept informed.

The first striking decision on tax evasion concerned the Curran scheme which had been developed in mid-1977. Estimates of the revenue lost varied from $500 million to $2000 million. In April 1978 the commissioner of taxation proposed that, since the Curran scheme was clearly a 'rip-off', the application of penalties should begin from the date of the previous budget. Howard, as treasurer, offered three alternatives to cabinet: to allow the legislation banning the scheme to take effect from the date of the previous budget in August 1977; to start its effect from the date of introduction; or to start from the date of introduction, but only allow the schemes already entered into to apply for the one financial year. Because the Curran scheme was blatantly artificial and the amount likely to be lost was massive, up to $1400 million, Howard recommended that the legislation apply from the budget date, even though it introduced an element of retrospectivity into the legislation.

Cabinet had wavered over its decision at earlier meetings on the desirability of retrospectivity, but in April 1978, concerned at the large potential losses of revenue, it agreed to apply the legislation to schemes entered into after the 1977 budget, with the treasurer to explain the reasons for the retrospective application. He was to emphasise the blatant nature of the scheme and the dimensions of the loss of revenue, and to provide a concise written statement to government party members. The cabinet was clearly concerned about the reception. After two weeks of fairly hostile public reaction, including a series of complaints from barristers and accountants and a co-ordinated group of letters from backbenchers, cabinet reaffirmed the decision. It also decided that in future the treasurer would obtain cabinet's consent to close off tax avoidance schemes as they emerged; the legislation was thereafter to operate from each date of announcement. This approach was, for instance, adopted in September when cabinet sought to prevent deductions for artificially created losses. The changes were not made without problems; the government's decisions on family trusts were contested by Anthony, who claimed the decisions were unjust if children were over sixteen.

Over the next two years tax schemes were outlawed one after another. In March 1979 the cabinet decided to review the general section of the tax legislation, section 260, and to establish a taxation advisory committee to advise on legislative changes. That redrafting took time; cabinet received progress reports in July 1979 and again in February 1980. There were considerable problems; as a briefing note to Fraser before the latter review said, a general anti-avoidance provision could be justified on economic, financial and tax equity grounds, but legal and logical arguments against it also abounded. It could be effective, it might act as a deterrent and indicate that the government was determined to protect the tax base, but it could also lead to acrimonious debate or criticism.

Yet there were constant opportunities for new loopholes to the tax law to be created. When a cabinet submission in September 1980 – presented in the election climate – proposed a new 150 per cent write-off for investment into Australian films, it was opposed by Treasury, Finance and the Tax Office because it would create a tax avoidance paradise and make a mockery of all recent tax-avoidance actions. Yet it was announced in the policy speech and approved in cabinet on 24 November, amid reminders that it could not be policed.

In May 1981 two submissions were brought to cabinet. The first was the final product of the long review of section 260, designed to provide a new general anti-avoidance provision by adding a new Part IVA that enabled the government to strike down artificial and contrived arrangements without casting unnecessary inhibitions on normal commercial transactions. Since the definition of terms like 'blatant' and 'contrived' was difficult, any scheme entered into for the sole or dominant purpose of avoiding tax was to be the benchmark.

The second submission was more controversial. In January, impatient at the slow progress of the redrafting, the Co-ordination committee had asked for a submission canvassing the possibility of selective retrospective legislation. It wanted to know if it was practical or desirable to announce that an arrangement later designated as tax avoidance would be legislated against with retrospective effect to the date of the initial general announcement. Fraser was impatient for action; in March he demanded to know when the two papers were to be presented.

The submission reported that the Treasury and the commissioner of taxation strongly supported the proposal for a general announcement as a deadly blow against the promoters of tax evasion schemes. But the author of the submission was Howard, who clearly did not like the idea. He argued that the use of the date of announcement as the starting point for the banning of specific tax schemes had limited tax avoidance and that a general statement would leave tax planning uncertain. He quoted the Liberal platform – 'The rights of the taxpayer are safeguarded by ensuring that taxation adjustments do not have retrospective effect' – and argued that the general avoidance measures of Part IVA were an alternative to a broad retrospective statement. He suggested that ministers should accept the legislative change as adequate. The submission was prepared under instruction, not from choice.

PMC supported both proposals, because they feared that there would be a question mark over the effectiveness of the new section for some years until the courts determined its scope. It also believed that a general retrospective statement would place the government's anti-avoidance stance beyond dispute.

In the tax sub-committee of cabinet Howard's view prevailed; the committee accepted the new clauses and the view that they would be sufficient. Cabinet endorsed those decisions and legislation was introduced. Nevertheless in some areas it was Fraser who was seen as the driving force. On 3 June 1981 the editor of the *Australian Tax Review*, Ian Spry, wrote to Fraser supporting his policies, but expressing concern about the ineptness of Howard. Spry thought Howard did not understand the legislation he introduced and could become a liability. He argued that the government's successes were due to Fraser, not Howard, and that Howard had made too many errors of judgement. That assessment did not take full account of the internal battles in the government.

The new section 260, now Part IVA, of the Tax Act was introduced in May. When coupled with the retirement of Sir Garfield Barwick as chief justice, and the passing of the Crimes (Tax Offences) Acts, the tax commissioner began to win cases in court.

By early 1982 the whole issue of tax was ready to explode. Fiscal drag was putting more people into a higher tax bracket. Estimates put the losses from tax avoidance as high as 20 per cent of income tax. In March Howard announced that the legislation banning two tax avoidance schemes would be backdated by three years to the date of the first announcement. The editorials in the *Age* on 12 February began to support the idea of retrospectivity. Liberal backbenchers in the party Treasury committee joined the campaign for tax cuts. The party room debate on the economy, after the Victorian state election defeat and the challenge for the leadership, swelled demands for tax reforms. The pressure for some dramatic action intensified.

Fraser was always inclined to search for the more striking points in response to circumstances and now sought to take up the attack. Whereas others wanted to see how circumstances developed, Fraser wanted to take the high moral and political ground. In April 1982 PMC sought to tone down the draft of an electorate address on tax evasion, which stated 'if it becomes necessary, we will not rule out taking retrospective action to protect the revenue and the community from tax cheats'. At least, they begged Cliff Walsh in the prime minister's office, tell the treasurer if the last 'dramatic' point was to be used. On 12 May Howard made a general statement promising that the government was prepared to introduce legislation backdated to that day to disallow any trust-stripping schemes. Then on 27 May the initiative was taken out of the federal government's hands. A report to the Victorian government, known as the McCabe–Lafranchi report after its two authors, identified large tax avoidance schemes and named many of those alleged to be involved. The details embarrassed the federal government. On 1 June cabinet asked the treasurer to bring forward another submission that examined options, including resort to criminal prosecutions, and again explored the possibility of future legislation that would be retrospective to the date of a general announcement.

On 2 June Fraser told the National Press Club that the government might legislate retrospectively if the tax evasion continued to flourish. Such an action, he agreed, might offend 'normally accepted principles' but might still be necessary. He regarded those who promoted the tax avoidance industry as being 'as anti-social and un-Australian in their approach as the activities of that minority of trade union leaders who sometimes seem to trample totally on the rights of communities of which they are a part'. Yet Howard was clearly unhappy about the notion of retrospectivity, a difference of opinion that was widely known.

It was six weeks before anything more happened, although Fraser was advised that, while the Tax Office hoped Part IVA would achieve its aims, a general announcement catching people who got around it might still be useful. Fraser was reminded that he wanted to raise the question of this general statement in Revenue committee. Co-ordination committee then agreed that the treasurer should develop proposals to support Part IVA in closing of tax avoidance retrospectively with a broadly based statement. The prime minister insisted that the formal decision be extensive, effectively including the bones of the press statement.

The next day, and after this urging from cabinet, the Tax Office's memorandum was ready. It argued that Part IVA was working, but its full success could not be guaranteed; therefore a policy of selective retrospectivity might be useful. It suggested that referral to a panel of practitioners for assessment might be useful. Cabinet agreed that if a tax scheme was found to be artificial, blatant or contrived, legislation should be effective from the date of general announcement; it asked for a statement to be drawn up, drawing on Howard's speech of 27 May 1981 and emphasising the distortion of relative tax burdens, the need for broad coverage and effective tests and the penalty provisions. Any retrospective legislation was to go through three stages; advice from practitioners, government decision and legislation. This decision was circulated only to Fraser, Howard, Stone and the commissioner of taxation.

Fraser again took the battle to the public, attacking the 'unmitigated evils'of tax evasion. As he put the dilemma to the Queensland Liberal party state conference on 18 July:

We are opposed to the general principle of retrospectivity, but we are also opposed to tax avoidance of the kind that has been pursued voraciously and with a total absence of morals and scruples.

Fraser was prepared to accept that the legislation announced by Howard to recover the millions lost through stripping company profits was retrospective because it proposed to collect company tax evaded before 1980 in the 'bottom of the harbour' schemes. But Fraser considered it justified because it was planned to collect $450 million. That decision put both Fraser and Howard on a collision course with several sections of the Liberal party.

Proposals to collect unpaid company tax also argued that tax should be collected from December 1980. Eventually Fraser and Howard agreed on a basis for the collecting of the tax and that agreement was recorded as a cabinet decision. Fraser was constantly prodding the treasurer to get reactions to advice he received from his network of contacts; he asked in particular whether the commissioner of taxation was using all the powers available to call in the tax under dispute. Howard sent over a Tax Office report explaining what the difficulties were. On 1 August Fraser sought to continue the fight through other channels, encouraging the treasurer to call a conference of state treasurers to discuss tax avoidance. But as only four states agreed to attend, the meeting was postponed until late September.

Howard and the Treasury were having difficulty drawing up the general statement. So Howard attempted to have the decision demanding it overturned. On 6 August he lodged a submission that sought to set aside the earlier decision; he argued that the Tax Advisory committee was opposed to a general statement and that he had considerable misgivings, as ministers were aware. A general threat of retrospective legislation had the potential to create uncertainty in the law, cast doubt on the effectiveness of Part IVA and even compromise the courts. He argued that while the action against the Curran scheme could be justified as action against a specific scheme, a broad proposal would abandon the pretence that the government was opposed to retrospectivity and run counter to the assurance that retrospectivity would be used only if all else failed.

Fraser's advisers were also having doubts about the earlier decision, because of its awkward relationship with Part IVA. They thought a detailed statement was too difficult, preferring a strong but short statement that would approve the government's preparedness to legislate retrospectively. However the public argument never took place, because the submission was never considered in cabinet. Fraser and Howard had several intense discussions, but not in cabinet. The proposal to reverse the earlier decision was listed as an under the line item on 5 August and then dropped after the arrival of the submission. The item was then listed to be discussed at Co-ordination committee, but not reached. Fraser asked for it to be listed on 16 August, but it was dropped from the agenda at the last minute. It was listed again for Tuesday 24 August, and again suddenly omitted. Howard then went away for two weeks. When he returned, the Cabinet Office put it on the agenda for 13 September. Beset by public uproar and advised by his office that it was still not an appropriate time to discuss it, Fraser crossed it off. It was put onto the pile 'to be taken at a future meeting'. It never was. Howard's view prevailed by default and no general statement was made.

This change of approach can be understood in the light of

circumstance. Liberal opposition to retrospectivity was growing, particularly in the Western Australian branch of the party, but Fraser told parliament that the government would not shift its stand. Then on 24 August the fights over tax evasion were fuelled by the Costigan report, the Royal Commission into the Painters and Dockers union. It criticised the Tax Office and the crown solicitor's office for failing to detect and follow up evidence of fraud. Several leading Liberals, particularly from Western Australia, were then named in parliament. In anticipation of the furore, Fraser had proposed to attorney-general Peter Durack the establishment of a special taskforce. Fraser began to campaign publicly and harshly against tax evaders, even those who were involved with the Liberal party. He defended the government at several Liberal state councils. On 29 August the federal executive of the Liberal party passed a motion favouring the battle against tax evasion, but recording its objection in principle to retrospectivity. At Fraser's insistence a letter stating that the motion had been misinterpreted was drafted, explaining that the executive gave unanimous support to moves against tax evasion, with the words 'particularly bottom of the harbour' added by Fraser to the draft. The statement conceded that the prime minister had made no concessions and that the executive respected and supported his stand.

The problem shifted from the general to the particular, and became even more uncomfortable. Several Liberals had been named either in the McCabe–Lafranchi or Costigan report, and Labor attacks turned onto those who held government appointments. The initial view of the ministry was that the naming of individuals was insufficient ground to remove them from public office. But the heat was gradually turned up.

Then the Dennis Horgan case enveloped cabinet in a week or more of bitter and extensive debates. Horgan was a commissioner of the ABC, chair of the finance committee of the Western Australian Liberal party and had been named by the McCabe–Lafranchi inquiry. On 13 September cabinet agreed that government appointees should be beyond reproach and those people identified as benefiting from tax evasion should not continue to hold statutory positions, but should be approached to stand aside. The general principle was accepted. But Horgan declined to resign and a group of cabinet ministers, led by Chaney, Carrick, Durack and Howard, saw no reason why he should. Fraser argued with them at length; Durack thought that Fraser 'worked in his usual style of overkill'. Cabinet was not prepared to commit itself to strong actions; it agreed only that Horgan should be persuaded to resign, and considered the possibility that he be removed from non-statutory appointments. The prime minister was given discretion to indicate the lines of the government's position. Two days later cabinet agreed to ask Horgan formally to stand down. The next day the prime minister was authorised to say that the cabinet was examining the rules. In all the cases above, the circulation of the decisions was nil, but cabinet had spent many hours arguing over the case – thirty or forty hours according to one account. Even if Horgan was being used as a test case, it illustrated how Fraser was prepared to argue at great length if he could not get agreement.

Although some of the political heat was reduced when the opposition over-reached itself in the unsubstantiated charges of tax avoidance against John Reid, a businessman appointed to hold an inquiry into the public service after 28 September, the cabinet pushed ahead with a plan to write to all appointees seeking assurances that they had not taken part in tax evasion schemes. Settling on the terms of the letter was not easy, as it came back for further drafting, including some suggestions from Fraser. The problem of Horgan remained unsettled; Fraser was never able to persuade him to stand down and cabinet even noted with regret in December that his attendance at three meetings of commonwealth boards was a breach of the understandings he had reached.

Throughout September and October cabinet and its sub-committee on tax met constantly to discuss the collection of avoided taxes, with the backbench arguing against any retrospective provisions. On 22 September 500 pages of documents were tabled; they illustrated the long history of the battle. One bill introduced on 23 September was attacked by backbenchers and opposed by the New South Wales and Queensland state branches because of the fear that it could catch innocent vendors. Fraser was prepared to fight the battle at Liberal party functions in Bradfield, at Liberal breakfasts in Queensland and addresses to the Chamber of Manufacturers in Sydney. He was not afraid to face and condemn those who might be involved. Observers spoke of his 'obsessive determination' to destroy the practice of tax evasion; his staff recall it as the one issue on which he was prepared to stake his leadership. On 14 October cabinet agreed to introduce fresh legislation, but on 20 October John Howard reported back to cabinet further objections from the party committee. Cabinet initially acceded to only one request, but after another party meeting more amendments were made. The push for legislation was constant, even if the political sensitivity had been partly reduced. Consultation with the party was extensive. A note in November explained in what areas tax avoidance schemes were still available. Apart from the self-inflicted example of the film industry, the memorandum listed gold mines, afforestation and the cash or barter economy as the main sources of evasion. The battle was not complete by any means when the government fell.

When the issue of tax evasion exploded after the publication of the two reports, Fraser calculated that the costs of opposing many in his party had to be met if the evils of tax evasion were to be ended. In part it was good political strategy because he was seen to be attacking even his allies when they were wrong, but it was also based on a deep distaste for the dubious practices that had been adopted. That distaste was translated into determined, unbending commitment to whatever action was required; the party opposition to retrospectivity was less important than the government's determination to destroy those schemes. Fraser's language was extreme; so were his feelings. His was the steel that maintained the commitment in the face of violent party opposition. He has still not been forgiven by many in the party for the events of those months.

Conclusions

Each case indicates different facets of Fraser's style and character. They collectively illustrate the difficulties that prime ministers must overcome to develop and implement policies.

Some policies, like the development of uranium, are inevitably complex, with strands interrelated, with sensitivities aroused and with power limited. Fraser had to manage the process and the presentation to ensure his satisfaction that the important questions were adequately answered. Even then the pace was determined by the speed with which the inquiry reported, the efficiency of the bureaucracy in providing answers, the degree of external opposition, the agreement of unions. Everything was contingent.

The Campbell inquiry illustrated both the capacity of a prime minister to push an issue along, and the inevitable limitations. He had to wait on others to provide the terms of reference and the working papers; he had to rely on the Treasury, whose power exercised through regulation was the subject of the inquiry, to produce papers on the way that progress could be made. The prime minister cannot do everything.

Often prime ministers must react. In the 35-hour week campaign Fraser could persuade or harangue; he could threaten or promise assistance; he could publicly declare what his government believed. But in the final resort he had no constitutional power to prevent the campaign succeeding. Outsiders were not always overawed and could play off federal and state governments. That did not mean that he chose to do nothing; it merely illustrates how often prime ministers must make bricks without straw, or policy without power. They improvise, they use what weight they have.

Even when they have the power there is no certainty that they will succeed. Tax evasion became the issue in 1982, even perhaps at a time when it was finally being controlled. Yet political importance had little to do with such factors. Fraser had to respond, even at the cost of upsetting his allies. He may have been too strident, too pushy for his colleagues, but it was finally a political calculation, determining the degree to which his government could escape the odour of its party connections. Political circumstances created the conditions in which Fraser had to operate. Prime ministers are rarely in full control of their environment. They do what they must, as much as they do what they want.

CHAPTER 11

DOMINATION AND CONSULTATION

MALCOLM FRASER AS PRIME MINISTER

This account of Fraser's activities has explained the multiple roles that prime ministers must play. They are national leaders, policy initiators, chairpersons of cabinet, leaders of parties, media figures, parliamentarians, electoral campaigners and administrative co-ordinators. It is easy to draw up lists of roles that appear distinct; in reality they are all interlocking. The different responsibilities often create contradictory demands. When Fraser negotiated with Bjelke-Petersen, should he give precedence to his position as head of the coalition government or to his role of party leader? Were decisions on expenditure made as economic manager or electoral campaigner? The diverse roles eventually are integrated into one: the position of prime minister. All of them have to be fulfilled, to a greater or lesser extent, at the same time.

The account has also illustrated the exercise of those powers that make prime ministers so important: the allocation of ministerial portfolios, the distribution of patronage, control over cabinet processes, access to information, the ability to call elections, the capacity to commit the government, the status of the position, the opportunities for persuasion. These powers are needed to persuade, to duchess, to encourage, to browbeat, to terrify others into taking action. Prime ministers have to act within institutional and political constraints; but even so, the mere listing of these prerogatives illustrate why those interested in exercising the full potential of the position can have a greater influence on the government than any other individual.

Yet these assessments are general, explaining what all prime ministers may do, what their potential may be. How they perform as individuals will depend on the circumstances and their personality. How they are judged will depend on the perceptions of outcomes and the perspective of the critics. Since there are no standard qualities that all leaders should have, there are no uniform judgements about what they have achieved.

Table 11.1: *Characteristics of Fraser*

Positive	Negative
Hard worker	Government by exhaustion
Interested in detail	Bogged down in minutiae
Consulted cabinet	'In the bunker' – too much time in cabinet
Understands all policy implications	Excessive interrogation, foreclosing options
Strong leader	Domination and fear
Widespread policy involvement	Meddling; unable to delegate
Swift reactions	Impatience; unnecessary pressure
Insisting on options	Creation of tension in the public service
High standards of ministerial behaviour	Poor management of ministers in trouble
Accessible to party	'Duchessing and strongarming'
Flexible	Opportunistic
Parliamentary determination	Political confrontationist
Precise use of words	Deliberately creating false impressions

The difficulty of assessing the impact of style or the desirability of its use can be shown starkly by pulling together different impressions of Fraser's style drawn from this book. The same events, the same personality and the same relationships are interpreted in very different ways. What for some observers are positive qualities, others see in negative terms.

The list could easily be expanded; all the descriptions are easily recognisable. Did he consult cabinet too much? Did he put much more emphasis on obtaining agreement? Were his interests in policy ideas too indiscriminate and wide-ranging? All these charges have been made. But then, turn each of these propositions around and the problems are immediately apparent: a prime minister who doesn't consult cabinet adequately; a prime minister who rides roughshod over cabinet colleagues; a prime minister uninterested in policy. None of these is desirable either.

What is the correct balance? It will depend on time and circumstance, on the nature of the issue, and on the strength of feeling of others. Fraser was accused of consulting others to lock in support at times of ministerial crisis. Would he not have been accused of acting arbitrarily if he had failed to consult? These points need to be emphasised before making judgements on Fraser or on anyone else. Leadership is relative to the time and the problems. If it is exercised within the constraints of a democratic system, and particularly a federal democratic system, there will be severe political and constitutional limitations on its use.

The public image of Fraser – the cynical, opportunistic, dominant, conservative and confrontationist prime minister – is not borne out by a more careful and informed picture of the way he worked. Fraser is a paradox, a set of apparent contradictions. He was a conservative; yet he was also a reformer. He was a traditionalist in foreign affairs with his commitment to the American alliance; yet he was more involved in north–south problems than any other Australian leader. He was confrontationist in much of his rhetoric; yet he was cautious and careful in the decisions his government took. He was prepared to seize opportunities for elections; yet he would never act alone in crises. He appeared all-powerful, and usually got his way; yet he consulted continuously and exhaustively. He insisted on high standards from his ministers; yet he was not trusted by some of them who regarded him as unscrupulous. He used the machinery and forms of cabinet, the patronage and power of the position and the force of his own knowledge and personality, to influence far more than any other individual the outcomes and policy choices of his government, but he did not make them by himself. Even if in the majority of instances he approved of the decision, he did not act unilaterally. He argued aggressively, interrogated ministers, pushed hard for preferred policies; yet he did not dictate or often demand. His policies may now be regarded as 'wet' (although that term was not given its political connotations by Thatcher until 1980); yet his reputation at the time was of being too harsh and unfeeling. He may have dominated; he did it through consultation. It is these contradictions that make him so difficult to label, apart of course from those easy slogans that do not require evidence.

A few of his contemporaries recognised both the strengths and the weaknesses of his style. To Paul Kelly, an acute journalist, Fraser

was larger than life. When he wanted to be cynical, when he wanted to buy votes, when he wanted to pander to an interest group, nobody did it as well as Malcolm. When he was committed to an idealistic policy, nobody could match with Malcolm's vehemence or ideological commitment.

Fraser's ministerial colleague Peter Baume thought him both 'a better, but not so tough, a man as the public image'.

How then should Fraser be assessed as a prime minister? Was he effective? The question can be asked in two parts, examining first the style of Fraser himself and, secondly, asking how far his performance reveals any of the problems of governing Australia: whether it could indeed be done differently, or more effectively.

Leadership is a matter of choices. Some prime ministers choose to lead by exhortation, standing out over the fray, leaving the detail to ministers, and becoming involved only when problems emerge. Others become constantly involved in the daily running of policies. Fraser fitted into the second group. He gave everything to the job, all day and often much of the night. He regarded it as a great responsibility to be borne. Work, problem-solving, an inability to relax, a concern for solutions: these were the continual pressures. David Barnett has argued:

Fraser was leading us out of a mess to the best of his ability and probably to the best of anybody's ability, given the climate ten years ago. In seven years with Fraser, I always felt I was serving my country and serving it well, not because of what I did, but because of the man I worked for.

Tony Eggleton thought that Fraser was prepared to lead, to determine what was required and push in that direction. 'He was a natural leader; people followed him. Once he made up his mind what he wanted, he went after it and carried people with him'. Chaney thought Fraser had 'gravitas'; Durack was impressed by his capacity to absorb information. Fraser himself believed that he ought to be the leader in terms of policy and ideas.

Fraser's style reflected his ambitions. The prime minister knew what was happening in all areas of government; he pushed ministers to consider the options. He left as little as possible to chance, exploring ideas and trying to assess the outcomes. He tested propositions by interrogating their advocates, trying to understand the basics of their arguments. He wanted to appreciate the way that policies might develop, arguing that an understanding of the detail was the necessary prerequisite for seeing the broader picture. He wanted to make ministers and officials perform at their best.

These positive characteristics – the understanding of detail, the interrogation of options and their advocates, the management of people – made him a dominant, constructive and involved prime minister. They also produced tensions.

Detail is necessary. Political crises occur as often because the detail goes astray as because the direction is wrong. A prime minister who is not able to master the intricacies of sensitive policies cedes authority and influence to those who can. Yet to become involved in too much detail across too many areas of policy may create problems. Ministers become more cautious as they are constantly aware that the prime minister might be looking over their shoulder all the time. It can breed a lack of confidence. If the prime minister is capable of doing everyone else's job, then ministers may lack the confidence to act independently. In Fraser's cabinet the able ministers were not affected, but the less competent and some of the average ones suffered. The problem, then, is in danger of becoming circular. Because the ministers lack the confidence to make independent decisions they bring them to cabinet, where their competence may be questioned. As a consequence the prime minister never develops trust in their judgement, and wants to maintain a closer oversight of what they are trying to achieve.

Fraser was not perceived by his ministers as trusting their judgement, allowing them independence. As a group they were probably rather better than the Whitlam ministers and not as talented as their successors, but the demands for collective involvement reduced individual initiative (quite apart from drastically reducing the time available for it). It is difficult for any prime minister to find that suitable balance between delegation and involvement, between trust and interest. Fraser's style put him firmly on the end of involvement and interest. It is easy to justify cabinet activities in the name of collective judgement. In retrospect everyone argued that cabinet was overloaded, that less time should have been spent in meetings and that less pressure could have been exerted. Fraser himself thought there should be less night cabinet meetings: 'it's amazing how much a combination of being tired and a couple of drinks makes people talk'. More contemplation and less activity, but neither Fraser's personality nor the nature of government encouraged contemplative styles. Playing tennis for relaxation may now seem a good idea; it is probably an option only in retrospect.

Fraser's style of dealing with ministers and officials had costs. Ministers were always conscious of the need to perform and felt rushed by the pressure to deliver. Those who understood the rules of the game – primarily those who with him frequently or were particularly confident in their opinions – were prepared to argue and to press their view. The less confident, or those whose style was milder even if their content no less valuable, had greater difficulty. Nervous anticipation may allow a minister or official to perform well; fear is likely to leave a muddled exposition.

Interrogation of proposals may lead to options foreclosed. Because the direction of the discussion was often dictated by Fraser, alternative solutions with which he had less patience were not pursued. The discussion on options was focussed and driven by the style of debate. For some ministers – and particularly for the less bold – there were clearly difficulties. Yet, as Sinclair comments: 'it's very easy to beat him about the ears and say everything was Malcolm's fault. But it wasn't all Malcolm's fault'. Others *were* there; they could have participated if they chose and changed the results if they had had the ability. If they did not, that may be a comment on *their* determination and weight. To change Fraser's mind was difficult, but not impossible. Acquiescence was for many an easier path.

Fraser's management of people was regarded by some colleagues as inadequate or poor. His style left him open to charges of bullying. He was inconsiderate of subordinates – not consciously but because of his impatience. He wanted answers immediately, and decisions yesterday. He would demand papers from the public service with a requirement for immediate delivery. When cabinet was unable to reach a decision, more papers would be required, even if they became effectively a rehash of existing information. Papers prepared in such a rush are never likely to be as thoughtful or as thorough as those done with greater care. Then, when ministers chose to delay consideration for two or three days, public servants could feel annoyed that they had been required to work through weekends to produce work that lay on the table.

A shy man, who found it difficult to encourage others with bonhomie and humour, Fraser dealt with colleagues by being single-minded and determined. Able to argue about policy, he was uncomfortable with individuals and their problems. When difficulties of personnel occurred – in ministerial crises, in particular – Fraser worked in part through intermediaries. The reaction from those who were in trouble was dissatisfaction; they felt they received inadequate support and loyalty and were not inclined to take their problems to Fraser. They respected him, lived in awe of him, appreciated his capacity to win and acknowledged his determination and skill; but they did not like him, nor were they prepared to show any vestiges of loyalty to Fraser or his memory. They felt that sometimes Fraser was more interested in his own survival than theirs. The unsurprising consequence of his style was that his achievements were denigrated, even by his own side, once he had gone.

Fraser had the ability, the desire and the drive to dominate the machinery of government. His commitment cannot be questioned. His involvement was so extensive, his interests so broad that little or nothing was done that he actively opposed. Because of his extensive control, in the end he approved most government decisions. His capacity has perhaps been unrivalled, even if some thought his involvement was too extensive. Nevertheless, the fact that Fraser was able to dominate the machinery and process of government is not usually in itself regarded as the same as claiming that he was a 'good' prime minister. Rather, leaders are judged by their output, by what they achieved. If it has been illustrated that Fraser was the dominant figure in his government, what was achieved?

At the crudest level – indeed at the level at which so many people choose to judge politicians, by their retention of office – Fraser must be regarded as successful. He was the second longest serving Australian prime minister; he won three elections, two of them with massive majorities.

In terms of monuments – those physical memorials that remain years after social and economic achievements are forgotten – the new Parliament House, the Defence Forces Academy and the Bicentennial Roads, provide clear indicators of decisions made by, and often attributable to, Fraser's own intervention. In social policy the introduction of family allowances, the land rights legislation, the administrative law that gave citizens some redress to bureaucratic decisions were all introduced by his government. The SBS and multiculturalism were established.

In foreign policy Fraser's commitment to the Third World was recognised by his appointment by the Hawke government as an 'eminent person'. In foreign affairs Fraser led Australian policy down unusual paths, while maintaining the centrality of the American alliance. In positive terms his achievements were substantial.

However, instead of praising his qualities, there is rather more of a tendency among his former colleagues to complain of what was *not* done and this reflects in part the style of the government and its caution. Ellicott argues that one measure of Fraser as a good prime minister was that 'he was rarely wrong in decisions on major matters. The one exception was the decision on wages in 1981 which led to a wages explosion. His real mistake was not making decisions which he should have made because he was overly concerned with staying in power'. Cuts, it is now widely argued, should have been more stringent, certainly in 1976, perhaps later too. There was no attempt to reduce tariffs. There was no redirection of the tax burden towards indirect tax. Deregulation was slow to emerge. Most of these criticisms are made with the advantage of hindsight, drawing on the perspectives of new policies in later years. If they have some force, it is not because the latter-day converts are necessarily wise, but because Fraser was in many ways more cautious than the image he presented. He was always conscious of the possible electoral outcomes (not necessarily a fault in a democracy); he believed that benefits to groups once granted could not be taken away. He was conscious of political advantages; although he appreciated the value of tax indexation, he preferred to opt for the politically expedient route of more explicit tax cuts. He was not prepared to risk the political costs of introducing a massive shift to indirect tax (any more than his successors have been; it may well be an impossible political move for any government, given three-year parliaments).

If some non-decisions were due to caution, others were a response to ideology. Fraser believed in an activist state, a government that tried to solve problems. To argue that governments were too large and intrusive was not to assert that they had no proper and necessary role. Fraser is happy to place himself in the tradition of Menzies and his belief in government action (although remarking that the Menzies government, now accused of being interventionist, was then attacked for doing too little). Nor did he believe that governments should sit back when action was possible. As a consequence Fraser was criticised for being too interventionist, the head of a 'fix-it' government. He did not believe, says John Howard, 'in the injunction that we should be godly and quietly governed which is contained in the book of common prayer'. Nor did others believe he had a consistent framework in his approach. Instead the government shifted from crisis to crisis, intervening where necessary. But then, claimed an economic adviser, 'maybe to have that sort of dynamic energy you have to have immediate goals and targets. Perhaps the person who sees the whole picture gets wracked with indecision'. To what extent governments should intervene to 'fix' problems is therefore an ideological question, with Fraser firmly committed to government action wherever necessary. He did not accept that a government should give up necessary economic weapons by floating the dollar or deregulating housing interest rates – at least not in the context of the time – and he should not be judged in any other context. His 'failures' were a result of caution and of ideology.

Fraser, it was also argued, lacked vision. Political opponent John Button thought he had a better idea of what he didn't want the country to be than what he wanted. Vision is an elusive concept. It is easy enough for political leaders to state that they believe in a fairer, more prosperous country or to maintain the belief in a 'light on a hill'; but that is often difficult to translate into specific policies. Margaret Guilfoyle argues, indeed, that there are too many limitations on the power of prime ministers and their options are too narrow for them to have any achievable visions. Yet she believed Fraser wanted to build up the nation, assisting particularly the Aborigines, handicapped people and migrants. Ian Macphee approvingly thought Fraser believed in a multiracial society and the freeing of world trade, but that in the face of domestic political pressures he found it difficult to spell out his vision. Chaney believed Fraser had a 'map of Australia' in his mind.

Few of his colleagues could be described as men or women

with long visions. As one official noted of the National party leaders:

They were tough guy negotiators, but not the sort of blokes who would give direction to a government. They were powerful, but powerful about getting immediate things, playing politics in terms of dams and airports.

Vision is eventually defined by policy. Fraser wanted a society in which individuals were free to make their own choices: how could it be achieved? If a well-defended, or a racially tolerant, society is required, then what policies need to be adopted? Vision was then reduced to solutions, with which Fraser was comfortable. A problem emerged; he tried to alleviate or solve it. It may not be a grandiose approach; but it is essentially practical and sensible.

His caution was in part created by the political climate. Having caused many of the tensions and divisions during the crisis of 1975, Fraser did not want to exacerbate them. Being elected under a cloud meant there was a constant search for legitimacy, a desire to govern without taking decisions that were divisive. Many in the community would not accept that picture; Fraser was seen as harsh, unsympathetic and confrontationist. The government was seen as too forceful, too tough, too uncaring. Nevertheless within the cabinet those perceptions of caution meant that, according to one minister, we 'did not act as firmly as we should have because we were concerned about divisions in the community'.

Most judgements select particular issues or policies as the criteria for success. They ask what specifically will the prime minister be remembered for in fifty years. The criteria by which Fraser would like to be judged are more general. He argues:

Government is not really about a series of unrelated events. There is a continuous job of administration to be undertaken . . . If somebody was prepared to make the judgement that the commonwealth was administered well during those years, without defining any particular achievement or area of government, I think it would be as much as anyone could expect. To me that would be better or mean more than one particular event. There is always one thing that somebody can do or that will be done well in terms of the government; that might also mean a lot of things have been done very badly.

This general impression that Fraser would like to portray is therefore that of a good manager, of maintaining tight budgets and responsible direction. It is an aspiration that acknowledges that much of what a prime minister does is about the routine of governance; it is a common aspiration of conservative leaders. It is worth comparing to the description of governing by the conservative political philosopher, Michael Oakeshott:

In political activity men sail a boundless and bottomless sea; there is neither harbour for shelter nor floor for anchorage, neither starting-place nor appointed destination. The enterprise is to keep afloat on an even keel; the sea is both friend and enemy; and the seamanship consists in using the resources of a traditional manner of behaviour in order to make a friend of every hostile occasion.

This description fits Fraser's approach to the role of governing. There were no permanent solutions, just the necessity for a continuous struggle to make the society work, to make it a better place.

Fraser was a leader who implicitly dealt in bargains with supporters and voters, a 'transactional' leader who tried to deliver success to his party and prosperity to the country – in exchange for support. He was not loved and had no charisma. He painted no vision except the need for belt-tightening and hard work; no promise that things would ever be easy. He had to deliver to survive.

It can be argued that for five years these ambitions were fulfilled. Government expenditure was reduced; there were costs but they were regarded as necessary for the broader goals of economic responsibility. There was no ministerial corruption, and even minor infractions of proper behaviour were punished severely. The government was hard working, but in the last term the appearance of administrative competence fell away. There was left the impression that the government failed to control its own processes: tax evasion scandals, the Greek conspiracy fraud in social security, the TV affair. These were administrative problems that left the taste of incompetence. With no alternative plan, with promises only of more of the same, the government could no longer offer the hope that the electorate required. 'We lost', argues Peter Baume, 'because we stopped projecting hope, purpose and confidence'. John Carrick believed that 'because of our tunnel vision, we missed the Pied Piper tune' that could tap into the aspirations of the electorate. Time, familiarity and a desire for change ended the term.

In another sense Fraser played a part in changing political expectations; his government can be seen as a transitional one. His predecessor believed in government expenditure as a means of solving problems; his successor, who was also head of a Labor government, largely continued Fraser's policy of trying to reduce public expenditure and discourage governmental solutions. It has gone much further in deregulation than Fraser's government did, but it would be unreal to suggest that widespread deregulation was seriously on anyone's political agenda in the late 1970s. Responsible economic management is now regarded as the fundamental requirement for government. 'The transformation of the Labor party into a party that is meant to be one exercising restraint, or which says it exercises restraint probably was our biggest victory', comments Fraser wryly. There is much in that claim. The intellectual climate has changed, but Fraser must be judged by the tenets of his time.

How inevitable was this style of governing? There may be a need to distinguish between pressures on governments and on prime ministers. As Sinclair has noted:

Governments get asked to find solutions. It's very difficult for us to say, that's not for us to solve. It's always easier to do something because you get blamed if you don't, particularly if the little people are hurt.

Indeed leaders who make mistakes trying to solve problems tend still to receive higher ratings than those who fail to act. It is a comment on expectations. Fraser largely accepted that conventional wisdom and as a consequence felt the need to react under pressure.

His experience, however, also tells us much about the Australian system of government. Cabinet government still means collective decision-making, because of the need to maintain support, because the authority and administrative capacity still lie with the departments, and because only cabinet government allows the variety of views to be expressed and tested. Even a dominant prime minister must choose to work with cabinet because it is the best system for policy making and survival. They can make individual decisions on some issues, but will lose support if they try to ignore cabinet too often. Whether they get their way in cabinet depends on their calibre and the quality of their ministers. Yet cabinet government need not be contrasted to prime ministerial government, as too often it is. The latter is seen as individualistic, the former collective. In practice a skilful prime minister may operate through the cabinet system, by determining who will decide and where decisions will be taken. All ministers may be collectively responsible for, even if only vaguely aware of, the government's decisions. Indeed, because of the advantages of gaining the consent, or at least acquiescence, of other ministers, prime ministers may be more influential if they work through their cabinet. However that requirement is time-consuming and often creates structural constraints – submissions, meetings, debate. In collective government that is a necessary cost. Influence is balanced against time. Fraser never acted individually, yet the prime minister's influence may have been the greater because of the process of ministerial involvement.

Cabinet, then, must be understood as a collection of meetings, in any of which authoritative decisions may be taken. The alternative is not between cabinet and prime ministerial decision-making; rather there is a need to understand in what way and how extensively the influence of the prime minister is applied. Individual styles become important because the decisions about involvement in detail may vary from one leader to another. Fraser and Hawke are distinct contrasts in the degree to which they chose to be involved across the range of policy areas and the discretion and independence they were prepared to give to their ministers.

Prime ministers must also deal with many other political forces that need to be managed and manipulated. They have little control over many of the forces with which they must deal, economic or political. Prime ministers have status that is not matched by the ability to command; power in Australia is widely dispersed. Parties create and support leaders; they need to be nourished. The state governments share powers, and often electorates; they need to be persuaded. Interest groups and the media have legitimate demands; they need to be duchessed or dealt with effectively. To ignore the sensitivities of any of these bodies is to invite political revenge. The greatest problem for prime ministers is to gain the support of different groups in several different fields at once, or no initiatives may be adopted; at the same time they must make the machine over which they have direct control operate smoothly. Only in international affairs, ironically, do prime ministers have the power to speak authoritatively and without so many constraints, and there Australia at best has limited influence.

The image of prime ministers is one of great power. That picture is true if the individual has the powers of persuasion, the skills of manipulation, the vision to direct, the ambition to drive and the energy to work. Then, and only then, may the prime minister turn all that potential into results. With its dispersed power, its collective procedures and its divergent interests, Australia is difficult to govern, even if someone is able to harness these talents. To use the prime minister's powers effectively and to the full is therefore an awesome challenge. Fraser was more interested across a wider range of policies than most leaders; he probably can be more directly identified with all the government's policies too. The fact that so powerful a leader saw the necessity to consult so often is a comment not just on the individual, but on the Australian political system.

SOURCES

Interviews

Interviews have been held with the following people: Doug Anthony, Tony Ayers, Peter Baume, David Barnett, Ken Begg, Peter Bowers, Neil Brown, Dale Budd, John Button, Brian Buckley, John Carrick, Richard Carleton, Jim Carlton, Ian Castles, Fred Chaney, David Charles, Mike Codd, Sir William Cole, Sir Charles Court, Jack Curtis, Alastair Drysdale, Peter Durack, Sir Llew Edwards, Tony Eggleton, Robert Ellicott, John Enfield, Wal Fife, Jim Forbes, Bernie Fraser, Malcolm Fraser, Petro Georgiou, Michelle Grattan, Alan Griffith, Dame Margaret Guilfoyle, Sir Rupert Hamer, Andrew Hay, Bill Hayden, John Hewson, John Hodges, John Howard, Ralph Hunt, John Hyde, Derek Ingram, Mike Keating, Paul Kelly, David Kemp, Michael Mackellar, John McLeay, Ian Macphee, John Moore, Hugh Morgan, George Nicholls, Peter Nixon, Laurie Oakes, Andrew Peacock, George Polites, Sonny Ramphal, Alan Rose, John Rose, B.A. Santamaria, Mick Shann, Ian Sinclair, Tony Staley, Tony Street, Ed Visbond, Cliff Walsh, Max Walsh, Sir Frederick Wheeler, Denis White, Reg Withers, Sir Geoffrey Yeend.

Additional information came from the interviews undertaken in 1979 and 1980 for the book written with Michelle Grattan, *Can Ministers Cope?* (Hutchinson, 1981). There are

SOURCES

other people I would have liked to have included in the above list but could not interview. That was not always for want of trying. Some requests were turned down, some people accepted but then were never available; some appointments were broken (in one case three times in two days!).

Where possible the comments have been attributed in the text to the speaker. Where a level of anonymity was preferred, the class of person has been indicated.

The Fraser papers

The following were the main files consulted. In the detailed references they are referred to by file and, where possible, box number.

M1254	'Blues': Binders of outward correspondence 1975-83 (from the department)
M1255	'Chrons': Binders of outward correspondence 1975-83 (from the private office)
M1256	Folders of political and personal correspondence 1976-83.
M1260	Folders of daily and weekly programs 1977-83.
M1263	Folders of speeches, notes and related correspondence 1973-83.
M1266	Files of correspondence with government ministers, senators and MPs 1979-82.
M1267	Folders of correspondence with Labor and Democrat MPs 1976-81.
M1268	Subject files, lexicographical series 1976-83. (Where possible, subject titles have been included in the specific references.)
M1269	Files of correspondence – overseas visits 1976-82.
M1272	Files of notes from principal private secretary 1976-83.
M1273	Folders of prime ministers' interviews 1974-82.
M1276	Folders of senior adviser's research material – first series 1975-77.
M1277	Folder of senior adviser's research material – second series 1977-80.
M1282	Record of discussions 1980-83.

SOURCES

M1333 Folders of letters from heads of government 1979-83.
M1334 Folders of correspondence with non-ministerial members in both houses 1976-79.
M1335 Folders of correspondence with ministers 1976-80.
M1342 Folders of correspondence with Liberal party branches 1975-83.
M1355 Subject files held by principal private secretary 1975-81.
M1380 Folders of prime minister's statements on tax evasion 1981-82.

Official files

Two sets of files were used: those of the Cabinet Office and those of the Department of Prime Minister and Cabinet (PMC).

Cabinet files were numbered sequentially throughout the period of the Fraser government and are prefaced by the letters LC. The decisions taken by the Fraser cabinet are also numbered sequentially from 1 to 19500. In the following references cabinet files are listed by number and usually also by title. PMC files are recorded as a year and a number. Thus 81/011695 Budget Figuring means the file was opened in 1981.

These official files were available to me at the request of Mr Fraser for the sole purpose of writing this book. Without his support I would have been unable to have any access whatsoever. Since the departmental papers deal with cabinet business, they are exempt documents under the terms of the Freedom of Information Act. Under the Archives Act they are closed to external access for thirty years.

Since these files are not available to other scholars or writers within that thirty years, I have chosen to consolidate the references. Many of the accounts in the text are constructed by meshing the information from several files which are maintained simultaneously. Rather than attribute every item or comment to its separate file or files, I have listed at the beginning of the relevant sections the files from which the account is compiled. Those lists will give an indication of the breadth of the material consulted.

SOURCES (pp. 1-7)

Chapter 1 The job and the man

1–3 For an account of the debate on whether cabinet government has become prime ministerial government, see Patrick Weller, *First Among Equals: Prime Ministers in Westminster Systems*, Allen & Unwin, Sydney, 1985, chapter 1. The main protagonists of the debate in Britain are John Mackintosh, Richard Crossman and George Jones. Mackintosh argues: 'The country is governed by the Prime Minister, who leads, co-ordinates and maintains a series of ministers' (*The British Cabinet*, Stevens, London, 1962, pp. 451-2). Crossman's statement is in the Introduction to Walter Bagehot, *The English Constitution* (first printed 1867, Fontana, London, 1965, p. 51.

By contrast George Jones argues: 'The British system of government cannot really be called prime ministerial government, nor cabinet government; the right term is ministerial government'; in 'The prime minister's aides', *Hull Papers in Politics*, 1979, p. 1.

2 The view that 'every cabinet minister is in a sense the prime minister's agent, his assistant' was expressed by Lord Home in the *Observer* on 16 September 1962, before he became prime minister. It is quoted in Crossman's introduction to Bagehot, *The English Constitution*, p. 52.

3 The comment on self-restraint is made by Richard Rose in 'Governments against Sub-governments: A European Perspective on Washington' in R. Rose, E. Suleiman (eds), *Presidents and Prime Ministers*, American Enterprise Institute, Washington, 1980, p. 340.

4 'The blank sheet of infinite opportunity' is the evocative phrase used by Michael Oakshott in *Rationalism in Politics*, Basic Books, New York, 1962, p. 112.

6–7 The debate on leadership and executives is extensive. For a full bibliography on the leadership of prime ministers, see Weller, *First Among Equals*. Particularly useful general studies are Anthony King, 'Executives', in Fred Greenstein and Nelson Polsby (eds), *Handbook of Political Sciences: Governmental Institutions and Processes*, vol. 5, Addison-Wesley, Reading, Mass., 1975, pp. 173–225; the review by Bert A. Rockman, 'Presidential and Executive Studies: 'The One, the Few and the Many', in H. F. Weisberg (ed.), *Political Science: The Science of Politics*, Adathon Press, New York, 1986, pp. 105–40; J. M. Burns, *Leadership*, Harper & Row, New York, 1978; Jean Blondel, *Political Leadership*, Sage, London, 1987.

7   See Fred I. Greenstein, *The Hidden-hand Presidency: Eisenhower as Leader*, Basic Books, New York, 1982; and Robert Caro, *The Years of Lyndon Johnson: The Path to Power*, Collins, London, 1982.

8   There are presently two biographies of Fraser. John Edwards, *Life Wasn't Mean to be Easy*, Mayhem, Sydney, 1976, provides an early picture of the then newly elected prime minister. Phillip Ayres, *Malcolm Fraser: A Biography*, William Heinemann, Melbourne, 1987, provides a recent and favourable account of his career. Denis White and David Kemp have edited a volume of extracts from his speeches, *Malcolm Fraser on Australia*, Hill of Content, Melbourne, 1986. On a more specific topic see Alan Renouf, *Malcolm Fraser and Australian Foreign Policy*, Australian Professional Publishers, Sydney, 1984, for a very hostile interpretation. The best account of Fraser as prime minister amid the drama of Australian politics is Paul Kelly, *The Hawke Ascendency*, Angus & Robertson, Sydney, 1984.

Fraser's entry in *Who's Who* gives considerable details on Simon Fraser's career.

For full details of Fraser's education and political career before 1975, see Ayres, *Malcolm Fraser*, chapters 1–13.

SOURCES (pp. 9-23)

9   Tange's comments are recorded in Ayres, *Malcolm Fraser*, pp.146, 162. So is the comment that Gorton regarded Fraser as a potential successor.

10   Fraser's resignation speech is in *Commonwealth Parliamentary Debates*, 9 March 1981, pp. 679-84.

11   His 1971 lecture was published by the Alfred Deakin Memorial Trust. This view on cabinet government can be found in 'A National View', in Ray Aitchison (ed.), *Looking at the Liberals*, Cheshire, Melbourne, 1974. His 1975 ANZAAS speech was entitled 'National Objectives: Social, Economic and Political Goals'.

11-12   Fraser's rise to the leadership is recounted in all the books describing the 1975 crisis; the best of them is Paul Kelly, *The Unmaking of Gough*, Angus & Robertson, Sydney, 1976.

15   The full quotation, taken from Bernard Shaw's play, *Back to Methuselah*, is 'Life is not meant to be easy, my child; but take courage; it can be delightful'. The first sentence was included in the Alfred Deakin lecture on 20 July 1971. Fraser spelt out the whole quotation to the Liberal party federal council on 31 May 1981.

16   Sir Hugh Ennor's request to Fraser to reduce his urgent requests is noted by Ayres, *Malcolm Fraser*, p. 198.

16-17   Kemp's article, 'A Leader and a Philosophy', is published in Henry Mayer (ed.), *Labor to Power*, Angus & Robertson, Sydney, 1973.

Chapter 2   Harnessing the machine: the system of advice

19-20   For the debate over support for prime ministers, see Weller, *First Among Equals*, chapter 7; for an internal view see Sir Geoffrey Yeend, 'The Department of Prime Minister and Cabinet in Perspective', *Australian Journal of Public Administration*, 38(2), 1979, pp. 133-50.

23   For a brief biography of Kemp, see James Walter, *The Ministers' Minders*, Oxford University Press, 1986, pp.

98–103. For Kemp on the role of the private office, see 'PM's private office supports "political" role', *Monash Reporter*, 6, 1983. Denis White's views of ministerial advisers can be seen in his article, 'Backup for Ministers', *Politics*, 23(1), May 1988.

23 Budd's analysis of the Canadian Prime Minister's Office is in M1255/4.

25 The explanation of the special position of the prime minister's office is in M1272/2.

26–7 The programs are in M1268/22 Programs. The identification of positions in square brackets has been added.

27 The record of the Heritage Commission's meeting with Fraser is in M1282/1.

29 Fraser's letters of thanks to Parvo et al. are in M1255/5.

The list of questions and briefings is in M1268/4.

30 The demands for changes to letters are in M1255.

34 Proposals for visits by members of the private office are in 1356/3.

35 The changes to the structure of PMC can be traced through the organisation charts in the department's *Annual Reports*.

36–7 The list of demands on 21 September 1977 is in M1268/24 Requests to secretary, PMC. The list for February 1980 is in M1255/11.

38 The instructions about monitoring parliamentary questions are in M1255/3.

40 Yeend's views are taken from his article, 'The Department of Prime Minister and Cabinet in Perspective'.

41 The brief on the Olympics is in 81/0103 Olympic Boycott. Peacock's views of PMC were stated in the speech justifying his resignation, see *Commonwealth Parliamentary Debates*, 28 April 1987, pp. 1609–10.

43 Codd's dispute over the speech was reported in the editorial of the *Australian Financial Review*,

SOURCES (pp. 44-72)

30 November 1979; the argument over ethnic functions is in M1272.

44 On the appointment of permanent heads, see M1266/2.

Chapter 3 'That big bastard': relations with ministers

62 In the Fraser correspondence there are few lighthearted letters. His notes to Chaney are an exception. When Chaney complained 'as a citizen' about a postbox stuffed with election brochures for the 1981 Curtin by-election (when he failed to get party preselection), Fraser responded 'Dear Citizen Chaney'. Another note recommended Chaney as a minister worth taking seriously; it was written to the lord mayor of Perth – who was Chaney's father. See M1266 for details.

67 Hodgman's note to Fraser on 28 February 1980 is in M1266. Other more flattering letters: his note on the 1977 referendum is in M1334 and his letter appreciating his elevation to the ministry written at Christmas 1980 is in M1266. All correspondence from backbenchers is in either M1266 or M1334.

Crossman's comment is in R. H. Crossman, *Inside View: Three Lectures on Prime Ministerial Government*, Cape, London, 1972, p. 46.

68 The list of permanent heads, with Fraser's comments and decisions, is in M1268/2 Appointments.

69-70 The letter to Kingsland is in 77/01523.

70 The split of DEIR is described in 78/0726 December 1978.

71 Cotton's imperialistic letter is in M1356/1.

72 Drafts of alternative AAOs in 1982 are in M1356.

The proposals for the establishment of a Department of Defence Support are in 70/01428 General Elections: Administrative Arrangements; 81/01 415; and in the

SOURCES (pp. 73-100)

PSB file 82/3319. Killen's letter to Fraser on the second minister is in M1266.

73-4   The account of the split of the Treasury is taken primarily from the Public Service Board file: 'Splitting the Treasury'. A consolidated chronology was compiled by a senior PSB officer and is the source of much of this account. Further details are in 76/02595 and LC 389 Administrative Arrangements Order. Letters complaining about economic advice are in M1268/3 and M1335/1.

76-82   The account of Lynch's resignation is taken from the Lynch Papers: Resignation 1977, held at the University of Melbourne Archives. The most detailed summary of these events was kept by Andrew Hay, Lynch's private secretary, and is kept in the papers. Searby's private opinion, the Chaney-Hyde letter to backbenchers and other papers are in M1268/SV.

82-7   The papers of Withers's resignation are in M1268/36 Royal Commission: Electoral Redistribution in Queensland; and in LC2050 Electoral Redistribution in Queensland.

87-91   A full file on Peacock's resignation and the preparation of the defence is in M1268/SV. Another set of the same papers is in LC3263 Peacock Resignation.

91-2   The TV affair papers are in M1266/4 and LC3647 Ministerial Resignations. For Ellicott's resignation, see LC1660 and M1356/3. For Nixon, see 81/01498 Royal Commission into the Meat Industry and M1268/SV

98   Budd's letter to Street's private secretary and to McLeay are both in M1255/6. The demand for an inquiry into social security and the dole is in M1268/21 Premiers (after Fraser was alerted by a state premier).

98-9   The request for a submission on refugees is in LC1366 Refugee Policy. The letter to Howard about a social security card is in M1254.

100   Carrick's letter to Fraser on 6 June 1979, stating that he

SOURCES (pp. 106-17)

understood the option of tertiary fees would not be taken up, is in M1335/1.

Chapter 4 'In the bunker': cabinet

106-33 The material on cabinet is drawn from several files, particularly LC2 Cabinet Procedures; LC294 Planning and Co-ordination Committees; LC272 Economic Committee; LC2542 Co-ordination Committee; LC2198 Review of the Cabinet System.

108 The Treasury's comment on controlling processes was made in *Royal Commission on Australian Government Administration*, AGPS, 1976, Appendix 1, p. 103.

109-16 The programs and arrangements are drawn from LC222 Cabinet Program for week of 18 September 1978; LC2234, 25 September 1978; LC2239, 2 October 1978; LC2250, 9 October 1978; LC2252, 16 October 1978; LC2283, 6 November 1978; LC2545, 7 December 1981; LC3560, 13 December 1981; LC3565, 12 January 1982; LC3566, 19 January 1982; LC3630, 6 April 1982; LC3641, 13 April 1981; LC3653, 3 May 1982; LC3662, 10 May 1982; LC3663, 17 May 1982; LC3672, 31 May 1982.

113-14 Anthony's special treatment is found in LC3663; the note explaining how the nuclear safeguards item was rushed through cabinet is in LC1868 Nuclear Safeguards. His request to discuss the IAC reports is in LC3672.

114 Howard's request on AUSSAT is in LC3643.

114-15 Fraser's instruction on the Commonwealth Games is in LC1520. His decision on listing the Olympics is in LC1520.

115 Fraser's letter to Yeend on the length of submissions and the timetable is in M1255/12.

116-17 The discussion of Lynch as agenda setter is part of the cabinet review by Yeend in LC2198.

117 Fraser's comment on the inadequacy of the submission

SOURCES (pp. 118-30)

on contingency planning is in M1255/12 and the note on the Canberra bus service is in M1254/20.

118 Tange's comments, widely repeated by officials, are contained in the Yeend reviews, LC2198.

The requests for quarterly reports are in LC1176 Progress and Achievements of the Fraser Government, and in M1254. The later requests are in M1352/1, M1254. Details of meetings of the ministry and the agenda are in LC2432 Ministry meetings: general discussions.

119 Discussion of access of ministers to cabinet is found in LC2.

119-20 Fraser's request from Lusaka for permanent representation is in LC2632 Diplomatic and Trade Representation in Zambia, while the foreign aid request is in LC553 Foreign Aid.

120 The note from Codd to the prime minister on the creation of SBS was written on 3 May 1980. See LC2197 Establishment of an Ethnic TV Service.

121 The book in question was *Documents in Australian Defence and Foreign Policy 1968-1975*, Walsh & Munster, Hong Kong, 1980. It was withdrawn from sale.

122 For the debate on the January cabinet meetings, see LC3641.

123 For details of the number of meetings over AUSSAT, see LC1702.

125 The details on the hours of meetings were prepared as part of the defence after Peacock's resignation and are in LC3263.

127 Fraser's comments on the committee system were made in 'Responsibility in Government' *Australian Journal of Public Administration*, 37(1), 1978.

129-30 For the agenda of the Co-ordination committee, see LC2542. The details of its activities were calculated after Peacock's resignation; they are in M1268/SV.

SOURCES (pp. 133-54)

        Peacock's criticism was made in parliament, see *Commonwealth Parliamentary Debates*, 24 April 1981.

133   The term 'partial cabinet' was coined by former British minister Patrick Gordon Walker in *The Cabinet*, Fontana, London, 1972, pp. 87-101.

142   The decision on the Coldham committee and the embarrassment of the Defence department can be found in LC1776 Committee of Reference for Defence Forces Pay.

143   The request for cabinet decisions on the Seas and Submerged Lands issue is in M1268/24: Requests to Secretary PMC.

144   The brief to Lynch is in the Lynch Papers: General Briefing.

147   Dell's comment is in 'Collective Responsibility: Fact, Fiction or Facade?' in *Policy and Practice: The Experience of Government*, Royal Institute of Public Administration, London, 1980, pp. 27-48.

Chapter 5   'Duchessing and strongarming': the party leader

150-1   The correspondence with backbenchers is all found in M1266 or M1334.

151   For specific subjects: Roger Shipton (Vic.) asked for the discussion on North West Cape on 26 August 1982; David Connolly (NSW) raised the proposal on legislation; Don Cameron (Qld) opposed TV licences; McLean and Hyde (WA) argued the case for cuts and Chaney (WA) for a minister for federal affairs.

152   The disputes over Anthony and TAA and Hunt's letter asking for assistance are in M1272.

153   For an example of the whip reporting on MHRs' absence, see the letter from whip John Bourchier to Fraser on 27 May 1976 in M1374.

154   Shipton's request for a separate party meeting is in M1266. The lists of party room agenda are in M1268/20 Party Meetings.

SOURCES (pp. 156-75)

156–7   For the papers on party committees, see M1268/4. For letters inviting John Knight (ACT), Kathy Martin (Qld), Vic Garland (WA), David Connolly (NSW) and Ian Macphee (Vic.) to join the arts committee, see M1266.

157   For Chaney's group on reform, see M1334.

157–9   Details of Tactics committee are in M1268/4&5 Committees and in the records of the committee.

159–60   The debate on whales is in M1268/30 Whales, in LC1827 Whales and in LC2044 Inquiry into Whaling.

161   For complaints about the challenge to Lynch, see Peter Falconer (Vic.) to Fraser, 14 December 1977 in M1334.

163   Copies of Falconer's letter to Peacock and Tuckey's note to Kramer are in M1266.

164   Lynch's draft letter is in the Lynch papers: Resignation 1982.

166   The monitoring of polls for the 1977 referenda is in M1356/3.

167   Eggleton's letters to Fraser about attendance at the federal executive in April 1981 are in M1272.

169–71   The main papers on the Gippsland dispute are in M1268/3 Coalition: relations between parties. Details of Simon's meetings with Fraser are in M1334.

171–4   The dispute with the Queensland division is documented in M1268/3 Coalition: Relations between parties and M1268/21 Premiers. The letters to Sparkes is in M1255. Cabinet's consideration is in LC2959 Coalition Parties in Queensland.

Chapter 6   'The highest authoritative source': the salesman

175   The title of the chapter comes from an article written by Warren Beeby in the *Australian* on 23 June 1976, describing a meeting with Fraser on the Great Wall of China: 'At the crest, on a misty battlement overlooking barren, craggy peaks, the press received a briefing by

a man who said he was to be referred to only as "the highest authoritative source".'

183   The memorandum from Eggleton to Fraser on 31 December 1975 and the subsequent strategic advice from the secretariat are in M1280/2.

183–4   The media monitoring proposals are in M1268/16 Media reports.

184–5   Details of the Public Information committee and its successors are in the Lynch Papers: Subject Files and in 78/0328 Public Presentation of Government Decisions.

185   Eggleton's advice is in M1280/2.

186   The media complaint about divided press conferences is in M1280/2.

190–9   Fraser's note to Peacock on 7 May 1976 about the leak is in M1335/6.

193   Strategy for the premiers' conference is in LC3167 1981 Premiers' Conference.

195–6   The letters to Warwick Fairfax are in M1255. The exchange with Packer over broadcasting legislation is in M1356/1. Details of meetings with proprietors over amendments to the Broadcasting Act are in LC376 Inquiry into the Australian Broadcasting System and in M1268/31 Broadcasting and Television Act.

196–9   All the ABC material is in M1268/1 ABC and M1356/1. Also in LC508 ABC Finance; LC ABC Programs; LC241 ABC Appointments. For a more general account of the problems of the ABC, see Glyn Davis, *Breaking up the ABC*, Allen & Unwin, Sydney, 1988.

199   The interview with Kramer is in 1282/SV.

200–3   The letter of 7 July for Lynch about the economic forecast is in M1295/5. All the material about the early election, including Eggleton's note about 'JK', is in 1268/32 Election Timing, July–October 1977.

204–5   Lynch's draft letter of resignation is in the Lynch Papers: Resignation 1982.

SOURCES (pp. 206-34)

206 For figures on the approval ratings, see Patrick Weller, 'The Anatomy of a Grievous Miscalculation', in H. Penniman (ed.), *Australia at the Polls, 1980 and 1982*, Allen & Unwin, Sydney, 1984, p. 276.

Lynch's proposal that Fraser should appear in more 'humane' positions is in M1335/3.

207-9 For the schedules see M1260/1980.

209-10 Clem Lloyd's comment is in 'The Media' in H. Penniman (ed.) *The Australian National Elections of 1977*, American Enterprise Institute, Washington, 1976, p. 262.

210 For the comment on St George's League Club see M1268/16 Media Reports.

212-13 Eggleton's interim report is in the Lynch papers.

Chapter 7 'Axing or taxing': the art of budgeting

214 'Malcolm is a taxer, not an axer' was a comment by Senator Withers in the *Australian Financial Review*, 14 August 1979.

216 The letter from Wheeler to Lynch in July 1977 and the notes from PMC officials are in 76/02457 Adherence to Budget Estimates.

218-34 The account of the 1976 budget is drawn from a wide range of files whose accounts constantly interconnect and duplicate each other. The primary files are: 75/03096 Expenditure Restraint December 1975; 76/0189 Expenditure Restraint December 1975; 75/01796 Budget Timetable; 76/0457 Budgetary and Fiscal Figuring 1976; 76/01138 Economic Measures May 1976; LC52 Government Expenditure Review; LC94 Economic Conditions and Prospects; LC102 Economic Consultative Group; LC115 National Wage Indexation 1976; LC148 Control and Review of Spending: Department of Social Security; LC199 Budget Estimates; LC212 Forward Estimates of Expenditure 1975-78; LC238 Budget Cabinet 1976, Arrangements and Procedures; LC411 Budget Outlays 1976/77; LC476 Expenditure Cuts 1976 (including the Lynch-Fraser letter of 14 May); LC477 Treasurer's statement on economic measures; LC593 Prospective Budget Outlays; LC667 Taxation reform; LC851 Budget Preview; LC867 Adherence to 1976/77 Budget Estimates; LC868 The Economy and Budget Strategy 1976/79; LC869 1976/77 Budget Figuring; LC870 Agreed Bids; LC871 Disagreed bids; LC 1971 Devaluation; LC2843 Tax Indexation.

224 Fraser's exchanges with the minister for environment, housing and community development are in M1254.

229 The Victorian submission, and the subsequent exchange of letters, are in M1268/21 Premiers.

231–3 The saga of Fraser's constant struggle to extract data from the Treasury can be found not only in the cabinet files, but also in M1356/3; M1255/5 and M1255/6. The reference to the *National Times* is in M1254/5.

234–44 By the time of the 1979 budget, the files appear to have been consolidated more effectively. This account is based on the following: 79/0117 Budget Policy and Figuring 1979-80; 78/0510 Monetary Policy; 78/0822 Budget Policy and Figuring 1978-79; 77/0862 Forward Estimates; 78/0294 Pre-budget Consultations; 78/0676 Budget Processes; LC2171 Budget Commitments for 1979/80; LC2339 Forward Estimates and Budget Cabinet Arrangements; LC2465 Budget Outlook 1977/80.

244 The comment by Michael Keating is in 78/0676 Budget Processes.

245–50 The Review of the Commonwealth Functions is recorded in 80/01605 RCF; 81/0943 RCF and LC3394 R.C.F.

250 The recommendation to end the building of the new Parliament House is Decision 14368 (RCF) in LC3098 Review of Commonwealth Functions: Department of Housing and Construction. The decision not to take up

SOURCES (pp. 251-83)

that recommendation is Decision 14984(C) in LC1387 New and Permanent Parliament House.

251–66 For the 1982 budget, see 80/01453 1981-82 Budget Procedures; 80/0189 Budget Policy and Figuring 1981/82; 81/01695 Budget Policy and Figuring 1982; 81/01696 Budget 1982/3: Procedures; 82/0717 Budget Outlays; 82/01023 1982/83 Budget: final consultation between prime minister, deputy minister and department; LC2 Cabinet Procedures; LC94 Economic Conditions and Prospects; LC1885 State Borrowing; LC3585 Budget Timetable: 1982 arrangements; LC3623 Budget Outlays and Figuring; LC3733 Securement of Payment of Overdue Income Tax. The Treasury's advice to the treasurer is in 81/01696. For the best secondary account see Paul Kelly, *The Hawke Ascendancy*, Angus & Robertson, Sydney, 1984.

258 The advice to Lynch from his department is in the Lynch papers: Subject files.

269 Fraser's notes to the Reserve Bank are in M1255/6.

Chapter 8   Treating with bandits: the federalist

277 Fraser's requests to Guilfoyle to attend the meeting of Victorian MPs and to Carrick to monitor legislation are both in M1271.

280 The negotiations over the Torres Strait are in LC235.

280–1 Griffith's note to Fraser is in M1268/1 Aborigines and M1268/10 Education.

281 On the call about the Gold Coast Casino, see Edward's affidavit to the Fitzgerald Inquiry, reported in the *Courier Mail*, 27 October 1988.

Baume's call can be found in M1272/2.

282 On the advice about attending Comalco's opening, see M1272.

283–90 The Aurukun and Mornington disputes can be explored in LC180 Aurukun; LC1981 Aboriginal Reserves in Queensland; 76/0421 Aurukun Bauxite;

75/01775 and 78/0643 Aboriginal Reserves in Queensland; 78/0284 Aboriginal Land Fund Commission; 78/0427 Aboriginal and Torres Strait Legislation. The Yarrabah dispute was taken from the same files and from 78/0643 Yarrabah. Additional material is also in M1268/1 Aborigines, M1268/21 Premiers; Viner's correspondence is in M1335/8.

284   Bjelke-Petersen's complaints about centralism in March 1976 are in M1268/5.

291   Griffith's advice to the acting prime minister is in M1268/12 Griffith. Chaney's letters to Fraser keeping him informed of progress are in M1268/1 Aborigines.

292   Fraser's note to Viner is in 78/0284.

293–302 The discussion of treaty-making is in LC1266 Treaties. Details of the Seas and Submerged Lands debates are in LC90 Offshore Legislation; 81/01417 Seas and Submerged Lands. The transcripts of all the premiers' conferences from 1976 to 1980 are in M1268/20.

297   Fraser's letter to Durack is in M1254/6.

304   The cabinet analysis of federal clauses is in LC1266 Treaties. Additional correspondence is in M1254 and M1268/21 Premiers.

304–11 The debate over the future of south-west Tasmania is drawn from LC3507 South-West Tasmania and 80/01422 Development of Hydro-electric Power in Tasmania. Fraser's letter to Lowe is in M1254.

307   Records of the meetings with the Heritage Commission and the Wilderness Society are in M1282/1.

Chapter 9 'Not without honour': foreign affairs

313   For studies of foreign policy under Fraser see Coral Bell, *Dependent Ally*, Oxford University Press, Melbourne, 1988. Alan Renouf's, *Malcolm Fraser and Australian Foreign Policy* is a hostile account that gives Fraser little credit for any achievement. Phillip Ayres, *Malcolm Fraser*, gives three chapters to Fraser's inter-

national role. It provides a useful account of the Lusaka conference and views of Fraser expressed by Michael Manley of Jamaica, Kenneth Kaunda of Zambia, Robert Mugabe of Zimbabwe and Valéry Giscard d'Estaing of France.

313   For letters to heads of government, see M1254.

314   For evidence of respect, see Henry Kissinger's foreword to *Malcolm Fraser on Australia*, and Valéry Giscard d'Estaing's foreword to Ayres's *Malcolm Fraser*. The fact that they even agreed to write the forewords is surely significant.

315-24   The account of policy towards South Africa and Zimbabwe is based on a wide range of files. They include LC1206 Zimbabwe Developments; LC1973 South African Sporting Contacts; LC2172 Recent Developments in Rhodesia; LC2632 Diplomatic and Trade Representation in Zambia; LC2512 CHOGM 1979: Key Issues; LC1363 CHOGM 1977; 71/01355 Zimbabwe; 77/0222 Pre-CHOGM Discussions with Pacific Leaders; 79/0616 Briefing for CHOGM 1979; 79/01394 Briefing and Record of Conversations CHOGM 1979; 78/0569 Rhodesian Information Centre; 80/0892 Aid to Zimbabwe.

318   Fraser's letter to Ramphal on 15 March is in M1341/1. For Fraser's letter to Datak Hussein Onn, 16 February 1977, see M1254.

320   For the contrary view that 'strangely there was never a discussion in cabinet of the problem facing South Africa', see D. J. Killen, *Inside Australian Politics* Methuen, Sydney, 1985, p.288.

321   Fraser's follow-up letters to Forbes Burnham, prime minister of Guyana, Michael Manley of Jamaica and Kenneth Kaunda of Zambia are all in M1255/5.

324   Griffith's letter to Fraser is in M1268/12 Griffith.

The correspondence with heads of government about CHOGM is collected mainly in M1333/SV.

SOURCES (pp. 327-67)

327 The paper on the Australian approach is in M1281/8. The daily reports are in M1356/1. So are the records of Peacock's conversation with the Tanzanian foreign minister and with Carrington, the notes of Fraser and Peacock's meeting with Thatcher and Carrington on 4 August and 4 February, and all Fraser's notes and annotations on drafts of the communiqué. The transcript of the background briefing prior to departure is in M1343/3.

333–4 Fraser's comment to the high commissioner-designate is in 80/0892 Aid to Zimbabwe.

335–44 The Sinai account is based primarily on LC3353 Sinai Peacekeeping; 81/0337 and 81/0934 Sinai Peacekeeping, and on other documents.

344–53 The Olympic Games boycott can be found in LC2773 Australian Response to Soviet Invasion of Afghanistan; LC2785 Overseas Visits of Prime Ministers and Foreign Ministers re the Invasion of Afghanistan; LC2843 Olympic Games; LC2867 Australian–USSR Trade Sanctions; 80/0105 Olympic Boycott. The collection of papers in M1268/7 and M1268/18 includes briefing notes and lists of boycotting countries. M1254/14 includes additional briefing notes and letters to heads of states. M1255/11 includes the analysis of letters; M1333/SV contains a letter from Thatcher. Ellicott's request for Fraser to ask Carter to contact Trudeau is in M1335/2.

354 For Coral Bell's views, see *Dependent Ally*, pp. 163, 178.

Chapter 10 Decisions, decisions

356–67 There is a great variety of files on the aspects of uranium development. The main ones used are LC1877 Uranium Development; LC1868 Nuclear Safeguards; LC1205 Uranium: Shipments and Industrial Relations; LC1862 Uranium Development in the Northern Territory; LC1870 Uranium: Production and

Marketing; LC1650 Uranium: Presentation of Decision; LC279 Aboriginal Land in the Northern Territory. The main departmental files are 76/02227 Uranium: Industrial Relations Aspects; 76/0527 Uranium: Officials' Committee; 76/0621 Uranium: Production and Marketing; 76/01504 Uranium: Shipments; 76/0739 Northern Territory: Land Rights: Uranium; 76/0238 Uranium Exports: Nuclear Safeguards Policy; 76/0372 Uranium Policy; 77/0982 Uranium: Public Presentation of Decisions: Policy. The massive technical material in these files has obviously had to be largely ignored. The interlocking complexity may be indicated by the fact that there were many more files dealing with other aspects of the policy. There is also a file of material in M1268/28 on uranium development.

365   For the attempt to counteract the statements by Professor Kerr, a member of the Fox inquiry, see M1268/28.

367   For accounts of the negotiation with Ranger see Felix, 'From Glass Beads to Gold Pens', *Legal Services Bulletin*, 3(6), 1978; R. Milliken, 'How the Aborigines Fared in the Ranger Agreement', *National Times*, 3–9 September 1978, which reports Dr Coombs's misgivings about the processes.

368–76   For details of the 35-hour week, see LC383 Wages Policy; 81/08 Wages Policy; 80/0763 35-Hour Week; LC2981 35-Hour Working Week Campaign.

371   The record of conversation with the MTIA is in 80/0763.

371–4   The transcripts of the interviews with ICI officials are in M1282/SV.

374   Ayres' judgement that Fraser 'stemmed the tide' is in *Malcolm Fraser*, p. 413.

376–82   The Campbell inquiry can be found in: 78/0327 Proposal for Enquiry into Capital Markets; 81/01825 Inquiry into the Australian Financial System: Task

SOURCES (pp. 381-406)

Force Papers, 82/0409 AFS: External Economic Policy; 82/078 AFS: Foreign Banks; LC1792: Monetary Policy; LC2525 The Campbell Inquiry.

381 Fraser's letter to Howard on 1 November 1982 is in M1254/23.

383–93 The tax avoidance debate is mainly derived from LC2834 Tax Avoidance Schemes: Policy: LC3749 Membership of Commonwealth Bodies; 79/01003 Tax Policy Avoidance; 81/01118 Taxation Policy. Fraser's statement and speeches on tax evasion in 1982 are collected in M1380. Collected papers on tax are in M1268/27.

384 The tax commissioner's comments on tax evasion are in M1268/27.

Chapter 11 Domination and consultation: Malcolm Fraser as prime minister

406 Oakeshott's description is in his essay 'Political Education', in *Rationalism in Politics*, Methuen, London, 1962, p. 127.

406 The concepts of transactional or transforming leadership were developed by J. M. Burns in *Leadership*, Harper & Row, New York, 1978.

INDEX

Aboriginal Affairs, Department of, 285–6, 288, 290
Aborigines, 116, 277, 280, 283–91, 358, 365, 367
Aderman, Evan, 66, 203
Administrative Arrangements Order, 60, 67
Administrative Services, Department of, 71
Administrative Review Committee, 220
Afghanistan, 344, 348, 353
Age, 73, 228, 230, 244, 265, 362, 373, 387
Amin, Idi, 320
Anthony, Doug, 16, 28, 29, 48, 63, 66, 68, 71, 83, 85, 88–9, 93, 96, 100, 111, 113–14, 118, 120, 121–2, 125, 136, 138, 141, 145, 152, 204–5, 208, 210, 224, 243, 245–6, 248, 258, 280, 291, 296, 299, 310, 337, 340–1, 344, 349–50, 356–62, 366–7, 380, 385
Arbitration Commission, 368–9, 371
Atwell, Sir John, 167, 202

Aurukun, 283–91
AUSSAT, 111, 114, 123, 134
Australian, 88
Australian Broadcasting Commission, 77, 115, 152, 155, 163, 176, 196–9, 391
Australian Council of Trade Unions, 360, 366, 368–71, 374
Australian Defence Force Academy, 248, 269, 272, 402
Australian Institute of Sport, 256–7, 269
Australian Olympic Federation, 345–50
Ayers, Tony, 40, 45

Barnett, David, 16, 29–30, 34, 53, 88, 95, 184, 201, 329, 399
Barwick, Garfield, 387
Batt, Neil, 298
Baume, Michael, 85, 157
Baume, Peter, 18, 65–6, 105, 141, 152, 157, 207, 281, 398, 407
Beale, Sir Howard, 79

INDEX

Begg, Ken, 178, 186-7, 193, 200, 204
Begin, Menachim, 314, 340, 343-4
Bell, Coral, 354
Bevan, Aneurin, 67
Bicentennial Roads, 135, 402
Bjelke-Petersen, Sir Joh, 27, 198, 276-91, 294, 298-301, 312, 348, 395
Bland, Sir Henry, 67, 197-8, 220
Bolte, Sir Henry, 79, 135
Bourchier, John, 170
Bowers, Peter, 34, 189, 191-4, 228, 244
Boyle, Raelene, 350
Brenchley, Fred, 195
Bridgland, Milton, 372-4
Britain, 2, 3, 317, 323-31, 333, 338-40, 346-8, 354, 361
Brown, Bob, 26
Brown, Neil, 65, 159, 160, 209, 230
Bonner, Neville, 289
Buckley, Brian, 78, 131
Budd, Dale, 15-16, 23, 25, 28, 30, 34, 47, 49-50, 55, 56, 98, 123, 184, 288
Budgets, 214-73; (1975) 14, 218; (1976) 217-31; (1979) 217, 234-44; (1981) 49; (1982) 217, 251-66; budget cabinet, 229, 242, 254, 261-2
Burnham, Forbes, 321, 334
Business and Consumer Affairs, Department of, 71, 72
Button, John, 404

cabinet, 15, 75, 106-47, 292; agenda, 109-12, 132; arrangements, 108-27; decisions, 90, 119-20, 139-40, 143-4; reviews, 125-7; schedule, 84-5, 110, 121, 123; workload, 118, 123, 125, 145
cabinet committees, ad hoc, 84-5, 110, 112, 113-14, 115, 128, 230, 236, 364-5; co-ordination, 90, 112, 126, 129-33, 210, 238-45, 250, 252, 259, 262, 268, 350, 373-4, 388, 390; economic, 127, 220-2, 224, 231; foreign affairs and defence, 111-12, 119, 128, 133, 319, 322, 326, 336-9, 342-3, 353; intelligence and security, 110, 128; general administrative, 110, 112, 126; legislation, 110-11, 126-7; machinery of government, 110; monetary, 33, 110-12, 128, 133, 254, 266, 377-81; public information, 184, 206, 370; review of commonwealth functions, 112, 128, 143, 246, 248-50; social welfare, 127-8; tax, 386
cabinet government, 1-4, 11, 408-9
Cabinet Office, 35, 89-90, 109, 113, 136, 143, 250, 390
Callaghan, James, 317, 361
Cameron, Don, 82-3, 157
Campbell inquiry, 33, 356, 377-82
Canada, 2, 23, 325, 332, 336, 338, 343, 346, 348, 359
Carleton, Richard, 186-7, 189, 198, 209
Carlton, Jim, 55, 65, 142
Carmody, Alan, 39, 74, 363
Carnegie, Rod, 29, 47
Caro, Robert, 7, 8
Carrick, Sir John, 65, 83, 100-1, 181, 203, 236, 238, 276-7, 299, 392, 407
Carrington, Lord, 323-31, 333, 338-9, 341-2
Carter, President, 314, 335, 344-5, 348-50, 360
Castles, Ian, 40, 45, 225, 243, 255
Castro, Fidel, 321
Chaney, Fred, 62, 66, 80, 85, 99-101,

INDEX

104, 122, 142, 145, 151, 156–7, 168–9, 265, 290–1, 392, 399, 404
Charles, Stephen, 80
Chipp, Don, 62–4
CHOGM, 119, 162, 315, 317–20, 323, 326–31, 341
CHOGRM, 87, 188
Clark, Andrew, 332
Clark, Joe, 325–6, 331
Clark, Professor Manning, 26
Codd, Michael, 40, 43, 45, 125, 235
Cole, Sir William, 70, 74
Coldham committee, 142
collective responsibility, 106, 144–7
Commonwealth, 315–34
Commonwealth Games, 114, 334
Confederation of Australian Industry, 370, 375
Cook, Michael, 24
Cordner, Dennis, 372
Costigan inquiry, 94, 144, 251, 308, 391
Cotton, Robert, 65, 71, 75, 203
Court, Sir Charles, 101, 193, 207, 276–7, 285–6, 293–4, 298, 300–2, 304, 312, 322
Crichton-Brown, Robert, 201
Crossman, Richard, 2, 67
Curtis, Jack, 138

Darwin–Alice Springs railway, 135
Davidson, Ken, 73, 230
Davie, Michael, 195
Defence, Department of, 72
Defence Support, Department of, 72
Dell, Edward, 147
Dolan, Cliff, 374–5
Drake-Brockman, Tom, 62
Drysdale, Alastair, 34

Duckmanton, Talbot, 166, 196–8
Duff, Sir Anthony, 329
Dunstan, Don, 298
Durack, Peter, 82–3, 85, 92–3, 116, 123, 140, 203, 297–301, 308, 391–2, 400

Edwards, Llew, 27, 172–2, 174, 278, 280–1, 290–1, 334
Eggleton, Tony, 76–8, 80, 83, 85, 90, 103, 156–7, 165–9, 180, 182, 185, 187, 196–7, 200–2, 204–5, 207, 212–13, 223, 317, 320, 324, 329–30, 399
Egypt, 335–44
Eisenhower, President, 7
Elections: (1975) 13; (1977) 158–9, 199–204, 210; (1980) 210–11; (1983) 189, 204–5, 211–13, 263
Ellicott, Robert, 26, 65, 75, 293–4, 346, 348–52, 363, 403
Elliott, John, 170, 259
Employment and Industrial Relations, Department of, 44, 70–1, 375
Enfield, John, 40
Environment, Housing and Community Development, Department of, 224
external affairs power, 293, 303–4

Fairfax, Sir Warwick, 195
Falconer, Peter, 163
Falklands, 116
family allowances, 225–32
federal clauses, 304
Fife, Wal, 31, 51, 93, 99–100, 134, 154, 203
Finance, Department of, 235, 248, 252–4, 308, 385

INDEX

Financial Review, 230, 244, 264, 371, 373
Flinders by-election, 164, 309
Forbes, Jim, 167-8, 205
Foreign Affairs, Department of, 309, 323, 331, 336
foreign banks, 379-82
Fox, Justice, 356-62, 364-5
Ford, Michelle, 351
Fraser, Malcolm:
  access to, 28, 187; administrative charges, 67-9; advice to, 23-4, 38-40, 46-58; 83; American alliance, 314, 337, 352; assessment of, 354, 395-409; briefs to, 35-6, 38-9, 133; British connections, 298-301, 312; and budgets, 217-18, 220, 234, 254; (1976) 220-31; (1979) 234-44; (1982) 255-66; and cabinet, 107-47, 235, 398; cabinet decisions, 140-2; campaigning, 206-13; and the Commonwealth, 315, 317-18, 320-34; consultations by, 21-2, 49-50, 54, 81-2, 89, 95, 99-101, 137, 139-40, 199-204, 397-8, 400-1; correspondence, 30-1, 310; and deregulation, 377-82, 403; economic ability, 270-1; economic policy, 214-66; economic record, 267-73; education, 8-9; election timing, 119-206; and electorate, 176; on external affairs power, 303-4; as federalist, 275-6, 293-4, 305-7, 310-12; impatience of, 47-8, 55, 82, 122; interrogative approach, 102-4, 137-9, 145-6, 400-1; leadership contests, 10-12, 80, 161-4; leadership views, 16-18; leaks, 190-4; lectures, 11-13; links with foreign leaders, 313-14;
  media relations, 89, 182-94, 209; and ministers, 61, 75-91, 100-7; as minister, 9-10; networks, 21, 28-9, 45; Olympic boycott, 344-53; in opposition, 10-11; patronage, use of, 94-7; and parliamentary party, 148-61; parliamentary performances, 177-82; and Liberal party divisions, 168-74; and party secretariat, 164-8; philosophy, 11, 17, 50, 403-4; policy advice and initiatives, 31-3, 355, 395; and premiers, 275-82, 283-92, 297-9; Premiers' Conference, 293-301; propriety, 81, 87, 95; questions from, 29, 36-7, 48-9, 52, 54, 98, 102, 118; and racism, 316, 321; reshuffles, 66, 68, 96; RCF, 245-54; schedule, 15, 25-7, 34, 46, 99, 111, 207-9; selecting ministers, 61-7; and Senate, 181-2; and Sinai force, 335-44; and South Africa, 316-20, 323, 335; and south-west Tasmania, 304-10; speeches, 31-2; style, 14-16, 18, 29, 49-50, 56-8, 81-2, 86-7, 95-6, 101-5, 131, 138-41, 145-6, 211-12, 395-409; support for, 21-45; and tax evasion, 362-3, 383-93; and 35-hour week campaign, 368-76; and Treasury, 44, 73-4, 231-3; and uranium, 356-67; vision, 404-6; workload, 46-7, 49, 55-6, 105; and Zimbabwe, 316-18, 320-33
Fraser, Phoebe, 160
Fraser, Tamie, 153, 195, 351

Garland, Vic, 65, 75, 168, 203
Georgiou, Petro, 32, 48
Gippsland dispute, 169-71

INDEX

Giscard d'Estaing, Valéry, 346, 349
Gorton, John, 9, 10, 45, 88, 90, 107, 165, 275, 293
Grange, Sid, 345–6
Grattan, Michelle, 186, 190, 201, 204, 329
Gray, Robin, 307–11
Greenstein, Fred, 7, 8
Greenwood, Ivor, 75, 224
Griffith, Alan, 280–1, 290–1, 324, 340
Guilfoyle, Margaret, 68, 85, 88, 103, 130, 134, 145, 190, 203, 209, 223, 225, 241, 245, 252, 254, 256, 265–6, 268, 277, 404

Haig, Alexander, 337–9, 341–3
Hamer, Dick, 100, 170, 206, 299, 302, 314
Harries, Owen, 33, 327
Harders, Clarrie, 121
Hasluck, Sir Paul, 79
Hawke, Robert, 27, 57, 180, 187, 205, 211–13, 354, 360, 366, 408
Hay, Andrew, 77–80, 164
Hayden, Bill, 14, 177, 179, 184, 204–5, 218, 266, 343
Henderson, Peter, 121
Herald (Melbourne), 196, 373
Heritage Commission, 27, 307, 309
Herron, John, 172, 174, 208
Hewson, John, 33, 378, 380–1
Higgins, Chris, 243
High Court, 277, 293–4, 296, 303, 307, 384
Hinze, Russ, 173, 279, 281–2, 289
Hodges, John, 97, 153–6, 162, 171, 180
Hodgman, Michael, 67, 154
Holgate, Harry, 27
Holt, Harold, 9, 65, 165

Horgan, Denis, 142, 391–2
Howard, John, 27, 62, 66, 77, 79, 80, 83, 85, 92–3, 96–9, 114, 125, 130–1, 154, 164, 190, 193, 235–6, 238, 240–5, 249, 253–7, 260, 262, 266, 299, 310, 377–8, 380–2, 384, 386–93, 404
Hunt, Ralph, 66, 68, 85, 135, 152, 179, 203
Hussein Onn, Datuk, 318, 320
Hyde, John, 67, 80, 85–6, 94, 150–2, 154, 157, 241

ICI, 87–8, 371–4, 376
Industries Assistance Commission, 71, 114, 368
Industry and Commerce, Department of, 71, 370
Inglis, Brian, 29
Irwin, Dudley, 9
Israel, 335–44

Johnston, L. B., 7, 8
Jones, Alan, 32, 347

Kampuchea, 87, 89
Kaunda, Kenneth, 315, 321, 325–8, 330–4
Keating, Michael, 40, 236, 238, 243
Keating, Paul, 212
Kelly, Paul, 186, 188–90, 211, 398
Kemp, David, 16–17, 23, 28, 31–4, 42–3, 50, 95, 102, 150, 157, 202, 373
Kerr, Sir John, 13, 90, 160, 184, 202
Killen, Jim, 72, 80, 85, 88, 140, 173, 203
Kingsland, Sir Richard, 69
Kissinger, Henry, 317
Kramer, Dame Leonie, 163, 199

436

INDEX

leaks, 190-3
Lee Kuan Yew, 87, 188
Lloyd, Clem, 209-10
Liberal party, 6, 61-7, 148-74, 201; backbenchers, 67, 85, 149-54, 241; committees, 156-7, 387, 393; federal executive, 166, 200-6; federal secretariat, 166, 223, 250; leadership ballots, 10-12, 80, 153, 161-4; party meetings, 154-6, 340-1; platform, 386; Queensland division, 82, 169-74; tactics committee, 156-9, 223, 255; Victorian division, 169-71; W.A. division, 142, 152, 160, 168, 391-2; whips, 153
Lini, Father, 26
Lowe, Doug, 300, 305-6
Lynch, Phillip, 28-9, 62, 70, 72-3, 75-82, 85, 87, 89, 104, 112, 116-17, 120, 125, 130, 134, 138, 144, 161-2, 164, 169-71, 184, 190, 203-6, 217-18, 220, 222-3, 227-8, 230-2, 236-8, 241-2, 245-50, 258, 296, 338, 373-7

McComb, Yvonne, 286
MacDonald, Flora, 332
McEwen, John, 68
McGregor inquiry, 83-5
McGuigan, Mark, 338, 341
Mackellar, Michael, 71, 76, 91, 95, 136, 150, 203
Mackerras, Malcolm, 202
McLeay, John, 75-6, 203
McMahon, Sir William, 162
Macphee, Ian, 71, 139, 157, 203, 316, 334, 404
McVeigh, Tom, 66
Manley, Michael, 314, 320, 325-8, 331, 334

Mara, Ratu, 332
Mathews, Russell, 229
Menadue, John, 22, 34, 39
Menzies, Sir Robert, 9, 11, 63, 65, 169, 194, 271, 316, 321, 403
Metal Trades Industry Association, 370, 371, 375
metal trades unions, 368-9
ministers, 19-20, 42, 44, 59-105; in cabinet, 107-47; resignations, 65-91; selection, 61-7; success of, 98-9
ministry meetings, 118-19
Missen, Alan, 157
Mitterrand, François, 340
Moore, John, 76, 91, 97, 280
Morgan, David, 262
Morgan, Gary, 166, 202
Mornington Island, 284
Mugabe, Robert, 315, 322, 333
Muldoon, Robert, 319, 321, 341, 349
Murdoch, Rupert, 196
Murphy, Justice, 300
Muzorewa, Bishop, 322, 324, 331, 333
Myer, Ken, 29

National Council of Women, 26
National Employers Policy committee, 228-9
National Gallery, 221, 257
National party, 6, 63, 66, 93, 172, 334, 405
National Times, 273
Newman, Kevin, 62, 154, 203, 309
Nixon, Peter, 42, 64, 66, 77-81, 83, 85, 87-9, 93-4, 101, 103-4, 120, 125, 129, 130, 138, 140, 154, 169, 170, 173, 178-9, 236, 240, 242, 245, 250, 268, 279-81, 284-9, 293-4, 364
Nkomo, Joshua, 315, 322, 333

INDEX

Nyerere, Julius, 315, 326-8, 331-4
nuclear safeguards, 358-60

Oakes, Laurie, 76, 184, 190
Oakeshott, Michael, 406
Office of National Assessments, 21, 331, 340
Olympic games, 41, 115, 344-53
opinion polls, 202-3, 206

Palestinian Liberation Organization, 340
Parbo, Arvi, 29, 259
Packer, Kerry, 123, 196
parliament, 27, 38, 83, 149-51, 177-82
patronage, 61, 67, 94-7
Peacock, Andrew, 10, 12, 26, 41-2, 49, 50, 64, 70-1, 76, 79, 85, 87-90, 94, 96, 113, 131-2, 143, 162-3, 190, 192-3, 203, 206, 212, 250-1, 280, 317-18, 322, 324, 326-7, 330-1, 340, 345-6, 349-54, 358, 361, 369, 371-4
Pearson, Keith, 83, 84
permanent heads, 44-5
Polites, George, 71, 222, 375
Porter, Charles, 279, 282, 286, 287, 290
premiers, 149, 275-7
premiers' conferences, 275, 296-302
press gallery, 185-94
Prices Justification Tribunal, 222, 246-7, 368-70
Primary Industry, Department of, 68, 159, 252
prime ministers, 1-7; assistance to, 19-20; and budgets, 216; and cabinet, 106-7, 117; criteria for assessment, 402, 406, 409; defeats, 10; federal leader, 274-5, 311; and foreign affairs, 313, 317-44, 353-4; need for assistance, 19-20; as party leader, 148-9; and policy, 355, 393, 395-8; roles, 20, 23, 57, 59-61, 351; as salesmen, 175-7; schedules, 25
Prime Minister and Cabinet, Department of (PMC), 27, 30, 34-43, 53, 55, 70-3, 89, 109, 115, 120, 128, 132-4, 159, 180, 184, 216, 219-20, 225, 229-42, 244-50, 252-60, 264-7, 280, 288-90, 297, 308, 319, 324, 357, 362-4, 368, 379-81, 387
prime minister's office, 21, 22-34, 36, 42
prime ministerial government, 1-7, 405
Pritchett, Bill, 121
Public Service Board, 21, 43, 44, 70, 72, 73, 249

Qantas, 236, 246-7

Ramphal, Sonny, 317-18, 320, 322, 325-31
Ranger inquiry, 357-66
Reagan, President, 273, 314, 339-42, 344
Reid, John, 179, 392
Reserve Bank, 128, 223, 226, 231, 233, 252, 260, 269, 277, 380-2
Review of Commonwealth Functions (RCF), 47, 49, 112, 128, 143, 217, 245-51
Rhodesian Information Centre, 323
Risstrom, Eric, 244
Robinson, Eric, 65, 75, 76, 80, 82-6, 105, 196, 203, 235-6, 238, 240, 243
Rose, Alan, 40
Rose, John, 33, 42, 200-1, 377, 380-1

INDEX

Sadat, Anwar, 335, 337–41
Santamaria, Bob, 28
Schmidt, Helmut, 346, 348–50
Scott, Doug, 66
Scott, Malcolm, 9
Searby, Richard, 80
Seas and Submerged Lands Act, 276, 278, 293–302
Senate, 6, 13, 158, 181–2, 201, 244, 251
Shiel, Glen, 66, 93
Shipton, Roger, 154
Simon, Barry, 88–9, 152, 157–8, 169–70
Sinclair, Ian, 64, 66, 75, 83, 93, 114, 119, 120, 129, 130, 137, 159, 177–8, 180–2, 203, 224, 238, 241, 401, 407
Sinai force, 49, 178, 335–44
Slatyer, Ralph, 307, 309–10
Snedden, Billy, 11, 12, 62, 79, 180
South Africa, 30, 315–21, 323, 353
south-west Tasmania, 26, 251, 304–11
Sparkes, Sir Robert, 172, 173, 208, 279, 281–2
Special Broadcasting Service, 120, 199, 247, 402
Spender, John, 340
Spry, Ian, 387
Staley, Tony, 12, 50, 55, 75, 77, 83, 155, 163, 201–3, 205
Stone, John, 73, 219, 240, 243, 255, 263, 389
Street, Tony, 16, 26, 56, 64, 68–71, 77, 79–81, 83, 89, 111, 120, 161, 169–71, 191, 203, 221, 308, 337–40, 360, 366
Summers, Anne, 204
Sydney Morning Herald, 223, 228, 244, 257

Tange, Sir Arthur, 9, 118
Tanzania, 119–20, 326–33
Tasmanian Wilderness Society, 305, 307
tax evasion, 30, 262–3, 383–93
tax indexation, 218, 225–7, 234, 237, 239, 272
Tax Office, 383–9
Thatcher, Margaret, 183, 273, 323–3, 332, 340–2, 345–50, 398
35-hour week, 49, 87–8, 368–76
Thompson, Lindsay, 277
Thomson, David, 66
Tonkin, David, 26
Toohey, Brian, 184, 190
Torres Strait, 280
Trade and Industry, Department of, 68
Trade, Department of, 252
Treasury, 28, 32, 44, 128–9, 134, 190, 214, 216–20, 223, 225–7, 229, 231–3, 235, 242, 252, 253–4, 258–9, 261–7, 270–1, 286, 308, 319, 376–82, 385; split of, 73–4
Trudeau, Pierre, 325, 339–42, 348–50, 359–60
Tuckey, Wilson, 116, 163
TV affair, 48, 90–1, 407

Uniting Church, 285–7
UK, *see* Britain
uranium, 37, 124, 356–7
Urban and Regional Development, Department of, 68
USA, 344–53, 359
USSR, 314, 322, 324, 335–7, 340, 345–9, 354
Utz, John, 72, 259

INDEX

Vance, Cyrus, 324, 326, 332
Vice-president of the Executive Council, Department of, 72
Viner, Ian, 70–2, 85, 203, 236, 245, 283–90, 292, 367, 375
Visbord, Ed, 40, 243, 377

wages policy, 221, 368–76
Walsh, Cliff, 32, 33, 253, 259, 265, 387
Walsh, Max, 189, 195, 209, 211
Warner, Ian, 168
Webb, Marius, 197
Webster, Jim, 66, 75, 203
Westminster principles, 4
whales, 159–60
Wheeler, Sir Frederick, 73, 74, 219
White, Denis, 24, 31–2, 45, 52
Whitlam, E. G., 12, 13, 177, 179, 182, 198, 218, 275
Wickham, Tracey, 350

'Williams, Mr', 28
Wilson, Ian, 157, 306, 308
Wiltshire, Kenneth, 26
Withers, Reg, 76, 80, 83–7, 90, 94–6, 98–104, 114, 120, 142, 158, 161, 163, 203, 234
Women's Electoral Lobby, 26
Woods, Alan, 45
Woodward, Justice, 93
World Heritage, 305–12
Wran, Neville, 298, 302, 373–4

Yarrabah, 290–1
Yeend, Sir Geoffrey, 28, 39–41, 43, 48, 56, 70, 83, 113, 115–16, 125, 143, 184, 235, 338, 342, 351, 362–3, 379

Zambia, 326–32
Zimbabwe, 315–33, 344, 349, 353

FOR THE BEST IN PAPERBACKS, LOOK FOR THE 🐧

PENGUIN

The Penguin History of Australia John Molony

A history for the people which is an enticing and comprehensive blend of social, political, cultural, economic and environmental history. Included are those so often neglected by historians, the 'ordinary' Australians whose class, race, age or gender rendered them 'unimportant'.

Here is the story of the making of a nation, the slow and painful process by which a people have come to identify with each other and with the land they inhabit. It tells of strangers and of the strange land which they encountered, confronted and, ultimately, came to understand and respect.

While John Molony deals with the strength of the British heritage, he is keenly aware of the richness resulting from its blending with other cultures. Although Molony is not blind to the failures and follies which followed the white peopling of Australia, his thoughtful and timely history is an acknowledgement of the considerable achievements of 200 years.

Don't Take Your Love to Town Ruby Langford

Ruby Langford was born on Bos Ridge mission, Coraki, on the north coast of NSW in 1934. She was raised in Bonalbo, and went to high school in Casino where she finished second form. At age 15 she moved to Sydney and became a qualified clothing machinist. Her first child was born when she was 17. She has a family of nine children and raised them mostly by herself. For many years she lived in tin huts and camped in the bush around Coonabarrabran, working at fencing, burning off, ringbarking and lopping, and pegging kangaroo skins. At other times she lived in the black areas of Sydney, and worked in clothing factories. Now 53, she is the grandmother of eighteen children, and works part-time at the Aboriginal Medical Service in Redfern.

FOR THE BEST IN PAPERBACKS, LOOK FOR THE

PENGUIN

Shouting from China Helene Chung

Helene Chung, Australian journalist born of ethnic Chinese parents, describes her term as the Australian Broadcasting Corporation's Beijing correspondent.

Based on the daily life of a foreign correspondent in Beijing, it gives a vivid portrait of China today – China's attitude to overseas Chinese, its dilemma in wanting to modernise through the importation of western technology without the importation of western ideas, and the problems of adequately reporting to the world on a vast country which is still such an enigma.

Katherine Mansfield Gillian Boddy

Katherine Mansfield was not only an extraordinary writer, devoted to her work, she was also a woman of great vivacity and strength, who led a brief but fascinating life from her birth in New Zealand to the literary circles of England and Europe. The leading writers of her age, people like Virginia Woolf and D. H. Lawrence, were a constant part of her life.

Gillian Boddy has drawn on her years of research to introduce to us a new Katherine Mansfield, not ethereal as has been the myth, but substantial, alive.

FOR THE BEST IN PAPERBACKS, LOOK FOR THE 🐧

PENGUIN

Shalom Compiled by Nancy Keesing

Some of the fourteen prominent contributors to this unique collection of stories – John George Lang, Harry Marks and Nancy Keesing herself – come from long-established Australian Jewish families. Others like Judah Waten, David Martin, Morris Lurie and Lilian Barnea are refugees of pogroms, revolutions and wars.

By drawing upon the diversity of their backgrounds and inspirations, well-known author and critic Nancy Keesing gives us an invaluable insight into Jewish life and thought in contemporary Australia.

Save Me Joe Louis Kate Jennings

'Twenty years of being a lovesick loon. Twenty years of careering through life like a horse loose in traffic. Enough is enough.'

With that realisation, Kate Jennings decides to change and in the process takes a clear-eyed and ruefully humourous look at her Riverina childhood, her years as a feminist activist, and her travels and current way of life in the United States. To make peace with herself, she sifts and sorts through subjects as diverse as school reunions, house-hunting in Connecticut, gender in Japan, and Australian drinking habits, weighing her options and reconciling the contradictions.

Old Worlds and New Australia Janis Wilton and Richard Bosworth

This topical book provides an overview of Australia's immigration policy since World War II: its impact on attitudes and lifestyles in Australia, as well as upon those who have brought to the new world their memories, dreams and conflicts.

FOR THE BEST IN PAPERBACKS, LOOK FOR THE 🐧

PENGUIN

The Immigrants Wendy Lowenstein and Morag Loh

Many Australians believe immigrants have made their fortunes running milk bars, delicatessens or small businesses. The reality is that most of them did the dirty jobs – jobs as cleaners, labourers, process workers – where the qualification is to be 'unskilled' and the reward is low wages. This is a compelling book that tells the real story of what immigrants to Australia between 1890–1970 found on arrival.

Captain Cook Chased a Chook June Factor

A fascinating study of the rhymes, games, insults and other folklore that make up the rich world of Australian children's culture. It explores the folklore of specific groups such as Aboriginal, colonial and migrant children; it also raises general questions about the nature of childhood, the way in which adult culture affects children and the future of children's play.

Born to Whinge Kerry Cue

From filling the baby's inner ear with mashed pumpkin to clothing teenagers with champagne tastes on a bubblegum budget, *Born to Whinge* is an hilarious celebration of the bizarre job of being a parent.

Best-selling author of *Crooks, Chooks and Bloody Ratbags* and *Hang On To Your Horses Doovers*, Kerry Cue has written Australia's funniest and most thoroughly unreliable guide for parents.

FOR THE BEST IN PAPERBACKS, LOOK FOR THE 🐧

PENGUIN

The Penguin Book of Australian Autobiography   John and Dorothy Colmer

A lively and stimulating introduction to more than forty Australians who write of their own lives. They include Kylie Tennant, Patrick White, Joan Lindsay, David Malouf, Henry Lawson, Judah Waten, Charles Perkins, Donald Horne, Albert Facey, Clive James, George Johnston and Mary Gilmore.

A Foreign Wife   Gillian Bouras

In 1980 Australian-born Gillian Bouras set off with her Greek husband to live in Greece. Her fellow villagers fondly regarded her, a migrant in their midst, as something of a curiosity. They in turn were the source of admiration and curiosity to her. This is her account of her experience in a 'small quiet world' which caused her so much perplexity and pleasure.

Edda's Diaries   Edda Walker

'I am determined to live until the moment of death.'

In this unusual and fascinating book we share a woman's journey – along the canals of western Europe with her family, through the crests and undertows of self-awareness; then her acceptance of life with cancer, and the ultimate rite of passage.

We come to know this remarkable woman through her diaries, her poems, her acute observations of people and places in Europe and Australia, and her compelling insights into herself.

As we come to know Edda, we come to know ourselves.